Arrested Development in Ethiopia

Arrested Development in Ethiopia

Essays on Underdevelopment, Democracy and Self-Determination

Edited by
Seyoum Hameso and Mohammed Hassen

The Red Sea Press Inc.
Publishers & Distributors of Third World Books

P.O. Box 1982
Trenton, NJ 08607

P.O. Box 48
Asmara, ERITREA

The Red Sea Press, Inc.

Publishers & Distributors of Third World Books

11-D Princess Road
Lawrenceville, NJ 08648

P. O. Box 48
Asmara, ERITREA

Book design: Saverance Publishing Services
Cover design: Ashraful Haque

Library of Congress Cataloging-in-Publication Data

Arrested development in Ethiopia : essays on underdevelopment, democracy, and self-determination / edited by Seyoum Y. Hameso and Mohammed Hassen.
   p. cm. Includes bibliographical references and index.
ISBN 1-56902-257-7 (hardcover) -- ISBN 1-56902-258-5 (pbk.)
   1. Ethiopia--Politics and government--1991- 2. Ethiopia--Economic condi-tions--1974- 3. Nationalism--Ethiopia. 4. Self-determination, National--Ethio-pia. 5. Oromo (African people)--Politics and government. I. Hameso, Seyoum Y. II. Hassen, Mohammed.
DT388.A77 2006
963.07'2--dc22   2006004467

When in the Course of human Events, it becomes necessary for one People to dissolve the Political Bands which have connected them with another, and to assume among the Powers of the Earth, the separate and equal Station to which the Laws of Nature and of Nature's God entitle them, a decent Respect to the Opinions of Mankind requires that they should declare the causes which impel them to the Separation.

Action of Second Continental Congress, 4 July 1776

The power of this book comes from the accord of the authors. As a unity of purpose among scholarly voices of the non-Abyssinian population and as an assembly of reasoned views, this book marks one of the beginnings of what must be understood as an emissary of a broader intellectual leadership networking to lay the knowledge base for a protracted effort towards a better future of the South. Hence, the very gathering of studious ideas is no mean achievement; the outstanding messages of refuting myths of the empire and exposing aggressive occupation are far reaching historical missives.

Asfaw Beyene, 2004

Table of Contents

Acknowledgements

The image of a human being whose hands are grotesquely tied symbolizes the central problem facing societies in an empire setting. On the one hand, the image conjures up the human condition under oppression; on the other hand, since no condition is permanent, it holds out the anticipation of freedom and hope beyond the empire state. It speaks volumes about the lack of freedom in Ethiopia without failing to point to indomitable human spirit to break the vicious problems of oppression, poverty and ignorance.

The contributors to this volume come from diverse backgrounds, and they are all keen on informing readers about arrested development in Ethiopia. They provide critical interpretations, which as a matter of necessity, diverge from the hitherto formalized approaches toward Ethiopian statehood. The concern of most of the contributors is based on the foresight of pathetic abuse of the resources of the Southern nations, a gradual erosion of their cultures and ways of life, the fragmentation of their societies, the arrested development of their peoples and the loss of prospect for posterity.

As one contributor eloquently argued in this book, the Ethiopian state has always suppressed the creative talents of its subjects. Individual potential to think, research and produce literary and artistic works critical of the existing oppressive order are censored or blocked. The subject people were dis-allowed from developing their talents, particularly when such talents reflected their identity or culture. They have been denied the right to freely determine not only the governance of their choice but also the pace and the direction of their socio-economic progress. In short, they are denied the right to improve their collective well-being. The contributors passionately believe that these problems are symptomatic of pernicious social and political formation, but they are neither inevitable nor insurmountable.

This work is intended to advance the cause of the oppressed people whose problems are neglected. It attempts to shed light where darkness and ignorance were knighted. In fulfilling their duty and responsibility on behalf of the silenced majority, the contributors express their views on crucial problems facing their people. They also share their own experience on forced migration and refugees whose rights are violated both individually and collectively, for it is well known that the fate of a people without state is often precarious.

The completion of this work could not have been possible without the encouragement from, and participation of, many people. Since the main goal of the work is to give voice to countless millions, our gratitude goes to those who paid sacrifice, in any shape and form, while resisting tyranny. We would also like to thank the contributing authors for sharing their cumulative knowledge and experience based on life-long scholarship and human rights activism.

Their commitment in terms of sharing their time and invaluable knowledge was of great value to make this effort enjoy the light of the day. If the strength of the exploration of the ideas contained in this book help dispel the myths and enable a better understanding of the problems faced by diverse peoples in Ethiopia, then our collective efforts are successful. Finally, we are indebted to Kassahun Checole, the president and the staff of the Red Sea Press, Inc. for their editorial assistance. Furthermore, Kassahun Checole, who published so many books on Ethiopia, Eritrea, and other African countries deserves special thanks for spreading knowledge about Africa and Africans throughout the world.

Seyoum Hameso and Mohammed Hassen
December 2004

INTRODUCTION

Seyoum Hameso and Mohammed Hassen

This book is a collective effort toward exploring the paradoxes one faces in the examination of historical inequities inherent in Ethiopian polity, the conflicts that ensued and the alternative proposals to resolve the problems rooted in the formation of the Ethiopian empire. The project was initiated for two closely related reasons (a) the need to give voice to the silent majority, and (b) the growing realization that the Abyssinian interpretation of history has contributed to the seemingly paradoxical developments in contemporary Ethiopia. Unraveling these paradoxes requires, as Alex De Waal opines, "a new set of paradigms.... which includes the recognition that the political symbolism used to interpret Ethiopia in the past was in fact founded more on obscurant myth than on social and economic reality" (De Waal 1994:39).

The history of the world is replete with examples of empire states replaced by progressive national polities in the process of creative destruction that is development. With the end of the Cold War, at the beginning of the 1990s, wretched contracts imposed by force were swiftly torn apart in different parts of the world. Yet Ethiopia stands as a symbol of equally wretched past in critical need of demystification and change. It is the belief here that the process of demystification should begin with unraveling the foundations of empire statehood.

To begin with, since its emergence in the last decade of the nineteenth century, Ethiopia's system of empire state had been based on the paradigm of conquest and domination. Throughout these periods, the patterns of systematic exclusion of subject peoples had been visible even when minor amendments were reported as revolutions. Again, throughout these periods, none of the regime changes could conceal the continuity of the main patterns of domination by the Ethiopian ruling circles who have shared values and beliefs with respect to the oppressed. All of them maintained unfair distribution of opportunities and wealth; all of them upheld the culture of despotism and the politics of violence vis-à-vis the oppressed; and nearly all of them intensified the misuse of resources and aggravated the abuse of human rights.

The official Ethiopianist discourse evades the true dimensions of the existing order. Instead of articulating the problem in its colonial dimension with a view to its resolution, it prefers to disguise it under "nationality question." Since the discourse evades the problem, the Ethiopianist elite do not fully recognize the impact of their policies on the colonized peoples. They know full well that there was no such a thing as the "Ethiopian nation" before the late nineteenth century's conquest save feuding armies and fiefdoms in the Abyssinian North. This being the case, subsequent regimes perceived the "colonial discourse" as a threat to the empire state and chose violent repression as a political means to prolong their rule, leading to the militarization of life and the subordination of society to militaristic ethos. The combined effect renders the contemporary Ethiopia being a mass of contradiction and contest revolving around the paradigms of oppression and liberation.

The aftermath of these contradictions and contests are decades of civil wars, massive poverty, famine and misery in monumental proportions. In this critical tension, the Ethiopian state plays a pivotal role in granting a hegemonic role for certain ethnic group(s) at the expense of heterogeneous peoples whose development is arrested. The latter face the stark realities of dispossession of their human and natural resources and the denigration of their cultures. Like the advocates of colonial rule elsewhere in the world, the Ethiopian rulers considered the oppressed people as backward lot who should be converted by abandoning their ways of life, cultures and belief systems.

The key problem in all this is the nature of the empire state—its formation, and its handling of competing national identities. The problem manifests itself in complete lack of national consensus on the nature of the state. In the eyes of the oppressed people, the machinery of the empire state is bent on undermining their social, economic and political survival. In its ideological leaning, the state has been totalitarian, often centrist and sometimes communist or a combination of all. Its operational principles remained coercion, conflict, domination, polarization, inequality and exploitation. In the eyes of the ruling elite and their political culture, the above operational principles are virtues to be defended not deformities to be changed. For the oppressed, they represented an agency of destruction in dire need of replacement.

In the meanwhile, the reasoned account of the history and politics of Ethiopian empire remains elusive as myth and misinformation are perpetually used to legitimize domination. Indeed, much of what has come to the public domain about Ethiopia is based on myth rather than reality. Many examples could be given, but two should suffice for our purpose here. First, the Abyssinian elite "too often and too easily hypnotized by the sheer myths and legends of 3,000 years of Ethiopian history," claim that Ethiopia has existed as one united country in its present form for [thirty centuries]. This is historically incorrect to say the least" (Hassen 1999: 119). There is no country in the world other than Ethiopia that claims history of three thousand years as a single nation and yet utterly lacking national consensus on the nature of the state! Second, the Abyssinian elite deliberately confuse historic Abyssinia with modern Ethiopia. Abyssinia, which constituted only one-third of what is today Ethiopia had rich and complex history. It was only King Menelik's colonial conquest (1870s-1900) which created contemporary Ethiopia and in the process historic Abyssinians (i.e. Amhara and Tigrayans) were transformed into what Professor Donald Levine described as "the true Ethiopians" (Levine, 1974: 8). Addis Hiwet, the most outstanding liberal Ethiopian historian observes that:

> . . . The deep-seated myth that has for so long enshrined Ethio-pia—both the name and country—still blurs genuine historical understanding. Ethiopia's existence as a 'modern state' does not... extend beyond the 1900s and into the limitless and ever-remote millennia. The same historical forces that created the 'Gold Coast' the 'Ivory Coast', the Sudan and Kenya, were the very ones that created modern Ethiopia too. And recognition of this fact makes modern Ethiopia no older than these African states (Hiwet, 1975: 1).

In reaching such a conclusion, Hiwet is an exception and most of the Abyssinian elite propagate myths that were fully absorbed by external observers of Ethiopia who failed to have a clear idea of the empire. This in itself is a problem since they end up supporting tyranny or denying support to legitimate claimants. Currently, the myopic rulers of the day attempt to make use of the external political environment of hostility towards international terrorism with a view to suppress the legitimate demands of the oppressed people. In the past, the ruling autocracies presented themselves as divinely ordained and wedded to their own account of statehood traceable to times immemorial. Far removed from such a myth, the contemporary Ethiopia comprises a significant Muslim and non-Orthodox Christian population. The core of the social-political history comprises of feuding warlords, the Abyssinian tradition, and the Coptic Church.

The true nature of the empire state is yet to be assessed critically by the Western discourse which, according to John Sorenson (1993:2) gave certain voices prominence while ignoring or silencing others. The Ethiopian elite, who do not admit the level of injustice and harm they inflict on the oppressed, fail to engage in constructive discourse about the demands for civil rights and national self-determination. On the contrary, the trend has been one of perpetuating myth, misrepresentation of reality and repression of popular aspirations. The distinction between myth and reality is becoming demonstrably visible with the passage of time and ever-growing wind of change. In this book, the task of demystification is conducted through passionate discussion of issues whose opinion formation has been suppressed.

It should be noted, however, that the book is not about Ethiopian history; it is rather about the hitherto ignored interpretations of contemporary Ethiopia's reality. The essays are based on the analysis and expression of lived experiences of people whose voices are faintly heard and whose development is arrested. The stories are told from different angles, yet the message is strikingly similar. The similarity of the narrations meant that repetition is an unavoidable possibility.

The work is intended to challenge the paradigm of domination which has denied voice and expression to the basic human rights of oppressed people. It proposes solutions from the perspective of the paradigm of emancipation whose goals are: a) to demystify the powers of oppression and, b) to articulate the case for national self-determination. The focal points for the emancipatory paradigm are what An-Na'im described as collective human rights, namely, the right to "self-determination (economic and cultural as well as political), existence, permanent sovereignty over natural resources, healthy and balanced environment, humanitarian disaster relief, cultural identity, freedom from coercive assimilation, schooling in mother tongue, and effective participation in public affairs" (An-Na'im 1998:15).

The prevalence of serious problems with human rights in Ethiopia created a gap between what its successive regimes proclaim (often for the sake of external consumption) and what they practise. For example, constitutions remained paper-based experiments destined for shelves not to be implemented. If one can dismiss the grant of a right of secession to the constituent republics of the U.S.S.R, as a piece of window dressing which lacks all political reality save its propaganda value, as Rupert Emerson (1960) observed, exactly the same could be said of Ethiopia today. There is no agreement on the rules, the incidence, transfer and exercise of political power in Ethiopia. The lack of agreement meant that the country continues to experience single party rule, dissent and repression. The state formation based on the paradigm of conquest bred a political culture that antagonizes democracy and the rule of law. The political rearrangement of the 1990s has not been able to remedy the serious problems mentioned above.

The story is, indeed, dismal and disillusioning. Ethiopia remains the poorest country in the world. The GNP per capita income is $100. Over 55 percent of the populations live in abject conditions below poverty line. About half of the children do not attend primary schools. Life expectancy at birth (which is a qualitative reflection of the quality of life in a country) stands at 44 years.

Disease, malnutrition and social unrest hugely impact on the quality of life and one's life expectancy. Deadly diseases such as HIV/AIDS and malaria epidemic spread their tentacles. Food insecurity and farmer vulnerability to famine are the hallmarks of the Ethiopian landscape. Wars and simmering conflicts ravage the poor. Human rights violations are rampant. The enlightened and conscious people who articulate the problems face unique violation of rights. The report by Human Rights Watch (2003:3) was accurate.

> Being educated can be a risky business in Ethiopia. Students and teachers, often among the most politically active elements of society, are frequent victims of human rights violations including extrajudicial killings, arbitrary arrest, and denial of freedom of association and expression.

Peaceful protests against government policies result in violent military action as in the case of the massacre of peaceful Oromo demonstrators in the town of Watar in Hararge in March 1992, the massacre of innocent Oromo in Nagle-Borana in 1996, and the killing of Addis Ababa University students in April 2001 and the massacre of peaceful protesters in Sidama on 24 May 2002. The litany of rights violations include arbitrary arrest and detention, ill-treatment of detainees, termination of employment to those who oppose the regime, restriction on assembly and association, interference with the privacy of individuals and homes, restrictions of freedom of press, and lack of fair trial. The country is prolific in producing and exporting refugees while millions of its subjects at home depend on international charity for survival. Certainly, this state of being cannot be considered as normal state of national being. Yet the empire state remains an arena of jealously guarded zone of unabashed privilege for certain ethno-national groups who receive the bulk of the rewards including leading positions in the state as well as the largest subsidies for economic and cultural projects while the rest of the subjects find themselves at a considerable disadvantage. The political domination of the empire state by economically poor and technologically less advanced groups engendered deep tensions, rivalries, and animosities which are by far more visible today than any time in history. The policy of forced assimilation of diverse peoples into Amharic culture has borne nothing but violence and backwardness to the great majority.

As the prospect for improvement in human condition become overwhelmingly disillusioning, generations have turned out to be aspiring and willing emigrants. At the same time, forced displacement caused by human rights violations and wars, have worsened an already precarious existence for those left behind often caught in the midst of man-made and natural disasters. The effect of brain drain on poorer societies is well documented. More importantly, the inability to provide food security and crippling dependence on food handout indicates that the Ethiopian power bears within it the seeds of its own destruction. Political corruption and decay eat into the basic fabric of the system.

When famine, hunger and resistance wrecked the feudal autocracy in 1974, a group of armed personnel, known collectively as the Derg, took over power and proclaimed a revolution. Its leader, a brutal army colonel, ruled the empire making use of Marxist-Leninist ideology. In the name of building a socialist state, the regime imposed severe repression, villagization, militarization, and massive poverty on the people. In this venture, it received significant military, economic and political support from the then "socialist block," yet, the regime faced inevitable collapse in 1991.

The ascendance to power of the Tigray People Liberation Front (TPLF) has slightly changed the make-up of Ethiopian polity. The most notable of this later phase is that no Habasha regime came closer to the correct diagnosis of the fundamental problems of the empire. Yet the very nature of the formation of the empire state precluded the TPLF leadership from reckoning with the past. In its initial bid to power, the TPLF regime consented to the fashionable rhetoric of "competitive" politics and free market economy. If true political democracy and freedom of economic enterprise were to become the rule of the game, the TPLF reckoned it will lose and it thwarted all genuine moves in that direction. The masters of deception, the regime's representatives made hollow claims about democratic reforms while there is hardly a place for mundane freedom of association, information, and the press. The overwhelming reality is one of severe repression, the creation and propping up surrogate parties, and unjust advantage of one region while others face policies of genocidal intent.

Taking extremely short-term perspective, the 'new' rulers presumed that a federal structure of their making answered the quest of various nations to national self-determination. They claimed to advocate decentralization but they abruptly switched gears and centralized the empire state when the elite they co-opted from the oppressed people began tilting towards their own people—their constituency. One external observer concluded that "... the most prevalent political development during [1991-2000] is the consolidation of a centralized party rule along with the formalization of a federal system, a development which implies an apparent paradox" (Aalen 2002:1).

The problem of nations under domination is not only a question of political identity but also a matter of survival. In the course of the struggle, which spans over three decades for some movements, it has become amply clear that reforming the Ethiopian empire in a democratic manner is an uphill task. If there is going to be a meaningful development, the Ethiopian empire state has to be decolonized, one way or the other. Decolonization through democratic self-determination is an urgent political agenda for the Southern nations.

The Ethiopian ruling elite's response to this quest is what one would expect of alien and hostile rule. They showed little effort to admit the past inequities and guarantee the demand for self-determination. They consider the empire state as legitimately independent while the majority of the constituent societies are internally colonized and they have no stake in the state to promote their social, economic and political rights. By approaching the problem from the perspective of subversion rather than seeking constructive solution, the response is often downright negative. As the result, subsequent attempts by the oppressed people to reform the Ethiopian state system have come to naught.

Nationalists and national liberation movements pursued different methods to restore the dignity and well-being of the oppressed people. The strategies ranged from peaceful resistance to armed struggle. Some movements felt that armed struggle was imposed on them as they were left with no other option except confronting the state-sponsored terrorism in kind. The struggle continues.

There is no claim that the contributions in this book are comprehensive or conclusive; they nonetheless represent a crucial step in demystifying the past. The belief is that the production of knowledge and information about alternative experiences will enrich what has been distorted and unbalanced view of reality in Ethiopia. Such an alternative view perceives the Ethiopian reality as an empire state "constructed as a result of a unique case of African imperialism" or where African circumstances are obtained in a combined way (Keller 1991:45; Curtin et al 1978:464). Ernest Gellner (1994a:85) described it as the "prison house of nations." The militarization and centralization of life mark the absence of the notion of civil society whereby "a single political economic-ideological hierarchy tolerated no rivals and one single vision defined not only truth but also personal rectitude" (Gellner 1994b).

The political centralization and ideological absolutism of the sort stands in stark contrast to the background of deep ethno-national diversity which has historical precedents traceable to the colonial era. Indeed, the colonial conquest is a markedly indicative notion to introduce the foundations of the contemporary Ethiopian polity for it is an invention of conquest or "largely a product of the past hundred years" (Keller 1994:15; see also Holocomb and Ibsa 1990). The consolidation of the colonial state was excessively partisan and conflict-ridden. While those who took part in the conquest of territorial expansion were rewarded with substantial grants of land and patronage, the Southern peoples were punished by enslavement, forced labor and other onerous burdens not to mention untold human suffering and arrested development. The same people were also deprived of their guardians as their organic intellectuals were subdued, exiled or killed. The essays tell a story of these people's lived experiences, their unstoppable struggle, their hopes and aspirations.

The essays are written for a general audience with a view to promote understanding about Ethiopian reality. Readers are forewarned to approach the problems at hand with critical and open mind. Sooner they realize that understanding the problems of people in conflict (on either holding or contesting the ground) is never an easy task. Parties to conflict situations are likely to disagree drastically in the evaluation of the problems and, more importantly, on their resolutions. The task of our contributors is providing collective voice and alternative analysis to problems facing diverse societies in this part of Africa. Some of the essays were initially published in 1997, in limited numbers and circulation, under the title "*Ethiopia: Conquest and quest for freedom and democracy.*" The current edition expands on the previous themes, this time with more contributions and a slightly different focus. What has changed since the first publication is the clarity of the nature of the Ethiopian statehood and the crises surrounding the peoples. Since then a devastating war was fought between Ethiopia and Eritrea; the crisis within the ruling TPLF elite worsened; and a vicious attack is taking place on the national identities of oppressed peoples. Large-scale famine and malicious forest fires hit the Southern areas with catastrophic effects on the people and the environment.

THE ORGANIZATION OF THE BOOK

The book is organized into three parts. In the first part, the contributors tell real stories about the predicament of their respective people. The starting point is Hamdesa Tuso's personal narrative, in which he humbly shares his own personal tragedy of what has happened to him, his family and his national group. "The tears of generations" is a powerful elucidation of how individual human rights are inextricably linked to collective rights of a nation; thus, the personal loss he suffered is in tandem with the national oppression that the Oromo people have endured. In chapter 1, Mekuria Bulcha goes beyond the individual to bring a collective, sociological perspective to bear on forced migration caused by the Ethiopian conquest. From his work, one can feel and imagine the temporal map of events that led to forced migration. His assessment of the experience of the Oromo people with involuntary displacement has strong currency and universal validity. Tragic as it may be, the experience of forced migration also provided the diaspora with the sense of achievement, if not trusteeship, and real opportunities that are not available to the oppressed people inside Ethiopia.

It is indeed the opportunities of enlightenment or the opening up, so to speak, of the oppressed peoples to examine the levels of oppression they were subjected to or stark knowledge of the degree of undue deprivation they suffered which compelled them to devise the means to change their wretched existence. As described in chapter 2, in the case of the Sidama, the structures of nationhood are developing despite the attempts by tyrannical rule and its genocidal policies. It should be recalled that whenever and wherever there is tyranny and injustice, there would be resistance and struggle. It is also a cardinal lesson in human history that, as human birth does not happen without pain, the inevitable victory of justice over the structures of repression does not develop without struggle. That is what the Ogaden people are doing, as Mohammed Mahdi explains in chapter 3. In chapter 4, Achame Shana chronicles the consequences of colonial rule on Shekacho people. Using crucial episodes in recent history, Achame intimates the fate of a people silenced by the politics of empire. Without exaggeration, the same pattern prevailed throughout the rest of the Southern nations, which is one of the reasons for the possibility of overlapping accounts by all contributors. The overriding rationale to allow such narrations is to enable the audience to understand the issues and the common patterns of the problem at hand.

The second part of the book deals with the political economy of arrested development. Chapter 5 looks into the nature of Ethiopian empire state formation. Seyoum Hameso underscores that informed debate on contemporary Ethiopia needs to begin at the watershed era when the empire took its present physical configuration. The colonial project was endorsed by the then European powers who were busy establishing and maintaining their own spheres of influence across Africa. Many African societies are still reeling from the effects of the colonial conundrum.

In chapter 6, Temesgen Erena relates the problems of development in Oromia to the militaristic ethos of Ethiopian empire. He opines that there is a marked incompatibility of Oromia's economic development and Ethiopia's colonial rule. The continued military occupation of the Southern nations, he notes, harms their long-term growth. The effects of bad governance on economic efficiency and social equity are self-evident. He sees colonial paradigm as an obstacle to meaningful national development.

In chapter 7, Trevor Trueman cites a series of human rights violations and genocide of the Oromo people. It is public knowledge that the TPLF/EPRDF regime commits atrocities on those who oppose it. Worse still, criticism from Western countries about human rights abuses has been muted because of the divergence of their interests from the needs of suffering people.

In chapter 8, Hamdesa Tuso positions the discussion of the political problematic of the crisis-ridden "Horn" of Africa region in the backdrop of super-power politics. Following an in-depth exploration of the impact of U.S. foreign policy towards Ethiopia, both during after the Cold War, he challenges policy makers to examine the assumptions that underlie the U.S. foreign policy toward the region. He tips policy makers of the futility of suppressing national movements and the validity of empowering weaker parties. It is now widely known that external interventions have affected the conditions of the oppressed nations and peoples since the inception of the contemporary Ethiopian state. Being one of the major participants in the scene, the U.S. has involved in the region with varying levels of commitment. The naming of this part of Africa as the Great Horn itself is believed to have American origins. Yet the policies of the U.S. administrations towards this region, and indeed to the whole Africa, are riddled with problems. For example, the United States Institute of Peace (2001:1) noted that the "U.S. foreign policy toward Africa has been one of the most daunting challenges for policymakers in the past 25 years. Inconsistency in policy formulation and implementation has had a correspondingly inconsistent effect on human rights in the region." The possible reason for this inconsistency is the problem of balancing the motives for promoting particularistic "national interest" with broader goal to defend universal human rights.

Such inconsistencies and external entanglements may complicate the problem, but regardless of the silence imposed from within and without, the oppressed people seem to have no option other than resisting tyranny, often by resorting to their own resources, cultures, traditions, languages, and in short their nationalisms. At stake are both the individual human rights and collective rights.

The third part of the book contains discussion on languages, nationalism and democracy. In chapter 9, Seyoum Hameso examines the key issues of languages, nations, nationalism in Ethiopia. In chapter 10, Mulugeta Daye situates the Sidama nationalism in relation to national identity problem in Ethiopia. In chapter 11, Mohammed Hassen traces the origin of contemporary Oromo nationalism to the middle of the twentieth century which started as a cultural phenomenon developing into political nationalism. In a prescriptive note, a very rare act by historians whose works dwells largely about the past, Hassen projects the future resolution of the Oromo national problem within the framework of the democratization of Ethiopian empire state on the basis of a federal arrangement. As a historian, he is not only keenly aware but also wary of the record of successive Ethiopian regimes that offered little room for competing national identities. He specifies some conditions for what he believes are "unsatisfactory resolutions" of the problems. Surely, the democratization path is pursued by nationalists who uphold a unique view pertaining to the resolution of the Oromo versus Ethiopian problem (see, for example, Lata 1999). What concerns nationalists is the realism of democratizing a colonial state that is in deep trouble.

Writing on a similar, but not the same, issue, Asafa Jalata (chapter 12), links the development of Oromo nationalism to the crises of the Ethiopian empire state. His conclusion that "Oromos and other colonized nations must ...be prepared to resolve these contradictions through creating a genuine multicultural democratic state" begs further scrutiny. The prime question in this position is how to imagine a blueprint for this kind of polity bearing in mind that the reading of the past hardly leaves room for much optimism. It may be a desirable outcome in the long term but the existing political raw materials are too raw to make it acceptable and workable in the immediate future. As far as the scholarly contributions are concerned, we feel that having diversity of opinion enhances the stuff of freedom, which needs to be entertained provided that such freedom would offer societies with vital and useful menu of options.

At any rate, however, the successful operation of struggle for self-determination requires national consensus on the problem and on the proposed solutions. Even though the debate may continue over the latter, there is consensus on the articulation of the problems as being caused by the colonial conquest of the Southern nations and the subsequent state formation. For example, there is no discord on the fact that the effects of the conquest are not yet terminated. It is widely recognized that the culture of conflict resolution among Ethiopian rulers is predicated on zero-sum politics, namely winning by destroying the other(s). There is no middle way, and no alternative form of conflict resolution. The result is the mutual de-recognition of the legitimacy and equality of respective demands. The logic of Ethiopian unity at any cost denotes the continuation of the philosophy of settler colonialism. One may note the desirability of national unity on the grounds of the benefits it is supposed to engender, namely collective security, social and economic development and political stability, but if it poses problems rather than enhancing these benefits, then it cannot be a frame of reference for conflict resolution. Hence, any model of sustainable resolution has to take the political aspirations of the respective peoples, their demographic composition, affiliations and preferences.

As far as the mainstream nationalists are concerned, it is known that the proposed resolution of the Ethiopian problem affects the content and the method of their struggle—the reason why intellectual effort should be exceptionally rigorous to take the social and the political reality into account. Theoretically, federation, as the outcome of bargain between the rulers of the central state and the leaders of its territorial sub-units, works if it appeals to both parties (Riker 1964). In the world of zero-sum politics of Ethiopian empire, a level-field fair play and a reasonable bargain are not feasible. It is visibly obvious that the recent Ethiopian constitutions failed to provide the basic minimum requirements of constitutional settlement within the same political roof. They failed, for example, to provide for equality and justice for all segments of the population, equality in sharing political power, economic and social development, and the enabling of each nation or people within the state to maintain and develop its distinctive cultural identity (An-Na'im 1993:106). The oppressed people are left with no choice other than demanding the full realization of their right to democracy and national self-determination.

The immediate response from the Ethiopian elite to this quest is what one would expect from alien and hostile rule. By approaching the problem from the perspective of subversion rather than seeking constructive solution, the elite's response is often downright negative. As Asfaw Beyene concludes in this book, "a sentiment of regret acknowledging the violent past of Abyssinian leadership is not in sight, and there is still a stern and fierce will of dominance." Indeed, the Ethiopian leaders and scholars, pampered with what Beyene calls "obnoxious ambition," which often comes across as "chauvinistic arrogance," are also characterized by lack of political vision. The outcome which emerges from such ambition and lack of vision is that given the history of domination and inherent inequity built into Ethiopian empire state system, the failure to realize self-determination or indeed the prolongation of ruinous polity is bound to invite far more misery and disaster. The issue now is how to reverse this outcome and make the transition more acceptable, less costly and permanent. The transition is known to be fraught with identity crisis within the Ethiopian empire at all levels, yet history has seen no shortcut to progress and no development without pain and investment.

In an epoch when comparatively similar modern empire states with Orthodox beliefs were changed in the Soviet Union and Yugoslavia, following the collapse of communism and the end of the Cold War, the unfinished business continues to haunt the Ethiopian state which needs complete transformation of the political and the social realm. The process of decolonization has already commenced, and as Beyene concludes in this book, "it is impossible to conquer a liberated mind." The tasks waiting for organic nationalists are manifold: they need to re-build on the existing raw materials to replace the archaic empire structures that failed to fulfill the aspirations of millions. It does not follow, however, that nationalists should fabricate new history, it means renewing the existing potential or collective will of their people. Finally, they have to make their aspirations known to those concerned to demonstrate "a decent respect to the opinions of mankind." This work is a contribution toward that end.

References

Aalen, Lovise. 2002. *Ethnic federalism in a dominant party state: The Ethiopian experience 1991-2000*, 2. Chr. Michelsen Institute Development Studies and Human Rights. Bergen: Chr. Michelsen Institute.

An-Na'im, Abdullahi. 1993. The national question, secession and constitutionalism: The mediation of competing claims to self-determination. In *Constitutionalism and democracy: Transitions in the contemporary worlds,* ed. Douglas Greenberg, et al. 105-125. New York, Oxford: Oxford University Press.

An-Na'im, Abdullahi. 1998. Human rights and the challenge of relevance: The case of collective rights. In *The role of the nation-state in the 21st century: Human rights, international organizations and foreign policy,* ed. Monique Castermans-Holleman, et al, 3-16. The Hague: Kluwer Law International.

Curtin, P., S. Feierman, L. Thompson and J. Vansina. 1978. *African history.* Harlow: Longman.

De Waal, A. 1994. Rethinking Ethiopia. In *The Horn of Africa,* ed. C. Gordon. London: University College of London Press.

Emerson, Rupert. 1960. *From empire to nation: The rise to self-assertion of Asian and African peoples.* Boston: Beacon Press.

Gellner, Ernest. 1994a. *Encounters with nationalism.* Oxford: Blackwell.

Gellner, Ernest. 1994b. *Conditions of liberty. Civil society and its rivals.* London: Hamish Hamilton.

Hiwet, Addis, 1975. *Ethiopia: from autocracy to revolution.* London: *Review of African Political Economy.* 2, 4:122-123.

Holcomb, Bonnie and Sisay Ibsa. 1990. *The invention of Ethiopia: The making of a dependent colonial state in northeast Africa.* Trenton: Red Sea Press.

Human Rights Watch. 2003. *Ethiopia, lessons in repression: Violations of academic freedom in Ethiopia.* 15, 2 (A), January. New York: Human Rights Watch.

Jalata, Asafa. 2001. *Fighting against the injustice of the state and globalization: Comparing the African American and Oromo movements.* New York and Houndsmills: Palgrave.

Keller, Edmond. 1991. *Revolutionary Ethiopia: From empire to people's republic.* Bloomington and Indianapolis: Indiana University Press.

Lata, Leenco. 1999. *The Ethiopian state at crossroads: Decolonization & democratization or disintegration.* Lawrenceville, NJ and Asmara: The Red Sea Press.

Levine, Donald. 1974. *Greater Ethiopia: The evolution of a multi-ethnic society.* Chicago: The University Press of Chicago.

Riker, William. 1964. *Federalism: Origin, operation, significance.* Boston: Little-Brown.

Sorenson, J. 1993. *Imagining Ethiopia: Struggles for history and identity in the Horn of Africa.* New Burnswick: Rutgers University Press.

United States Institute of Peace. 2001. *U.S. human rights policy toward Africa: Special report.* Washington, 9 August.

Prologue
The Tears of Generations

Hamdesa Tuso

I am an Oromo who was born and raised in the Rift Valley, around Arsi-Nagel-lee and Shashamanne area. I represent the third generation in my family whose lives have been dramatically affected by the ongoing conflict in Ethiopia. My grandfather, Ulla Tulle, was gunned down in one morning on a wedding occasion at the foot of Mt. Duro. With him, five persons (family members and neighbors) also perished. My grandmother lost her first son, Bariso, in that onslaught; however, she managed to run away with four of her remaining children who were too young to comprehend that dramatic event. The government confiscated the entire cattle and property of the family and that of relatives and neighbors.

My grandmother was my first history teacher on the subject of the conquest and subjugation of the Oromo and many other population groups in the periphery of the Ethiopian Empire. The wound, which remained in her soul, was indelible in my memory through her tears over the slaughter of her son, Bariso. It was agents of the government who undertook this act of atrocity. It was done under the pretext that my grandfather had failed to pay taxes. This took place during 1930s, about four decades after the Oromos were conquered by Emperor Menelik II. This was the period in which the colonial administration employed various drastic pacification measures. One such method was eliminating the leadership among the Oromos. It happened to be that my grandfather was a leader in his community.

My father, one of the four children who escaped death due to the courageous act of my grandmother, grew up in terror and was further terrorized as a peasant under the regimes of Emperor Haile Selassie and the Derg. In the district of Arsi-Nageelle, the entire land, with a few exceptions, belonged to Her Imperial Majesty, Etege Menen. In addition to numerous unfair and abusive obligatory duties, the peasants of the colonized subjects had to endure in Haile Selassie's

Ethiopia. My father, as the government policy demanded of all subjects on the royal family owned lands, had to pay taxes to Haile Selassie's government as well as to the office of Her Imperial Majesty. Yet the West embraced Emperor Haile Selassie as "the wise and modernizing Emperor."

The Derg emerged claiming to be a pro-peasant, socialist government. The then socialist world embraced it as a truly revolutionary regime which cared about equality and socialist justice. However, in due course, the Derg emerged as one of the most brutal regimes in the world. Among its chief cruel policies toward the peoples in the periphery of the Ethiopian Empire, was the resettlement of the new *naftanya* (colonial settlers) to the South, the imposition of price controls on the agricultural goods of the peasants, and most of all, the introduction of forced villagization on Oromo peasants of the generations of my father and his children. Indeed, this scorched earth policy was meant to achieve the ultimate goal of the colonial conspiracy: to complete the final dispossession of the Oromo people of their resource, their national identity and cultural heritage!

The educated Oromos who, for the most part, represent the first generation literate segment in the Oromo society, did not fare any better. The Derg systematically and indiscriminately persecuted Oromo professionals and intellectuals through intimidation, imprisonment, torture, and physical liquidation.

In 1991, between May and July, I witnessed the dawn of a new era, the rise of the Tigrean power. Also, I witnessed in disbelief the coronation of Meles Zenawi and his Tigrean cohorts, the successor of the Derg, by the West as "the new agents for democracy and protectors of human rights" in the new political order of the post Cold War Ethiopia. On May 22, I learned from National Public Radio (U.S.) about the flight of Col. Mengistu Hailemariam from Addis Ababa. Like many who were following events in the Horn of Africa, I was taken by surprise by that extra-ordinary development in Ethiopia. After a few days, the U.S. State Department announced that it was hosting a peace conference in London, UK, on the political future of Ethiopia.

This announcement excited me for several reasons. First, on May 6, I had organized a colloquium on the same general topic hosted by the Institute of Conflict Analysis and Resolution at George Mason University, Fairfax, Virginia—the idea came from the course I was teaching about the conflict in the Horn of Africa at the time. The participants included the representative of the Eritrean People's Liberation Front (EPLF), the representative of the Oromo Liberation Front (OLF), the representative of the Tigray People's Libation Front (TPLF), the representative of the Embassy of Ethiopia in Washington, D.C., the representative of the U.S. State Department, and the representative of the USSR Embassy in Washington, D.C. A dialogue format was selected for the discourse. Professor Christopher Mitchell, an internationally recognized scholar on deep-rooted conflicts, served as the moderator. Three other colleagues from the faculty of George Mason University joined him in asking questions designed to facilitate dialogue. It so happened that the same parties would be invited to attend the London Peace Conference about two weeks later. At the London Peace Conference, Mr. Herman Cohen, Assistant Secretary for Africa, U. S. State Department, was the convener of the peace talks. The representative of the Soviet Union attended the conference as an observer.

Second, the London Peace Conference was significant in that peoples of the periphery of the Ethiopian Empire were represented for the first time in a major international arena since the conquest which took place during late 19th century and early 20th century. At least symbolically, the presence of the OLF at the conference was a historic event. It would be recalled that in 1941 when the British expelled Italy from Ethiopia, Oromos wanted to be given a chance to rule themselves; however, it was the London government which surrendered them to Emperor Haile Selassie against their will. Indeed, the event was a clear demonstration that the attempts by the successive Abyssinian regimes to obliterate the Oromo nation from the political landscape did not succeed.

Third, the U.S. played a pivotal role in the incorporation of Eritrea by Emperor Haile Selassie. Fourth, the involvement of the U.S. government in the peace process gave new hope because there prevailed an expectation that the U.S., freshly freed from its preoccupation with the Cold War, might ensure some measure of democratic process and might provide a new source of legitimacy for the peoples of the periphery.

Finally, I was invited to attend the London Peace Conference as consultant to one party in the conflict. I flew out of the Dulles Airport in Virginia on May 27 overnight and arrived in London in the morning. By the time I reached my destination in London, the conference was already over. On that evening, I watched on CNN the dramatic announcement by Mr. Cohen that the U.S had already unilaterally endorsed the TPLF to enter Addis Ababa and take charge. All of a sudden, the mood changed from that of hope to a new level of anxiety for peoples of the periphery. Having witnessed the hope that the Peace Conference would usher in a new era of equity and mutual respect for the various national groups in Ethiopia was dashed, I flew back in a mental condition of alarm and anxiety. Having witnessed the beginning of a new drama unfolding, I gave a speech in Minneapolis entitled, "The *utuba* has fallen: Will the Oromo create their own or remain a *galtu?*"

Now I wish to explain the two metaphors, *utuba* and *galtu* which were used as the central pieces relative to symbolic representation of the realties as I conceived them at the time of that speech. The term *utuba* in Oromo language is the central pillar that holds up the roof—of course, we are thinking about a traditional wooden house in an African setting for which grass is used as a cover. In such a house, there are other *utabas* which play subsidiary roles in upholding the structure. The term *galtu* (also an Oromo term) is used to describe a person who cannot make it on his own; instead he becomes dependent on another person. For example, a *galtu* cannot build his own house, cannot have his own farm; thus he becomes a dependent on someone else. He survives by providing some sort of service for the family on which he depends. More importantly, his very survival always depends on the mercy of that family.

Now placing these metaphors in the context of the politics in the Ethiopian Empire, I conceived the term *utuba* to represent the Amhara power structure which had played pivotal roles in the Abyssinian political landscape. The Amhara rulers, although they promoted Amhara dominance in all manners, somehow deflected the image of Amhara control by insisting that all peoples in the empire were Ethiopians and identification with any ethnic group was a "tribalistic" tendency and as such a manifestation of political "backwardness." Even more seriously, such notions were castigated as anti-unity of Ethiopia and not to be tolerated. The Amhara rulers were able to lure the educated class of the subordinate nationalities, for the most part, through varied forms of reward system (e.g. intermarriage, high posts, feudal titles, acceptance to the social class, etc.). They also, as we will discuss later in this work, employed brutal repression to crush anyone who manifested any semblance of challenge to their power.

Thus such a twin system of control—reward and punishment—provided the aura of security of the Ethiopian state, and projected an illusion that the political system in Ethiopia would be a viable one. In particular, the minds of the educated elite of subordinated nationalities were pacified by this twin system of control. Therefore the question in 1991 was, now that Amhara power has collapsed, what will keep Ethiopia together?

The metaphor *galtu* has a particular significance to the Oromo in their history of a century old colonial experience. Since a *galtu* ranks higher than a slave and a servant, how would he represent the social position of the colonized population? However, this metaphor represents the experience of the peoples of the periphery (i.e. their subordinate status) in some fundamental ways.

First, it is to represent the psychological and social condition of the educated elite of the subordinate nationalities. Because of their relatively higher status in the social order due to their formal education and socialization, they, for the most part, escaped the brutality perpetrated against the peasant class. However, they remained the classic *galtu*, perpetually dependent psychologically, culturally, and socially. They were the psychologically castrated class of the Oromo society. During the last century, the social phenomenon of *galtu* has been haunting the Oromos. Indeed, towering personalities such as General Gobana Daci played a crucial role in the conquest of the Oromos (he surrendered them to Emperor Menelik II, but the latter showed his gratitude by eliminating the General himself once the war of conquest was won). Gobana came to symbolize the ultimate Oromo quisling. Fitaurari Habte Giorgis who served as Minister of War during the reign of Empress Zawuditu, while Teferi Mekonen was still a political novice, refused, according to some accounts, to take power when the opportunity presented itself. Then there is the history of the Bale armed movement which rekindled Oromo nationalism and a quest for self-determination. There too, it was Oromo generals such as Jagama Kello and a few others who helped defeat the movement.

Second, toward the late 1980s, the TPLF began, in some vague manners, preaching about "unity based on equality" in the new Ethiopia to be ruled by the TPLF. Yet in 1990, it created the Oromo Peoples Democratic Organization (OPDO) out of prisoners of war for the purpose of undermining the legitimacy of the Oromo Liberation Front (OLF). Oromos in the Diaspora and at home universally condemned this move. As the London Peace Conference was adjourned abruptly and unilaterally by the American host of the Peace Conference, dashing any hope of creating some kind of equitable system of government for the post Derg Ethiopia, this author flew back from London thinking "who and which Oromo group will be the new Gobanas—the new *galtus*!" Little one imagined that Meles Zenawi would create a ceremonial presidency and recruit a highly educated Oromo, Nagasso Gidada, and of all things, a former supporter of the OLF, as his highest point of deception in creating an illusion of participation by the peoples of the periphery in the post-Derg Ethiopia.[1] Neither did one conceive that Oromos would universally reject the OPDO and label it as a *matanne*. *Matanne* in Oromo language refers to an object which does not possess the necessary structural qualities to stand on its own strength; instead, it attaches itself and crawls, so to speak, around a stronger object to accomplish its major functions. Metaphorically speaking, in the Oromo worldview, this represents the ultimate form of dependency.

Thus my choice of the term *galtu* as metaphor was conceived to represent these complex realities. In the Oromo notion of social realities, both of these metaphors, *galtu* and *matanne* signify in some clear ways dependence, lack of self-confidence, and lack of accountability. However, the designation of the term *matanne* to represent the relationship between the TPLF and OPDO illustrate a much stronger social disapproval on the part of the Oromos towards the rulers and their PDO's (People's Democratic Organizations).

There was another episode, a symbolically powerful one which I still vividly remember from that week—it was the tears of the fourth generation! During that week, upon returning from London, I talked to a lot of people about the political development in London as well as in Addis Ababa about the future of Ethiopia. During the same week, the Tigray People's Liberation Front (TPLF), with the support of the Eritrean People's Liberation Front (EPLF), was marching into Addis Ababa routing the remnant of the Derg soldiers.

One evening, I was discussing these rapidly unfolding events with a young Oromo woman. I will call her Shaggitu. She was a refugee awaiting a decision from the U.S. Immigration and Naturalization Service on her application for political asylum. All of a sudden, she broke into tears. I was lost as to what to say. She kept on crying, louder and louder. What confused me was the fact that she was, for all intents and purposes, an apolitical person. After sometime, I asked her why she was crying.

She calmed down and softly began talking. "You don't understand, you don't understand!" she replied. Her voice started to rise again. "You will never understand what will be happening to the people in Ethiopia," she added. "You are lucky; you were outside during the Red Terror!" she continued. Then she carefully explained to me her thesis. She said, "You see, the Derg was a minority political group. It was not accepted by the people. So in order to be accepted, it killed so many and destroyed so much. Then she went on. "You see, this group is another minority. So, they are going to kill so many and cause so much damage to impose themselves on the people."

Shaggitu had direct traumatic experience with the Derg. As a teenager, she lived in Addis Ababa during the years of the Derg. The Derg killed her older brother during the Red Terror. She almost lost her own life when the agents of the Derg raided her apartment one morning to capture her brother who was eventually killed. Her father died of stroke as the result of the stress he had experienced from the tragic loss of his son and the mounting social turbulence during the Red Terror. He left behind ten children and a widow who did not have much education. Suddenly, Shaggitu's world collapsed before her watchful eyes. Just like my grandmother, she sustained emotional scars from the legacy of violence during the brutal years of the Derg.

The Red Terror was a violent conflict between three political entities—the Derg, the Ethiopian People's Revolutionary Party (EPRP), and MEISON (the All-Ethiopian Socialist Movement). Essentially, the central issue in the conflict was who would have exclusive control over political power in the post Haile Selassie Ethiopia. All the three political organizations, for the most part, were controlled by the Amharas.[2]

For the Oromo students, the Red Terror had a special significance in two major ways. First, since the leaders of these contending political organizations (the Derg, EPRP, Meison) were very conscious of the fact that Oromos were the majority, each perceived that any organization that would gain Oromo support would be in a more advantageous position to attain the goal of winning supremacy in the a new political order.

Second, the ghost of the Oromo Liberation Front was increasingly looming over the political landscape of the empire. Consequently, Oromo students became suspects by all three groups, leading to the targeting of Oromo students either for recruiting them for one's political organization or eliminating them through physical liquidation.[3]

The tears of Shaggitu represent the tears of the fourth generation of Oromos whose lives have been dramatically shattered as the result of conquest and colonization. Indeed, Shaggitu's predictions came true. The Tigrayans, once they took over Addis Ababa, imposed themselves through sheer military might and violence. The rise of Tigrayan power has had profound ramifications for the Oromo society. The TPLF, the successor of the Derg, systematically aborted the internationally advertised elections of June 1992, successfully purged all the genuine Oromo organizations, and then declared war on the Oromos. Meles Zenawi is now conducting genocide against the Oromos in his wars from the Red Sea to the Indian Ocean. In his war with Eritrea, he has been using Oromo peasants as cannon fodder.[4]

As if controlling some thirty million Oromos in Ethiopia is not enough, he has recently occupied half of Somalia. His agents, "as agents for democracy and protectors of human rights," in the new political order in post-Cold War Ethiopia, have penetrated the heartland of Kenya to terrorize Oromos, even those who are Kenyan citizens.[5]

Early studies about Ethiopia have been exclusively about the Abyssinian kings and the power based Orthodox Church, the deadly rivalry among them, their conquest of the periphery, and their intrigues with the external powers. The conflict which dominated the scene during the 1960s and early 1970s, was essentially between the young educated *habasha* intellectuals and the old upper class represented by the Emperor, the nobility, and the Orthodox Church. The major story that grabbed the attention of the international community during the 1980s, for the most part, was about the conflict between the Amhara dominated regime in Addis Ababa and the two Tigrayan political organizations (TPLF and EPLF). Now in the 1990s, the major story of the conflict in the post-Derg Ethiopia is about the new conflict between two Tigrayan groups—TPLF of Tigray and the Eritrean government in Asmara.

The personal narrative I have attempted to present here can be told by hundreds and thousands of other families in the periphery of the Ethiopian Empire. I relate this personal narrative in the hope of making a point: the population in the periphery in Ethiopia comprises about 70 percent; yet the analysis which predominates the social scene in Ethiopia has been almost exclusively about the Abyssinian core and it is usually exclusively about the machinations of the Abyssinian ruling class.

In my view, this historically skewed treatment of the political development in the Ethiopian Empire, invariably in support of the narrative of the Abyssinian core at the expense of the overwhelming majority populations in the periphery, has created a distorted view of the realities of the ever-raging conflict in the collapsing empire of Ethiopia. As the African proverb goes, "When elephants fight it is the grass beneath the feet which suffers." I believe the record will show that it has been mainly the people in the periphery who have been the grass beneath the feet of the giant elephants in the struggle for exclusive power in the Ethiopian-state. It seems that *habashas* have managed to dominate the international scene by effectively occupying the two opposing positions in the universe of the ongoing social conflict. In one category, the winner campaigns in the world arena for recognition and in another category, the loser runs around the world as the victim asking for sympathy.

To be sure, as a student of social conflict I readily recognize resolving deep-rooted social conflict such as the one in Ethiopia will be an arduous and complex undertaking if there will ever be some reasonable and just resolution. However, it is my strong view that any new attempt to make peace in that overheated, complex social order has to be preceded by assembling reasonably representative and accurate information which could result in some sound diagnosis. Thus far it is very clear, at least from my point of view, that the analysis of social change in Ethiopia has missed the mark by a significant margin (this may be an understatement of the problem).

Ethiopian studies not only ignored the story of the majority in the periphery—the bloody conquest, the subsequent subjugation, and the perpetual exploitative relationships between the core and the periphery—they even failed to sufficiently recognize the deadly inter-group conflict within the Abyssinian core which has been driving the political discourse in the empire. The level of ignorance and the extent of mis-diagnosis on the part of external powers about politics in Ethiopia has been just as stark, and to some extent, even worse than that of the Ethiopianists. It is hoped that in some small way this work will reflect, the social realities' perspective from the periphery of the deep-rooted and protracted social conflict in Africa.

Notes

1. The Oromo view relative to the ascendancy of Nagasso Gidada to the ceremonial presidency in the post-Derg Ethiopia was well captured by the title commentary by Tadesse Fida which appeared in Urjii, an Oromo paper in Addis Ababa. The

title read, "What a joke? In the ascendancy of Nagasso Gidada to [Presidency], the Oromo nation has been disgraced." See *Urjii* Vol. II, No. 24 (August 29, 1995), p. 7.

2. The conflict during the Derg, particularly the Red Terror, has been well covered by different authors. One source comes from the members of the participants themselves. (See Tola, 1989; Tadesse, 1993; 1998. See also Wolde Giorgis 1989:31-34).

3. I have collected valuable information over the years through interviews from Oromo students and professionals who lived in Ethiopia during the Derg on this aspect of the conflict.

4. See "Atrocities and abuses against Oromo in Kenya" a detailed report inserted in a Press Release issued by Oromia Support Group, August - October 1999, No. 29; See also Said Wabera, "Town tense as trader Is killed," 15 August 1999.

5. See David Hirst, "In Tsorona, On the Eritrea-Ethiopia Border," The Guardian, 18 May 1999. For a summary of a first hand account as related by conscripted Oromos in this war see "Fighting talk: Students and captured soldiers tell of forced conscription and horrors of battle", Sagalee Haaraa, Oromia Support Group Newsletter, No. 28 (May-July 1999), pp. 4-5.

Part I

Social and Political History

Chapter 1

Conquest and Forced Migration: An Assessment of the Oromo Experience

Mekuria Bulcha

INTRODUCTION

Forced migration and uprooting are not sufficiently researched and acknowledged even though they have been part of Oromo history since their conquest by the Abyssinians at the end of the nineteenth century. During the last one hundred years, the chain of events that were directly or indirectly related to the conquest have spurred internal and external displacement of the Oromo population. Thus many Oromos were forced to move from their places of residence to become refugees in their own country and abroad or were taken and sold as slaves. Although slaves and refugees are separate sub-categories of involuntary migrants, both are victims of forced migration. The social and psychological deprivation caused by forced migration across international borders affect both categories of migrants.

While the main concerns of this chapter are internally displaced persons and refugees, some remarks will be made on slavery only when needed for comparison. The flow of Oromo refugees, which was sporadic in the past, has become more or less continuous since the 1960s. Hence, the latter part of this chapter deals mainly with the predicament of contemporary Oromo refugees.

CONQUEST AND UPROOTING

The largest uprooting and displacement in the history of the Oromo people was probably that caused by the Abyssinian conquest which took about 30 years to accomplish. Between the 1870s, the date of the conquest of Wallo in the north, and the subjugation of Boorana in 1899 in the south, large numbers of Oromos were uprooted as they left their home areas to seek shelter in the yet unconquered parts of Oromoland.

Large scale looting of property both in Oromoland and in the neighboring territories conquered by the Abyssinians exacerbated uprooting and other negative consequences of the conquest. Even within its own territory, the Abyssinian state was always predatory. Its kings, nobility and soldiers thrived on looting rather than on legal taxation of their peasants. From the time of the conquest and until the mid-1930s, the predatory habit of the Abyssinian state and soldiers became the most destructive instrument of warfare against the people of the South.

The Abyssinian armies took all transportable property and burnt homes, food stores, crop-fields and other properties which they could carry away. Herbert Austin, who passed through one of the newly conquered districts in September 1898 witnessed the destruction caused by the Abyssinian army in Gamu Gofa in the South, had this to say:

> .. the Abyssinians had recently devastated the whole of this region ... we could obtain no food at either Murle or Kerre, the people of whom were starving. The Abyssinians had done their work thoroughly. They had scoured both banks of the river, carried away all the cattle, goats, and sheep, cut down crops, burnt down the granaries with their store of food, and taken away captive men, women, children (cited in Hickey 1984:48).

What followed this indiscriminate destruction was famine that in turn caused massive death and displacement in various parts of the Oromo country. The 1889-92 famine which coincided with the conquest and in several regions, in fact, has no parallel in the history of the Oromo. It is said that hyenas attacked and devoured human beings who were enfeebled by starvation and unable to defend themselves. In Wallaga, in the west, a myth about a man-eating beast and half-human monster called *adi* is part of the history of that period and famine.[1] In Hararge, in the east, the period is remembered as the time when God was no longer kind and did not care for the weak (Hassen 1979:9).

Reports by European travelers visiting what is today the southern half of Ethiopia present unanimous impression of the results of the conquest; the travelers saw everywhere abandoned villages and other "signs of vanished population" (Darley 1926:198-99). They were struck by the destitution of the people they met (Smith 1896:123-27). Some of them estimated that the Oromo population was reduced to almost half of its pre-conquest size. The Russian officer Lt. Alexander Bulatovich, who was a guest of Emperor Menelik and who visited most of the conquered areas following Ras Wolde Giorgis and his army of 30,000 men on an expedition to Kaffa and Maji noted the demographic consequences of the conquest in Ilu Abba Bor as follows:

Ten to twelve years ago this countryside was completely settled, and of course, there wasn't a piece of good land left uncultivated. But cattle disease led to famine, and *destruction of the population during the subjugation of the region has half depopulated it*. Riding through, every minute you come across straight lines of ... cactus among the overgrowth, indicating former property boundaries or the former fence of a farmstead. Now the territory all around is completely overgrown with bushes... Rarely, you can come upon a Galla [Oromo] settlement ...On November 16, we ... spent the night at the home of a Galla. The family consisted of the host (the father of whom was killed by Abyssinians during the subjugation), his mother and two wives. ... The host himself, apparently, was reconciled with his fate, but his mother looked on Abyssinians [escorting Bulatovich] with fear and anger and sat by the fire all night long (Bulatovich 1897:13-14). [Emphasis added]

The Abyssinians carried out constant raids in the conquered territory using the maintenance of law and order as pretexts, but they used the raids to capture slaves. During the conquest, slavery became in itself an important cause for both internal and international displacement of its population. Menelik and his armies were able to round up, in a single expedition ten times as many captives as the slave-raiders all together were able to capture in a couple of years a decade earlier.[2] Most of those who were captured during the war or the slave-raiding expeditions were taken to the north to serve the Emperor and other members of the royal family, and in the households as well as on the estates of land-lords or were sold in the markets. The Ethiopian slave export increased significantly during the second half of the nineteenth century. Available information from the period indicate that a large proportion of the so-called Abyssinian or Ethiopian slaves sold in the markets of northern Africa and the Arab countries were Oromos.

INTERNAL AND EXTERNAL DISPLACEMENT

Nearly all regions of Oromia were affected by the conquest, and internal as well as external displacement of population took place in one form or another. Both oral traditions and written records confirm that even regions whose rulers submitted without much resistance did not escape the destruction, exploitation and displacement caused by the conquest. According to these traditions, not only economic production but also social reproduction was thwarted. The following verse quoted from a *Geerarsa* (a genre of the traditional oral Oromo poetry expressed in song) sang by a bachelor who lived in one of the regions which initially submitted without resistance, to console his fiancée who was aggrieved by the postponement of their marriage expresses the situation.

> When I was ready for marriage,
> Dajjaach Birru descended upon us.
> I gave him all my money to save my life,
> And I am left only with the tatters on my ass.
> Even the married think to separate to day,
> Be patient, you have yet a long time to wait.
> (Author translation from Oromo language)

Dajjaach Birru in the above quote was the governor of Leeqa Qellem in Western Oromia between 1918-1927. Jote Tullu, the mooti (king) of Leeqa Qellem, was among those Oromo leaders who submitted to Menelik without armed resistance in 1886. Jote was made Dajja(zm)ach and was allowed to continue to rule his territory with some degree of autonomy. However, the initial peace between Jote and Menelik did not last long. When the imposition of the *gabbar* system was also met great resentment from the people, conflict broke out and Jote was removed from his post and imprisoned in 1908. His imprisonment led to open rebellion and the defeat of the Abyssinian army. It was to put down the rebellion and to re-establish Abyssinian rule that Dajjaach Birru was appointed from Addis Ababa and "descended" upon Leeqa Qellem accompanied by 7,000-8,000 soldiers in 1918. The punitive measures he took are said to have caused large-scale displacement of the Oromo population. Alessandro Triulzi who has recorded and analyzed protest songs from the same region and period wrote regarding forced migration and displacement that:

> ... the prosperous and seemingly contented condition of the country witnessed by Major Austin in 1900 had quite changed by 1918 when the *gabbar*, many of whom had left their homes and gone to the forest on individual basis, started to flee *en masse*. Some 9000 moved up north to the fertile Begi highlands, under the patronage of Sheik Hojäle al-Hasan ... (Triulzi 1980:179).

The war of conquest had generated refugees who fled to neighboring territories then under European colonial rule. However, records about the fate of these refugees or those who were sold into slavery are few and scattered. One of the written sources relates the fate of a prince, Firrisaa Abba Joobiir, and his followers. Firrisaa was the crown prince of the Guuma kingdom (today a district in Ilu Abba Bor) which was one of the five Oromo states in southwestern Oromia. Upon the annexation of Guuma by the Abyssinians in 1882, Firrisaa fled with some of his followers to Massawa on the Red Sea coast where they stayed for more than a decade (Cerulli 1922:45).

Enrico Cerulli has also recorded that around the years 1899-1900, Firrisaa went through the Italian colony of Eritrea to the Sudan. He assembled some of the Oromo refugees who lived along the Ethio-Sudan frontier, and entered the newly created Ethiopian Empire at Anffillo. From Anffillo he proceeded eastward to Guuma. On arrival in the land of his ancestors, Firrisaa invited all of its chiefs to a meeting and proclaimed Guuma independent of Abyssinia and himself its king. War broke out between the Oromo and the Abyssinians and Firrisaa was victorious in the initial stages. However, the Abyssinians came back with reinforcements and supplies of new weapons. After two and a half years of struggle, the pressure of well-equipped and well-supplied Abyssinian forces proved effective and the Oromo army was defeated; Firrisaa was killed; and the Abyssinians were able to consolidate their position in the region (Cerulli 1922:52). Fought in one of the remote corners of the Ethiopian empire at the end of the nineteenth century, Firrisaa's freedom struggle remains unknown even among researchers on Oromo history.

Uprooting and forced migration from Oromia did not stop with the end of conquest and the consolidation of Abyssinian rule. The harsh rule which the Oromo were subjected to, continued to spur uprooting and displacement almost at regular intervals. There are many oral accounts about families and communities who took refuge in inaccessible lowlands and perished because of malaria. Although not comparable to the internal displacement, there is some evidence to confirm that the conquest also caused cross-border migration all along the borders of the Ethiopian empire at the turn of the century. Dennis Hickey (1984:42), who had studied documents from that period wrote about the peoples of the southwest thus:

> A certain minority of these peoples avoided enslavement through defensive migration, either to a 'protected' agricultural zone of the southwest, or across the Sudanese border. In all probability, the flight of the Uduk from Beni Shangul (...), far from being an isolated phenomenon, had distinct parallels along the entire frontier. ... The depopulation often perceived by contemporary observers was more a product of [cross-border] out-migration and tactical retreat [internal displacement] than accurate indication mortality and captivity rates.

With regard to "cross-border" displacements in the South, one of the earliest records about Oromo exodus caused by the Abyssinian conquest is found in British colonial archives. It concerns the fate of about 4,000 Oromos who fled across the borders newly created by the British and the Abyssinians to British East Africa Colony in 1910. This occurred just about a decade after the conquest of the Boorana region and was induced by the harsh rule imposed by the Abyssinian *naftanya* administration. Describing the reaction of the Boorana Oromo, Margery Perham (1969:314) has noted that

> The population [in Boorana] was not large and the soldiers pressed so hardly upon the *gabbars* allotted to them that many of these fled

to the bush or into British territory. The governor [of Boorana],
urged by his soldiers, pressed the British authorities to round up and
send them back.

Correspondence between the Ethiopian Government and the British Ministry for Foreign Affairs during the period indicates the many attempts made by the former to get back the refugees and the humanitarian gestures of some of the British colonial officials of that time. Some British colonial officials both in Kenya and London argued that forced repatriation of refugees "could not be condoned on either moral or diplomatic grounds and would cause enormous damage to British prestige in East Africa."[3] However, some of the 'pragmatic' officials within the British colonial administration maintained that sentiments should not to be allowed to interfere with policy, and that the refugees should be used as a bargaining chip in the efforts to secure territorial agreement with the Abyssinia (Maud cited in Hickey 1984:145-46).

Fortunately, for the Oromo refugees, there were also influential officials within that administration who saw forced repatriation as morally objectionable. From London, Louis Harcourt, the British Colonial Secretary wrote in 1910 that "it would be objectionable to approve of the Boorana and other tribes being returned to the Abyssinian government, and their being submitted again to extortion which ... is the fate of most subject tribes under Shoan rule."[4] In fact, as one source put it, the British officials saw the *gabbar* system as "a far worse evil than slavery" (see *The Times*, 18 April 1931). Thus, the Oromo and other refugees were allowed to stay in the British colony.[5]

Documents in Kenyan and British archives show that over the next two decades (i.e. from 1910), the Ethiopian government never abandoned its claims on the Oromo refugees in Kenya but raised the question of their forcible repatriation on many occasions. The Abyssinian officials argued that "the provincial administration's viability was directly threatened by the flight of the gabbars and the erosion of its base of taxation." The Ethiopian government did not pay salaries to its soldiers and administrators but gave them a number of (depending upon the rank of the soldier) Oromo families as gabbars upon whose labor they lived. Hence its officials argued in their correspondence with the British that the land is useless without the Oromo gabbar, and insisted that the soldiers and administrators of Boorana province could not be provided for unless the refugees are sent back.

Although the Oromo refugee problem continued to cause some diplomatic problems for their colonial administration, the British Foreign Office refused to hand them over to the Ethiopian administration. In fact, for these refugees, their flight into the British colony was just a matter of internal displacement. The Boorana territory straddled the border between the Ethiopian empire and the British colony of Kenya; and for the Oromos, both the British and the Abyssinians were alien intruders. Hickey has argued that when the burden under *pax Amharica* became unbearable, an increasing number of Booran families took their stocks and moved south to the shelter of *pax Britannica*. Although it would be illogical to construe that any sort of colonialism is a promoter and guarantor of peace, the displaced Oromo were forced to stay in the territory occupied by the less oppressive colonial power—the British.

The overthrow of Lej Iyasu's government in 1916 also caused internal displacement of a significant number of people, mainly Oromos. The opposition that the Abyssinian nobility and clergy showed Iyasu's government was important because its contribution to perpetual conflict among religious and ethnic groups in Ethiopia than for the forced migration it caused at that time. Lej Iyasu was an offspring of a political marriage which the invading elite entered into with some of the indigenous Oromo elites. His father was an Oromo leader and his mother the daughter of the architect of the Ethiopian empire—Emperor Menelik II.

On the death of Menelik, Iyasu became heir to the throne and tried to go beyond the political marriage of the few elites from the ruling and subject nationalities and create a political integration of the various peoples, religions and cultures of the Ethiopian empire. As Hans Lockhot (1994:13) has aptly remarked, Iyasu found it humiliating and discriminating against a major part of his subjects if he allowed the prevailing ethnic and religious hierarchy to continue. Therefore the "Crescent had to be incorporated into the imperial crown as well as the Cross; and new heraldic figures had to be added to the national flag."

Thus, Iyasu's main aim became building a nation out of empire, and he was convinced that his policy of equality of all religions and ethnic groups before the law would reduce the empire-state's chronic conflicts and enhance economic and social development (Marcus 1994:113-14). Had it succeeded, Iyasu's policy could have probably reduced not only the ethnicity or nationality-related conflicts but prevented the mass-exodus of refugees that Ethiopia has been generating over the last seventy years. However, his vision of ethnic and religious pluralism and nation-building became a serious threat to the interests of the Abyssinian nobility and the Church. His religious policy was also a challenge to the so-called Tripartite powers—Britain, France and Italy—whose colonial territories shared borders with Ethiopia. Fearing that Iyasu's co-operation with the Muslim population of their colonies in Africa would prove subversive, they co-operated with the Amhara (in this case Shoan) nobility, providing them assistance including a "large consignment of machine guns" to bring him down (Lockhot 1994:23). Later Iyasu was unable to seek asylum in the neighboring colonial territories ruled by the British, the French and the Italians. Hence he became an internal displaced person, or a refugee within his own country with many of his followers. He roamed the hot Afar lowlands for five years. He was captured in 1921 and was kept in prison until 1935, where at the outset of the Ethio-Italian war, Haile Selassie had him killed. Some of his Oromo followers had fled to the British East Africa colony. Still today there are families in Tanzania who are descendants of those refugees.[6]

PEASANT UPRISING, COMMERCIAL FARMING AND DISPLACEMENT

The number of Oromos in the diaspora began to increase significantly in the 1960s when Oromo refugees crossed international borders in large numbers. First the suppression of the Macha and Tulama movement, a pan-Oromo voluntary association, produced some refugees who went to the Sudan and Somalia. But the largest flow of refugees was caused by the repressive measures of the Imperial government to crush peasant uprisings in the Bale and Sidamo regions (from 1963-70). Extensively bombarded by Ethiopian air and ground forces, thousands of Oromo peasants and pastoralists from Bale and Sidamo "crossed the border (into Somalia) in fear and awe of the huge silver birds that dropped fire on their huts and harvests" (Anon, Horn of Africa 1981:13)

Both the Macha and Tulama and the Bale movements had significant influence on the development of Oromo nationalism and the mobilization of Oromo against the Ethiopian regime. Particularly the Bale uprising had inspired a number of young men who crossed oceans to seek asylum in other parts of the world. These young men, who had Organic education, migrated to the Middle East, particularly Iraq and Syria either to seek further education or to receive military training for guerrilla activities to be waged against the Ethiopian regime. Many of them went back to join the struggle in Oromia in the early 1970s while the rest of them migrated further to Europe and North America.[7]

The 1960s was also the decade when commercial farming was introduced on large scale in Ethiopia with disastrous effects for sections of both the pastoralist and peasant populations. Numerous Oromo communities became victims of evictions and internal displacement. The involuntary migration caused by the eviction of peasants and pastoralists from their ancestral homelands may seem less dramatic or may not involve cross-border movements as those caused by war and political persecution, but it did cause trauma for the affected individuals and communities.

Before the 1960s, land without gabbars was considered as "tef meret" (wasteland), and irrespective of whether it is arable or not, such land was considered as lacking in value. Therefore, when land grants were made by the Imperial government, what was "given" was not just any piece of land, but "lem meret" or fertile land with gabbar or peasant cultivators. In the rural areas, the grant was measured not in square meters or hectares, but the number of gabbars cultivating it. Since they did not farm, the grantees were often absentee landlords to whom the gabbars were required to hand over the bulk of their crop as well as to provide personal service. The introduction of mechanized farming changed the relations between the landlords and gabbars in some parts of the Oromo country in the 1960s. As the tractor made farming a profitable activity, absentee landlords became interested in agriculture or rented their lands to others who went into commercial farming.

The new trend which Rene Lefort (1981:20) called "mechanized feudalism" made the gabbar dispensable, and took away the little land security he had in the previous system. The result was that thousands of the gabbar households were forcibly evicted from the lands which they cultivated for generations. The development affected even poor peasants who owned their plots of land and pastoralist also became victim of eviction, unemployment and involuntary migration.

Large scale eviction started in the Upper Awash Valley, where land used by the Jile and Karrayu Oromo for centuries was leased by the Ethiopian government to the Dutch HVA Company which owned extensive cane sugar estates in the area since the 1950s. Since the Imperial government considered all land in the lowlands the Crown or state property, peasant and pastoralist households, whose farming and grazing lands were taken over by commercial farms were not given any compensation. They were rather simply pushed into drier and less hospitable zones where their stocks diminished rapidly and their way of life destroyed. For example, John Markakis and Nega Ayele (1978:56) have noted that the Jile Oromo community disintegrated and disappeared as a group because of displacement.

The state continued to grant or lease large tracts of land to large and small commercial farms and individual farmers until 1974. According to Patrick Gilkes (1975:132), there were twenty-seven large and medium size agro-industrial enterprises in the valley in 1973. The number of pastoralist displaced by these plantations was conservatively estimated to be about 20,000 (Kloos 1982 cited in Jalata 1993:93). The Koka Dam and the Awash Game Park which are located in the Upper Awash Valley also uprooted thousands of Oromo pastoralists in the 1960s. Since the peasants and the pastoralists who were displaced in this manner were denied access to the waters of the Awash River, thousands of them perished in the famine which hit the northern Ethiopia in the period 1973-74 (see for example, Bondestam: 1984).

The problem of population dislocation caused by mechanized farming was not limited to the Awash River basin, but spread also to other regions. Edmond Keller (1987:144) has indicated that between 1941 and 1960 imperial land grant which averaged between 60,000 hectares per year rose between 1960-

1974 to an annul average of 175,000 hectares. The granted lands were either occupied by peasants or were grazing lands used by pastoralists. Those who were affected most by forced migration accompanying the land grants were perhaps the Arsi Oromo.

Generally, tenure insecurity which was caused by the evictions and involuntary migration of thousands of Oromo households, had its roots in the Abyssinian conquest of the South in the 1880s. This was the case in the Arsi region more than anywhere in the empire. Since Menelik's principal objective was permanent pacification of territories, he directed a ruthless policy of conquest when opposed which crushed the resisting areas. The result of fierce Arsi resistance was born by their descendants (Cohen 1987:50). The Arsi were not only severely punished for their stiff resistance which cost thousands of lives on both sides, their land was confiscated and distributed by Menelik among his army and Christian settlers from the North.[8] The Arsi became gabbars to the conquerors and to the new comers and continued to work on the land which they once owned. Many of them fled into arid lowlands.

Upon the introduction of mechanized farming in the region, thousands of Arsi peasants lost even the little right they had as gabbars, that is, the right to cultivate the land and feed their families, and they were forced to leave their homes. To oust the peasants from their holdings, the land owners destroyed the crops and bulldozed the homes of their former gabbars or tenants. The number of commercial estates in the awuraja (province) increased from one in 1967 to 126 in 1971 (Gilkes 1975:126). By 1971, five years after the introduction of commercial farming in the highlands of Chilalo, eviction was estimated to affect between twenty and twenty-five percent of the indigenous inhabitants. In some districts such as Itaya, the eviction rate was over thirty percent (CADU 1972). The majority of these peasants and pastoralists evicted by the "green revolution" moved to the regions of Hararge and Bale, and the Rift Valley lakes area.

The rate of eviction was even greater in the Rift Valley districts than in the highlands of Chilalo and other awurajas, and the Arsi Oromo pastoralists who inhabited the region between Maqi town in the north and Lake Hawaasa in the south were severely affected. Many of these pastoralists were pushed into the lowlands from their traditional grazing grounds in the highlands when the land grants to settlers from the north was accelerated by the state in the area after the Italian occupation (1936-1941). However, migration into the lowlands did not save them from land insecurity resulting from the Oromo defeat by the Abyssinians in the 1880s. Although the Oromo pastoralists paid tax on the land, the state and members of the royal family owned all land in the area. Fertile soil and asphalted highway which bisects the area from north to south, proximity to Addis Ababa and other facilities made these lowlands attractive to those who wished to make quick profits by commercial farming. According to Patrick Gilkes, there were 85 mechanized farms in the Shashemene district alone in 1972 and all of them have been started since 1968. Many of the farms were owned by "week-end farmers"[9] who were engaged in other occupations and were settled in Addis Ababa and other and urban centers.

The number of people evicted by commercial farming in the Rift Valley lakes area is unknown; but it seems to be greater than anywhere else in the empire. By 1973, the number of indigenous households living in the area was greatly reduced. Gilkes maintains that the rate of eviction was about 200 families a year in the Shashemene district alone. The rate for the whole area was without doubt much larger. Although little research is done regarding their fate, the evicted peasants and pastoralist generally left their home areas to seek land in other provinces (Bjeren 1985:83). That families carrying small children and driving their livestock south were common sight along the Addis Ababa-Awassa highway in the early 1970s.[10] This indicates that for many of the displaced households the destination was either Bale or other Oromo areas in the region.

The Imperial system of land tenure and the expansion of private commercial agriculture in Oromia were brought to an end with the military takeover. However, the eviction and internal as well as external displacement of Oromos did not stop. In all its ramifications, involuntary migration among the Oromo reflected their relations between them and their conquerors. The revolution hardly changed the basic characteristics of these relations.

The next, and so far the most, significant Oromo exodus from Ethiopia was sparked by events that followed the seizure of power by military Derg in 1974. Since I have discussed these events at length elsewhere (Bulcha 1988, chapter five in particular), suffices to mention here that the political and religious persecution, war, forced conscription into the military, forced labor, and economic policies pursued by Ethiopian military regime (1974-91) created the largest number of refugees to cross international borders in the history of the country. Oromos constituted a large proportion of these refugees.

Staffan Bodemar, one time head of the United Nations High Commissioner for Refugees (UNHCR) office in Mogadishu, estimated that out of the 350,000 Ethiopian refugees sheltered in camps in Somalia in 1979 as many as two-thirds were Oromos (Svenska Dagbladet 1979). Ulrich Braukämper (1982/83:4) who conducted a study in 1981, wrote that according to UNHCR estimates the number refugees in Somalia was about 700,000—"roughly one-third of whom may be Oromo, i.e., approximately 200,000 to 250,000." In addition, the "villagization program", by which the Mengistu regime forced millions of peasants front their traditional habitat into hastily set-up strategic villages, sent about 140,000 Oromo refugees to northwest Somalia in 1985-86 from the Hararge region alone.[11] More than two thousand of these "villagization" refugees perished because of starvation, and cholera epidemic that broke out in the over-crowded camp near the border town of Tug Wajale in northwest Somalia.[12]

All in all, there were, during the 1980s, between one and half to two million Ethiopian refugees in the neighboring countries, particularly, Somalia, Sudan and Djibouti. At least 360,000 of them were Oromos. Up to 1990, over 90 per cent of the Oromo refugees were in Somalia while the rest sought asylum mainly in the Sudan, Djibouti and in other African countries such as Kenya and Egypt. A small fraction of the Oromo refugees went to the Middle East, Europe, North America, and Australia.[13]

OROMO REFUGEES IN THE 1990S

The exodus of refugees from a country can be seen as that country's political malaise. One hundred years after its creation, Ethiopia today is showing no significant progress in terms of political development or respect for human rights, and the flow of refugees from the country seems to have no end. The exodus of refugees from Ethiopia in general, and of Oromo refugees in particular, did not cease with the fall of the Mengistu regime in 1991. The present regime's failure to respect basic human rights is still creating Oromo refugees and internally displaced persons. Many of the Oromo, who now flee Ethiopia, are businessmen, intellectuals and public servants. Since the violations of human rights is on the increase under the current regime, the repatriation during the previous decades is also made impossible (see among others the annual and country reports of Amnesty International (1991-96); Tronvoll and Aaland 1995; Pollock 1996:5-16).

Sudan which has a very generous refugee policy, has accepted thousands of Oromo refugees over the years. Still today refugees are crossing into the Sudan from the western regions of Oromia. In the 1990s, there were tens of thousands of Oromo refugees in Northeast Africa. Unfortunately, generosity towards refugees is not an expressed policy of all the African states in the region; particularly Djibouti. Since 1974, several thousand Oromos have sought refuge there but from 1983 onwards, the Djibouti government has followed a policy of refoulment (forcible deportation) of refugees to Ethiopia (see among others, Greenfield 1983:53-54). Roberta Aitchison (1983:21) has noted that the impression one gets of "the desperate poverty in this harsh, desert place is stark. But more distressing was the utter vulnerability of refugees." For many refugees, life in Djibouti is a nightmare because of the "violent rafles, detentions, and rape by border guards and city police." Aitchison (1983b:4) described the raffs (pronounced as "ruff") as routine sweeps whereby refugees are "seized from the streets of Djibouti city detained by local police, held overnight and brought by force in the mornings to work on local construction projects" or are deported to Ethiopia.

In another article focusing on sexual abuse of refugee women in Djibouti, Roberta Aitchison (1984:26) has also pointed out that refugee women can be picked up from the street or even from their homes for any reason and raped at any time by police. She added that sexual abuse in job situations is a big problem and it is the fate of many female house servants. "If the woman says no, she is automatically fired; and the chance in finding a new employment without this requirement is minimal." For many female refugees, the ordeal starts the moment they cross into Djibouti territory where border guards often separate girls and women from male asylum seekers. The guards not only detain or rape these women, but also often keep their victims at the isolated border posts for days or even weeks. Roberta Aitchison (as above) reported:

> Lensa, one refugee, agreed to talk about her experience after two years of silence. At the age of 18, she arrived from the two-week trek through the Danakil desert physically exhausted, badly dehydrated, and with blistering sorts from exposure on her feet and body. But the most terrible part of her ordeal, she points out, was the three days she was held at the border jail and raped repeatedly.

The humiliation of rape affects not only the women themselves, but often also the mates of refugees from whom they are separated at the border posts and molested. When men who are in the company of these women are relatives or husbands, rape becomes even collective predicament. The powerlessness felt by men-folk to protect their family members from such horrendous disgrace as rape leads to guilty feeling and loss of self-respect which they may not overcome in their lives. The tragedy may not end with that, it could also cause family disintegration. Today, there are still a large number of Oromos who flee to Djibouti in order to escape political persecution in Ethiopia. Obviously few, if any, are aware of the tribulations that awaits them en route or on the country of asylum. Many refugees flee to Djibouti with the intention of using it as a gate to other countries of asylum. However, the majority do not have the possibility of seeking asylum elsewhere, but linger in Djibouti with the hope that political changes will take place back home and that they will return.

Although the turmoil that followed the fall of the Barre regime and the disintegration of the Somali state in 1991 had forced most of the Oromo refugees who lived in Somalia in the 1980s to disperse in all directions, some of them have stayed in Somalia and are still there in spite of the chaos and lack of protection by the international community (Challa 1992). Many of the former Oromo refugees in Somalia fled to Kenya where they were repulsed by the Kenyan authorities and thus deported to Ethiopia. Kenya has continued to threaten Oromo political refugees in 1996 with deportation to Ethiopia (Inter Press Agency, 10 April 1996). Recognizing the danger that these refugees would face in Ethiopia, Denmark, Germany and Norway have accepted and resettled some of them. Roughly estimated, there are between fifteen and twenty thousand Oromo refugees in Europe and North America and perhaps about the same number in the Middle East. Australia has resettled several hundred Oromo refugees since the mid 1980s. A large proportion of the Oromo refugees in Europe and North America are educated while the majority of those who live in the Horn of Africa are peasants with little or no formal education. However, irrespective of their background and their countries of asylum, these refugees go through similar experience or face similar predicaments: i.e. uprooting, deprivation and crisis of discontinuity.

THE PREDICAMENTS OF EXILE

Uprooting is more than a physical absence from home. It is a predicament which concerns the inner balance of the individual. In other words, it involves an emotional crisis caused by the individual's separation from his/her natural physical and social environment and a psychological problem of adjusting to the new one. Refugees see or experience their situation in different ways: some see it as a curse, others feel it as bereavement. In a letter to the UNHCR magazine, *Refugees* (1985:8), a twenty-one-years-old Angolan refugee expressed his predicament as: "we refugees are the most accursed people on the Planet Earth. And many people in the world do not know how this curse affects us." Although psychologists, sociologists and anthropologists who have studied refugees and refugee communities have described the magnitude of their problems, the inner crises and bereavement that refugees feel are often concealed from and are beyond the cognition of non-refugees.

One way of getting an insight into this aspect of life in exile is through literature, music and art produced by refugees. Such works often mirror the inner (mental and emotional) reactions of refugees to this loss. In her study of Ugandan refugees in Southern Sudan, Barbara Harrell-Bond (1986:286) has noted that the themes of songs composed by Ugandan refugees "showed preoccupation with death, suffering, hunger, and violent revenge." She added, "Many songs are dirges. ... [and] are now performed as part of social events much more frequently than they were in Uganda." Perhaps for similar reasons, music composed by involuntary migrants and by their descendants are often nostalgic. The melancholic tone which characterizes black music such as blues, gospel music, and spirituals underline the perennial nostalgia felt by Afro-Americans about homes and roots from which their ancestors where violently uprooted and taken to the New World by slave-traffickers as well as the agonies which they suffered by the treatment which the slave owners and racial discrimination in

America. Songs and poems composed by Oromo refugees, as we shall discuss later on, reflect not only physical and political hardships but the overall potential problems felt because of uprooting bereavement.

In general, uprooting and forced migration creates a "crisis of discontinuity" (see for instance, Baskauskas 1981:278). The crisis of discontinuity concerns the multiple disruptions of life-goals and the loss which characterize the lives of refugees. One such a disruption concerns marriage and family life. Among Oromo refugees in the West, the ratio of unmarried single men in their late forties is still quite large, and it seems late for many to build a "normal" family life. The unsettled characteristic of life in exile and the demographic profile of the Oromo refugee population are contributory factors to this situation. Up to the mid-1980s, single young men constituted the vast majority of Oromo refugees; women were a minority. For example, in the Scandinavian countries the proportion of Oromo male to female refugees was about five-to-one in the 1980s and for many men it was impossible to find a partner for marriage. Even the demographic profile of Oromo refugees I studied in Sudan in the early 1980s showed the same structure (Bulcha 1983). My findings were confirmed by a study which Virginia Luling (1986:131-420) conducted among Oromo refugees in the same region in 1986. Today, however, the demographic profile of the Oromo in the diaspora is changing as more Oromo women are becoming refugees.

Flight also leads to disruption of careers and education. In countries where it takes several years for a refugee to get a residence permit, this concerns life in limbo for a long time, because without residence permit, it is impossible to work or study in many of these countries. The following poem, "All in My Thought", composed by Giddi Abamegal, an Oromo refugee in Kenya and published in Tilting Cages: A Collection of Refugee Writings, edited by Noomi Flutter and Cari Solomon (cited in Refugees, No. 105 1996:11), reflects this feeling of loneliness, uncertainty and rootlessness which permeates the lives of refugees everywhere.

> In front of my tilting cage,
> that little hut of plastics,
> so not to suffer from loneliness,
> I traveled far and wide,
> all in my thought.
>
> I went back to the remote past,
> our home and its vicinities,
> grandma and her stories
> of my great-grandfather,
> those mighty warriors

from whom I inherited
intolerance and pride.
I traveled far and wide,
all in my thought.

I went far into the future,
into my dreams and high hopes.
To see what was there,
where this changeless passage of time,
where this endless kick of my heels,
could possibly one day lead.
I traveled far and wide,
All in my thought
I also traveled to eternity,
to see my soul at the end of this mess.
I traveled far and wide,
all in my thought.

The majority of African refugees are from rural areas. Many Oromo refugees, particularly most of those who live in the countries of the Horn of Africa, have their origins in traditional rural communities where social relations are closely knit and life is based on a strong sense of solidarity and interdependence. In those communities, members are oriented to one another cognitively and emotionally. Among the Oromo, this cognitive and emotional orientation is reflected in the three concepts of *warrummaa* (family hood), *ollummaa* (community) and *firummaa/soddummaa* (affinity) which are considered as crucial for the well-being of both the individual and society. The family is integrated in the community and the individual is part of a mutual support system which characterizes these forms of social relations. Uprooting and flight disrupt the individual's state of belonging to an immediate social environmental which is mainly the family and community. It impairs the solidarity the individual enjoys and the support he/she receives from these social networks. Left more or less alone, a refugee has to cope with a new environment which is often different and strange. Having stepped into anonymity one loses ones old identity and faces the difficulty of forging a new one. Hence, flight involves far-reaching loss incurred in order to attain physical security. The latter is obtained at the cost of social security which the individual enjoyed as member of a family and the community in his or her homeland. It is obtained at a great loss which often becomes difficult to repair as the life in exile becomes longer and longer

The type of loss that results from flight is often a cause for grief. This is a feeling which is expressed in a poem composed by Tahir Umar, an Oromo refugee, who fled to Djibouti in the late 1970s. In this poetic song composed in 1981, Nu Haqaaf Lolla ("We Struggle for Justice"), Tahir Umar grieves over his situation not only as his personal bad luck but collective predicament of all Oromos both in exile and at home. He relates the deprivation he suffers in exile to the general deprivation of the Oromo nation under an alien and oppressive administration. Tahir laments being uprooted, the loss of his roots and his homeland, and he deplores the suffering of his compatriots under the rule of alien aggressors who have occupied his country. Chanted in chorus and in a low rhythm and melancholic tone which seems to merge rhythms and tones of the *wadaaja*—the traditional Oromo communal prayer—with Qoranic religious songs, the taped version of this 20-page long narration also seems to express the quintessential feelings uprooted and displaced Oromos everywhere—at present and in the past.

The song brings to mind biblical lamentations of the Judaic Diaspora who paraphrase Psalm 137, prayed and wept by the sides of the rivers of Babylon as they remembered Zion from where they were uprooted and taken away. The graphic description of the geography and natural resource of Oromia, the cry about the misfortunes of Oromo nation, as well as the passionate appeal to Oromos to unite and bring an end to the causes of the collective predicament and exile reflects the sort of nostalgia and lamentation exile entails. An extract from the song goes:

> Thou knowst Waaqayyo (God), we're crying for justice,
> Thou knowst best, we need not tell Thee that;
> Our homes and our land, we are dispossessed by force;
> By force have enemies occupied our motherland,
> Dividing among themselves all her most productive parts.
> We lament the fate of our people enslaved,
> Hoping for Thine Solidarity, Thine unfailing Help.
> (in chorus)
> We rise up and beg Thee, Oh! Lord Mighty,
> To help us go back home to our country.
> (Author's translation from Oromo to English).

Research conducted among survivors of natural and man-made catastrophes has repeatedly confirmed one thing—their feelings of guilt. Survivors tend to indulge in self-blaming for what has happened to non-survivors. Researchers have also observed the same phenomenon among refugees. Flight seems to cause the feeling of guilt for different reasons. Many refugees feel guilty because of what they failed to do. They feel guilty for their failure to fulfill roles to which they are bound by family obligations. Men and women who left behind their relatives, often including their children, wives and husbands, and young people whose aging parents are left behind without support enhances the feeling of guilt.

> Oh! listen Oromo, brothers and sisters
> Those who like me are homeless refugees,
> Deprived of your country by the colonizers
> Tell me what is best, advise me what is wise;
> Can we forget our land and lead healthy lives?
> Or forsake our country, which is our paradise?
> Those who stayed behind, our fathers and peers,
> Children of the same womb, and all our compatriots,
> They truly are suffering amidst awful distress,
> And while we are alive and are in good health,
> Can we ignore them or have any peace to rest?
> They are anxiously waiting from us to hear,
> In their affectionate thoughts, and hopeful dreams.
> Let us in solidarity go back to our land
> (in chorus)
> Oh! Almighty God, lead us to freedom.
> Give us solidarity, our cause is just.
> Help us go back home to our motherland.
> (Author's translation from Oromo to English).

Refugees who live and work in Western countries and the oil-producing states of the Middle East send money to assist their parents and relatives and keep contacts by telephone. However, it is not possible to mend the attenuated family relations by making expensive telephone calls across continents and oceans once in a while, or to compensate for filial obligation by sending sums of money now and then. Telephone conversation does not compensate for the satisfaction that parents usually derive from having their offspring around them. Even if it is an expression of a primordial duty and is very important for the survival and comfort of its recipients, money sent by refugees to their aging relatives cannot compensate for the social, emotional and psychological security that children provide to their parents in traditional societies such as the Oromo.

Furthermore, since most refugees in Africa come from places where there are no post offices, telephones or they live in remote refugee camps and rural settlements, they cannot make any contact with their relatives. In many cases, the disruption of contact with their relatives is total. Nearly 50 percent of the 413 refugees I interviewed in eastern Sudan in 1981-83 had no contacts whatsoever with relatives after they left their homes in Ethiopia. In 14.5 percent of the cases, those who were left behind at home were children, spouses, and old parents (Bulcha 1988:217). This is an experience that they share with millions of refugees in Africa and other parts of the world. For example, in a study I conducted in the settlements of Ulyankulu for Hutu refugees from Burundi, and Likuyu for Mozambican refugees in 1994 in Tanzania, I found similar degrees of lack of contact with relatives in the countries of origin. Although the Hutu refugees left their homeland 20 years ago, their worries about relatives left behind and the desire to return home to find out what had happened to them in the meantime was still very acute.

In traditional societies such as the Oromo, one of the most important social obligations of a son or a daughter is providing a decent funeral to deceased parents. A funeral is a sacred ritual which demands the presence of the deceased person's kin and kith. Paul Baxter (1978:15) has described the Boorana Oromo society as one that sometimes seemed to float on a river prayers and blessings (*eebba*), who celebrated the values that are central to their culture. *Eebba*, as conducted by elders and in some cases also by the qaalluu (traditional ritual leaders) in other parts of the Oromo country, is also a deep rooted ritual reflecting on peace, fertility, rich harvests, health, long life and a decent funeral. One of the many phrases which is commonly recited when a person is the focus of such a ritual is, "dhukkubsatee kan si gaafatu, duutee kan si owaalu hin dhabin" ("may you have someone who takes care of you when ill; may you have someone who gives you a funeral").

According to this traditional ritual, those who have children are blessed because they have someone who takes care of them when they are sick and also give them decent funerals when they die. In other words, "someone" in the above *eebba* is a euphemism for a child, and being a son or daughter is to be ritually charged with the social and moral responsibility for aged parents. Not to do so for one's parents is a great failure in a person's life. But such a failure in filial duty is an unavoidable corollary of uprooting and flight. Consequently, for many Oromos, the inability to be at the side of sick parents or to mourn and give them a proper funeral when they die causes a sense of lingering grief. The predicament associated with life in exile is felt and hurts most when, as often the case is, one hears the death of one's own child, spouse, parent or sibling a long time after it had happened. The inability to share happy moments such as marriage and birth with family and relatives is also the cause for a deep sense of deprivation among the uprooted.

HOMELESSNESS AND NOSTALGIA

Loss caused by uprooting is also associated with nostalgia about the place of origin and events and objects that are associated with such a place. Uprooting causes a cognitive disorientation that tends to affect the emotions and psyche of the uprooted. Edward Shils (1978:405) commented on the relation between uprooting and nostalgia as follows:

> There is much sentiment about the place of origin but it becomes articulate usually after departure from that place ... perhaps no awareness of attachment arises until there is an actual or threatened displacement. Generalised appreciation or attachment to a place of past location occurs only after the loss of the object itself.

Generally, the Oromo are quite sentimental about their *qeyee* or heimat. Compared to their neighbors such as the Gurage, the Amhara, the Tigrayans, the Somali, the Oromo seem to be more reluctant to settle elsewhere. The Oromo peasant, for example is, particularly reluctant to leave his *qeyee*. Hence, there has been very little rural-urban migration among the Oromo before the 1970s. For an Oromo, his *qeyee* is more than a place. It symbolizes both the physical space which he/she inhabits and the social life that is embedded in it is a crucial part of ones identity. An Oromo peasant abandons his *qeyee* only when conditions become extremely unbearable or life threatening or when opportunities for education, public employment, etc. in the place of destination are deemed significantly attractive. In fact, "qeyee koo'ttan du'a" ("I will die in my qeyee"), is a common Oromo saying. This seems to be the case even among the semi-nomadic Boorana Oromo pastoralists who inhibited the southern part of their country. They move within a defined territory which has its *olla* (camp sites), *ella* (water-holes), *hawicha* and *fura* (grazing fields), *hora* (salt-leaks), burial mounds, and ritual sites. Their life which follows, a more or less regular and patterned movement within a sort of spatially oversized qeyee disturbed by major droughts and war or by interference from state authorities. When such disturbances occur and the Booran are pushed out of their environment, and as is the case sometimes, their life becomes disoriented and destitution is often the result.

Being sentimental about one's place of origin as indicated by the dictum "east or west, home is best," is a feeling which is common to human beings everywhere; of course, with varying degrees. But awareness and sentiments about the place of ones origin usually become acute when one is forcibly displaced and the possibility of returning home becomes uncertain. With that comes also a generalized, often exaggerated, appreciation of the place of birth, a home. Although home and homelessness are familiar themes in the myths and legends of different societies and nations, they seem to be more frequent among those who have known long histories of uprooting.

Notions of homelessness and "roots" tend to be frequent in the discourse, music, prayers and lamentations of slaves and refugees than those (of voluntary migrants and are traceable in written records and traditions from the past. The psalmodic lamentations of the Judaic Diaspora mentioned above is an example of such a discourse. Similarly, there are records from the past that indicate the longing expressed by Oromos sold into slavery for their relatives and homeland.

One such record consists of letters exchanged in 1840 between two Oromo youth, Akkafedhe and Aaga, who were sold into slavery and were taken to Germany, via Gondar, Gallabat and Cairo around 1839.

Akkafedhe wrote to Aagaa:

> O do not think, my brother, that thou wilt not be able to see thy family again, as 'butter fallen into the fire comes not back'. Many Gallas [slaves] who went from the hands of their mothers and fathers sit with weeping hearts; though thou shouldst not see thy mother and thy father again, be comforted! Better pray for them, that God may let them live as happily as possible. (Tutschek 1845:90-91)

Apparently seeking to encourage Aaga, but probably also reflecting his own dreams of returning home one day, Akkafedhe added:

> ... Who knows whether thy master, when thou art grown up and able to go alone, will not send thee into thy father-land! O my brother, at that time what will thy mother say when thou tellest her: was sold and carried to a country that I did not know; and there a man took me to himself and educated me, and when I was grown up he said: 'seek now thy mother and father'. On that day thy relations and brothers will pour out to meet thee (Tutschek 1845:90-91).

Akkafedhe persuaded Aaga to pray for his parents and relatives. Akkafedhe's dreams were never fulfilled. He died a few months after he wrote the above letter. Concerning the preoccupation of the uprooted with thoughts about family and homeland, the Swedish missionary, Lundahl, who sent the Oromo ex-slave Onesimos Nasib to Sweden for education, wrote from his station at Massawa to his colleagues in Stockholm, "...the young man might now and then lie awake far into the night praying for his people and his native country."[14] The dream about home which preoccupies the minds of many of those who experience forced migration, could also pass from one generation to the next particularly when assimilation in the new country is hindered by racial factors. Thus "projects" like the "Back to Africa" movement which Marcus Garvey propagated among Afro-Americans during the first decade of the last century, and works which, like Alex Haley's famous book, *Roots*, express the homelessness and nostalgia felt by those who have, not often directly but indirectly experienced the bane of forced migration.

It was only after becoming refugees that many Oromos started to feel, to see, to talk, to write about and to sing the natural beauty of their country and the abundance of its natural resources. The appreciation for Oromo culture, language and history was strengthened, and in many cases born in exile. The following passage from Tahir Umar's poem expresses such sentiment.

> Blessed Oromiya which God has given us,
> You are a heaven on earth, our own paradise,
> We know of no land which matches your bounty
> Where one need not suffer or complain for being thirsty
> Where heat or cold causes no discomfort or despair
> Where need doesn't arise, for buying cool wholesome air
> Exile has taught us the truth about what you are.
> (Author's translation from Oromo to English).

Being in exile, Tahir Umar discovers that his homeland is a paradise. The host country which is not named in the text but is obviously Djibouti, is hell-like in many ways. Those who caused his flight have driven him and his compatriots from paradise into hell. One who listens to Tahir's poetic song in its entirety gets not only a clear image of the landscape, natural beauty and pleasant weather of Oromia, but also the bareness of his host country where great discomfort is caused by scarcity of water and an extremely hot climate. Perhaps no language has all the right words to adequately express the loss and suffering one might experience in exile or the disgrace and humiliation one often feels when one "walks the stairs of others" in search of safety, but Tahir's nostalgic narrative, when read or heard in its original language also expresses the nostalgic longings of the Oromo diaspora and hopes with remarkable clarity. It is not only those Oromo who sought refuge in the arid lands of the Horn of Africa who express this sort of intense feelings and longing for their homelands in songs and poems, but also those who found safe havens in Europe and North America.

OPPORTUNITIES AND THE CRISES OF UPROOTING AND EXILE

From what is said above, it is quite clear that life in exile is harsh and bitter. However, that should not be construed to mean that exile is only an endless story of deprivation or that refugees are a collection of lost and pathetic individuals. Exile can also offer an opening to new opportunities. Many people discover or realize their own individual potentialities only when faced by great challenge; and such a discovery often leads to optimism about the future of individual or collective life. Ulrich Braukämper who conducted an anthropological investigation among Oromo refugees in Africa and in Germany in 1981 argued that the Oromo refugees seem to see the future in terms of a kind of unconscious dialectic, the former life in their country of origin being the thesis, the existence as a refugee the anti-thesis, and the new society which is to be created after the time of exile being the synthesis. What Braukämper is referring to is the hope and dynamism that characterizes the attitudes of refugees everywhere.

The creation of a new society after exile requires the participation of the refugees, both in the struggle against the cause of flight and in the preparation of new foundation on which the new society is to be founded. In fact, exile has provided a stage for a struggle against the cause of flight and for the reconstruction of new society in the future.

Like all repressive systems, the Ethiopian state has always suppressed the creative talents of its subjects. Thus, individual potentials to think, research and produce literary and artistic works which are critical of the existing order, were censored. The Oromo were not allowed to develop their talents, particularly when such talents reflected Oromo identity or culture. Exile has given many Oromos an opportunity to do what they were forbidden to do in Ethiopia. It gave them the freedom of expression; freedom to work only for a political change in their country of origin, and for the development of Oromo culture and language, and to make research into Oromo history even if most of the time the resources were not there. More importantly, exile enabled them to organize themselves as free individuals and Oromos, to carry out these objectives.

OROMO ORGANIZATIONS IN THE DIASPORA

The large scale exodus of Oromo refugees in the 1970s and 1980s gave birth to several Oromo organizations in the diaspora. The characteristics of these organizations varied according to the policies of the countries of asylum. In Somalia, Djibouti and Saudi Arabia where refugees were allowed to set up their own associations, underground Oromo youth, women, workers and relief organizations have existed since the early 1980s. In Sudan, where refugee organizations were not only tolerated but even enjoyed support from the host authorities, the Oromo Relief Association (ORA), and *chaya ummattaa* (mass associations) "have been able to put up an efficient network to meet the material and psychological needs of the exiled Oromo—and to some extent also of other refugee groups, such as the Koma and Berta, who were not able to establish their own associations" (Braukämper 1982/83:10).

In Europe and North America, Oromo organizations came into existence in 1974 with the creation of Tokkummaa Bartoota Oromoo Awrophaa (Union of Oromo Students in Europe TBOA), and Tokkummaa Oromoo Amerika Bitaa (Union of Oromos in North America, UONA). By 1977, TBOA did set up branches in several European countries; it also established contacts with the Oromo Liberation Front. By the beginning of the 1980s, branch unions were also organized in the former Soviet Union and several of other communist countries in Eastern Europe which gave scholarship to thousands of students from Ethiopia. In North America, the first union was established in Washington D.C. and spread to other states and to Canada which has received and resettled thousands of Oromos since the mid-1980s. Writing on political refugees in general, Egon Kunz (1981:46) has suggested that

> Believing that they share a cause with the majority of their compatri-
> ots left behind, many feel guilty for not sharing also their fate with
> them. This sense lead some to perceive the existence of an "historic
> responsibility" which is placed on them, impelling them to work
> for the cause and compensate for their freedom, by speaking up for
> those silenced at home.

The major objectives of TBOA and UONA was precisely this "historic responsibility" and sense of commitment which Kunz has pointed out. Particularly TBOA has, in its bylaws, stated that it aims:

1. to work for the revival and promotion of the Oromo people's culture;
2. to research into Oromo history and struggle against the existing oppressive system and forces that are suppressing the Oromo culture and language and distort Oromo history;
3. to provide support for the Oromo national struggle and uphold the banner of independence in cooperation with the OLF; and,
4. to introduce the Oromo people to the international community and make their plight known in order to solicit moral, economic and political support.

The objectives mentioned under (1) and (2) were considered most important and were given more focus by both organizations. Their importance lies in the fact that knowledge of Oromo culture and history was essential to define and articulate Oromo identity. Knowledge of Oromo history was required to define the Oromo question in comprehensible terms to the international audience and members of Oromo communities in the diaspora. In fact, these Oromo organizations turned exile into school. Many Oromo refugees decided to cut off the colonial chain that tied them to Ethiopia and started to look seriously into their cultural and historical heritage. For many of them, flight from Ethiopia had turned into a pilgrimage to their roots, and the destination of their flight a rendezvous with the culture, history and language of their ancestors. They started to study and use their language and culture as much as the exile situation allowed them. They went back to the sources of their own history although they were (are) physically far from their homeland. Thousands of Oromo refugees learned to read and write their own language through the literacy classes conducted by these Organizations. This was an opportunity they were denied in Ethiopia.

It was also interesting to note that there were even some refugees who learned to speak the Oromo language in exile; while in Ethiopia they spoke only Amharic—the language of the dominant nationality. In Sudan, regular schools were even established by ORA to provide education for refugee children. Regarding a refugee settlement in Yabus, Sudan, Roberta Aitchison (1985:10) has noted:

> Most Oromo refugees who are literate learned from classes conducted by ORA or the Oromo Liberation Front. ... Considering that there are 20 million speakers of this ... tongue; it is remarkable that the only schools that teach in Oromo language are in the liberated areas of Oromia or in exile. The teaching at the new school in Yabus, therefore, is more significant than what meets the eye.

More significantly it was the experience gained and the work that was accomplished, particularly in the areas of Oromo language and literacy, by these refugee organizations and the OLF which became the foundation for the revival of Oromo culture and language at home following the demise of the Mengistu regime in 1991. Ironically it is not the first time that uprooting and forced migration has become a platform for the development of literacy in the Oromo language. As I have discussed elsewhere (e.g. in Bulcha 1995) it was the work that Onesimos Nasib and his Oromo language team accomplished in the 1880s which became the first and until the 1990s the most significant step towards creating an Oromo literature. Onesimos and his colleagues were freed from Abyssinian and Arab slave-traders by the humanitarian acts of individuals, and Italian colonialists who then controlled parts of the Red Sea coast in Northeast Africa. Supported by Swedish missionaries at a place called Geleb in the Italian colony of Eritrea these ex-slaves toiled to make *Afaan* Oromo a written language. Their aim and hope to return one day to Oromoland and spread literacy among their people was partially fulfilled as they were finally able to repatriate and open the first schools and spread literacy in western Oromia during the first three decades of the last century.

The expansion of Oromo literacy came to abrupt end in 1942 as a result of the Haile Selassie government's Amharisation program which banned the use of Oromo language for teaching, preaching or administration. This ban lasted for decades and the gains made in Oromo literacy before 1942 were more or obliterated; and in the 1980s, the Oromo diaspora had to start the work of Oromo literacy from the scratch. Over the last 20 years, exile also became school where many Oromos got the chance to appraise their own history.

In the introduction to his book, Mohammed Hassen (1990) argued that the ruling Abyssinian elite have perceived the danger of the large Oromo population to their empire and have systematically depicted them as a people without history, and belittled their way of life, and their religious and political institutions. He maintained that it "is no exaggeration to say that no people have had their history as distorted and human qualities undervalued as the Oromo have been in Ethiopian historiography." He also pointed out that the denigration of the Oromo was necessary for the Abyssinian elites to justify their rule over the Oromo. Naturally, Oromo intellectuals have been contesting the policies which denigrate their culture, language and history. However, they did not have the opportunity to openly express or publish these contestations in Ethiopia. It is only exile that this became possible.

As mentioned above, the revival of the Oromo culture and research into Oromo history were, from the very beginning, some of the main objective of the Oromo organizations in the diaspora. Hence, dozens of seminars, workshops, and international conferences were conducted by TBOA and UONA on Oromo culture, language and history in Europe and North America in the past 20 years. Some of the outcomes of these endeavors are quite interesting and concrete. Among the more significant results is the creation of an international Oromo Studies Association (OSA). In addition to half a dozen conference proceedings, OSA has been publishing the Journal of Oromo Studies since 1993. A number of works were published on Oromo history, language, politics and culture by Oromo scholars in the diaspora. These works have not only added new titles to literature on the Oromo, but have expanded the frontier of knowledge about them. Ethiopian historiography which has depicted the Oromo as intruders and barbarians is effectively challenged. This does not mean that the causes or uprooting and forced migrations from Oromia are resolved.

CONCLUSION

This contribution dwelt on forced migration and Oromo society. Uprooting and forced migrations have been part of the Oromo experience since the conquest of their land by the Abyssinians in the nineteenth century. Focus is made on slavery, cross-border flight, and internal displacement of population caused by war and the empire state's socio-economic policies all of which form a chain of events. The predicaments caused by uprooting are also analyzed alongside the opportunities availed by exile such as freedom to learn and to use own language, freedom to organize, freedom to write, etc, opportunities that have been denied in the Ethiopian empire.

Notes

1. The myth about this monster was widespread in western Oromia.

2. J. G. Vanderheym who accompanied Menelik during an expedition to Walayta in 1894, and who himself captured 11 slaves, wrote that Menelik's army captured 18,000 slaves, one-tenth of, which were considered the Emperor's share and the rest the property of the soldiers. Vanderheym, "Une expedition avec le negous Menelik", Paris 1896, p. 90, cited in R. Pankhurst, *Economic history of Ethiopia 1800-1935*, Addis Ababa 1968, p. 105.

3. Louis Harcourt's letter ref: F0-3711822, Colonial office to Foreign Office, 2 December 1910, cited in Hickey 1984, p.146.

4. Major P. Maud, "Notes on Mr. Thesigers's Despatches. Dated October 17 and October 29 1910, and on Gwynn's Remarks Thereon..." cited in Hickey 1984, p.146.

5. The Oromo were not the ones to cross the colonial borders to escape Abyssinian pillage. Citing British Colonial Office documents, Hickey, (1984:197) wrote that in 1924 "... some three thousand Degoda Somali with 30,000 heads of stock, crossed the boundary to escape the exactions and mutilations of Fitaurari Walde Gabril Lej Belai who were free to tax and raid at their discretion."

6. Personal communication. In 1995, some descendants from those refugees came to the OLF office in Nairobi to enquire about the situation in Oromia and to express their solidarity with their kinsmen.

7. Interview with Tahir Yousouf, Berlin, 29 August 1995.

8. For a detailed study of Arsi resistance and Menelik's revenge on them, see Abbas Haji, "The history 1880-1935", B. A. Thesis, Department of History, Ababa University, 1982.

9. Weekend farmers were high-ranking state officials who run their farms by hired labor and bank loan and visited them during weekends for inspection.

10. Personal observation; the author spent the summer months of 1971-1973 in the area.

11. Thomas Zitelmann wrote that "We have nobody in the agencies!": Somali and Oromo responses to relief aid in refugee camps (Hiraan region/Somali Democratic Republic)" Sozialanthropologische Arbeitspapiere, FU Berlin, Institut fur Ethnologic 1989. p. 5.

12. See Peter Godwin, "Thousands flee Ethiopian regime", *The Sunday Times*, London 18 May 1986. Tala Skari reported that in the spring season of 1985 alone, cholera claimed 1,100 lives in the camps for the "villagisation" refugees. See Refugees, No. 21, September 1995.

13. Many Oromos who went to Europe and North America to study before or after the revolution became refugees as persecution was intensified.

14. Lundahl to Pettersson 18 September 1816, cited in Gustav Aren, Evangelical pioneers in Ethiopia, Stocholm, EFS Förlaget 1978, p. 249.

References

Aitchison, R. 1983a. UN starts forcible deportation of Djibouti refugees. *New African.* November.

Aitchison, R. 1983b. "Forced repatriation of refugees to Ethiopia in February 1983." Report prepared for the refugee research project for the Horn of Africa, *Cultural Survival.*

Aitchison, R. 1984. Reluctant witnesses: The sexual abuse of refugee women in Djibouti. *Cultural Survival Quarterly.* Summer, 8:2.

Aitchison, R. 1985. Oromo refugees in Yabus: A brief view, Minneapolis.

Anonymous. 1981. Ethiopia: Conquest and terror. *Horn of Africa.* 4,1:8-19.

Baskauskas, L. 1981. The Lithuanian refugee experience and grief. *International Migration Review.* 25, 1-2.

Baxter, P. 1978. Boran age-sets and generation-sets: Gada, a puzzle or a maze? In *Age, generation and time: Some features of East African age organizations,* ed. Baxter, P. and Almagor. London: University of London.

Bjeren, G. 1985. *Migration to Shashemene: Ethnicity, gender and occupation in urban Ethiopia.* Uppsala.

Braukämper, U. 1982/83. Ethnic identity and social change among Oromo refugees in the Horn of Africa. *Northeast African Studies.* 4, 3.

Bondestam, L 1974. *Den Dömda Dalen: Om kapitalism och människor i nordöstra Etiopien.*

Bulatovich, A. 1897. *From Entoto to Baro: Report from a journey through the Southwestern areas of the Ethiopian empire 1896-1897.* St. Petersburg.

Bulcha, Mekuria. 1988. *Flight and Integration: Causes of mass exodus from Ethiopia and problems of integration in the Sudan.* Uppsala.

Bulcha, Mekuria. 1993. *Some notes on the conditions of Oromo, Beria and other refugees in the Kurmuk district of Blue Nile Province, Sudan.* Khartoum.

Bulcha, Mekuria. 1995. Onesimos Nasib's pioneering contributions to Oromo writing. *Journal of African Studies* 4, 1.

Cerulli, E. 1922. Folk-Literature of the Galla of Southern Abyssinia. *Harvard African Studies III* Cambridge, Mass.

CADU, *General agricultural survey 1972.* Chilalo Agricultural Development Unit.

Challa, A. 1992. Report on the situation of repatriated Oromo Refugees, April, ORA, Ontario.

Cohen, J. 1987. *Integrated rural development: Ethiopian experience and the debate.* Uppsala.

Darley, H. 1926. *Slaves and Ivory: A record of adventure and exploration in the unknown Sudan, and among the Abyssinian slave-raiders,* London.

Dibaba, T. 1996. *The Situation of Oromo refugees in the Sudan.* Oromo Relief Association. Delmenhorst, March.

Gilkes, Patrick. 1975. *The dying lion: Feudalism and modernization in Ethiopia.* London: Julian Friedman.

Greenfield, R. 1983. Djibouti refugees left defenceless. *New African*, July.

Harrell-Bond, B. 1986. *Imposing aid: Emergency assistance to refugees.* Oxford: Oxford University Press.

Hassen, Mohammed. 1979. "Menelik's conquest of Harar, 1887, and its effect on the political organization of the surrounding Oromo up to 1900." Paper presented on the Cambridge Conference, 19-21 July.

Hassen, Mohammed. 1990. *The Oromo of Ethiopia: History 1570-1860.* Cambridge: Cambridge University Press.

Hickey, Dennis. 1984. "Ethiopia and Great Britain: Conflict in the southern borderlands, 1916-1935", A Ph.D. Dissertation in history, Submitted to the graduate school, Northwestern University, Evanston, Illinois.

Inter Press Service, 1996. "Ethiopian Refugees: Unwanted abroad, under threat at home", Nairobi 10 April.

Jalata, Asafa. 1993. *Oromia & Ethiopia: State formation and ethnonational conflict, 1868-1992.* Boulder: Reinener.

Keller, Edmond. 1987. *Revolutionary Ethiopia.* Bloomington and Indianapolis: Indiana University Press.

Kloos, H. 1982. Development, drought, and famine in the Awash Valley of Ethiopia. *The African Studies*, 25, 4.

Kunz, Egon. 1981. Exile and resettlement: Refugees theory. *International Migration Review.* 15, 1-2

Lefort, Rene. 1981. *Ethiopia: An heretical revolution?* London: Zed Press.

Lockhot, H. 1994. *The mission, the life, reign and character of Haile Selassie I.* New York: St. Martin Press.

Luling, Virgina. 1986. Oromo refugees in the Sudan town. *Northeast African Studies* 8, 2-3.

Marcus, H. 1994. *A history of Ethiopia.* University of California Press.

Markakis, John and Nega Ayele. 1978. *Class and revolution in Ethiopia.* Nottingham: Spokesman.

Perham, P. 1969. *The Government of Ethiopia.* London: Faber and Faber.

Pollock, S. 1996. Ethiopia: Tragedy in the making. *The Oromo Commentary* 6,1:5-16.

Shils, E. 1978. Roots. The sense of place and past: The cultural gains and losses of migrants. In *Human migration patterns and policies,* eds. McNeil, W and S. Adams. Bloomington: Indiana University Press.

Smith, D. 1896. Expeditions through Somali land to Lake Rudolf. *Geographical Journal* 123-27.

Svenska Dagbladet, Stockholm 13 November 1979.

Tronvoll, K. and Aaland, O. 1995. *The process of democratization in Ethiopia: An expression of popular participation or political resistance?* Oslo: Norwegian Institute of Human Rights, Report No. 5, August.

Triulzi, A. 1980. Social protest and rebellion in some gabbar songs from Qellem, Wallaga. In *Modern Ethiopia: From the accession of Menelik II to the present*, ed. J. Tubiana. Rotterdam: Balkema.

Tutschek, C. 1845. *A grammar of the Galla language.* Munich.

Chapter 2

The Sidama Nation:
An Introduction

Seyoum Hameso

> To appreciate a people's explanation of life and misfortune, one
> needs to have a general picture of the wider framework of their exis-
> tence (Brøgger 1986:21)

Little is known about the Sidama nation, its people, its history and culture.
Sidama studies were virtually non-existent even for academic purposes.
There are many reasons for this. First and foremost, the emergence of enlightened nationalists and the promotion of Sidama nationalism were late and slow
in comparison to other regions. Secondly, the Ethiopian historiography had no
room for the promotion or development of non-Habasha cultures and peoples.
Worse, still, it had circumvented and undermined knowledge production and
dissemination of the latter. The combination of these factors engendered ambiguity about the past and uncertainty about contemporary developments.

The ensuing lack of critical scholarship, as William Shack noted, had "distorted the human achievements of conquered peoples including transformations
of their social, cultural and political institutions" (quoted in Jalata 1995: 95). A
lot has to be done to reverse this scenario and to revitalize the Sidama studies.
Without pretending to offer a definitive source of knowledge about the subject,
this effort constitutes the onset of a multi-disciplinary research agenda.

The Sidama people, like their counterparts in Africa, have rich historical traditions that remained largely unrecorded, a problem, which is being overcome
with the advance of time and education.[1] For the time being, informed debate
on Sidama history is bound to rely on oral tradition, rituals, and symbols most
of which remain matters for further inquiry. Written records are not only far
and between but they are also fairly recent phenomena. From a scanty literature
made available by expatriate scholars, different names had been used to describe

the Sidama people. A browse, for example, through the works of John Hamer, Jan Brøgger, Ulrich Braukämper, G. Hudsen, S. Stanley, Enricho Cerulli and Klaus Wedekind indicate the use of different names at different times.

John Hamer (whose works on social anthropology I draw on heavily here) noted the problem of nomenclature in his later works and settled on the name used by the people themselves, i.e., Sidama. Other names mentioned by scholars in reference to the Sidama people include Sadama, Sidamo or one of the Cushitic-speaking people of Southern Ethiopia. The term "Sidamo" is also used to describe the Cushitic language groups which, in addition to Sidama proper, includes Hadiya, Kambata, Alaba, Gedeo and Bambala and sometimes to their neighbors to the west: the Ometo, Kafa, Gibe, and Janjero.

The problem of nomenclature is not confined to scholarship; it is common in public perception as it is influenced by Ethiopian polity which imposed the term "Sidamo." This term is no more than a geographic dispensation given to a southern region that included Sidama, Boorana, Gedeo, Burji and Wolayita nations. Such misrepresentation is undertaken to suppress Sidama identity and to dissolve the collective identity of the people. The misrepresentation of reality and the problems of nomenclature are related to the history of the conquest of Sidama nation.

THE CONQUEST

The Sidama are one of the ancient human groups to live in their present environment with the inevitable internal and external population movements affecting their settlement. They form part of the great Cushitic civilizations that produced significant achievements in this part of Africa. They share many similarities in terms of language, culture, values, and psychological make-up with their fellow Cushitic neighbors. They also share the common history of conquest by the army of Menelik of Shawa in the late nineteenth century which is by far the most critical and perverse event in Sidama history. The conquest of Sidamaland in 1893 had impacted the Sidama world in many ways. It brought about the colonial system of tenant-settler relationship. It also resulted in the promotion of authoritarian ethos and the consequent demotion of the local systems of governance inculcated in *halaale* principle. It imposed a hegemonic system of rule by undermining the *luwa* system which was based on consultative decision-making. The values inherent in *halaale* or the principle of truth and the *luwa* systems have contemporary validity among Sidamas despite the assimilationist policies of subsequent Ethiopian governments (Hameso 2004).

The political subordination of Sidama people caused their economic dispossession and inevitable resistance followed by severe coercion against dissent. The sense of consultative egalitarian underpinning of local governance

58

was replaced by authoritarian Abyssinian values. A unique combination of the actions of the Abyssinian state and the church caused physical, cultural and spiritual supremacy in the colonized lands.[2] As the timing and the patterns of Abyssinian conquest coincided with European colonial rule in Africa, its effects were also similar. Like colonialism elsewhere, this one too undermined people's culture and their tools of self-definition. It led to "the destruction or the deliberate undervaluing of their literature and the conscious elevation of the language of the colonizer" (Thiongo 1986:16). However, unlike European settler colonialism, which relinquished power and physically departed from the scene in the mid-twentieth century, the Abyssinian colonial rule remained in Sidama now over a century without creating the material foundation for progress for itself or for the subjects.

The legacy of domination and exploitation were maintained by the "modernizing" autocracy of Haile Selassie. The collective memory of the Sidama nationals of this epoch was the modernization of oppression; namely the honing of the methods of tax collection, recruitment of coercive army and bureaucratic personnel. The period is characterized by land dispossession, feudalism, force, myth and external support—the means through which the spoils of the conquest were maintained.

The impact of the Abyssinian conquest and domination were reinforced by tumultuous developments of the 1970s and 1980s. The relative backwardness of the imperial era meant that cultural impositions were resisted as much as they were repulsed. For example, Menelik's direct attempts at forced baptism were ignored. The concern during Haile Selassie shifted to economic exploitation and gradual consolidation of central power without undue confrontation on the cultural and spiritual arena. In the 1960s, while the imperial government encouraged the short-lived self-help associations to take over the local judicial and administrative functions, it actually re-centralized the controls and eliminated all creative autonomy (Hamer 1996:548-9). The same legacy of conquest was bequeathed to the military junta of the 1970s-1980s and the TPLF militia of 1990s.

THE PEOPLE, THE NATION AND THE ECONOMY

The Sidama nation[3] is situated in northeastern Africa (Southern Ethiopia) where there is deep contest and conflict over identity, including the population size. The Sidama population is estimated to be 4.5 million.[4] The Sidama people believe they belong to *Sidamigobba,* the Sidama country. They do not call themselves Sidamo, a term which confuses their name and suppresses their identity. The conquest and the suppression of their identity went hand in hand with underestimation of the nation's numerical strength. Sidamaland has shared borders with Oromia in the northeast, Wolayita in the west and Gedeo in the south. The northern border extends from Lake Hawassa to Dilla town in the South. The eastern boundary starts at Mount Garamba and extends westward to Bilaatte River in the West.

Sidamas had practiced mixed horticulture and cattle herding for the last several hundred years while for much of the twentieth century they were engaged in farming. Agriculture is still the mainstay of Sidama economy and society. Land is the most important asset to which the people have intense attachment. Before the colonial adventure, each member of the Sidama society was entitled to land ownership. Private ownership of land was buttressed by communal land or *dannawu baatto* earmarked for grazing and other collective purposes including reserves for new comers and young couples. The local councils or *songo* determined the use and distribution of community land. The land holding system based on egalitarian ethos helped maintain fraternity, peace and the moral order in society until it was replaced by feudalism during the introduction of the *naftanya* system from the north.

The Sidama landscape involves lakes, rivers and different climatic zones suitable for various flora and fauna. Sidama is home to indigenous plants like *weese* which resembles a banana tree. It is grown in the highlands and midlands where the climate conditions are characterized by high rainfall. It takes three to six years for the plant to mature and to be processed as *waasa*, a staple food item. Once it is properly planted, the *weese* plant does not require labor-intensive work. Planting and weeding is carried out by men while the task of readying the plant for consumption is finalized by women. The production techniques of *waasa* are anachronistic and labor intensive. Major technical change is required in the form of research and development if the situation of women is to be improved. Women are also responsible for the upkeep of milk and milk products. Cattle are reared for milk, meat or as symbols of status.

Sidamaland grows several crops including coffee. The production, exchange and consumption of coffee has direct bearing on the socio-economic welfare of the people and political arrangements within and outside Sidama. While coffee is the main cash crop and the biggest source of revenue for the Ethiopian state, the coffee farmers are one of the least beneficiaries. In the 1970s and 1980s, the Derg regime had adopted the policy of fixed coffee pricing which determined a rate well below the world market prices. On the other hand, farmers were forced to pay heavy taxes and rising prices for industrial products and services with perverse terms of trade.

In an economy which is predominantly agricultural, the majority of people depend on this sector for their livelihood and employment. However, this sector and the rural population were neglected by Ethiopian policy makers who emphasized the exploitation of land and labor instead of investment on both. Agricultural activity remains, by and large, rain-fed without proper investment and suitable land use policy.

In the post-Derg Ethiopia, the skewed distribution of income against Sidama meant that revenues from Sidama are diverted to finance projects in the hometowns of the ruling elite, namely Tigray. Different political and administrative measures discouraged Sidama entrepreneurs because of the regime's fear of their potential political influence. More often than not, it is the members or supporters of the regime who had the opportunity to acquire economic enterprises as per the government's "privatization" program. Despite their natural and human resources, the majority of Sidama people remain poor and susceptible to diseases and famine.

Health facilities are inadequate in relation to the size of the population. Until recently, the capital city, Hawaasa (also called Awassa), had no hospital. The only hospital in Sidama was the Yirgalem Hospital built in the 1950s by foreign aid. Access to health services in general is extremely poor. Most rural communities do not have access to social amenities. In 1994, it was estimated that only 18% of school age children attended school which is one of the lowest rates in Ethiopian standards and considerably below the average for sub-Saharan Africa. The situation for girls was even worse. The government policy of education adopted in 2001/02 restricts access by rural residents and their children to higher education.

Trade, industry and tourism and other social services are confined to urban areas. Unemployment and related benefits do not exist. Rural residents have no pensions where deprivation is extreme. Modern infrastructure such as transport and communication are undeveloped. Very few towns have electricity while most remote areas have no roads. The roads that exist are the ones designed to facilitate the transportation of coffee export. Most of them are dilapidated due to lack of maintenance. There is only one highway in Sidama which connects Addis Ababa and the town of Moyale in the South. There are neither railway lines nor international airports. There are barely industries. A textile factory, set up in the 1980s catering for external market, had little linkage to the local economy. There are no modern coffees processing plants except raw coffee washing plants.

LANGUAGE, CULTURE, BELIEFS AND INSTITUTIONS

Sidama is a potentially rich nation impoverished by the culture of conquest and domination. It prizes of relatively distinct language and cultural entity. The Sidama language, one of the Cushitic languages, is spoken by most Sidamas.

Like other comparable communities, the Sidama people trace their origins to common ancestors. Oral tradition had it that Sidamas descended from two ancestral fathers: Bushee and Maldea. Successive generations worshiped ancestor spirit, *Annuwate ayaana*. It is believed that the dead retain their individual identity and continue to play an active role in society. Like elsewhere in Africa ancestor veneration is important to religious beliefs and practices (Howard 1996:314).

Sidama's holy places associated with the founders of major groups are known as *akaako darga*. Some of these include Teellamo, Wonsho, Buunama, Aroosa, Hallo, Guushala, Beera, Goida, Bansa Illaala, Saafa and Cirfa. The followers of Sidama traditional religion emphasize that they do not worship *Akaako*, but a creator sky deity, *Magano*, who once lived on earth, but returned to sky after people complained about having to make a choice between reproduction and eternal life (Braukämper 1992:197, also Daye 2001). Since then, God is approached through the brokerage of lower level deities. In other words, *Akaako* is the mediator through whom the people approach the Supreme Being.

Stanley (1966:219) noted that:

> The Sidama religion is basically monotheistic combined with ancestor worship.... Even the worship of the tribal forefathers is largely based on the belief that they are powerful protectors of the clans, as effective intermediaries between God and their people.

Through ancestor worship, the living and the dead occupy interconnected worlds as the spirits of the dead visit the living from the realm of ideas, mainly through dreams. The notion of reincarnation and life after death that is actively sought after in other belief systems existed in Sidama. Different sacrifices are offered to "feed" the dead. The sacrifice of animals on sacred sites (such as burial places and forestlands), the prohibition of eating pork, and the responsibilities of the first born to offer sacrifice at the funeral of one's parents have similarity to other religions. The older persons being close to the dead, and thereby close to God, occupy temporal space between ordinary being and the supernatural. In Sidama worldview, old age commands respect and recognition, as the advancement of age is often associated with experience and wisdom. This is common to other cultures since the "values drawn from the past do ... have contemporary relevance and a hold in all our imagination" (Baxter 1983:183).

Sidama's monotheistic belief tendency in divine creation, *kalaqo*, augured well with the teaching of other monotheist belief systems, partly explaining the ease with which Christian missions were received in Sidama. The missions were aided by modern education and the tendency to expand their numbers by proselytizing and converting members of other faiths to their own followers (See also Braukämper, 1992:195-7). It has to be noted that the introduction of cash crop economy and the spread of Christian values have undoubtedly influenced the activities, beliefs, and attitudes of the Sidama people (See Hamer and Hamer 1994:188).

The pre-conquest Sidama society had rich and complex social and political institutions. The people had developed their cultural ethos on the basis of community life with complex moral codes, laws, conventions and sanctions with predictable mechanisms of enforcement. John Hamer pointed out that Sidama's gerontocratic social structure is based on generational class system which tends to facilitate the implementation of elderhood authority. It contains a "group of specialist mediators who are leaders of the major clans (*mote*), the generational classes (*gadaana*), and a few esteemed old men who have survived two cycles of the generational class system (*woma*) (Hamer 1996:526; 1994:128). Jan Brøgger (1986:114) described them as the system of age-grades.

In this system, age has important implications. For example, the division of labor is predicated on age meant old men and women are respected members of the community. From old men comes *cimeesa*, an equivalent of a ritual leader who is chosen according to his age while from old women emerges *qarricho* chosen again by age. Even though the society is largely paterlineal and women are not formally members of the *luwa* generational system, but they are integral to its survival through their responsibility for the reproduction of household and the management of much of its subsistence labor. Women do not participate directly in councils of elders, but they are represented before the council by a spokesman of their choice, whenever having grievance. Jan Brøgger cited an example where elderly women behave with self-assurance, even smoking water pipe which is regarded as the prerogative of male elders, consistent with the increase in their authority (Brøgger 1986:54). On the other hand, male elders are empowered to legislate, take administrative actions to meet emergencies, mediate disputes and enforce decisions. They

> reach their position settling disputes of everyday life, making policy rules about production, assisting the government in collecting taxes, and performing the rituals that negotiate the changing meaning of the cultural code. Indeed, they are the ones closest to the influential dead elders who, through dreams, remind the living of their obligations to that code (Hamer 1994:128).

The moral code referred above is known as the *halaale* code which plays an important role in religious and politico-cultural systems. The term *halaale* means "truth" or "a true way of life." The code forms the foundation for *halaale* ideology defined as the principles of moral code governing the relationship between people (Hamer 1994, 1996). It involves specific values such as the importance of generosity, commitment to truth in conflict mediation, fairness in delivering blame and punishment, avoiding disruptive gossip, responsible use of money, respect for property boundaries and avoidance of adultery and sexual promiscuity. The significance of wealth acquisition relates to the status and esteem achieved through reputation for generosity by redistributing wealth through hospitality and the support of one's kin.

According to *halaale* moral code, greed and arrogance are not viewed favorably as they invite jealousy and fear. The task of guarding and interpreting the moral order and code resides in the hands of elders. Since life is a continual process, the halaale code does not end with the death of elders who continue to influence the living by reappearing in dreams. The latter are believed to remind the living elders not to fail in upholding halaale and not to neglect "feeding" them animal sacrifice at appropriate shrines (Hamer 1994).

In the past, the halaale code worked effectively well through social sanctions. The code is also supported by interrelated administrative and cultural institutions of *buude, jirtee* and *seeraa*. Recourse to ultimate sanction takes the form of curse believed to be effective. From among such sanctions, the feeling of alienation will have a marked effect since the ostracization by *seera* leads to social rejection by both the social and supernatural worlds. A comparable phenomenon in the contemporary Western society is incarceration in prisons which is a complete physical removal of persons from society. The Sidama world knows no capital punishment; murder is punishable by *guma* or blood compensation. Neither do the elders and their council possess direct physical forces of coercion at their disposal. Jan Brøgger (1986:109, 111) noted that:

> the style of behavior and demeanor of everyday life .... is clearly not based on threat of physical force. It is not the cowed subservience based on fear of whips, gallows and dungeons which is displayed, but it clearly demonstrates a concern for public opinion and sensitivity to criticism.

Without the use of physical force and violence, the moral order had worked well for centuries in preserving the institutions and the moral code itself. It linked a household to community, generation to generation, and men to women, on a complementary basis. The moral code also conformed to another side of Sidama ethos, that of decentralized decision-making and consensual rule. Hamer (1998b) compares the practice of community participation and rational discourse with the authority of the Western style polity devoid of justice whose alternative, he suggests, could be Sidama's personalized and decentralized form of gerontocracy.

Three institutions dominate the Sidama political and cultural space. They are (a) kingdom (*woma*), (b) principality (*mote*) and (c) the *Luwa* systems. The woma institution is the earliest form of political institution in Sidama governance. The term *"woma"* is associated with wisdom whose role in production and organization is considered to be sophisticated. The *woma* presides over a council or *songo* (what Brøgger compared to a senate with strong authority whereby "pressure on the individual is not exerted by the invisible hand of the market" (Brøgger 1986:108). *Womu-songo*, or the king's council, is the senate chaired by a woma.

The position of woma in society varied from place to place and from clan to clan. While the presence of a woma is essential in all parts of Sidama, as bees have a queen, the age and the method of electing him varied from region to region. In most parts of Sidama, including in Alata where there are several clans governed as federations, gerontocrats are elected from different sections of society to the role of a *woma*. In other places, such as Holoo and Sawolaa, the *woma* institution is dynastic and familial, hence inherited. In this case, when a *woma* dies, his son replaces him regardless of the age of the latter. If the son is too young and unprepared for the assumption of authority, he is helped by regents and other advisers (Hoteso 1990:146-47).

The *mote* institution is another form of authority relation with explicitly political role. The leader is called *moticha* and he is elected to the position of administration and leadership on the basis of age and knowledge. His election takes place after thorough consultation with members of several local councils. *Mooticha* is responsible to look after the national council which also subsumes independent units of local councils such as the *ollaa songos*. Members of the *songo* are selected from the body of "wise persons," or *hayoo*, elected from different clans. These councillors are, mainly but not necessarily, gerontocrats whose job is to advise the *songo*, to represent a person in dispute, to take ones case or appeal to the *songo* of the higher order or to lobby for assorted causes. The councils are run according to customary laws. Members of the local council need to memorize the law by heart including the crime typology and the relevant punishment. While the most routine and relatively simple tasks were performed at the local level, the higher and controversial issues or disputes required the meeting of the *moote songo*. In such cases, the *mooticha* resorts to halaale and those persons who stand in front of his court to tell a lie were perceived to die. The fear of death compels suspects to reveal truth.

The *woma* institution had experienced decline through time with the emergence of the feudal Ethiopian rule while the powers of the *mote* had waxed (Hoteso 1990). The role of the woma was reduced to the level of non-interference in political and administrative matters and consultation on cultural and religious issues. Today, the position of a *mote* itself is largely undermined by the existing political system and attendant changes.

The *Luwa* system is an age-related institution performing ritual, cultural, and political roles. This institution has several similarities to the *gada* system of the Oromos.[5] Writing from a Marxist anthropological vantage, Hamer (1998b:6) describes the *luwa* as the generational "class" system of structuring society. Each "class" consists of three sets of people—elders, initiates, and pre-initiates—where all men are linked to one another in a junior-senior relationship throughout the life cycle. Age-grades are a compromise between chronological age and generation (Brøgger 1986). There are five rotating age grades: Darrara, Moggisa, Hirbbora, Fullaasa, and Wawaasa. Members of different grades pass through time cycles (every seventh year) and their life status changes accordingly. The Luwa congregation takes place at sacred sites, usually camps where the initiates stay for two months fed by *Luwa fathers* away from labor and sex. (Luwa fathers are cultural fathers who are not necessarily the biological fathers of the initiates). The initiation follows the appointment of a leader *gadaanna* by a panel of eight individuals. Panel members conduct the selection under strict secrecy. As a matter of principle, they assume no prior knowledge of each other; neither should they have contact with the young man they choose.

In the process of recruitment, they consult *masalto* (philosophers) and *qalichas* (fortunetellers) to identify the right person. The panel also sets the criteria (or the job description, so to speak) of the would-be leader's character and physical features. Being the first-born male, preferably from the first marriage is an added advantage. Ideally, the person should be physically and morally fit to symbolise the rituals of power on behalf of the group. The desirable qualities of leadership include ones wisdom, circumspection, and ability to mediate disputes. The final selection is based on the elder's majority vote. The *gadaanna* is appointed for the term of seven years. These years are associated with his name since it is part of the Sidama culture that "the points in history will be identified with reference to the *gadaanna*" (Brøgger 1986:114).

The cyclical feature of the *luwa* system means that all males will progress from a youthful status of providing service to senior positions of redistributing wealth and knowledge. Initially, the youth learn skills by attending council meetings where elders make decisions. With unavoidable sense of paternalism and trusteeship of the moral code, the elders have a direct bearing on the youth who constitute the productive forces and the basis of wealth creation.

All these reinforce the place of elders whose roles are as diverse as consultation, decision-making, conflict resolution, monitoring social cohesion and the assurance of continuity amidst change. As for conflict resolution and the elders' role, it had been customary that land and property disputes occupy most of their time. The authority of the elders to solve conflicts and policy-making is stamped by resort to curse and to the supernatural involving heavy sanctions. The usefulness and the relevance of age-related systems in general and of gerontocracy in particular depends on its ability to positively contribute towards the economic, political, social, educational and belief systems of contemporary society.

In times and in a society where story telling is a necessity, where spoken rather than the written word holds significance, where illiteracy is widespread, where the economic base is confined to subsistence agriculture, the problem of informing or educating the youth remains in the hands of those who possess useful information at their disposal. From earlier stages in life, women teach their children in several ways. Then, through rituals and meetings, old men pass on knowledge obtained from ceaseless struggle for survival in a harsh environment. The lessons add confidence to the young generation about the wisdom of their past contributing to their efficacy to solve contemporary problems.

Several forces threaten gerontocracy in Sidama, both external and internal. They include the expansion of the cash economy, the dissemination of religious missions, and ever present political pressure from Ethiopian empire state. It is reported that, elsewhere in Africa, age systems faltered in the face of external influences, modern education, capitalist cash economy, and state intervention (Kurimto and Simonse 1998:25). For example, in the Masai speaking Samburu of Kenya, gerontocracy was imperiled by external influences. The British colonial administration controlled the Masai peoples' dispute settlement processes, imposed taxes, and required the sale of cattle through official channels. But then the influence of an imposed colonial administration was limited and the Samburu continued their traditional gerontocratic authority over herding and community life since there was no other environmentally appropriate means of survival (Spencer 1965).

In the case of Sidama, most external influences entered through Christian missionaries, the aid agencies and schooling. The expansion of Lutheran, Evangelical, Roman Catholic, and Adventist churches in the mid-twentieth century allured several social groupings to Christian preaching. The fact that the churches, particularly Catholic and Adventist, were based in the rural areas indicates their keenness to acquire more members by demonstrating their usefulness to the needs of the rural population. In most areas, these churches were accompanied by schools and health clinics offering educational and health facilities. While competing with the local values, the churches have also played complementary role. Some preached in Sidama language or translated or wrote books in Sidama. In their works, the priests and the churches did not face insurmountable obstacles since the halaale code has messages that reinforce that of the Bible. Yet the task of interpreting truth shifted from the Sidama wise men to learned priests who were keen to allure the youth, and through them their families to differing ways of life. The end result, either way, was to change the worldview of the would-be followers who no longer resort to local norms and practices including ancestral veneration.

The work of aid agencies has never been prominent in Sidama until recently. For one, the self-sufficiency ethos of the moral code precluded any tendency to be dependent on external alms. Begging is morally unacceptable and immediate support comes from the community itself when needed. Secondly, it is highly unlikely that aid agencies would be permitted to pass the Ethiopian centre and carry out development-oriented programs in Sidama. Neither has there been a widely publicized emergency situation worth attracting the attention for food aid as in the northern Ethiopia. Nevertheless, minor aid programs had filtered through church groups with a notable exception of Irish Aid which started its functions in the early 1990s. The social and economic effects of this and other externally funded programs are yet to be seen.

The Sidama social organization and cultural underpinning was further undermined by the upheaval of military dictatorship.[6] The role of customary sanctions were relegated and replaced by communist-structured, strictly hierarchical administrative units. The customary village council or *ollaa* was replaced by administrative units known as *qebele (*also spelt as kebele), while the roles of *murichas* (event organizers and informants) and *cinanchos* (work co-ordiantors) were taken by *qebele* administrators. The *qebele* administration instituted by the Derg had little to do with the Sidama customary law and procedures, *seera*. *Qebele* appointees became part and parcel of the Derg administrative apparatus. At the same time, the regime denigrated the Sidama belief system and it worked to undermine the *Luwa* system. Sacred forests and public assembly-point trees (*gudumaales)* were destroyed and replaced by cash crop plantation and draconian communist villagisation programs. The burden on the Sidama society was only worsened by economic oppression associated with heavy taxation and low fixed coffee prices.

Given the centrist tendency of the Derg, the consensual authority of elders virtually ceased to exist except in conformity with government edicts and unless practiced clandestinely. The communist style of socio-political organization that spreads its tentacles from the core to the villages, and the physical force that accompanies militaristic bureaucracy distorted the politico-cultural airwaves of the Sidama world. It undermined the social complementarity between elders and youth as well as between genders. At the same time, the consensual authority of elders was transferred from local songos to corrupt imposition of *qebele* committees. The government policies of taxation and marketing controls became more oppressive, making life worse and destabilizing to the internal mechanisms of survival. Devastating were also the practices of collective farming and villagisation coupled with forced conscription of youth into the army to fight endless wars with neighboring countries and nationalist insurgencies.

The regime that replaced the Derg in 1991 was less enthusiastic in supporting elders' councils fearing that they might undermine its authority. The problem is more than lack of enthusiasm since the TPLF regime introduced pervasive inter-generational conflicts. By selective and manipulative arming of the youth, the regime has exacerbated a generational divide. Upon assuming power, it promoted a decided minority of youth with the least knowledge and experience of the Abyssinian political machination while excluding those with a through knowledge of the system. Worse still, as soon as the less experienced youth gathered substantive knowledge and start asking the inevitable, they were sacked, imprisoned or replaced by far the less experienced ones or by those more cowed and confused. This practice enabled the TPLF regime, at least temporarily, to manipulate the overall process of governance. At the same time, attempts at co-opting the local leaders and elders were made possible at the expense of corruption and loss of respect to their moral authority.

What happened then is the social disorientation and lack of moral direction. For example, politically motivated semi-religious fanatic groups covered the ground emptied of the moral code. Fundamentalist churches went on taxing the poor while taking the youth away from work, education and the protective shields of their parents and elders. Seemingly freed from the shackles of tradition, the youth roam around the country engaged in endless congregations. A generation that lost its initiation rites and rights recompenses itself by a new form of religious initiation. In personal communication to this author, John Hamer (1998b:7) noted that

> considering the experiences of youth in being removed from the land, impressed into conflicting military organizations, and losing the authority and instruction of the elders, it was not surprising that a condition of cynicism, even nihilism, engulfed much of the young generation.

Similar pervasive role of state was also noted in the case of the Orma people, in Kenya. There, state interference in production, marketing and distribution led to the stratification of social life, favoring wealthy individuals, and a decline in the redistribution process. Competing interests were no longer negotiated through consensual agreement and the Orma increasingly came to rely on the sanctioning force of the state (Ensiminger 1990, 1996; See also Hamer 1998b:10). John Abbink opines that the Gada system of government, once grafted on an agropastoral way of life, is susceptible to changes in social scale, economic life and external contacts. He further argued that the system "will not work in a stratified society with economically specialized groups, such as modern society [and it] serves mainly as a symbol of Oromo political ethos and achievement, as well as illustration that there were traditional constitutional limits on the exercise of power." In brief, the "traditions of political organization, customary law and cultural autonomy provide elements of a value system and a fund of collective memory and identity" (Abbink 1998:161, 163).

Changes to tradition are also effected by education. The establishment of literacy in garrison towns initially aimed at educating the siblings of settlers later spread to the rural Sidama through Christian missionary schools. With uneven distribution of schools and schooling, the outcome of such literacy was beneficial to the northern settlers and not to the Sidama society. Lately, those Sidamas who made it to higher education were hindered from promoting their social and political heritage, and they were removed from Sidama to work or live in other areas. Some Sidamas managed to migrate to the outside world forming and strengthening the Sidama diaspora. The progress of the political movements, national awareness, and further studies complemented the efforts in Sidama itself.[7]

CONTEMPORARY POLITICS

The political arrangement that replaced the Derg in 1991 drew its social base from Tigray, led by the Tigray People's Liberation Front (TPLF) which obtains its inspiration from Albanian communism. In rhetoric, and in order to rally support, the Front bandied about the "nations, nationalities and peoples", decentralization and federations, and the use of national/local languages, issues that needed real reckoning. As the centralizing tendency of the Ethiopian polity worked against any realization of such goals, the regime revived the main thrust of the Ethiopian past. Indeed, the half-hearted pronouncements were made to ensure the social and political supremacy by the TPLF.

On the front of political organization, soon after the assumption of power, the TPLF patched up surrogate parties such as the Sidama People's Democratic Organization (SPDO) to serve one and only one purpose: to become its puppets. The core members of SPDO were prisoners of war taken during armed confrontations with the Derg army. The membership later expanded to include primary school teachers (who suffered from low morale and low pay), aggrieved personalities, and the unemployed youth who were not accustomed to Abyssinian machination and treachery. It armed, supported and financed the SPDO elements while terrorizing other groups and individuals. By promoting the mediocre, the TPLF demoted independent, creative and well-informed personalities as well as nationalist elders. The regime's supporters were promoted as models to be followed while creative and critical thinkers were discouraged and undermined. The regime has progressively excluded true nationalists from decision-making process. The regime's propaganda tools presented intellectuals and business persons from the South as enemies of the people or anti-people.

The SPDO is supervised by another satellite organization created by the TPLF, namely, the Southern Ethiopian People's Democratic Front (SEPDF) which is a member of the EPRDF. According Lovise Aalen

> The TPLF's strong regional and federal position is a stark contrast to the position of the southern EPRDF partner, the SEPDF, which is disempowered at both regional and federal level. Since the ruling party at federal level is Tigray dominated, Tigrayan interest are pursued and Tigray regional state maintains an exceptional position in the federation, while the governments of other federal units, including SNNPRS, remain weak and practically ineffective (Aalen 2002:94).

Through the so-called the Southern Nations, Nationalities, and People's Regional State (SNNPRS) and the SEPDF, the TPLF sought to control the Sidama national capital, Hawaasa. The complicated agenda for the city resulted in the growth of urban slums, the spread of diseases, environmental pollution and civil strife. The ill-defined policy to make Hawaasa the regional administrative capital, supposedly under the control of the central government, harnessed insecurity among Sidamas culminating in popular protest and brutal massacre of hundreds of Sidamas by the government army on 24 May 2002. Known as the Looqe massacre, this is the most grave and historically significant event in recent history. The massacre, which is apart of the ongoing process of genocide took place as the TPLF government security forces opened fire on peaceful demonstrators who were protesting the destabilizing policies of the government. Over hundred lives were lost, and nearly all were Sidamas. The regime was criticized by human rights organizations and national governments. The Looqe massacre remains in the collective conscience of the Sidama public.

Throughout the nation, state-sponsored conflicts continue to claim lives and property. Times were when the regime creates conflict (even warfare) while it joins the game as a non-partisan mediator. Several prominent Sidamas lost their lives in these incidents. This is in line with the old colonial style of divide-and-rule whereby the colonized are separated from each other so that they cannot plausibly mount common struggle. It has been one of the measures to encourage the elites from oppressed people to be oblivious of, if not openly hostile to, the neighbors (i.e., the Oromo, Kaficho, Wolayta, Hadiya, etc.) while they are compelled to master the culture, language and the values of the oppressors.

In recent times, the Sidama nation experienced severe famine conditions. The government gave little or no attention. Most relief effort was provided by Irish Aid under the supervision of the independent local NGO, the Sidama

Development Corporation (SDC). The SDC is a grass root non-profit organization established in July 1997 to help reduce poverty and foster sustainable development in Sidama. Its express mission was to harness the human and physical resources of Sidama so that the people could address the fundamental obstacles to development. The idea to establish SDC came from the Sidama people including those working in Sidama Development Programme (SDP) funded by Irish Aid since 1994. The Irish Aid program has assisted in the establishment of SDC both in terms of creating the critical awareness among the population through integrated rural development program and making the resources available for the establishment of the organization itself. The director of SDC, Wollassa Kumo, made significant effort to secure external resources to help development efforts in the land most neglected by Ethiopian authorities. He was forced to resign in April 2002, prior to the Looqe massacre, and fled the country subsequently.

The development of Sidama nationalism owes its origins in the conquest and the growing discontent and deep-seated malaise caused by Ethiopian empire statehood. The spontaneous rise and fall of peasant uprisings and protests in Sidama in the past is progressively replaced by informed nationalist program that relies on written word. Literacy reinforces permanence and preservation of national treasure. The dispersal of Sidamas throughout the world is also strengthening the network of unity and nationalism in information age.

Notes

1. Currently, the Sidama studies are developing in the Sidama Diaspora. *The Sidama Concern* online has established contacts among Sidamas and other scholars keen on Sidama studies.

2. The Coptic Orthodox Church is the main architect of religious affairs of the northern ethnies. In the south, it was based in urban areas and garrison settlements where the majority of settlers spoke Amharic language. Braukamper (1992: 197) attests that the orthodoxisation campaign failed to go beyond the sphere of influence of the military colonists from northern Ethiopia.

3. The term "nation" here refers to people who share common descent, language, culture, history as well as subjective identification with the political peoplehood. Yoram Dinstein noted that peoplehood is contingent on two separate elements: an objective element of being an ethnic group with a common history, a cultural identity, and a subjective element indicating itself as a people (Dinstein 1976:104). I dwelt on the terminology of nations and nationalism in other publications. See, for example, Seyoum Hameso, (1997a, 1997b).

4. The survey carried out by The Sidama Development Programme in 1995 indicated that Sidama had a population of 3.7 million. See also The Hutchinson Encyclopae-

dic Dictionary, 1991, p.368; and The U.S. Department of State, Country Profile: Ethiopia, The Bureau of African Affairs, 4 December 1997.

5.   See *The Sidama Concern,* Vol. 2, No. 1, 1997, pp.6-7 for comparisons. Gada is an age-grade system of governance. It is based on consultative decision-making with constitutional limits on the exercise of power. The oral law for Sidamas and Oromos draw from the same word, *seeraa,* acting as a social sanction. There is also an assembly system which aims to reach consensus under a shed of a tree known as *odakoo* for Sidamas, and *odaa* for the Oromos. The assembly system is cultural heritage shared by both the Sidamas (*xadoo*) and the Oromos (*gummi*). (See Legesse 1973; see also Bassi 1997).

6.   In the same year of disturbance, 1974, a Mogissa age-set was initiated following the Hirbora age set.

7.   The Sidama Liberation Movement (SLM) as the forerunner of the Sidama Liberation Front (SLF) was formed in the late 1970s. For most of the last decades, it operated from outside Sidama, but joined the TPLF/EPRDF dominated Transitional Government of Ethiopia in 1991 and was expelled from TGE shortly after. On academic and the media field, *The Sidama Concern* focused on promoting the national, regional and international awareness about Sidama.

References

Aalen, Lovise. 2002. *Ethnic federalism in a dominant party state: The Ethiopian experience 1991-2000,* Report R 2002: 2. Chr. Michelsen Institute Development Studies and Human Rights. Bergen: Chr. Michelsen Institute.

Bassi, Marco. 1996. Power's ambiguity or the political significance of Gada. In *Being and becoming Oromo: Historical and anthropological enquiries,* ed. P.T.W. Baxter, J. Hultin, J. and A. Triulzi. 150-161. Uppsala: Nordska Africa Institute.

Baxter, P.T.W. 1994. The creation and constitution of Oromo nationality. In *Ethnicity and ethnic conflict in the Horn of Africa,* ed. K. Fukui and J. Markakis. London: James Currey.

BCA. 1991. *The Hutchinson encyclopedic dictionary.* London: BCA.

Braukämper, U. 1992. Aspects of religious syncretism in southern Ethiopia. *Journal of Religion in Africa.* XXII, 3:194-207.

Brøgger, J. 1986. *Belief and experience among the Sidamo: A case study towards an anthropology of knowledge.* Oslo: Norwegian University Press.

Dinstein, Yoram. 1976. Collective human rights of peoples and minorities. *The International and Comparative Law Quarterly.* 25, 1:102-120.

Ensiminger, J. 1990. Co-opting the elders: The political economy of state incorporation in Africa *American Anthropologist.* 92:662-675.

Ensiminger, J. 1996. *Making a market: The institutional transformation of an African society.* Cambridge University Press.

Hamer, John. 1970. Sidamo generational class cycles. A political gerontocracy. *Africa.* 40:50-70.

_____and I. Hamer, 1994. Impact of cash economy on complimentary relations among the Sidama of Ethiopia. *Anthropological Quarterly.* 67:187-202.

_____ 1994. Commensality, process and the moral order: An example from Southern Ethiopia. *Africa.* 64, 1:126-144.

_____ 1996. Inculcation of ideology among the Sidama of Ethiopia. *Africa.* 66, 4:526-551.

_____ 1998a. The Sidama of Ethiopia and rational communication: Action in policy and dispute settlement. *Anthropos.* 93:137-153.

_____ 1998b. Gerontocracy as a tradition and a mirror for the future. *The Sidama Concern.* 3, 3:5-11.

Hameso, Seyoum. 1997a. *Ethnicity in Africa: Towards a positive approach.* London: TSC.

_____ 1997b. *Ethnicity and nationalism in Africa.* New York: Nova Science Publishers.

_____ 2004. *The Sidama nation and the solidarity of the colonised nations.* In *State crises, globalization and national movements in North-East Africa,* ed. Asafa Jalata. London: Routledge.

Hoteso, B. 1990. *Sidama: Its people and its culture.* Addis Ababa: Bole Printing Press, [in Amharic].

Howard, Michael. 1996. *Contemporary cultural anthropology.* New York: Harper Collins.

Jalata, A. 1995. The struggle for knowledge: The case of emergent Oromo studies. *The African Studies Review.* 39,2:95-132.

Keller, E. 1987. *Revolutionary Ethiopia: From empire to people's republic.* Bloomington and Indianapolis: Indiana University Press.

Kertzer, D. I. and O. B. Madison. 1981. Women's age-set systems. in Africa: The Lutuka of southern Sudan. In *Dimensions: Aging, culture, and health,* ed. C.L. Fry. New York: Preager.

Kurimto, E. and S. Simonse, eds. 1998. *Conflict, age and power: Age systems in transition.* Oxford: James Currey.

Legesse, A. 1973. *Gada: Three approaches to the study of African society.* New York: Free Press.

Spencer, P. 1965. *The Samburu: A study of gerontocracy in a nomadic tribe.* Berkeley: University of California.

Stanley, S. 1966. The political system of the Sidama. In *The proceedings of the third international conference of Ethiopian Studies.* Addis Ababa. Vol. III.

Stanley, S. and D. Karsten. 1968. The Luwa system of the Garbicco sub-tribe of the Sidama (Southern Ethiopia) as a Special case of an age set system. *Paideuma* 14:93-102.

Stanley, S. 1970. The political system of Sidama. *Proceedings of the third international conference of Ethiopian Studies, vol. III.* 215-228. Addis Ababa: Institute of Ethiopian Studies.

The U.S. Department of State. 1997. *Country profile: Ethiopia.* The Bureau of African Affairs, December.

Thiongo, Ngugi. 1986. *Decolonizing the mind: The politics of language and African cultural literature.* London: James Currey.

Wedekind, Klaus. 1980. Sidamo, Darasa, Burjii: Phonological differences and likenesses. *Journal of Ethiopian Studies.* 14, 131-176.

Chapter 3

The Ogaden Past and Present

Abdurahman Mahdi

The Ogaden Somali territory lies between Oromia to the west, Afar to the northwest, the Republic of Djibouti to the north, Kenya to the south and the Somali Republic to the East. The Ogaden people are agro-pastoralists and they speak Somali language.

The Ogaden Somali people were independent and powerful until European colonial powers came to Africa and started arming the Abyssinian chiefs in the north. Using the arms and expertise provided by the colonialists, the Abyssinians captured Harar in 1887 and started raiding villages in that area, killing men and selling women and children as slaves. From their base in Harar, the Abyssinians invaded the region of Ogaden. The Ogaden Somalis vehemently resisted the encroachment of the Abyssinian expansionists and succeeded in halting their advance. Even though the Abyssinian military campaign to conquer the rest of the Somali territory failed, the colonial powers recognized its claim over the Ogaden Somali land and signed treaties with them.

From 1896 to 1948 Abyssinia (renaming itself Ethiopia) waged a constant war of conquest against the Somalis but failed in gaining any further foothold in the Ogaden. In 1935, Italy invaded Abyssinia and captured it along with the Ogaden and the territories of other nations in the area. In 1941, the British defeated Italy in the region, and administered the Ogaden for eight years until it transferred part of the Ogaden (Jigjiga area) to Ethiopia for the first time. The other parts were transferred in 1954 and 1956. Ethiopia then gained control over the Ogaden without the knowledge or the consent of the Ogaden Somali people. From then onwards, successive Ethiopian regimes mercilessly suppressed the Ogaden people and whenever the liberation movements seriously weakened and threatened Ethiopian colonialism, a foreign power directly intervened to re-establish the colonial rule over the Ogaden.

Ethiopia has been characterized, since the beginning of the last century and up to now, by a single ethno-nation using the powers of state to subjugate and exploit all the other nations. For almost one century, the Abyssinians have abused the concept of sovereignty and statehood to deprive the rights of other peoples living under the oppressive rule.

Ethiopia is a state founded on colonial doctrine. Its rule is based on the use of force and emergency measures for oppressing the majority of the people and exploiting them. Whereas Ethiopia inherited the Ogaden territory from the colonial powers, at the same time, it boasts to be the only African state that was never colonized. The fact remains that Ethiopia has been a participant and a partner with the colonial powers that divided Africa among themselves but, unlike other powers, it has never relinquished its colonial possessions.

To maintain such a colonial state, the rulers had to build massive military machine and embark on forcefully maintaining one of the most vicious authoritarian rules in the third world. The resultant resistance from the people and the inevitable taxing of material and moral resources of the oppressive elite became Ethiopia's Achilles' hill and brought about the downfall of its successive regimes. Both Haile Selassie's rule and that of Mengistu's military junta were brought down by the relentless resistance of the colonized nations and the consequential resource drainage.

After the fall of Mengistu Hailemariam, the Ethiopian Peoples Revolutionary Democratic Front (EPRDF)—a new name adopted by the Tigray Peoples Liberation Front (TPLF) to camouflage its narrow ethnic base and rule in Ethiopia—succeeded in capturing Addis Ababa with the help of Eritrean Peoples Liberation Front (EPLF). Although most of the nations under Ethiopian colonial rule contributed to the weakening and the downfall of the Derg politico-military machine, TPLF captured the seat of power and succeeded in gaining international recognition.

At first, the new Ethiopian rulers, feeling weak and aware of the international climate and the demise of totalitarian regimes, forwarded a reasonable and plausible program for addressing the burning issue of Ethiopian colonialism and its solution through recognizing and granting the right of nations to self-determination through peaceful process.

EPRDF agreed to the charter program which recognized the right of nations to self-determination up to secession and stated that a transitional period of two years has to relapse before the nations could exercise that right. Thus, EPRDF recognized the colonial nature of Ethiopia in principle.

Considering the burden of the long struggle of the Ogaden Somali people and cognizant of the value of resolving the long standing conflict between Ethiopia and the Ogaden people through peaceful means, the Ogaden National

Liberation Front (ONLF) decided to give peace a chance and avert a costly and unnecessary war.

But it became obvious that EPRDF was only buying time and was laying the ground for keeping the colonial legacy it inherited and was scheming to attain the submission of the Ogaden Somalis to its colonial rule through demagogy and token democracy. In doing so, the EPRDF grossly miscalculated the gravity and depth of the Ogaden versus the Ethiopian problem.

The EPRDF, blinded by its sudden and unexpected victory and the temporary absence of challenge and armed opposition from the ONLF, grossly miscalculated the severity and gravity of the conflict between the Ogaden people and Ethiopia and the unbending desire of the Ogaden Somalis to regain their sovereignty and independence. Again the EPRDF, forgetful of the bitter experience of its people under the previous rulers and despite its rhetoric of being committed to democracy and the rule of law and respecting the right of nations, began the construction of its politico-military structures to maintain the colonial empire of its predecessors.

Hence, all people concerned in ending the long-standing conflict lost an excellent opportunity and EPRDF planted the seeds of the next cycle of bloodshed and violence in the region. It started by trying to divide the Ogaden Somali people and undermine the leading role of the liberation movement by creating pseudo-organizations based on clan lines. At the same time, it spread its intelligence network and military garrisons in Ogaden. In early 1992, the EPRDF government masterminded the killing of the leadership of the ONLF. Then it attacked the headquarters of ONLF in an effort to wipe it out but withdrew after sustaining high casualties and postponed its plans.

In spite of all the intrigues and harassment of the EPRDF, the Ogaden Somalis persisted in avoiding confrontation and continued rebuilding their political and administrative institutions. In September 1992, they went to the polls to cast their votes in a free and fair election, for the first time in their long history, to elect their district councils and representatives for the regional parliament. EPRDF strongly campaigned for its surrogate parties and members, but in a landslide victory, the ONLF won about 84% of the seats in the newly elected regional parliament.

In mid-1993, the regional government complained to the government in Addis Ababa about its flagrant interference in the day-to-day affairs of the Ogaden region, an act that contradicted the commitment to regional autonomy and devolution of power to the regions. The EPRDF retaliated by freezing the regional budget, diverting international aid, discouraging international non-governmental organizations (NGOs) from working in the Ogaden, and obstructing all initiatives and projects deemed necessary for the development of the region. In the late 1993, the Ethiopian security forces arrested the president, the vice-president and secretary of the Regional Assembly, and transferred them to a prison in Addis Ababa. They were released after ten months without trail.

Finally, when the EPRDF established itself as the government of Ethiopia in the eyes of the international community, and its military and economic resources were enhanced, it felt confident enough to mount a military campaign against the Ogaden Somalis at the end of the transitional period. Moreover, in order to get the *raison d'être* for its campaign of terror and subjugation of the Ogaden people, the EPRDF dictated to Ogaden Somalis an unacceptable choice. It told them to endorse a compulsory constitution that would legalize the colonization of the Ogaden people by Ethiopia and the participation in an election where their role would be to endorse the EPRDF nominated candidates. The EPRDF strategy was to deceive the Ogaden Somalis into sanctioning its colonial rule while at the same time eliminating themselves from the political structures it intended to maintain its hegemony over the nations and avert any future threat. In addition, if the Ogaden Somalis oppose what it proposed, the aim was to acquire the pretext for declaring war on the Ogaden people and extricate itself from honoring the pledges it entered in its moment of weakness and maintain the Ethiopian colonial legacy.

After deliberating on the moves and intentions of the EPRDF and understanding the choices put forth by the EPRDF, the Ogaden people decided that it was unacceptable to succumb to the designs of the EPRDF and forgo their quest for self-determination for which so much blood was shed and so many have suffered. The Ogaden Somali people had to decide either to relinquishing what they had fought for so long or to continue fighting. They wanted peaceful resolution of conflict but war was imposed on them by the TPLF regime.

On 28 January 1994, at a press conference in Addis Ababa, ONLF called for referendum on Ogaden self-determination. On 22 February 1994, a cold-blood massacre took place in the town of Wardheer, where more than 81 unarmed civilians were killed by TPLF militias, who tried to kill or capture alive the chairman of the ONLF, Mr. Ibrahim Abdalla Mohamed, who was addressing a peaceful rally in the center of the town.

In February 1994, the regional assembly passed a unanimous resolution, in accordance with the Transitional Charter. It demanded a referendum on self-determination and independence for the Ogaden people under the auspices of international and regional bodies such as the United Nations, the Organization of African Unity, the European Union, and other independent non-governmental organizations.

The EPRDF government reacted swiftly overthrowing and virtually disbanding all democratically elected institutions in the Ogaden, including the regional parliament. Like their predecessors, the president of the parliament, vice-president and several members of the parliament, were arrested and transferred to prisons in Addis Ababa. Mass arrests and indiscriminate killings took place.

On 17 April 1994, the Ethiopian government launched a large-scale military offensive against ONLF positions and detained many suspected supporters of ONLF. Since 20 April, the combatants of the ONLF and Ethiopian forces are fighting bloody battles and Ethiopia is vehemently denying the engagements with the liberation forces. Certainly, the ongoing suppression of the struggle for self-determination and independence in the Ogaden continues to cause human suffering and are the basis of instability and tragedy in the Horn of Africa. On 28 April, at a press conference in Addis Ababa, the then TPLF defense minister Siye Abraha claimed that all resistance movements in the Ogaden had been destroyed and stamped out. In a petition addressed to the president of the Transitional Government of Ethiopia (TGE), Ogaden elders asked the TGE to stop the military offensive against the people and seek a peaceful dialogue to resolve the conflict, instead of opting for a military solution which complicated an already explosive situation.

In May 1994, the government sponsored a new surrogate party called Ethiopian Somali Democratic League (ESDL) which is one the satellite People's Democratic Organizations (PDO) which exists throughout Ethiopia within the EPRDF framework. The first congress of ESDL was held in Hurso under the patronage of the then prime minister of TGE, Tamirat Layne (now in jail with a prison sentence of 18 years for corruption), who appointed a member of the EPRDF coalition as a chairman of the new pro-government party.

On 25 January 1995, the EPRDF government hastily arranged a meeting in the town of Qabridaharre to convince the ONLF to participate in the upcoming elections. The meeting which was chaired by the then president Meles Zenawi (the current Prime Minister), failed when the EPRDF refused to allow independent arbitrators to participate in a negotiated settlement. Then the ONLF broke off all contacts with the EPRDF government, closed down its office in Addis Ababa and boycotted elections in 1995.

In the Charter of 1991 and the Constitution of 8 December 1994, the EPRDF claimed to guarantee the secession of a people if they are, "convinced that their rights are abridged or abrogated." Indeed, the right of the Ogaden people is constantly abrogated and the process of negating this demand proved too costly to the ruling junta in Addis Ababa.

The tyrannical regime in Ethiopia started a propaganda campaign and public relations stunt in order to convince the international community of its democratic nature by announcing that it was conducting elections in the Ogaden. It also wanted to legitimize its continued presence in the Ogaden even after the people requested to exercise their right to self-determination. Ogaden people thwarted its attempts and yet the regime announced that elections were held and its bogus surrogates had won the seats in Ogaden. At the same time to further its treachery, it formed its own ONLF party and unashamedly declared that ONLF had taken part in its sham elections. This was a clear indicator of its lack of confidence and inability to hide its failure to control the Ogaden. From that time onwards, Ethiopia has been molding and remolding sham representatives in the Ogaden, the so-called parties and Ogaden parliament, more than five times but up to this day it is unable to manage the situation. After failing to intimidate the people to go along with its colonial program, the EPRDF has embarked on a war of attrition with ONLF, and indiscriminate and inhuman tyranny against the Ogaden people. The EPRDF militias killed and imprisoned thousands of civilians and looted their properties. Hundreds of women were raped and for the first time in the history of the Ogaden people, male children were raped.

Thus, the new Ethiopian colonial state headed by the EPRDF has used every trick in the books of colonial strategy but it could not obliterate the armed national struggle of the Ogaden people and has been forced to occupy only the major towns and move in heavily armed convoys.

Then Ethiopia frantically resorted to human rights violations such as killings, imprisonment, forced conscription, exiling, intimidation and harassment, suppression of basic democratic rights which highlight the suffering of the peoples. The regime's policies of systematic underdevelopment include economic sabotage, irresponsible plunder of resources with no regard to sustainability of the environment, denial of educational opportunities, socio-cultural dismantling and subjection to conflict-ridden political and administrative structures.

Moreover in the Ogaden, the EPRDF forces and Tigrayan dealers who have been given concessions and licences by the Ethiopian government dominated by ethnic Tigrayans, are devastating the poor and the fragile ecological balance by widespread exploitation and depletion of forests for military purposes, firewood and charcoal. The rich wildlife, including game birds, forests and water resources have all suffered irreparable damage in the Ogaden under the Ethiopian government.

After it became obvious to the EPRDF that it could not destroy the national resistance of the people and that it was gaining momentum, the EPRDF attacked stateless Somalia and captured three regions following the strategies of its predecessors. The regime is intending to find scapegoats to blame for its failure in subduing the Ogaden people and their rejection of its colonial lust, in order to divert attention and bid to maintain its credibility both inside and outside Ethiopia. It is also actively engaged in sabotaging the reconciliation of the Somali people and building of a Somali state. At the same time, Ethiopia is hosting summits for the Somali leaders posing as a mentor to the Somali people and collecting funds from the UN on that issue.

The Ethiopian destabilization plan is not limited to the Somali nation. Ethiopia attacked Eritrea on the pretext of retaking two Eritrean territories but in reality it is intent on recapturing Eritrea and colonizing it again, but it received lessons from Eritrea it did not bargain for.

Ironically, the Ethiopian government which violates the very basic human rights of all citizens in the empire-state of Ethiopia, including the Ogaden Somalis and wages wars against its neighbors, poses itself as a champion of democracy and human rights in Africa.

Finally, the following sentences sum up the views of the Ogaden Somali. Ethiopia has colonized the Ogaden people and it is viciously continuing that colonial legacy in spite of the change of regime in Addis Ababa. Therefore the people categorically state that the present regime is not different from its predecessors in substance. The Ogaden people, as a sovereign nation, have the right to be masters of their destiny, and are intent on actualizing that right.

The people's struggle will continue as long as the Ethiopian state remains intransigent to the rights and wishes of the people and continues pursuing its inhuman oppressive policies. They will not participate in the bogus elections Ethiopia periodically conducts as a public relations exercise to beguile the local and international communities and hide its colonial and authoritarian nature. Nor will they be taking part in its colonial administrative structures.

The international community is informed that the Ethiopian government is violating the basic human rights of Ogaden people and is systematically exterminating them. Ethiopia is being encouraged to commit genocide against the Ogaden people by the lack of censure from international community over its human rights violations, and holding its rulers responsible for the gross human rights abuses perpetrated by its army and security forces in the Ogaden. Furthermore, Ethiopia is using international aid for military-political programs directed at oppressing the Ogaden Somalis and other nations under its colonial rule and in its expansionist policies against its neighbors. Whenever its war coffers are depleted, Ethiopia appeals for international aid in the name of natural disaster victims. At the same time, Ethiopia has the means to attack two neighboring states and maintain a huge colonial occupation army in the Ogaden, Oromia, Sidama and in the territories of other oppressed nations.

Chapter 4

The Shekacho People: Untold Stories

Achame Shana

The Shekacho live in the Kaffa region which is in the southwest of the Ethiopian empire. Shekacho territory has its southern border with the Bako river, and the Baro river to the north. Its western and eastern borders are the Sudan and the river Gojeb, respectively.

The Shekacho people have a common culture, language and history. They once enjoyed common social, economic, political and religious institutions and they were known for their highly organized state and administrative system. In 1898, they were conquered by the Shawan Amhara and incorporated by force into the Ethiopian empire. The people speak Sheka language which they share with Kafficho people, with dialectical differences. Sheka language is different from Amharic, Ethiopia's official language. Only 5% of the Shekacho people can read or speak Amharic. The majority are illiterate and their only contact with government officials is through interpreters. The language is not developed in its written form.

In 1993, the population census estimated that the Shekacho population is about 1 million, of which approximately 75% are female and 25% are male, 66% are under 30 years of age. These unbalanced demographic figures are due to political and military events which will be outlined later.

About 98% of the population are engaged in subsistence agriculture. About 1.2% of the population are involved in trade while 0.6% are crafts people working as potters, blacksmiths and, occasionally as miners. Only 0.2% of the population have formal education. The policy of successive Ethiopian administrations is to keep the people away from education as much as possible. They were worried that education will give the Shekacho people self-awareness and power that would threaten the Ethiopian dominance. Furthermore, they try to keep those few individuals who have managed to educate themselves away from their people, thus depriving the population of an educated class who could organize and represent the Shekacho people.

The Shekacho people live in a fertile land. They could provide enough food for other areas with the introduction of scientific knowledge and suitable technology. Sadly the potential is far from being realized. At present, the area produces a good proportion of Ethiopia's coffee exports (the word "coffee" is derived from the name of the province, Kaffa), and other products such as honey, gold and fruits. Although there has never been any scientific study, it is believed that the area is rich in minerals such as phosphorous, potassium, gold, coal, copper and uranium.

Until 1984, about 78% of the land area of Kaffa was covered by tropical rain forest. Since 1984 the Northern Ethiopian rulers and their surrogates have been systematically deforesting the area, cutting trees for timber destined for internal and external consumption (largely to the Middle East). The forest area has now been reduced to about 40% of the land area. This drastic depletion of the forest cover seriously threatens many indigenous plants and animal species.

There are seven large rivers in the area including the Baro, the Gojeb, the Gangi and the Gemadro. There are also 20 small rivers. These, if sensibly utilized, could produce large amount of electricity; and they could as well be used for irrigation.

The Shekacho people have been—and still are—subject to cruel governance, they suffered largely at the hands of northern Ethiopians and their surrogates. The following is an outline of political events of the history of the Shekacho people.

In 1898, the Shekacho people, together with their kins, the Kaficho people, were conquered by the Abyssinians, helped by Oromo collaborators from surrounding areas. Shekacho's elaborate defence were overrun by the well-armed invaders and their last king was taken to Addis Ababa, where he was held in silver chains until his death.

From 1897-1912, the Shekacho people frequently opposed the invading forces and were devastated for their resistance. It is believed that tens of thousands of people lost their lives.

Between 1912 and 1924, as the Northern Ethiopian grip on Shekacho society tightened, the people lost control over their land and resources. The Shekacho aristocracy was eliminated and the common people were uprooted; hunted down and sold into slavery. It is estimated that more than 160,000 people were sold into slavery from Shekacho region of Kaffa alone.

In 1924, the Ethiopian government attempted to show the League of Nations that it had abolished slavery and stopped the slave trade in Ethiopia.

Though slavery and the slave trade continued, theoretically the Shekacho people gained their human dignity. And yet they continued to be treated as if they were still semi-slaves.

After Italy invaded Ethiopia in 1935 and Emperor Haile Selassie fled the country, the northern landlords who owned 99% of Sheka land fled the area, fearing that the Shekacho people would attack them. With the oppressive central imperial power removed, the Shekacho people enjoyed a brief period of autonomy and begun to restore their shattered society.

In 1941, with the defeat of the Italian army, Haile Selassie was restored to power by the British government. He took cruel revenge on the Shekacho people ending the brief interlude of freedom. His army was stationed in Shekacho land and the area was used as a detention center for his political opponents and critics. One such political prisoner was a well-known writer, Abe Gubegna, who spent most of his exile life in Shekacho land. In the following years, corrupt civil servants and military officials who were guilty of criminal activities in other provinces were sent as part of their punishment to govern the people of Shekacho. This corrupt clique did whatever it wanted with the Shekacho people. Thousands of Shekacho people suffered and died at the hands of corrupt Ethiopian officials. The outside world remained unaware of the situation in this area as access to it was only through powerful, mostly corrupt, individuals whose allegiance was to the northern Ethiopian imperial power. Even scholars who came to Ethiopia for "scientific" and anthropological works had to rely on northern Ethiopian mediation which was biased and contemptuous towards the Shekacho people. This is still the case as far as European perceptions of Ethiopia are concerned. Western aid agencies have their priorities determined by Ethiopian authorities who ignore Kaffa and similar southern areas.

In 1968, an incident occurred which was typical of the usual brutality with which the Shekacho people were ruled. An Amhara regional governor called Inqu Selassie, toured the Shekacho area using his private car. The entire population of the area were press-ganged to build an 18 k.m. road for his convenience. However, the car soon got bogged down in mud. Shekacho men were forced to carry the car on their shoulders for the rest of the journey using two heavy logs, while the governor sat inside the car. Shekacho women were forced to clap and shout in praise of the governor as they watched their men begging to be released from their torment. About eight people died from injuries sustained during this cruel incident and many others were crippled.

In 1974, when the people in other parts of Ethiopian revolted against the imperial domination, the Shekacho people were jubilant and supportive of the overthrow of Haile Selassie's regime. The military regime known as the Derg came to power and issued a proclamation which on paper freed all the land and resources of the country from the Amhara landlords promising to restore them to the original rightful owners. This development came as a great surprise to the Shekaho people and they wholeheartedly supported the decisions taken by the military regime which promised to guarantee freedom and equality to all of the people of Ethiopia. However, sadly the military regime reneged on its promise. As a result, the Shekacho people were denied their freedom and the basic right of owing their own land. The northern settlers in Shekacho land continued to dominate every aspect of Shekacho life.

Between 1977 and 1979, in order to fight its wars with Eritrea and Somalia, the Derg regime introduced forced military conscription, compelling all males over the age of 18 to join the army. Many Shekaho people joined the army; about 15,000 went to fight. At the end of the war, Somalia was defeated but most conscripts died. Those who survived, all of whom wanted to return to their homes, were forced to serve the army in the northern battle fronts. Instead of giving the Shekacho people freedom and self-government, the Derg demanded more resources and manpower from them. A permanent army recruitment centers were established in the region and thousands of young men were press-ganged and sent to the war fronts. These innocent young men, who had no reason to fight in the internecine war between the northerners, were deployed in the provinces of Tigray, Eritrea, Gojam and Gondar. More than 100,000 young Shekacho men were sent to fight in this war. An army of northerners was permanently stationed in Shekacho land and people were rounded up at gunpoint to fulfill quarterly quotas. The people as a whole were taxed far beyond their means.

In 1980, the Derg initiated a policy to teach Amharic language to every one above the age of five. To the outside world, this was presented as a benevolent scheme to improve literacy in the country. However, Amharic—like the languages of Tigray and Eritrea—is a Semitic language and is unrelated to the Cushitic and Omotic languages of the south. It is difficult to learn and it is not used for international communication and scientific learning. In reality, the literacy program was an attempt to consolidate the cultural hegemony of the north. In any case, the mass "literacy" campaign was superficial and its "success" was demonstrated to the gullible outside world when individuals were produced who were but able to write and sign their names.

In1982, for the first time in their long history, the Shekacho people began to die from starvation in their own fertile lands. The demands for work force and increased taxes had severely disrupted the agricultural cycle. International efforts to relieve the Ethiopian famine were channeled only into the northern areas. Southerners had no access to international agencies; and about 8,000 people died at this time. This was kept secret from the rest of the world by the Derg regime.

Between 1984 -1987, the military regime began a soviet-style policy of settling northerners on Shekacho land. It issued a proclamation that all native people had to leave their homes and build new settlements for themselves to give way to 100,000 northerners, who were brought into the region. The army was sent into the region to force the people to accept this policy. Thousands of houses were burnt, money, cattle and belongings were looted by the troops. This caused a intense anger and for three months there was a civil strife in the region. More than 22,000 men, women and children were killed and thousands of others wounded. The northerners who were brought to settle in the region were given combat training and weapons to protect themselves from native people. They were provided with food, clothes and money. Most of the wounded in this war died from infection caused by an absence of any medical care. The policy of forced internal migration was opposed by the international community but no practical help was given to the people who suffered from it.

Between 1988 and 1989, in order to shore up its waning authority, the Derg regime changed its policy and granted autonomy to several regions of Ethiopia. Tigray, Eritrea, Ogaden and other areas seemed to gain from this. The Shekacho region was one of the many areas which did not. A governor was appointed from the north on the pretext that after years of oppression and violence, the Shekacho people lacked an educated class who could provide leadership in the way that was possible in the northern areas.

The government policy was to provide little or no educational resources. As mentioned earlier, literacy programs were superficial and designed to increase Amhara cultural domination. Nevertheless, a few individuals did manage to earn the degrees of higher education. They started by traveling hours each day to poorly equipped bush schools, where they had to sit at the back and pick up Amharic while it was being taught to the children of residing northern officials. A few went on to higher education, in some cases to Eastern European universities. While studying, these few individuals were kept under strict supervision and any deviation from the support of the government was punished. For example, visa extensions were refused in the middle of degree courses and the government requested that diplomas and certificates to be handed directly to the authorities rather than to the individuals who earned them. By 1990, most of the few Shekacho scholars who were abroad were refused permission to return home for fear that they would help their own people find a voice. As always, government policy was to hide the situation in southern Ethiopia from the eyes of the world.

In 1991, with the encouragement of the United States government, TPLF/ EPRDF and the EPLF took over power replacing the Derg regime. Most of these organizations, as their names show, had as their priority the liberation of their own nations. In the middle of 1991, the TPLF/EPRDF armed forces were deployed in the town and villages of Shekacho people. They asked local people to come forward and set up their own party and participate in the new government of Ethiopia. They said that they understood the Shekacho people's hesitant approach because of their treatment at the hands of previous Amhara rulers. They promised that they would do everything they could to help the Shekacho people to come forward in an organized way. After lengthy discussions and a call from the TPLF leader, the Kaffa People's Democratic Union (KPDU) was formed with the aim of representing the people and restoring their freedom which was lost in 1898. The leaders of the KPDU produced a written program to begin tackling economic, political and social problems besetting their region. The KPDU was given two seats in the Council of Representatives as were most southern Ethiopian peoples. However, most seats went to the TPLF and its surrogates such as the EPDM, OPDO and other PDOs. The Charter of the Transitional Government involved most of the people of Ethiopia. The Charter promised freedom, equality and the rule of law.

The Transitional Government was dominated by the TPLF/EPRDF. Since economic, social and political issues were controlled by the TPLF/EPRDF, policy was biased towards the benefit of the northern Ethiopians. The EPRDF began to loot what remained in the south and move it to the north. Bridges were dismantled and taken to Tigray, the only bridge built by the Italians in 1937 was taken by the EPRDF from the Baro river. When local people objected, they were told to shut up. They were told the KPDU represented only an insignificant minority.

Similar problems were experienced by other southern parties. In response to these smaller parties joined together to create the southern Ethiopian parties. For a while, the parties managed to make their voice heard in parliament, but this was seen as threat by the EPRDF. It decided that the Southern Ethiopians should be represented by new political parties created by the TPLF. Using the resources available to the groups of central government began to manipulate the situation. The KPDU was banned from operating in the Shekacho and Kaficho regions, although an office was kept open in Addis Ababa for the benefit of foreign observers. In this way, the EPRDF drafted a new constitution; recruited about 20 local people and gave them three months' training in law, politics, administration and sent them to the South as their government officers. Members of the KPDU were jailed and ordered to join the EPRDF surrogate parties. The surrogate parties created or manufactured by the TPLF in May 1992 were given a name: Southern Ethiopian Peoples Democratic Front. By this means, the divisions of Ethiopia into de facto two regions was re-established. In the South, the people are now "represented" by the TPLF's surrogate parties which do little apart from rubber stamping decisions made by the dominant Northern elite. On the other hand, in the north the people are well organized and able to direct resources for their own benefit. Money provided by Western governments and various charities were used to further enrich the Northern ruling elites and their supporters.

In 1993-1994, there were different planned election events in the Shekacho land for district representatives. The people were hopeful of electing their own representatives on their own free will. However, the TPLF/EPDRF prevented the free and fair election and it installed its own appointees who are easily manipulated and controlled. While the people were demanding the rule of law and democracy without interference, the TPLF is always busy at interfering in all wakes of life. For example, Bitew Belay, once a high TPLF official and today a prisoner after the crisis within the TPLF, was appointed as a regional governor to oversee and control the political and economic developments in the region. No official or non-official meeting of PDOs was held without his presence, knowledge and direction. The interference resulted in conflicts between the people and the EPDRF/ TPLF.

In 1995, there was a general election. When the people wanted to elect the individuals that they thought would work for their own interest and sought to indicate whom they want to elect, they were denied the choice as the EPDRF blocked the path to free and fair election and prematurely declared itself as a winner. All opposition groups were denied to be included in the election process and were detained. Due to popular resistance, the EPDRF considered the area as a hostile territory to their policy of domination. Following this and other events, the Shekacho Zone was incorporated to Kaffa Zone without the consent of the Shekacho people. The aim of this was to deprive the people the privilege of self-administration and primary economic developments associated with the zone arrangements. The main advantage of zone administration is a direct contact with regional council and access to regional offices for any development and administrative issues. The EPDRF has imposed various layers of bureaucratic arrangements on the people in their affairs. Complicated administrative arrangements were imposed while other zones in Ethiopia enjoy the limited freedom granted by the TPLF. Heinous crimes were committed in the Shekacho land and the people were repeatedly denied justice.

Between 1996 and 1997, the Shekacho people seriously opposed the above measures and procedures. Various demonstrations and meetings were held against the transfer of zone administration to the Kaffa region. Petitions were collected and sent to the Prime Minister's office to overturn the decision. In addition, they elected elderly people to lodge appeals on a personal basis to the Prime Minster and the regional council. The elderly men stayed in Addis Ababa for three months which is several hundreds of kilo meters away from their home. However, the Prime Minister's office ignored elderly people and their appeal. They were seen as simple beggars that have come to waste their time. The Council of Representatives ignored the plea of Shekacho elders. Ignored by the Prime Minister's office as well as by the Council of representatives, the humiliated Shekacho elders returned to their land. The EPDRF officials demonstrated that they are the new masters whose orders should be obeyed.

Between 1997 and 1998, the government facilitated a major scale deforestation and timber trade for the use in the construction industry in the north and central areas. Besides, many commercial entrepreneurs were given densely forested land in the Shekacho area in the name of developing Tea farms and organic coffee production. As a result of these activities, real climatic change and environmental degradation is being noticed (reduced amount of rain fall and famine). The Shekacho people derived no benefit from these activities and were worried that the scale of environmental disaster that was imposed on them is having significant deleterious effects. Many people died of starvation. Again, the people elected their own elderly delegations and tried to represent their case to the Prime Minister's office as well as to the regional council. The delegations achieved nothing. Once again, they were humiliated and intimidated.

In 2000, the campaign for the election of members for the House of Representatives and regional council representatives started. As in previous elections, several opposition groups' members and individuals who did not belong to the ruling party were detained, some were killed. The people clearly voiced their dissent to continued unfair representation and mistreatment of their rights. Various demonstrations and rallies were carried out against the hand picked puppet representatives in the House of parliament and the regional council. Also they demanded the unconditional restoration of the Shekacho zone administration. These demands were denied and shame election was held and its out come was the foregone " victory" for the ruling party.

In 2001, owing to the continued resistance of the people, the Shekacho zone administration was restored in theory. However in practice, military administration from the centre has replaced local civil administration.

The year 2002 witnessed the continued and systematic subjugation of the Shekacho people by the TPLF regime in Ethiopia. The Shekacho people continued their peaceful resistance, which was met with violence. As the result, 1800 people were killed and more than 1,117 houses and property burned in a day in Tepi area alone. According to local observers, the TPLF regime in Ethiopia is playing double games. On the one hand, the regime kills those who stand with the masses and reflect the interest of people. On the other hand, the regime also kills those hated individuals, its own instrument in Shekacho land. The purpose for killing its local agents is to blame the mass murder its army had committed against the Shekacho people. In fact, since the mass massacre of 20002, the regime has imposed curfew in Shekacho land, where its soldiers are engaged in rape of girls and married women.

CONCLUSION

Since their conquest and incorporation into the Ethiopian Empire, the Shekacho people suffered under successive Ethiopian regimes. Before 1935, the Shekacho people were treated as slaves. From 1941 to 1974, there was very little development activities in Shekacho land. During the period of military rule, Shekacho people continued to suffer under brutal regime. The TPLF dominated government that replaced the Derg has shown itself to be unsympathetic to the needs and hopes of the people in the South. The Shekacho region is reduced to poverty-stricken wasteland. Those men who had been forced to fight for the *Derg* and survived, struggled back to their homes found themselves with no food, no clothes, no shelter, or no families. Little better than beggars in their own land, many experienced jail and torture. Some went into hiding and in desperation started robbing ordinary people and government officials. The EPRDF sent its militia to capture or kill them. The government officials called a meeting in the area and relatives of the those individuals were summoned and killed. Their bodies were left by the roadside to terrorize the living.

Part II

Contemporary Political Economy

Chapter 5

Myths and Realities of the Ethiopian State

Seyoum Hameso

The political foundation of Ethiopian state is a matter of mythology as much as legend (Legend, here, implies to unauthentic story handed down by tradition and popularly regarded as historical. Myth is a fictitious narrative, magnified by tradition, usually involving supernatural persons or events and expressive of primitive beliefs). The perpetuation of myth commences with a reportedly glorious past of ancient kingdom. Known until the 1930s as Abyssinia, Ethiopia is a country whose

> dominant tribe, the Amhara,[1] were converted to Christianity in the fourth century and have adhered to it ever since to the Coptic Church.... Europeans heard legends of the wondrous kingdoms of Prester John, lost somewhere beyond the horizons. But the reality was less glorious. Ethiopia was remote and poor, and its rulers fought constantly against other tribes... Explorers of the 19th century discovered a land of extreme poverty and ignorance, whose paranoid rulers imprisoned their sons for fear they would rise in revolt (Brogan 1992:28).

For the pre-sixteenth century Portuguese travellers, Abyssinia was known as the land of Prester John, a Christian island in the midst of Muslims. It should be noted, however, that today out of an estimated population of 70 million, about 45 per cent are Muslim. Christian denominations include Coptic Orthodox, protestant, Catholic and others.

Menelik, who lived as a prisoner for a decade during Tewodros' rule (1855-1867), had gained control over Abyssinian fiefdoms in the late nineteenth century. In 1865 he became the king of Shoa (also referred as Shawa or Shewa) and then turned his attention to the nations of the South unleashing a series of assaults against the peoples and their political formations. The war booty enabled Menelik and his *ethnie* to write a self-congratulatory version of history. According to Tronvoll, this version identifies Ethiopia "with the ancient Abyssinian cultures" of Amhara and Tigray, in both governmental presentation and foreign understanding" while the "range of other ethnic groups in Ethiopia has scarcely been visible, and until recently little interest has been shown towards understanding their traditions and cultures" (Tronvoll 2000:5).

This legend of antiquity ignored the complex and rich cultural and political history of the Southern peoples. Research into the latter was discouraged. To nullify the voices and historicity of the oppressed groups, the dominant historiography, extended its longevity of unified empire statehood to three thousand years which is but a combination of legend and myth.

MYTH AS HISTORY

The myth of Solomonic line is based on a fairy tale of a certain Queen's (referred to as Saba or Sheba) visit to ancient Israel who returned pregnant with the son who was to become Menelik I. The story, according to Edmond Keller, was written in the book of *kebra-negast* and translated from Arabic with quotations and illustrations from the Bible, the Quran and from elsewhere (Keller 1991: 47-8). The myth served a purpose: it helped justify the mutual exclusion of Northern *ethnie* to rule their warring fiefdoms while keeping other people on the margins or away from competition for power.

Another myth surrounds the perception of modernization. (Modernization, here, relates to expansion of education and building "modern" institutions along Western lines). This myth is particularly associated with the early twentieth century "modernizing monarchy." The modernization drive focused on three objects: a) upgrading the army, b) bureaucratization, and c) assimilation. The imperial regime was alerted to the importance of establishing these institutions of control of conquered areas through trained and paid soldiers (in contrast to emergency-based ad hoc traditional militia) and loyal bureaucratic personnel. These, in turn, required the introduction of military training centers and other schools as sources of recruiting people to help administer and collect taxes. What was in effect modernized was the apparatus of coercion and control whereas education was used as a tool of assimilation into Abyssinian culture and values (Keller 1991).

The modernization myth was thus merely a disguise for honing the methods of subordination, exploitation and control over colonized nations. Contrary to organic development that accompanied modernization elsewhere in the world with a view to improve the living standards of respective people, modernization in Ethiopia was sought precisely for the defense of the empire state and what it came to represent. In that sense, modernization was merely a self-serving goal and it had little to do with engendering equitable and fast economic growth or social and political transformation commonly associated with the modernization literature in the West.

Any progress that had occurred was extremely uneven since most of the new institutions were clustered in and around the capital. For example, it was reported that in the early 1970s, about 70 per cent of industrial activities were clustered in Addis Ababa and Asmara. In 1972, out of 61 secondary schools in the empire, 25 were in Shawa, mainly in the capital, Addis Ababa. The Addis Ababa University, formerly named after Emperor Haile Selassie, was located in the capital grooming largely the Abyssinian ruling class. By the end of Haile Selassie's reign in the 1970s, the empire was as ancient as feudalism itself, where the rulers continued to believe in annual rituals involving human sacrifice to maintain the power that flows from divine ordination, and not from the people.

Another myth surrounds the representation of black independence. At the time of the wind of change in Africa which culminated in the formal decolonization of African countries, some in the West believed in this image of Ethiopia symbolizing a never-colonized black nation in Africa. This perception contradicts the absence of freedom and self-determination for the people who fell under Abyssinian colonial rule. Again, this imagery was used by the rulers to secure external support—both financial and diplomatic. The Emperor hoped, by presenting the image of an advocate of African unity and independence, "to avoid international pressure on Ethiopia to grant the right to self-determination being demanded by disparate ethnic [groups] within the empire, especially by the Eritreans and the Ogaden Somalis" (Keller 1991: 93).

Asafa Jalata contends that the perception of Ethiopia as a symbol of freedom was shared among the African Diaspora but it lacks critical understanding. Accordingly,

> this uncritical position emerged from lack of understanding that the Ethiopian empire was created by the alliance of Ethiopian colonialism and European imperialism during the 'scramble' for Africa by enslaving and colonizing Oromos, Sidamas, Somalis, Wolaytas and other ethnonations in the Horn of Africa (Jalata 2001:4).

The reality is that the stateless nations of the present-day Ethiopia are the colonies of former Abyssinia. Africanist historians have clearly affirmed this position. In their book entitled *African History*, Philip Curtin, S. Feierman, L. Thompson and J. Vansina wrote that:

> Ethiopia in the twentieth century was not so much an exception to the normal pattern of African history as it was a country where historical trends found elsewhere combined in a particular way (Curtin, *et al* 1978:464).

The point about what had happened in reality is made abundantly clear by examining the history and the nature of Ethiopian empire and its state formation. Slightly over a century ago, after seizing power as the king of Shoa, Menelik II annexed territories beyond the domains of the traditional feudal Abyssinia. Between 1868 and 1876, he had gained control of Wallo in the northeast. In the next decades, he had turned his attention to the South by conquering areas such as Gudru, Horo, parts of Leqa, Botor, Badifolla, and the kingdoms of Limu-Enarya, Guma, Gera, Goma and Jimma-Kaka in 1882. By 1887, Gurage, Arsi and Harar had fallen providing him access and control over important trade routes and resources. In the period between 1890 and 1906, he added Ogaden, Bale, Sidama, Wolayta, Kaffa and Illubabor by which time the present configuration of the empire came into existence (Keller 1991: 36).

In other words,

> The empire Menelik built had a Christian core area whose people spoke Semitic languages like Tigrina [and] Amharic; but it did not include all such populations, and the majority came to be non-Christian and non-["Semitic"]... Menelik's conquests included a fringe of Nilotic peoples to the West, the Sidamo states to the South, the Muslims of the Eastern highlands... the vast Somali speaking semi-desert of Ogaden...and finally the nomadic people of the Denakil lowlands (Curtin *et al* 1978: 464-65).

The war of conquest was extremely brutal in areas where resistance was fierce due to well-established indigenous authority structures. Justification for genocidal cruelty was derived from the Abyssinian book of kibre-negest which codified brutal terror to be directed against those who resist alien rule. Following a prolonged resistance in some of the Southern kingdoms including Kaffa and Wolayta, their population were sold into slavery and targeted for degrading treatment. Whatever followed the Abyssinian victory was the formation of the "victor-vanquished" relationship that reigned for much of the twentieth century. It is also this relationship which brought about the contemporary Ethiopia which is but a modern invention of the conquest of the nations of the present-day Southern Ethiopia.

In order to accomplish the conquest, Emperor Menelik had raised substantial army, mainly from the North and collaborators from the South. He also received substantial foreign aid in the form of military and technical assistance inviting Europeans to his court to assist in the training of his men. Edmond Keller noted that the military advisers were:

> mainly French and Russian and their activities were largely confined to instruct [his] soldiers in the use of certain weapons. Some of these

individuals even accompanied Ethiopian military units as advisers during campaigns of conquest in the South (Keller 1991: 39).

With the support of foreign armaments and expertise, atrocious wars were conducted against relatively less armed Africans not to mention the later confrontation with the colonizing Italian army.[2] As far as the external world was concerned, it was only the "black-white" confrontation which received attention whereas inglorious conquest and what one might call domestic colonialism was hardly told or were told in a different light. To cover up the reality and to defend its status, the empire state assumed a satellite status to one or other global powers, dubbed correctly as a dependent state in this part of Africa (Holocomb and Ibsa 1990). Today, dependence is so complete that what one would consider as fundamental need for food self-sufficiency is far from being achieved.

EXPANSION OR COLONIALISM?

The direct annexation of territories of Southern nations lies at the center of the process of Ethiopian empire building. That process had begun at the time of the European Scramble for Africa. The history of annexation was written, re-written and translated by palace historians rather mildly as imperial expansion to the South or even "re-unification" as if there had existed a unified entity before. The motives and the pretext for the conquest were bluntly expressed by Emperor Menelik who related to Europeans that:

> I have no intention of being an indifferent looker-on if the distant powers have the idea of dividing up Africa for Ethiopia has been for more than fourteen centuries an island of Christians in the middle of the sea of the pagans (Menelik's letter of 10 April 1891, quoted in Pakenham 1991: 470).

Through that message, he justified the scramble for African nations by an African who would trace his descent from outside Africa. It is accurately noted that "Ethiopia, particularly under Menelik, was itself a participant in the colonial scramble for Africa, enlarging what we know as Ethiopia substantially between 1882 and 1906 … incorporating [the] newly acquired territories" (Keller 1991:36). In the words of Lovise Aalen

> Menelik expanded his rule from the central highland regions to the south and east of the country and established the borders of Ethiopia that we find today, a country including more than eighty different ethnic groups. He defeated powerful traditional kingdoms, some of them had been not been under the rule of the central highlanders before, such as the Oromo, the Wolayita, the Sidama, the Gurage and the Kafa (Aalen 2002:3).

The case becomes more explicit when one looks into the borders that were artificially carved in accordance with agreements between the local notable, Emperor Menelik, and different colonial powers including Italy (26 October 1896), France (20 March 1897) in the north and east, and Britain (14 May 1897) in the south and the west. These artificial borders had no regard to the social environment. Time and again, they remained a permanent cause for conflict.[3]

Viewed from the point of view of the conquest of the Southern nations, Menelik's expansion was by no means different from colonial adventures elsewhere. Indeed, "like the European empires in Africa, Ethiopia was a conquest state" where territories were amassed by sheer force with the aid of imported military arsenal (Wilson 1994: 19). Why a colonialist state claims independence? There are explanations for the desire to be regarded as the only black African state to escape European colonialism. Edmond Keller is of the opinion that

> During the most critical phase of the struggle for African independence under Haile Selassie's tutelage, Ethiopia sought to establish itself as the ultimate champion in the cause of African independence and self-determination. Indeed, an effort was made to portray Ethiopia as the epitome of African independence, a stable and integrated community amid a continent of new states characterized by chronic political instability. These were, however, myths that could not stand the test of time. They had been introduced mainly for the symbolic support they might elicit for the legitimacy of the Ethiopian empire in the world community and for the promotion of the desirability of unified, multi-ethnic African nation states (Keller 1991: 1).

In theory and practice, the resultant state formation was based on the Jacobin notion of territoriality of state and acquisition of land with little or no consideration to the social environment and human settlement. This is precisely what the colonial scramble for land did to Africa. In fact, the outcome of Abyssinian expansion was quite similar to the outcome of the Berlin Conference in the rest of Africa. What made the Ethiopian case unique is the fact that it is an African colonialism perpetrated against African nations, a kind of black-on-black imperialism. This position stands firmly in contrast to the view of the only African country that escaped colonialism—the view which the ruling elite and Ethiopianists would like to entertain.

In unison with the rulers, advocates of Abyssinian historiography describe Emperor Menelik's move as expansion or unification rather than colonialism. They draw parallels between historical precedents of capitalist development in Europe on the eve of colonialism and the pre-feudal or feudal formations of Abyssinia. European colonialism, unlike that of Abyssinia, was preceded by technical and military advances. The late nineteenth century Abyssinia had not been capitalist nor had it mastered advanced technology. On the contrary, it had been ruled by anachronistic feuding warlords whose outlook did not coincide with the buoyant motives of the protestant era of capitalism except the ruthless use of natural access to sea and to the procurement of armaments. With these armaments, the warlords schemed and fought first among themselves and then against others.

The political motive for external support to Abyssinian warlords was largely dictated by broader historical events in Europe and its ramification in the Scramble for Africa than military strength or weakness within the empire. Prior to the scramble, Emperor Tewodros of Gondar died in April 1868. Then Ras Kassa, later Yohanes of Tigre and, according to Thomas Pakenham, the principal collaborator with General Napier against Tewodros, had received ammunition and stores worth half a million pounds (Pakenham 1991: 470-71). In all their internecine feuds, the warlords had been at ease neither with themselves nor with their neighbors. Pausewang clearly noted that:

> ...It is not true that Ethiopia is the only African country that escaped European colonialism. The truth is that Emperor Menelik claimed a place among the colonial powers for his Ethiopia which became the only African colonial power the Europeans hesitatingly recognized [and] [t]he weapons Menelik used to conquer the areas in the South, and later to defend against the Italian invasion—came from Europe... It subjugated pastoral or peasant communities to a centralized political structure which follows the principles of European colonial rule (Pausewang 1993:159).

Thus irrespective of the modernity or anachronism of rule, colonialism is nothing but colonialism, defined in the dictionary as a policy of acquiring or maintaining colonies and a policy of economic exploitation of people. According to Ngugi wa Thiong'o, the most trenchant critic of colonialism in Africa:

> The real aim of colonialism was to control the people's wealth: what they produced, how they produced it, and how it was distributed; to control, in other words, the entire realm of the language of real life. Colonialism imposed its control of the social production of wealth through military conquest and subsequent military dictatorship. But its most important area of domination was the mental universe of the colonized, the control through culture, of how people perceived themselves and their relationship to the world. Economic and political control can never be complete or effective without mental control. To control a people's culture is to control their tools of self-definition in relation to others. For colonialism this involved two aspects of the same process: the destruction or the deliberate undervaluing of a people's culture, their art, dances, religions, history, geography, education, orature and literature, and the con-

scious elevation of the language of the colonizer. The domination
of a people's language by the language of the colonizing nations was
crucial to the domination of the mental universe of the colonized
(Thiong'o 1986: 16).

The above description of colonialism and its effects are all too apparent in
contemporary Ethiopia just as it is the case of colonized people elsewhere in
the world. In what unique ways did the Abyssinian colonialism manifest itself?
Typical of colonial rule, what followed the conquest was ruthless repression of
civil rights and the disappearance from official history books of the long historicity of political and cultural tradition of the colonized people. Such nations
as the Oromo, Sidama, Shekacho, Wolayta and their corresponding authority
structures were subordinated to anachronistic autocracy, feudalism, force and
tradition tied by manipulative family formations. By imposing itself on diverse
modes of existence, the Abyssinian colonial rule corrupted the *gada* system of
the Oromo, the *luwa* of the Sidama and similar cultures of other nations forcing
them into what Pausewang (1993: 159) calls "anarchic accommodation of individual self-interest."

In equally typical manner with colonial style, people in the South were confiscated their properties and deprived of their land becoming tenants to settled
soldiers and representatives of the crown from the North. By taking over land
and property, the colonial system reduced the indigenous people to complete
serfdom none other than personal servants. The settlers were largely drawn from
northern highlands, mainly but not exclusively Amharic speakers and other collaborators most of whom were assimilated to Amharic culture.

THE PAST AS PRESENT

What followed this process of colonization was the subordination of the
majority South to the minority ruling elites from a Northern ethnic group. This
relationship of domination had always been maintained by force, violence and
authoritarian polity. Subsequent regimes, since the formation of the empire,
perpetuated the same past with varying levels of cruelty which eventually led
to their downfall.

The outcomes of the scramble soon became the territorial configuration of
what Emperor Haile Selassie inherited. True to the word, the political and class
structure of the regime was imperial and feudal. The Emperor was an absolute
monarch who legitimized his authority on the grounds of divine ordination. The
personalized nature of the state was such that officials owed their position to the
person of the Emperor who was never meant to be accused or reprimanded.
The continuation of the conquest enabled a class of landed nobility (referred to

as absentee landlords) to own fertile agricultural land throughout the country. These landlords

> ... did not reside in the countryside but exercised ownership rights over its property through a system of surrogate agents. In the countryside itself, the local gentry which owned considerable land in its own right, served as the chief government agent, serving as administrator and judge at the level of the sub-province and district. Most farming peasants did not own the land they tilled but were tenants of the landed classes or the state. Under a variety of classifications, the state held vast tracts of agricultural land in the country. Some of this land was given to persons who had rendered or were expected to render loyal service to the state. The offer was conditional and could be withdrawn at any time. Other holdings of the state were farmed by tenant farmers who handed over a portion of their produce to the state agent in the form of rent. In theory, all the land in the country belonged to the state, and under the ancient principle of eminent domain the state had the right to claim land held under private ownership and to dispossess any person or institution (Rahmato *et al* 1999:14).

It should also be said that the system of land holding in the North was different from the South. In the former, the system known as 'rist' (a combination of communal and individual land ownership) was maintained. The aftermath of conquest introduced settler-tenant relationship to the South. After owning land, the very basic element of survival for the rural poor, the Abyssinian state kept the latter dispossessed, poor and insecure. Moreover, as those who rendered loyal service to the conquest were largely drawn from the distinguished ethnie, they owned what was left off the state and the church holdings leading to the system of tenant farming which

> ... was most widespread on land owned by the landed classes. It was the main form of tenure for farming peasants in the southern part of the country. The landed nobility were not only absentee owners but were for the most part northerners whose rights to land in the southern regions was based ultimately on conquest and political domination. For the peasant, tenancy was onerous and exploitative. The farmer not only paid rent, usually in kind, for the use of the land, but had to render a variety of services including labor to his landlord. While frequent evictions of tenants was not a regular practice, most tenants had no sense of secure holdings. In the latter part of the 1960s and the early 1970s, a good deal of tenant evictions did take place due to the expansion of large-scale mechanized agriculture (Rahmato *et al*, ibid.)

In this way, for much of the twentieth century, the Ethiopian empire was ruled by elite group drawn mainly from Amharic speakers who literally owned the state so much so that Amharic culture and language were presented as one and the same as Ethiopia. The rest of the people who constituted a majority, were considered as clusters of people without history, culture, language and by definition without power—and thus just like raw materials ready to be converted. The same historiography suppressed ethnic diversity through centralized polity buttressed by personal rule and patronage whereby handpicked persons run administrative districts whose territorial boundaries had little resemblance to social demarcations.

In 1974, when the emperor was deposed, imperial power changed hands from feudal autocracy to the military dictatorship known as the Derg causing a shift in the country's ideological and foreign policy directions. To many it sounded like a revolution but there was hardly a fundamental change in the imperial nature of Ethiopia. Ernest Gellner noted that, after removing a less agile emperor:

> [the Derg] promptly announced, as new rulers are liable to do, that henceforth all ethnic groups were equal and indeed free to chose their own destiny. These admirable liberal sentiments were followed fairly soon by a systematic liquidation of intellectuals drawn from non-Amhara group.... (Gellner 1983:85).

The only semblance of radical change was in relation to land and even that was due to the short-lived participation of the Southern liberals who initiated the demand for reform. According to Rahmato *et al* (1999:15):

> Initially, the reform was received with a good deal of support; it appeared as an emancipatory reform designed to enable the peasantry to become an independent class. But subsequent policies aimed at the socialization of agriculture alienated the peasantry and soured the relations between it and the Derg. Moreover, the reform gave rise to frequent redistribution of land and as a result created a high degree of tenure insecurity.

Thus, in the name of Marxist-Leninist ideology of proletarian hegemony and aggressive militarism, centrist policies were pursued to the extremes. Marina Ottaway pointed out that "change was controlled from the top, and the military, not the people, came to occupy center stage. The revolution brought neither social justice nor economic development" (Ottaway 1990:1).

By and large, very little has changed as far as the fundamentals of centralism and ethnic domination are concerned. In fact, old policies were pursued with vigor, now with the disguise of ideology and partisan external support. In the name of building a socialist republic along scientific Marxist-Leninist ideology, the Derg took some measures without changing the tradition of centralism. Initially, it adhered to the fourteen provinces, renamed as "Administrative Regions." In 1988, cognizant of the unavoidability of the problem but unwilling to concede, it introduced five "autonomous" regions and twenty-five "administrative regions." The arrangement had more to do with administrative expediency than social or geographic configuration. Once again, the amendment did not deter hostilities between the Derg and the rebellion movements operating in Eritrea, Ogaden, Tigray, Oromia and in many other areas. Eventually, it was the "coalition" of such regional and ethno-national armies that effectively brought an end to the Derg rule.

What followed the Derg's departure requires a book in its own but a few points should be cited here. The empire's underlying Northern core still remains, ruling largely by force and expropriation of the resources of the South. It seeks legitimacy and foreign support by pretending to pursue half-hearted programs of federalism and a "free" market economy, while leaving the empire status largely intact. The report from the Government's own Federal Civil Service Commission showed that Amhara still hold 57 per cent of posts in the state bureaucracy, and Tigreans 12 per cent. The Oromo who account for nearly half of the country's population, hold only 14 per cent (*Ethiopian Herald*, 8 April 1996). This is only a minute way of indicating an inherent bias within Ethiopia's state machinery. Young (1996) indicated that "the public bureaucracy remains, as it was under the Derg, deeply conservative, resistant to change, preoccupied with national security, and seriously in need of reform."

This particular epoch is fraught with the most obvious contradictions the Ethiopian empire came to represent. The verdict of one external observer is perceptively accurate.

> Whether it is the product of the country's feudal traditions or the result of a government which, after five years in power, still does not feel secure in its capital city, the EPRDF leadership appears remote, and has little interaction beyond a select group of political allies, most of whom are Tigrean. The EPRDF presides over what is still an authoritarian state which it shows little interest in reforming [it] than was the case during its first five years in power (Young 1996:541)

The TPLF/EPRDF employs five methods to exert influence over sham federalism:

> First, the direct representation of the EPRDF on state councils, as currently exists in Afar and Benshangul Gumuz states; second, there are key EPRDF 'advisers' in each state, who play an active, and some claim decisive, role in political affairs; third, the EPRDF provides a

> wide range of courses and educational functions for state and party officials and bureaucrats, disseminating and streamlining an EPRDF 'way of thought'; fourth, the EPRDF can directly discipline members of its affiliated organizations and remove them from their political positions, and finally, the EPRDF controlled army has assumed, or tries to assume, direct control in various 'unstable' peripheral parts of the country .... (Young, quoted in Tronvoll 2000:21)

The regime of Meles Zenawi presides over an authoritarian state, committing human rights abuses bordering on genocide.

Looking into the *modus operandi* of subsequent Ethiopian rule, the term "empire state" continues to hold currency, as far as the content and the procedures of the state that was formed as the result of conquest of nations continues well after the era of the emperor. The current regime differs from the previous ones in openly accepting the Ethiopian problematic presumably seeking constitutional redress but in reality buying time to revert to the paradigm of domination. In relation to this hypocrisy, Kjetil Tronvoll was tipped by an insider that:

> One must understand that the Constitution is only meant for foreign consumption, and not for internal implementation. Thus, to analyze the 'EPRDF Ethiopia' on the background of the Constitution alone, will not at all give a representative picture. Some policies might have changed from the former regimes of Haile Selassie and the Derg, but one thing always remains intact in Ethiopia: politics is run from the center with a top down control. This is also the case today (Tronvoll 2000:5).

If constitutions elsewhere are designed to limit the powers of rulers and safeguard individual persons and groups against arbitrary and despotic government, in Ethiopia they are destined for shelves and for fleeting if not selective reference for external propaganda purposes. The political crises within the TPLF leadership that followed the conclusion of the Ethiopia- Eritrea war[4] in 2001 further undermined the constitutional references in favor of personalized rule by the TPLF faction led by Meles Zenawi.

While states elsewhere provide for mechanisms of collective protection, conflict-mediation, and re-distributive agency focused on people's needs, the Ethiopian state is distinguished by perpetuating poverty, famine, and war. The vast majority desperately struggle for survival amid devastating famine and the collapse of local economies. Today, the Tigrayan phase of colonialism is attempting to keep the Ethiopian empire economically and politically segmented always fraught with contradictions. For example, while centralism is a fact of life, federalism (sometimes reported as ethnic federalism) is claimed for propaganda purposes. The contradictions rendered Ethiopia's official speak being very different to the real life lived and felt by the majority of the population.

More alarmingly, the TPLF/EPRDF single party dictatorship has changed into personal dictatorship encapsulated under dubious notion of "Revolutionary Democracy" whose direct effect could be the perpetuation of genocide on a large scale. The symptoms of this are already being observed in the actions and policy pronouncements of the regime. The unintended consequence of this is a further promotion of nationalism among oppressed people who find it necessary to strengthen their demands for democratic rights and for the achievement of national self-determination. More than any time in their history, the urgency of decolonization is heavily felt. As An-Na'im attests "human societies are entitled, and do in fact seek, to follow their own path to self-determination in accordance with their world-views and visions of the public good (An-Na'im, 1992:267). If patterns of conquest and the paradigm of domination are to continue, the future of the empire is no different to that described by Thomas Hobbes (1660) in his Leviathan of the mid-seventeenth century whereby:

> ...There is no place for industry, because the fruit thereof is uncertain, and consequentially no culture of the earth, no navigation, nor use of the commodities that may be imported by sea; no commodious building ... no account of time; no letters; no society; and ... worst of all, continual fear, and danger of violent death.

The authors of the following document are prophetic about future:

> In the twenty-first century, only nations that share a commitment to protecting basic human rights and guaranteeing political and economic freedom will be able to unleash the potential of their people and assure their future prosperity. People everywhere want to be able to speak freely; choose who will govern them; worship as they please; educate their children—male and female; own property; and enjoy the benefits of their labor. These values of freedom are right and true for every person, in every society—and the duty of protecting these values against their enemies is the common calling of freedom-loving people across the globe and across the ages (White House 2002:iii).

As far as the Ethiopian problem is concerned, the question remains if it is possible for the prison house of nations to extricate itself from this past. The answer lies in how the problem—a tension between a colonized people's struggle for national self-determination and the attempt by the state to exercise its hegemony over those people—is resolved. If a resolution is found without destructive confrontation, which is already the case, it is a significant achievement for all involved.

Notes

1. It was arguably the Tigrayans, who were converted to Christianity in the fourth century. The Amhara ethnic identity was formed during the 10th and 11th centuries.

2. The Italian army was defeated in 1896 at the battle of Adwa. The second round of armed confrontation took place in 1936. The occupation by Mussolini's army lasted until 1941. When Italy was defeated by the Allied Forces in 1941, Emperor Haile Selassie, who spent five years in exile in Britain, returned to the throne. Italy lost its colonial possessions in Africa including Abyssinia, Libya, Somaliland and Eritrea. It is recalled that Eritrea was an Italian colony from 1890 until 1941 by which time it was administered as a UN/British protectorate. The trusteeship ended in 1952 when Eritrea had been federated with Ethiopia. In 1962, Haile Selassie dissolved the federation triggering Africa's longest war for independence which culminated in a de facto freedom in 1991 and formal independence in 1993.

3. For instance, the wars between Ethiopia and Eritrea, between Somalia and Ethiopia were initiated or exacerbated by these artificial borders as well as the processes of domination. No time has this been as explicit as the most recent Ethiopia-Eritrea war where an estimated 123,000 people were killed on both sides. An equal number were displaced and significant damage was sustained by economic and social institutions.

4. The war started suddenly in May 1998 and continued until February 2000. It was stopped by significant external involvement and mutual exhaustion by both parties culminating in the signing of Algiers Peace Accord in June 2000 and subsequent border ruling, on 13 April 2002, from the Hague-based Boundary Commission.

References

Aalen, Lovise. 2002. *Ethnic federalism in a dominant party state: The Ethiopian experience 1991-2000*, Report 2. Chr. Michelsen Institute Development Studies and Human Rights. Bergen: Chr. Michelsen Institute.

An-Na'im, Abdullahi. 1992. Civil right the Islamic constitutional tradition: Shared ideas and divergent regimes. *The John Marshal Law Review*. 25:2, 267-293.

Brogan, P. 1992. *World conflicts: Why and where they are happening*. London: Bloomsbury.

Clapham, C. 1995. Ethiopia and Eritrea: The politics of post-insurgency. In *Democracy and change in sub-Saharan Africa,* John Wiseman. London and New York: Routledge.

Curtin, P., S. Feierman, L. Thompson and J. Vansina. 1978. *African history*. Harlow: Longman.

De Waal, A. 1994. Rethinking Ethiopia. In *The Horn of Africa*, ed. C. Gordon. London: University College of London Press.

Gellner, E. 1983. *Nations and nationalism*. Oxford: Basil Blackwell.

Hobbes, Thomas. Leviathan. 1660. available <http://oregonstate.edu/instruct/phl302/texts/hobbes/leviathan-contents.html>

Holocomb, Bonnie and Sisay Ibsa. 1990. *The invention of Ethiopia: The making of a dependent colonial state in northeast Africa.* Trenton, NJ: The Red Sea Press.

Jalata, Asafa. 2001. *Fighting against the injustice of the state and globalization: Comparing the African American and Oromo movements.* New York and Basingstoke: Pelgrave.

Keller, E. 1992. *Revolutionary Ethiopia: From empire to people's republic.* Bloomington and Indianapolis: Indiana University Press.

Ottaway, Marina. 1990. Introduction: The crisis of the Ethiopian state and economy. *The political economy of Ethiopia,* ed. Marina Ottaway. Praeger Publishers. New York.

Pakenham, T. 1991. *The scramble for Africa.* London: Weidenfield and Nicolson.

Pausewang, S. 1993. A new world order for Third World peasants? In *Africa within the world,* ed. A. Adedej, et al. London: Zed Books.

Rhamato, Dessalegn and A. Kidanu. 1999. *Consultations with the poor: A sudy to inform The World Development Report /2000/01 On poverty and development (National Report, Ethiopia),* July. Addis Ababa.

Sorenson, J. 1993. *Imagining Ethiopia: Struggles for history and identity in the Horn of Africa.* New Burnswick: Rutgers University Press.

Thiong'o, N. 1986. *Decolonising the mind: The politics of language and African literature.* London: James Currey.

Tronvoll, Kjetil. 2000. *Ethiopia: A new start?* Minority Rights Group International Report. London: MRG.

White House. 1992. *The national security strategy of the United States of America.* <http://www.whitehouse.gov/nsc/nss.pdf>.

Wilson, H. 1994. *African decolonisation.* London: Edward Arnold.

Young, John. 1996. Ethnicity and power in Ethiopia. *Review of African Political Economy.* 70, 531-542.

Chapter 6

The Politics of Underdevelopment and Militarism: The Case of Oromia

Temesgen Erena

This essay dwells on the political conditions prevailing in Oromia under the Ethiopian domination. It argues that these conditions have enormous impact on prevailing development crisis since the political force that affected Oromia's history in the last century continue to undermine the efforts of its people towards national self-determination. In the early 1990s, the old settler colonialism was replaced by "federal colonialism" and the phase of exploitation seemed to take on new dimensions. The pattern of domination had remained the same since it started a century ago with the Berlin Conference of 1884-85 which had enabled the scramble for Africa among European colonial powers. It was a time when the Ethiopian empire was given a mandate of Christianizing and "civilizing" the native people. It remains a historic irony how a backward empire was to "civilize" the peoples whose development levels and potentials were diverse and even better.

The very idea of Christianizing and civilizing was projected and supported by external protagonists. In the pre-1974 Ethiopia, this took the form of substantial military and economic aid from the U.S. and Europe. During the Cold War, the oppression of the Oromos was maintained by fresh military aid from the then Soviet Union intent on spreading its influence and its ideology to Africa. In the contemporary "new world disorder", the support has got new momentum in which the old Christian missionaries are replaced by an army of western neo-classical economists who peddle a "free market" ideology which they hope, will take care of the imprisoned market agents.

According to the new gospel, the Tigrayan colonizers are given the mandate and the necessary financial backing to pursue "economic liberaliza-tion" while keeping strict control that Oromia remains the Ethiopian colony. It is no wonder that the political and economic prescriptions that the Ethiopian colonial rulers implemented or pretend to implement are in line with the advice of the International Monetary Fund and the World Bank and the U.S. administration's "The Horn of Africa Initiative" all of which have exacerbated the problem of the Oromo nation.

The sad reality is that mutual interest and solidarity between the West and the Ethiopian colonizers are impoverishing the people. Given this, the people's last resort to defend their own interests is the exit option or to retreat from the colonizers. The need to rely on the Oromo initiatives to solve the Oromo problems has become more apparent than ever. The Oromo poor need to defend themselves from the free market crusaders and their fanatic local allies. This is necessary, since, in the absence of freedom and democracy, no free market economic gimmickry is able to reverse the tragedy. It is within this context, that we discuss how the Ethiopian colonial rule, in collaboration once with socialism and now with the global capitalism has impoverished one particular community in Africa, the Oromo nation.

THE POLITICS OF UNDERDEVELOPMENT

Economists are prompt to point out the importance of political factors couched in terms of "governance" and its role in economic development. Recently, their concerns about political factors in economic development is revitalized because of the failure of economic reform programs to produce definite success, particularly, in Africa. Poor governance is identified as the main problem (World Bank 1989; Moore 1992). There are three different aspects to the concept of governance:

1. the form of political regime (independent, colonial government, multi-party democracy, authoritarian, etc),
2. the process by which authorities exercise power in the management of the country's economic and social resource; and,
3. the willingness, the competence and the capacity of the government to design, formulate, and implement genuine development policies, and, in general to discharge developmental government functions.

While there is no discord concerning the proposition that "good" governance is an important and desirable ingredient of development, scholars are cautious not to attach specific regime types and political reforms to good governance. Broadly, however, good governance is legitimated by developmentalist ideology while poor governance is characterized by "state elite enrichment" (Jackson and Rosberg 1984), the "rent seeking society" (Krueger 1974) or "politics of the belly" (Bayart 1993; Tolesa 1995) (such as Ethiopia, Nigeria and Zaire). The latter are characterized by sclerotic behavior and are obstacles to development.

We are never going to understand development problems in Oromia, much less contain it, as long as we continue to think it as an economic problem. What is before us now is fundamentally a political problem whose economic outcome are staid. Not only the problem is inherently political in character, it is also political in origin. It arose largely from Ethiopian imperial conquest and its associated political disposition which is characterized by reliance on sheer force, authoritarianism and violence.

The story goes back to the days of Menelik II who had seized the territory and resources of Oromia, making concerted assault on the latter's history and culture in the name of civilizing the "non-believers." One implication of the doctrine of the "civilizing mission" of Menelik was that the Oromos needed to be ruled by Ethiopians and could not responsibly be granted civil liberties. Authoritarian as it has always been, the Ethiopian colonial rule in Oromia whether under Menelik II, Haile Selassie, Mengistu Hailemariam and currently under Meles Zenawi has been characterized by the "politics of the belly." Their underlying ethos remains self-aggrandizement and they are alien to growth whereas their politics have been tainted by corruption, brutality and grotesque incompetence. Time and again, they siphoned off Oromia's wealth and indulged in conspicuous consumption and stashing millions of dollars in remote secret accounts.

While the Ethiopian colonial settlers in Oromia do not want and support policies that promote development, they find external military support to stay in power. In more than one time, this anti-development force has been strongly reinforced by external forces (Holcomb and Ibssa 1990). Despite generous foreign assistance, they hardly commanded legitimacy to mobilize the colonized masses behind their rule. To the contrary, their rule has been fiercely resisted by people who have waged legitimate struggle to reclaim their freedom, cultures and history (Bulcha 1995; Lewis 1983).

Oromos had their own political power which was fully operational before they were colonized and incorporated into Ethiopia and brought under the control of Ethiopian empire state. Their political system was based on Oromo democratic tradition known as the *gada* system which has been the foundation of Oromo civilization, culture and world view. The *gada* political practices manifested the idea of real representative democracy with checks and balance, the rule of law, social justice, egalitarianism, local and regional autonomy, and the peaceful transfer of democratic power (Jalata 1996). The system also facilitated the right to property, stability, the expansion of commerce, improved farm techniques and agricultural settlements and gradual diversification of division of labor.

However, since the last decades of the nineteenth century, the Ethiopian colonial class and its state outlawed the *gada* political system and expropriated the Oromo basic means of subsistence and it established an Ethiopian system of rule over Oromia. Productive relations were imposed through the process of commodity production and extraction between those who control or own the means of duress, the state, and those who do not. Those who control the means of coercion had the opportunity to re-organize productive relations through dispossession of the colonized population in order to facilitate more produce extraction.

The process of dispossession is multi-faceted and far-reaching. As result of it, the Oromos have been denied power and access to education, cultural, economic and political fields while at the extremes, the Ethiopian colonialism has been practiced through violence, mass killings, mutilations, cultural destruction, enslavement and property expropriation. Jalata (1993) sees the Ethiopian colonial domination as the negation of the historical process of structural and technological transformation. This is the case where the Ethiopian colonial class occupies an intermediate status in the global political economy serving its own interest and that of imperialists. The Oromos were targeted to provide raw materials for local and foreign markets. Inside the empire, wherever they go, the Ethiopian colonial settlers built garrison towns as their political centers for practicing colonial domination through the monopoly of the means of compulsion, wealth extraction and cultural dissemination.

The main mechanism of produce extraction was tribute collection. Thus the Ethiopian social system was more cognate to a tributary system whereby the rulers extract tribute and labor from colonized lands. The Ethiopian farmers supported their households, the state and the church from what they produced. After its colonial expansion, Ethiopia maintained its tributary nature and established colonial political economy in Oromia and in the Southern nations. Although the colonial state intensified land expropriation and produce extraction from colonized peoples, capitalist productive relations did not emerge. Gradually with the further integration of the Ethiopian empire into the capitalist world economy, semi-capitalist farms seemed to emerge by extending their roots mainly through tenancy, sharecropping and the use of forced-labor. The colonial exploitation has been maintained under Mengistu's so-called socialist collectivization and villagization campaigns and in the current Meles's regime under the mask of "free" market economic system (Jalata 1993).

It should also be mentioned that in addition to authoritarian and coercive rule, Ethiopian colonialism depended on Oromo collaborationist agents that were essential to enforce Ethiopian colonialism. These agents are merely an expendable appendage, who devote most of their energy in picking up the leftover in economic and political advantages. The main task of this class is to ensure the continuous supply of products and labor for the settlers, yet this class is not always loyal to the Ethiopian state (Jalata 1993).

The state itself is a battlefield for two exclusive claims to rulership and political competition among the Ethiopian colonizers, the Amharas and the Tigreans. In effect, this makes the Ethiopian colonizer politics effectively a zero-sum game and the very practice of politics become a negation of politics.

The Ethiopian rulers, who have inherited power used to believe that their interests were well served by depoliticizing, muting and suppressing the Oromos' and the Southern peoples' quest for national self-determination under the guise of maintaining the unity of the Ethiopian empire. They convinced themselves and tried to convince others that there were no serious socio-political differences and no basis for political opposition. Apoliticism has been elevated to the level of ideology while the political structures become ever more monolithic and authoritarian.

The political structures and political ideologies which have been used to effect suppression and depoliticization are all too familiar. The main aim of depoliticization is to deny the existence of differences, to disallow their legitimate expression and, therefore, to deny collective negotiation. Whatever the degree of repression, the process did not remove the differences. The ensuing frustration and resistance led to further repression, the latter becoming an important feature of the Ethiopian political life and domination as its salient political relationship. As political power proves particularity important, the struggle to seize it becomes singularly intense.

There are two major ways in which this situation has severely thwarted development in the past. The first problem lies in the incompatibility between the pursuit of development and the quest for reproduction of the existing forms of domination. The damaging effect of this incompatibility is that it leads to misuse of human resources, inefficiency and corruption. Invariably, appointments into positions of power, even when they are positions which demand specialized knowledge, tend to be made by political criteria, particularly by regarding these appointments as part of survival strategy. Each time such appointment is made, the conflict between political survival and economic efficiency and development surfaces. The damage to efficiency and development arises not only from the performance criteria and likely incompetence of the persons so appointed but also from the general demoralization of the technically competent people serving under them who are often frustrated by their subordination to the supervision of people who are powerful but inept. Here lies the role of Ethiopian ministries and parastatals, incompetent personnel that obstruct the productive use of resources. Wasted are also competent people who lose at both ends. In the midst of waste, the Oromos have been denied basic civil and political rights and the right to development. The related economic problem, the very rights over which the people are fiercely struggling, was imposed by alien leaders who channel the meager resources into unproductive uses.

Cases abound where important development projects were initiated for the wrong reasons; they may, on account of political considerations, be located in places where they are least beneficial both economically and socially. One could cite familiar cases where important contracts and licenses have been given to politically significant people. Sometimes, higher positions are created just to give jobs to people whose political support is considered important. Oromia pays for all these disservices. In some cases, the Ethiopian bureaucrats are overpaid creating demoralizing disparities between reward and effort. That is how, the maintenance of Ethiopian imperial domination is jeopardizing the whole notion of development.

The question is, can the people of Oromia try to function and develop their economy in this state of siege? The question is important and relevant; but the answer is doubtful as it is impractical. Development strategies as such are comprehensive programs of social transformation. They call for a great deal of ingenious management, confidence in the leadership and commitment. They require clarity of purpose for a society at large; they need social consensus especially on the legitimacy of the leadership. Yet these are not common features of an institution which does not represent the society. Besides, development is about change and that change may not work to the survival of the rulers. In this sense, it runs against the instincts of the rulers whose preoccupation is to maintain its dominant position.

One of the most amazing things about development discourse in Ethiopian empire is how readily it is assumed that the rulers are interested in development particularly when they profess commitment to development and negotiate with international aid organizations for development assistance. People making this assumption forget the primacy of maintaining colonial power and its conflict with other social and economic goals.

Why the Ethiopian rulers embark on a course of social transformation just because it is good for the nations under its empire if they perceive it to be bad for their survival? Since development is about society at large, the paradox is that it is often the leaders who are not in a position to think of the objective interest of the society. Thinking in this way entails profound democratic commitment which cannot usually be expected of colonial rulers. Because of their position, colonial rulers suffer the disadvantage of confusing what maintains the existing social order, which they dominate, and the need for progress, they are suspicious of change. And all the more so when it comes to fundamental change.

One has to remember some of the implications of development with respect to alien rule. As it has already been mentioned, Ethiopian rulers are more interested in taking advantage of the social order inherited from their predecessors rather than in transforming it. The Oromos have been oppressed and humiliated for over a century. The political history of the last hundred years of colonial rule of Oromia has vividly indicated that the Oromos lacked freedom, that they did not have control over the products of their labor, that their natural resources and environment were tarnished by others, and eventually it meant that they witnessed chronic poverty and destitution (Bulcha 1995).

In these circumstances, it is not surprising that where development is pursued in Oromia, if at all, it is full of ambiguities and contradictions and it is a mere posture. Even taking these postures on their face value, in so far as one is critical of development strategies, ones criticism runs in the direction of their sloppy conception and hence their failure to come to grips with the obstacles of imperial domination. Looking into the contradiction between political survival and social transformation, one begins to see that it is doubtful if development has ever been on the colonizers' agenda for Oromia.

The other aspect of economic consequences of domination has been militarism which is but the outcome of the over-valuation of political power. Associated with it is the intense struggle to capture and keep it. Then, the politics of empire will be sustained by warfare. In this atmosphere, force is mobilized and deployed: the winners are anxious to take absolute power into their hands while the losers forgo not only power but also lose their liberty and even life. As politics rely solely on force, its vocabulary and organization advocates coercion. For that matter, the Ethiopian empire is a political formation of armies in action and this is in itself a development problem. In an institution in which the political formations are organized as warring armies, differences are too wide and far, the scope for co-operation is limited; there is too much distrust; and life is too raw to nurture commerce and industry in subject nations. Currently the militarization of life and politics reached its logical culmination in military rule which hinders the course of development in Oromia.

The Ethiopian colonial classes view the economy as a pie of fixed size, hence they can cut for themselves a bigger piece or all of it, but only by taking away a portion or all that originally belonged to others. They have not even seen the possibility that the size of the pie itself can be increased so that all can have larger and more slices.

The Oromo people are the objects of development in every sense. If development means anything at all, it is development of people's potentials, not development by outside agencies whose interests and intentions conflict with the development needs of the people. Furthermore, whenever pursued, development should be participatory. If it is not, it can only be the development of alienation and domination.

The people who talk most about development and who make and implement policies are the alien leaders, their agents and supporters. But these are not the people who understand the peoples development. Most importantly, the interests of these groups are at odds with those of the subordinate peoples. Therefore, the development of Oromia should involve the liberation of the Oromos from the conditions of deprivation and oppression. In this context, the development of Oromia essentially requires freedom as a prerequisite and that freedom involves, firstly, the national freedom which is the ability of Oromia's citizens to determine their own future, and to govern themselves. Secondly, it is freedom from hunger, from disease and poverty. Thirdly, it involves personal freedoms; namely, the right of the individual citizens to live in dignity and equality with others, freedom of speech, freedom to participate in decisions which affect their lives and freedom from arbitrary arrest.

Thus, the people of Oromia should be left free to choose both their political and development destiny. History teaches us imperial conquest and domination whether "the Scramble for Africa" or "The Forward Movement" in South East Asia hardly brought development to its subject people except depriving their liberty and plundering their resources. The reality is the reflection of this historical fact. The Oromos should have their own political rule in order to tackle development problems in their own particular environment. What keeps them in development crisis is their powerlessness to remove predatory colonial rule. At the same time, since political and economic crisis are fused, it is futile to solve one without the other. Conceivably, the colonial settlers would not concede freedom and do not promote genuine development. Therefore, political independence is necessary for Oromia before economic development is possible.

Studies have examined the causes for economic performance and social welfare. Attempts were made to measure systematic interaction of economic performance and welfare indicators with both the quality and quantity of production inputs such as labor, physical capital, human capital, knowledge and technology. It is noted that an important thematic weakness of conventional economics is its concentration on the above variables and their interactions. In the nations like Oromia and the empire state of Ethiopia, institutional factors such as militarism (building a military force or the use of occupation army and the forces of torture for the purpose of social control) usually escape empirical attention.

The correlation and regression test on militarism-economic growth link focuses on defense spending. Studies by Ball (1983), Deger (1986), Faini et al. (1984), Lim (1983) and Smith (1977) found defense spending which they referred to as consumption good, as having negative effects on the performance of the economy. It does so by spreading inefficiency, decreasing investment and expenditure on research and development. On the other hand, Benoit (1978), Fredericksen and Looney (1982) and Melman (1988) argued that the performance of the economy can be stimulated by defense spending via the creation of effective demand, enhancement of human capital and increasing productivity due to technological progress. It should be noted, however, that correlation does not mean causation.

Further empirical works have investigated the nature of causal link between defense spending and economic growth but arrived at mixed results. While Joerding (1986) has identified the presence of causal relationship between the two variables, Chowdhury (1991) found the causal link to be statistically insignificant.

The essence of the above empirical works examined the relationship between militarism, economic performance based on time series econometric analysis in Oromia and Ethiopian empire for the period 1960 to 1998. In this context, militarism is captured by proxy variables such as the size of armed forces and defense spending. For the sake of simplicity, economic performance is approximated by quantitative increases in per capita output, commonly known as net economic growth (gross output growth minus population growth). Output growth is taken as an indicator of economic performance and the level of welfare because without improvement in production capacity no increase in real income, more jobs and investment can be generated. Without it, the qualitative aspects of development such as a higher social welfare and improved quality of life cannot be realized. In the light of the above literature, proper consideration is given in limiting the arguments to the link between output growth and militarism.

In repressive polities such as that of the Ethiopia, it can be hypothesized that militarism retards output growth and as means of social control it is welfare reducing. Militaristic repression reduces the chance for life assurance, self-esteem, and the freedom to choose among a variety of options that sustain and improve the level of economic and social welfare. In the particular case of Ethiopian empire vis-à-vis the colonized nations such as Oromia, the army which can be termed as occupation army, increasingly uses force to suppress the quest for self-determination. The army and the security forces possess extra judiciary powers to torture, execute, and loot the properties of the peoples of the occupied territories. The presence of occupation army alienates the colonized Oromos from the entitlement to their land and natural environment; it also restricts their right to improve their quality of life.

What contribution can this chapter make? At the crudest level, it should be noted that none of the previous studies were specific to Oromia and Ethiopian empire. This chapter seeks to use an econometric methodology.

This section is organized in such a way that the basic concepts are discussed, and the militarism and the accompanying economic deceleration in Oromia and Ethiopian empire are reviewed. The study here refers to the econometric methodology set out in Erena (1997) and empirical tests performed and results obtained in the same work and subsequent studies conducted in Erena (2001). The implications of these empirical studies are presented in this work.

Militarism as a concept is often described as excessive influence (legitimate or illegitimate) of military institutions, policies, and values on civil society and occupied territories (Odetola 1978:4-6; McAlister 1976:850-64). The deplorable use of militarism had been practiced, for instance, in Napeolic France, Hitler's Third Reich, Mussolini's Italy and Stalinist Soviet Russia, in Ethiopian empire, ex-Yugoslavia, Nigeria, Zaire, and Indonesia).

In the literature, it has been argued that militarism can play positive role to promote economic development. The military structure is considered as disciplined, hierarchical, and based on specialization of functions and skills akin to industrial based organizations perceived to make rational decisions. In broader terms, this decision-making system mobilizes a country's human and material resources, allocating most efficiently in the development process. Since the capacity to develop requires a government ability to administer and co-ordinate diverse activities nationwide, the military according to this argument, is the best political organization suited to the vast task involved (Erena 1997: 123-140).

Keynesian economists have considered defense spending as a component of a demand side macroeconomic variables which has a positive multiplier effect on economic growth. In this context, defense is taken as an essential public good and its expenditure is beyond an economic calculus because it is the most basic rationale for government to provide national defense from outsiders (Kasliwal 1995:319). Therefore, it is claimed that it is difficult to optimize the amount of defense in the sense that the marginal social benefit of the last penny spent on the defense equals the benefit of the last penny spent elsewhere in the economy. However, scholars have questioned the vast and seemingly uncontrolled expansion of such expenditures and militarism (Kasliwal Ibid: 320). The World Bank, in its 1998/99 World Report, states that "high military expenditure and dysfunctional behavior of military personnel (in the absence of other checks and balances) have been other important impediments." Consequently, it is described as the root cause of state failure.

While the impact of militarism in society may vary from country to country, the broader case against militarism rests on the assumption that it is parasitic and inimical to growth. According to this line of thinking, military by its very nature is "apolitical, institutionally conservative force, untrained in the tactics and strategies of civilian rule", thus, incapable to promote economic development (Odetola, 1982:4). Lieuwen (1964b), Huntington (1968), Welch (1970), Price (1971) and (Murray, 1966) share similar views. According to McAlister (1966) militarism is aberrant and abnormal. It consumes large amount of resources for non-productive purposes. Odetola (1982) provides invaluable survey of analytical literature.

Historical experience of colonized nations like Oromia indicates that occupation armies are agents of colonialism imposing colonial institutions which are alien to local democratic traditions. The Ethiopian militarism, in particular, has devastated the entire civilization of colonized peoples. Militarism, from this experience is the source of insecurity, and impoverishment. Militarism makes society incapable of commanding their material and social life by depriving them the rights and opportunities to command.

International development agencies such as the United Nations Development Program (UNDP) and International NGOs like OXFAM have focused on the relief of poverty in the developing world. They maintain that people and the quality of their lives should be at the center of developmentalist agenda. The UNDP has emphasized the perspective of economics that incorporates human development.

In the context of Oromos, what is more important than mere growth or decline in Gross Domestic Product (GDP) is how human capabilities are improved or worsened, and in turn, how people utilize their capabilities. Harvard's economist and the Nobel prize winner Amartya Sen stressed that economic development is a process of expansion of positive freedom that people enjoy (Sen 1983:745-750). The real problems in the developing world in general and in Oromia in particular are reduced lives, rather than low income as such, though the latter contributes to the former. Sen (1983: 745-750) interprets economic development as a process that expands the "entitlements" and "capabilities" of people "in a ways we have reason to value."

The lower level of welfare and abject poverty we observe in Oromia can be understood not just as a matter of relative impoverishment compared to the others, but lack of access to the very basic material and social well-being; that is, the failure to have certain minimum "capabilities" and "entitlements." In this context, poverty is not only about lacking material goods but also depravation in social wealth such as liberty and national freedom.

The criteria of minimum capabilities and entitlements are "absolute" not in a sense that they do not vary from society to society, or over time, but peoples' deprivation is judged absolutely, not simply in comparison with the deprivations of others in that society. If a person is seen as poor because he is unable to satisfy his/her basic material and social need, then that diagnosis of poverty cannot be altered by the fact that others too may also be hardly at the position of satisfying their basic needs (so that this person may not be, relatively speaking, any worse off than most others). A person's advantage is judged in this approach by his/her capabilities and entitlements, viz., what he can or cannot and entitled to do (Sen, 1983).

In terms of conventional definition, the aggregate domestic production per capita and total supply of goods in Oromia is by far higher than that of the Ethiopia (Abyssinia) and other "Horn" of Africa regions. However, in the context of welfare models, the Oromo people whether as individual or as a nation are categorically poor because they have been deprived of those critical minimum entitlements and capabilities to satisfy their basic needs for material and social goods. This has happened because of the colonizing and aggressive Abyssinian rule that has been institutionalized through militarism.

MILITARISM AND ECONOMIC PERFORMANCE

The Ethiopian Empire state, since its formation in the 1880s, rules on the basis of repressive occupation army. The state has built a system of military control to maintain authority over the occupied territories. In the first decades of the twentieth century, Ras Teferi (Ras is the classical military status), later emperor Haile Selassie took power in a palace *coup d'etat* at the helm of Oromia's capital. Haile Selassie was claimed to be "modernizing" monarch. However, Ethiopianist scholars such as Clapham (1985:259) argue that modernization was akin to the creation of mechanisms for central control of occupied territories. Moreover, modernization for Haile Selassie meant

> ... a cash-crop economy whose product were channeled through the capital and government controlled ports, whence they could be sold to raise government revenue; a communications network which radiates from Addis Ababa; a central bureaucracy and the educational system to man it; and most obvious of all, a large standing army (Clapham 1985:259).

This centralizing process was supported by political institutions such as partially elected parliament and the court. There were no political parties. The so-called modernizing institutions and bureaucracies were not only "traditional" and corrupt but also "inward-looking", "immobilist" and "undynamic" (Clapham 1985:260).

In 1974, the armed forces came to power after toppling the 82-year-old Emperor with allegation of corruption, abuse of power, and so on. Lieutenant Colonel Mengistu Hailemariam assassinated the next two head of the Empire State (General Aman Andom and General Teferri Bante) before he assumed power in February 1977. The Mengistu regime was overthrown by another armed guerrilla group in May 1991.

Armed campaigns to take control of the Ethiopian Empire state had contributed to the overthrow their preceding repressive regimes. All the Ethiopian regimes had attempted to crush those who challenged their rules and none of them had a consistent policy regarding economic growth and development. The only consistency is the use of human and economic resources to build up their military forces to their particular purposes. These purposes have been manifested in the priority of the regimes to consolidate the hold on power, while ensuring their military capabilities to crush the quest for democracy and self-determination of occupied territories.

Table 1: Growth parameters and the Size of Armed Forces

Economy	Armed Forces "000"	GNP Per Capita Income (US $)	Unemployment Rate(% of labor force, 1994)	Ranks in the world health league table (as of WHO 2000)*
South Africa	75	2880	33	175
Ethiopia	600	100	30	180
Sudan	100	290	30	134
Angola	95	340	15	181
Nigeria	76	300	28	187
Eritrea	350	200	5.80	158
Uganda	50	310	N/A	149
Zaire	50	110	N/A	188
Zimbabwe	40	610	45	155
Rwanda	40	230	N/A	172
Tanzania	35	210	N/A	156
Chad	35	230	N/A	178
Kenya	24	350	N/A	140
Cameroon	13	610	25	164
Zambia	21	330	N/A	182
Madagascar	21	260	N/A	159
Mozambique	14	210	50	184
Mauritania	1	410	20	162
Burundi	35	140	N/A	143
Cote D' Ivoire	15	700	14	137
Senegal	13.35	530	N/A	59
Burkina Faso	10	240	N/A	132
Congo	10	690	N/A	166
Guinea	9.7	540	N/A	161
Djibouti	9.6	726	30	157
Guinea-Bissau	7	160	N/A	176
Namibia	8	1940	35	168

Economy	Armed Forces "000"	GNP Per Capita Income (US$)	Unemployment Rate(% of labor force,1994)	Ranks in the world health league table (as of WHO 2000)*
Malawi	8	200	N/A	185
Botswana	8	3600	25	169
Mali	10	250	N/A	163
Ghana	7	390	10	135
Togo	12	330	N/A	152
Sierra Leone	5	140	N/A	191
Niger	5	190	N/A	170
Central African Republic	5	300	30	189
Benin	8	380	N/A	97
Gabon	10	4170	N/A	139
Swaziland	3	1400	15	177
Lesotho	2	570	35	183
Equatorial Guinea	1.32	1060	5.90	171
Cape Verde	1.1	910	26	113
San Tome and Principe	0.9	250	N/A	133
Comoros	0.8	510	15.80	118
Gambia	1	340	N/A	146
Schelles	0.3	6450	9	56
Liberia	0	725	48	186

Source: Kessing's (1995 and 1996). *Record of World Events: Annual Reference Supplement*, vol. 41 and 42. London: Cartemill Publishing, *Word Bank: Word Bank: Word Indicators, 2000, WHO report* (2000): www.who.int/wh: Special report on the guardian network at www.guardianunlimited.co.uk/nhs.

*   Health system in Oromia and Ethiopia takes 180th in the world. The figure is based on the WHO assessment of five indicators: Overall level of health, Health inequaities, Patient satisfaction, How the system responds and how well-served people feel.

The militarism of the Ethiopian polity is a set back to the economy. It has been associated with economic and institutional decay. For a long time, Abyssinian rulers have maintained personal rule, curtailed political participation and set and enforced the policies of genocide. The occupation army has left civilians of the occupied territory with large financial debt and social burdens. Of course, it is evident that militarism occurs in many parts of the world but it does appear to have been particularly pervasive in occupied territories of Ethiopian Empire.

Figures from the World Bank indicate that the Ethiopian Empire is the poorest of the poor states in the world. Its annual per capita income was one of the lowest with $110 in 1990 (Meier 1995:50) and $100 in 1998 (Word Bank 2000) which was declining over the period 1965-1990 on average by 0.2 per cent. Between 1990 and 1998, it declined by 10 per cent, from $110 to $100 (World Bank 1997:162). Thirty per cent of the 22 million labor force were unemployed (Keesing's 1995). In the reverse, the military size of the Ethiopian empire is one of the largest in Sub Saharan Africa (See Table 1 above).

The 1998 data which is the latest available shows that the Ethiopian empire's Gross Domestic output was $6.1 billion whereas for the same year it owes ,10 billion as foreign debt (Keesing's, 1996 World Bank 2000; CIA in WWW, 2000). Infant mortality is one of the highest in the world, 107 per 1000 live births in 1998 (World Bank 2000).

Life expectancy is also one of the lowest in the world, namely 40 years (CIA WWW 2000); disability weighted life expectancy is below 40 (WHO 2000). Overall health system attainment is one of the lowest in the world, 186th in the ranks of 191 countries (WHO 2000).

The over all net economic growth for Oromia and Ethiopia empire can be shown in table 2 below:

Table: 2. Average Annual Growth Rates in Constant Prices

Year	Net Average Growth Rates*
1970-80	- 1.0
1973-80	0.0
1980-91	-1.5
1990-93	-3.3
1965-90	-0.2
1965-98	-0.5

* The figures are adopted from World Bank (Various years) and Kessing's (1995) by taking into account population growth rates of 2.7 and 3.1 for the periods 1965-80 and 1980-90 respectively.

The militarization of the economy and ordinary life meant that millions of lives have been lost including children, women and elders. Millions of dollars are wasted on the purchase of armaments. Accordingly, the negative militarism and economic performance link that have been identified in our empirical test and the result is the confirmation of all these development distortions. The Ethiopian militarism is not only income reducing but also welfare and life reducing (in terms of social goods). The occupied territories are denied the freedom of trade, the freedom to develop their own natural resources, markets, capital, industrial capacity and democratic institutions. It is by using of sheer force, violence and military supremacy that has once been Amhara ruling class and and now the Tigrayan is able to steal the natural and human wealth of Oromia, extort tribute, undermine their cultures, destroy their villages and towns, eliminate their creativity, crafts and industries.

The forces opposed to freedom have the ability to deprive large number of people of subsistence requirements. They use hunger, poverty and neglect, as a means of political intimidation and control which is to subjugate the unwilling colony.

Freedom is the ultimate goal of social and economic arrangements and the most efficient means of realizing general welfare. In politically independent and democratic societies, social institutions such as markets, political parties, legislatures, the judiciary, and the media contribute to development and individual freedom and in turn social values. Social values, development and freedom are closely related. Hence, the size of Oromia's collective economic wealth depends on the size of national and individual ability to live as the people should treasure. Individual and national freedom, social justice and human rights must be social commitments that a just state can guarantee and safeguard which are absent under the present Ethiopian conditions.

The Ethiopian militarism is the cause of repression and negative welfare. It has emerged as the main pillar of colonialism. It has repeatedly relied upon repression. It has deployed Oromo conscripts as "mine sweepers and cannon fodder" in the war with Eritrea. (IRIN News Briefs, 1 June 2000). This is part of genocide against the Oromo people.

When we consider the insecurity in itself, the latter causes scarcity to Oromos and other occupied societies. Their action for emancipation does not constitute counter-peace, separatism, or narrow nationalism as the coercive rule would have them believe, but a struggle for survival against such force and its state. In the dialects of oppression and in the oppressed and the oppressor connectivity, it is only where the latter ends that free and civil society begins.

The Abyssinian militarism, systematic and violent repression whether in the nineteenth or twentieth or in the early twenty-first century, have never been isolated phenomena. They are invariably linked both instrumentally and structurally to the global militarism and its goal of mastering spaces (the 19th century scramble for Africa, imperialistic competitions, cold war superpower competitions, direct intervention, proxy war, arms trade and military assistance, post cold war (new) world disorder, etc.). The mutual interests of the TPLF and the global actors have reinforced the domestic and international connectivity of militarism and provide conducive environment for militarism and the whole system of repression. Given such systematic and global link of repression, the arms embargo on Ethiopia during its war against Eritrea was a special case, a surprise. But it exhibited that the positive links of local and global militarism was at risk in the Horn of Africa or it was no more positive.

The Oromo checking force, defense power and security system must be a precondition to change the status quo. There must be an Oromo security mechanism that can check the welfare reducing militarism, the force of torture and state terrorism. Hence, national and democratic freedom can be nurtured and its positive economic and social after effect will be propelled.

The decolonizing force must be consolidated and grow stronger along with active political struggle which is drawn to the cause of national freedom. Historically and presently, the Ethiopian militarism has deployed the oppressed as cannon fodder from occupied territories. Oromos and other peoples under occupation should also resist being used as tools by others and should stop joining the TPLF militarism toward sovereign neighbor countries. Oromos should increase their social commitment by making momentous engagement in diverse activities of national freedom. The oppressed people need to fight for freedom, justice and development.

Oromos perceive the Abyssinian rule over Oromia through its methods of rule. In Oromia, attention to the local-level perspective leads naturally to a focus on the TPLF's implements of coercive rule. As in the past, the present colonialist made militarism and coercion as a business. The TPLF warlord politics is using coercion to control resources and trafficking it to Tigray. There has been an intensive development in the Tigray, core of the colonist which is at the expense of extraordinary underdevelopment in Oromia and in the South. In a nutshell, the domobilization of the repressive occupation army is a necessary precondition to facilitate civilized institutions and democratic process which in turn hoped to reverse the down ward spiral of economic performance and negative welfare.

References

Ball, N. 1983. Defense spending and development: a critique of the Benoit study. *Economic Development and Cultural Change*. 31, 507-24.

Bayart, J. 1993. *The state in Africa: The politics of the belly*. London: Longman.

Benoit, E. 1978. Growth and defense in developing countries. *Economic Development and Cultural Change*. 26, 271-80.

Bulcha, M. 1995. Freedom, bread and peace. *Oromo Commentary*. 5,2.

Chien, H. 1993. Causality between defense spending and economic growth: the case of mainland China. *Journal of Economic Studies*. 20, 37-47.

Chowdhury, A. 1981. A causal analysis of defense spending and economic growth. *Journal of Conflict Resolution*. 35, 80-97.

Clapham, C. 1985. Ethiopia: A Marxist military regime. In *The military dilemmas of military regimes,* eds. C. Clapham and G. Philip. London: Croom Helm.

Deger, S. 1986. Economic development and defense expenditure, *Economic Development and Cultural Change*. 35, 179-96.

Erena, T. 1997. Militarism and economic performance in Ethiopia: Evidence from time series econometric analysis. In *Ethiopia: Conquest and the quest for freedom and democracy*, ed. Seyoum Hameso, Trever Truman and Temesgen M. Erena, 123-140. London: TSC.

Erena, T. 2001. The precarious balance: Abyssinian militarism, economic and welfare conditions in Oromia and the Ethiopian Empire. *Oromia Quarterly*. IV, 1 &2: 20-41.

Faini, R. Annez, P. and Taylor, L. 1984. Defense spending and economic structure, and growth: evidence among countries and over time, *Economic Development and Cultural Change* 32, 487-98.

Fredericksen, P. and Looney, R. 1982. Defense expenditure and economic growth in developing countries: Some further empirical evidence. *Journal of Economic Development*. 7, 113-24.

Gillis, M. et al. 1983. *Economics of development*. New York: Norton.

Holcomb, B. and S. Ibssa. 1990. *The invention of Ethiopia: The making of a dependent colonial state in Northeast Africa*. Trenton: Red Sea Press.

International Institute of Strategic Studies. Various years. *Military balance*. London: Oxford University Press.

International Moneary Fund. Various Years. *International financial statistics*. Washington, D.C. Oxford University Press.

Jackson R. and C. Rosberg. 1984. Personal Rule: Theory and Practice in Africa. *Comparative Politics*. 16, 4 :421-442.

Jalata, A. 1993. Socio-cultural origins of the Oromo national movement in Ethiopia. *Journal of Political Economy and Military Sociology*. 21, 267-86.

Jalata, A. 1996. Reinventing an Oromian state: A theoretical Analysis. *Urjii*. 1, 1:21-25.

Joerding, W. 1986. Economic growth and defense spending. *Journal of Development Economics*. 21, 35-40.

Kasliwal, P. 1995. *Development economics*. Los Angeles: South-Western College Publishing.

Keesing's 1995. *Record of world events: Reference supplement*, vol. 42. London: Cartemill Publishing.

Krueger, A. 1974. The political economy of rent-seeking society. *American Economic Review* 64, 291-303.

Lewis, I. ed. 1983. *Nationalism and self-determination in the Horn of Africa*. London: Ithaca Press.

Lim, D. 1983. Another look at growth and defense in less developed countries. *Economic Development and Cultural Change*. 31, 377-84.

McAlister, L. 1976. Recent researches and writings on the role of military and non-military regimes, *American Political Science Review*. LXX, 850-64.

Meier, G. 1995. *Leading issues in economic development*, Sixth Edition. Oxford: Oxford University Press.

Moore, M. 1993. Declining to learn from the East? The World Bank on governance and development. *Institute of Development Studies*. 24, no.3:1-3.

Murray, R. 1966. Militarism in Africa. *New Left Review*. July—August, 33-57.

Odetola, O. 1978. *Military regimes and development: A comparative analysis in African societies*. London: George Allen and Unwin.

Price, R. 1971. Military officers and political leadership: the Ghanaian case. *Comparative Politics*. XXIII, 399-429.

Sen, A.K. 1983. Development which way now? *Economic Journal*.December.

Smith, R. 1977. Military expenditure and capitalism. *Cambridge Journal of Economics*. 1, 61-76.

Tolesa, A. 1995. Literature on the quest for self-determination and democracy: The case of Oromia and Ethiopia. *Oromo Commentary*. 5,2.

Welch, C. 1970. *Soldier and state in Africa*. Evanston: Northwestern University Press.

World Bank, Various Years. *World development report*. Washington, D.C.: Oxford University Press.

World Bank 1989. *Sub-Saharan Africa: From crisis to sustainable growth*. Washington D. C.

Chapter 7
Genocide Against the Oromo People

Trevor Trueman

BACKGROUND

The Oromo and other non-Abyssinian peoples of Ethiopia[1] claim they have been colonized and oppressed since the incorporation of their territories into the present day Ethiopia at the end of the nineteenth century. The nationalist movements among these peoples, especially the Oromo Liberation Front (OLF), contributed alongside the liberation fronts from Tigray and Eritrea, to the downfall of the communist military dictatorship of the Derg. The OLF and other nationality-based political bodies were initially part of the transitional Ethiopian government in 1991. They were barred from effective power sharing (Lata 1999:xiii), despite the OLF being the most popular and established party among the 25-30 million Oromo, at least 40% of the population of Ethiopia (Baxter 1996:7). They withdrew from the June 1992 elections because of "widespread arrest and intimidation of candidates" (Norwegian Institute of Human Rights 1992). OLF offices were then attacked[2] and staff killed (Lata 1999: 63-67). OLF troops, encamped away from towns for the elections, were attacked and overrun, despite international guarantees for their safety (Lata 1998:61-64). Between 20,000 and 45,000[3] suspected OLF supporters were detained in harsh conditions and hundreds killed (Africa Confidential 1996:3; Lata 1999:60).

STATED GOVERNMENT POLICY

Oromo nationalism is perceived as the greatest threat to the ruling government party (the EPRDF, an umbrella party, led and dominated by TPLF).

The ruling party journal, *Hizbaawi Adera* stated that:

> to defeat narrow nationalism . . . must be part of our struggle.... In
> order to have a lasting solution to our problem . . . we have to break

narrow nationalist tendencies in Oromia ... we have to fight narrow nationalism to the bitter end ... to smash it in a very decisive manner. ... fighting the higher intellectual and bourgeoisie classes in a very extensive and resolute manner. .... The standard bearers of narrow nationalism are the educated elite and the bourgeoisie. [W]e must be in a position to eradicate all narrow nationalists ...[4]

EXTRA-JUDICIAL KILLINGS, DISAPPEARANCE, ARBITRARY DETENTION, TORTURE AND RAPE

Since 1991, suspected Oromo nationalists have been killed, tortured, raped and made to disappear. The Oromia Support Group has received credible reports of 2,754 extra-judicial killings and 842 reports of disappearance, since it was established in 1994.[5] The U.S. State Department reports that suspicion of belonging to the OLF is the most common cause for detention in Ethiopia. The report for 2000 states that the Ethiopian government "continued to detain persons suspected of sympathizing with or being involved with the OLF" (U.S. State department 2001).

Officials of the International Committee of the Red Cross visited 10,000 detainees in Ethiopia, nearly all in official prisons.[6] Clandestine human rights organisations in Ethiopia claim that ten times that number were being held in unofficial detention centres. A defecting official from the Ethiopian Security Ministry, confirmed the existence of secret detention centres; underground cells for solitary confinement in military camps and "ghost houses" in Addis Ababa,[7] as reported many times by correspondents and interviewees to the Oromia Support Group or OSG (see OSG PR 1-34). Amnesty International reported that torture and disappearance are more likely to occur in these centres than in official places of detention (Amnesty International 1995). After his defection, Yonatan Dhibisa, the Minister of Justice in Oromia Region stated that 30,000 Oromo political prisoners were being held in official detention centres in Oromia.[8]

According to several hundred reports sent to OSG and over thirty inter-views with victims and their relatives, beating of detainees is routine. Torture, especially arm-tying, beating of the soles of the feet, suspension of weights from genitalia and mock execution, is commonplace, at least in unofficial places of detention (OSG PR 32 2000:8-9; OSG PR 33:11,14). Female detainees esti-mate that 50% of women are raped during detention, often by several soldiers or policemen on several occasions (OSG PR 32 2000:9). The Minnesota Center for Victims of Torture has surveyed over 500 randomly selected Oromo refu-gees. The majority had been subject to torture and nearly all of the rest had been subject to some kind of government violence (Johnson 2000).

Members of the EPRDF surrogate Oromo party, the Oromo Peoples Democratic Organisation (OPDO), are also subject to purges, if they complain of lack of investment or of human rights violations in Oromia Region. Hassan Ali, the vice-president of the OPDO, escaped to the USA after an assassination attempt by security forces. He reported other killings of OPDO officials, because they were suspected of holding nationalist sentiments.[9]

Members and supporters of OLF are pursued to neighbouring countries— Djibouti, Sudan, Kenya, Somalia, Somaliland—where they have been detained, tortured, killed and subjected to *refoulement* back to Ethiopia (OSG PR28, 1999:12-14; OSG PR29 1999:18-22; OSG PR30 2000:16-19; OSG PR31 2000:24-27, OSG PR33: 2001:18-19). Several were killed in South Africa in 1998 and 1999 (OSG PR30, 2000:20-23).

In late 1997 and early 1998, all board members of the Human Rights League were detained in Addis Ababa. The Human Rights League was a newly formed body of Oromo, working legally which held workshops on human rights and which intended to report violations. Most board members of the Macha-Tulama Association, a 37 year old Oromo cultural and self-help organisation, and the Executive Director and other staff of the Oromo Relief Association, an indigenous relief and development agency caring for over 300,000, were also detained, along with journalists, doctors and nurses. Amnesty International regarded many of these as prisoners of conscience.[10] In all, 61 were still facing conspiracy charges (OSG PR31 2000:12-14), punishable by the death penalty, when after over three years of detention and over 20 court appearances, 28 were released in May 2001 (Human Rights Watch 2001). One had disappeared in detention (OSG PR29 1999:3-4). Two detainees, held at the same time in Karchale Central Prison in Addis Ababa, died during detention (OSG PR31 2000:14), at least one from torture injuries (OSG PR28 1999:3).

Detentions of Macha-Tulama Association members continued. The vice-president was detained incommunicado for two weeks in August 2000 and eight other members were kept in detention.[11]

JUDICIARY

Successive U.S. State Department country reports state that prolonged pre-trial detention is partly due to a shortage of trained judges. Judges report intimidation, dismissal and detention, if they release or attempt to release detainees suspected of supporting the OLF. For example, all of the Oromia State Supreme Court judges were dismissed in March 2000 (OSG PR33 2001:11). Trials are frequently unfair. For example, in March 2001, 33 OLF members held in Zeway military camp were sentenced to 15-25 years imprisonment on evidence given solely by soldiers who guarded them in the camp (OSG PR33, 2001:8-9).

Decisions by judges to release detainees because of lack of evidence are frequently reversed by military and security personnel. For example, 230 detainees in Batu military camp were ordered to be released in January 2000. The detainees wrote of their being in their sixth year of detention, in March 2001 (OSG PR33, 2001:7-8).

PRESS

The government, using an ambiguous press law, has succeeded in forcing most of the private press which flourished in 1991, into dissolution. Non-government newspapers are effectively banned outside of Addis Ababa. Vendors are harassed and papers confiscated.[12] Frequent fines, detention of journalists, punitive bond payments and escalating prices of material have got rid of every indigenous Oromo magazine and newspaper.[13]

The last newspapers written by Oromo were *Urjii* and *Seife Nebelbal*. *Urjii* ceased publication in late 1997 after three of its journalists were detained (as prisoners of conscience, see above). The editor of *Seife Nebelbal* wrote from exile in Kenya in January 2001, having fled Ethiopia with eight outstanding charges against him and fearful of another term in prison.

The persecution of the remaining, non-Oromo, press continues.[14] One journalist was driven to suicide in January 2000, apparently fearful of repeated detention.[15]

Ethiopia has imprisoned more journalists than any other country in Africa in each year since 1993.

CULTURAL RIGHTS

Use of the Oromo language has been discouraged for over 100 years. In 1991, when the Minister of Education was an OLF official, text books in the Oromo language became available for the first time in Oromia Region.[16]

After the OLF withdrew from government, teachers of the Oromo language and the Latin script have been detained, tortured and killed.[17]

Cassette tapes of Oromo songs are confiscated from shops and premises often destroyed.[18] Oromo singers have been killed, tortured, detained and raped. Ebbisa Addunya was shot dead in his home by security forces in Addis Ababa, in August 1996.[19] Amnesty International has reported the detention of Oromo musicians and singers.[20]

The last remaining Oromo band, the *gada* band, were forced into exile after refusing to perform at the 25th anniversary of the TPLF, in February 2000.[21] Personal interviews with singers have corroborated reports of torture and rape.[22] Dramatists and writers have also been detained, tortured and driven into exile.[23, 24]

LIFE CONDITIONS

Development and Commerce

Government budget allocations to Oromia Region are less than those to the smaller Tigray Region and, as most projects are cancelled in Oromia, most of the allocation is returned to central coffers. Roads are deteriorating in Oromia and electricity is restricted in Addis Ababa. In Tigray, new hospitals, universities, medical schools and an airport have been built and Tigrayans enjoy continuous electricity.[25, 26]

Offices of the Oromo Relief Association were closed in 1995 and 1996. The government announced that a larger organisation, their own Oromo Self Help Association, was needed because development needs were large in Oromia Region. The Oromo Self Help Association was dissolved in early 1999 and its assets were transferred to a branch of the Relief Society of Tigray.[27] The Relief Society of Tigray, Tigray Development Association and Endowment Fund for Rehabilitation of Tigray are controlled by central committee members of the TPLF. Through these companies, the TPLF and its members own most major business enterprises in Ethiopia.[28]

Investment by mining companies, for example the Canadian, Canyon Resources Corporation which mines for gold in Oromia Region, benefits the central government. Even employment is not offered to the local population.

Successful Oromo traders, businesspeople, farmers and hotel owners are particularly likely to be detained and tortured. Nearly all detainees report confiscation of property.[29]

Education

Educational establishments flourish in Tigray, while the famous school of agriculture in Haromaya, Oromia Region, has been dismembered and parts transferred to Tigray.[30] Although the largest nationality in Ethiopia, few Oromo are given places at Addis Ababa University.[31]

Medical facilities

Rural areas in Ethiopia have never enjoyed adequate access to health care. Two incidents indicate that medication and supplies are deliberately withheld from Oromia Region. An Oromo doctor, exiled to the USA, reported by interview in August 1998, that vital intra venous fluids were withheld by the Health Ministry from Hararge Zone, Oromia Region, during a cholera epidemic. A helpful NGO supplied the fluids.

A former reporter for the Ethiopian News Agency, interviewed in the USA, investigated a malaria outbreak in Jimma, Oromia Region, at the end of 1996. He reported that 400 died in a two month period, because medication was not supplied by the Ministry of Health. He was later forced to report that the government had the outbreak under control.[32]

Famine

Famine in Ethiopia has long been associated with and believed to be due to warfare and denial of human rights.[33] In 2000, the Ethiopian government stated, with agreement from the World Food Program, that at least 10 million were in need of food aid in Ethiopia. Areas which had never lacked food before were affected and the population was said by NGO officials to be more at risk than during the 1984-85 famine.[34]

Several correspondents complained that food aid was being denied to suspected OLF supporters and their families, to families who refused to present their sons as conscripts for the war with Eritrea and to families who refused to register for the May 2000 elections.[35]

Forced Conscription

Local correspondents and foreign journalists corroborate information obtained from prisoners of war. Youngsters, as young as 13, were rounded up from schools, markets and public meetings. Many schools closed because students stayed away, fearing conscription. Even Sudanese and Somali youths were caught up in forced conscription. At least two were killed for resisting conscription.[36]

The prisoners of war described the human wave tactics used by Ethiopian commanders to breech fortified positions held by Eritrea and reported being forced at gunpoint to cross minefields, acting as human minesweepers as most of them were mowed down by Eritrean fire. Ethiopian media now put the Ethiopian death toll for the two year war at 123,000.[37]

Security Network

Any of the Oromia Support Group press releases and the report from Sue Pollock's information gathering trip to Ethiopia in December 1995 and January 1996 portray the extent and depth of penetration of Oromo society by the government security apparatus. Whenever farmers take their produce to markets, they are liable to harassment and confiscation of their goods and vehicles.[38] Many who report being arrested from their homes, also report their goods and vehicles being confiscated.

Villagers travelling to nearby villages report being questioned on arrival by OPDO militia, who then hand them over to TPLF security men for interrogation.

The government security apparatus is able to track suspects across the breadth of Ethiopia within one or two days.[39] Nearly all accounts from former detainees include that their release is conditional on signing documents, agreeing that their life is forfeited should there be OLF activity in their area or they be showed to have involvement with the OLF. They are usually ordered to attend security offices every week.

FIRES AND PROTEST IN 2000

Possibly the most serious abuse of human rights, because of its long term effects on the environment and livelihood of civilians, is the deliberate burning of one sixth of Oromia's forest and of forests in Sidama, Ogaden and in Benishangul. Deforestation for commercial purposes already claims 100,000 hectares per year, according to the Ethiopian Agricultural Bureau.[40]

The fires were nearly all started on the same day, 30 January 2000, by Ethiopian government officials, according to informants across Oromia and elsewhere. They wrote that the government was flushing out armed opposition movements in each of these areas and punishing the local population. Large areas of primary forest, including endemic species and other species of international significance, were destroyed. Villages and farms were razed. Farm animals were killed and beehives lost. At least 600,000 hectares of forest were burned in Oromia alone.

The government claimed that the fires were started by farmers clearing land or honey collectors smoking bees out of their hives. However, these practices are long established and have not caused large fires before. Areas which have previously never been subject to fires were involved. Furthermore, it is not normal practice to clear land by fire at the end of January, especially if the December rains have been poor. Similarly, honey collectors only operate in October and November. The fires only occurred in areas which support armed opposition movements (Oromo Liberation Front, Ogaden National Liberation Front, Sidama Liberation Army).

Initially, government spokesmen stated that the fires would have to be left burning until the rains began in April. One month later, responding to pressure from students and media, international assistance was sought and 350 Addis Ababa University students were allowed to help. They reported being harassed and intimidated. Thousands of students from other educational establishments were refused permission to help extinguish the fires. Villagers put out the majority of fires in inhabited areas but inaccessible tracts of primary forest in the Bale mountains continued to burn until put out by the onset of rain on 10 April.

The fires precipitated unprecedented civil disturbance across Oromia. Four were killed at the first student demonstration, in Ambo on 9 March, including 12th grade student Getu Diriba, who was beaten to death by police.

Subsequent demonstrations were not only against the government's complicity in the fires. Students protested against forced conscription for the war with Eritrea, killings and beatings at other demonstrations and the organising and arming of Amhara settlers (the *Galla Gadaye*—"Oromo Killer"—groups).

Despite the use of violence to prevent demonstrations, including the killing of at least one student, Alemu Disassa, in Jimma, Illubabor Zone, protests occurred in Guder, Ginci, Gedo, Mandi, Nakamte, Gimbi, Dambi Dollo, Nejo, Arjo, Horro Guduru, Ayra Guliso, Gori, Qilta Kara and Begi. Secondary schools and higher education establishments were closed "from Addis Ababa to Asosa" and only re-opened in August. At least seven students were killed. Diribee Jifaar, a young teenager, was among two shot dead in Dembi Dollo on 2 April 2000. Many were injured and hundreds of demonstrators were detained, especially after a widespread round up of demonstrators at the end of April 2000.

At least one of the 350 Addis Ababa University students, Terefe Ejere, disappeared. Terefe was taken from his dormitory on 2 May and was held *incommunicado* for several weeks. Other students who attended the fires have been intimidated, had their identiy cards confiscated and restricted to the campus.

The unrest continued into June. In May 2000, there were killings and detentions in Wollo and Hararge when civilians resisted forced conscription. Demonstrators were also detained in Shashemane.

On 5 June 2000, after the fifth extra-judicial killing of a civilian within two weeks in Waliso, Showa, 6000 demonstrated at the funeral. Soldiers were called in from Ambo and Sabbata and "there was gunfire all day", with many wounded. Over 100 were detained.

On 11/12 June 2000, civil unrest in Ambo, Guder and Gindaberet resulted in severe damage to army barracks and the police station.[41]

POLICE ATTACK ON STUDENTS

Amnesty International appealed on 12 January 2001 about police invading the campus of Addis Ababa University and severely beating Oromo students in their dormitories. After being severely beaten at least 150 students were detained. Several were hospitalized. The action was precipitated by a clash between Oromo and Tigray students, following which ten Oromo students disappeared from the campus, according to a statement issued by the students. The statement continued

> The same night turns into a nightmare when Tigrean police and security ... break into the dorms through doors and windows terrorizing the students. Doors that led out of the dormitories get locked and students from the other building cannot respond to the screams and cries of students in the locked rooms. Students who were in the rooms report that they got beaten and kicked with rifle butts, police batons . . . The men (with the aid of the Tigre students in

campus) then proceed to look for the people whom they had come to collect.[43]

PROVOCATION OF VIOLENCE BETWEEN OROMO AND OTHER NATIONALITIES

Formal inauguration of *Hagere Fikir* groups has occurred, at least in Nairobi, Kenya, and Johannesburg, South Africa. *Hagere Fikir* means "love of mother-land/country." The organization was initially established by Haile Selassie, re-juvenated by the Derg in 1989 and again re-established by Ethiopian embassies, during the war with Eritrea, in 1998. Its stated purpose is to attack any opposition to the Ethiopian government. Although it is run by the TPLF, it uses Amhara opposition to Oromo nationalism; its functionaries are mainly former Derg members or soldiers. The group has been responsible for killing, robbing, harassing and intimidating Oromo refugees in Kenya and South Africa.[44, 45]

The government refused to publish investigations into the reported massacre of Amhara in Bedeno in 1992, by the OLF.[46] The OLF asked for the investigation, claiming that advancing government troops, fighting the OLF, had committed the atrocity. Many Amhara believe the massacre was the work of the OLF. Amhara settlers are encouraged to go to Oromia Region and have precipitated violence from Oromo peasants because of environmental damage they have caused in Wallega zone.[47]

Oromo in Borana zone complain that their land and water resources are being given to Somali Region and report eight being killed by Garre clansmen in March 2001.[48] Over 150 were reported killed earlier in the year.[49] In June 2000, the Ethiopian press reported the massacre of 39 Oromo by Issa clan in Harage zone.[50]

Whenever clashes of this sort are investigated, Ethiopian government troops are implicated. Degodia settlers who clashed with Boran Oromo in northern Kenya which resulted in over 50 young men being killed by Kenyan ground troops in May 2000, are reported by Oromo residents to have been urged on and armed by the Ethiopian government.[51] Fighting apparently between Guji Oromo (Borana zone) and Gedeo people in 1994 was found by an investigating journalist to have been attacks by disguised TPLF soldiers on Guji Oromo. Captured soldiers, found killing animals, could not speak the Gedeo language and Gedeo people resided many miles from the incident. In December 2000, 12 Oromo were killed in North Wajir, Kenya, by Garre clan members, according to the Ethiopian embassy in Nairobi. Two soldiers who were killed in the fighting were wearing Ethiopian army uniforms.[52]

GENOCIDE

The UN definition of genocide, from the convention on its prevention and punishment, is that the term means any of the following acts committed with intent to destroy, in whole or in part, a national, ethnic, racial or religious group:

1. Killings members of the group;
2. Causing serious bodily or mental harm to members of the group;
3. Deliberately inflicting on the group conditions of life calculated to bring about its physical destruction in whole or in part;
4. Imposing measures intended to prevent births within the group, and forcibly transferring children of the group to another group.[53]

It is the author's view that events in Ethiopia are consistent with its government committing genocide against the Oromo and other peoples of Ethiopia.

In *The Roots of Evil,* Professor Staub lists pre-conditions for genocide, including, "difficult life conditions, devaluation of sub-groups (scapegoats), hierarchical social structure, monolithic, not pluralistic culture, [and] strong ideology."[54] These conditions exist in Ethiopia today. As the third poorest country in the world, with a declining standard of living, Ethiopia may be said to have difficult life conditions.

Stereotypically, Abyssinians, i.e. Amhara and Tigrean people, regard the Oromo as animals who don't eat grass. Anti-Oromo racism is a fundamental part of Abyssinian culture and of the conflicts between the Amhara and Tigrean peoples and the Oromo. Racist attitudes towards Oromo became more integral to Amhara/Tigre culture when Oromia was colonized in the late nineteenth century. As it became necessary in Europe to justify the colonization of Africa through the "civilising mission," regarding Oromo as animals became necessary for Abyssinians. The devaluation and scape-goating of Oromo, especially those who uphold nationalist views, is still inherent in "Ethiopian" polity.

Ethiopian culture, as presented to the West, is Abyssinian culture. Unlike the long-standing democracies which belong to Oromo and other peoples' cultures, Abyssinian culture is based on feudalism and imperialism. No Abyssinian leader has assumed power peacefully. Their society, at family and civil levels, is strictly hierarchical.

Under the present TPLF regime, zero-sum, winner-takes-all, politics prevail. People are punished unless they show uncritical allegiance to the dominant party whose agenda is narrow and whose control is extremely profitable to a tiny elite.

Society in Ethiopia is militarised and brutalised. The TPLF-controlled media whipped up frightening hatred of Eritreans during the recent conflict. Over 80,000 were deported. The ideology of "Ethiopia First" struck familiar chords throughout Abyssinian society. These conditions are typical of those in which genocide occurs.

Deep wedges are being driven between different peoples of Ethiopia, especially between Amhara and Oromo. The TPLF have rejuvenated the ultra-nationalist *Hagere Fikir* organisation—whose targets are primarily Oromo.

At the Oromo Studies Association meeting in Toronto in July 2000, Dr Mekuria Bulcha estimated that up to a quarter of a million Oromo died needlessly in the previous year, because of TPLF oppression.[55] The scale of abuse is greater than at any time since the Oromo population was reduced from ten to five million in the late 19th century, by the Amhara hero, Menelik II.[56]

BYSTANDER EFFECT: WESTERN INFLUENCE

The role of bystanders is critical. Criticism from western countries about human rights abuses has been muted because of their strategic interests in Ethiopia and the Horn of Africa.

According to investigative journalist and director of a consortium of Swiss NGOs, Peter Niggli, two thirds of Ethiopia's budget comes from foreign aid.[57] Ethiopia enjoys more aid from the European Union than any other country in the world.[58] In 1997, Susan Rice, the former assistant Secretary of State for Africa stated that Ethiopia was the second largest recipient of aid from America in sub-Saharan Africa and that Ethiopia was to be praised for its progress in human rights and democratisation.[59] The UN arms embargo against Ethiopia was lifted in May 2001. The World Bank, International Monetary Fund (IMF) and the Paris Club of creditor nations have cancelled and rescheduled most of Ethiopia's debt and the remainder is to be alleviated by the Highly Indebted Poor Country initiative of the World Bank and IMF. If the present situation is allowed to continue, that is, if the West continues to prop up the TPLF regime, genocide on a much larger scale is a real possibility.

CONCLUSION

The Ethiopian government is deliberately and systematically destroying all serious political opposition, using its extensive and sophisticated security apparatus. The Oromo and other southern peoples believe themselves to have been colonised and oppressed since the incorporation of their territories into Ethiopia. In 1992, they were represented in the transitional administration, established at the downfall of the Derg military dictatorship, by their nationality-based liberation fronts. Since 1991, Oromo nationalists have been targeted for human rights violations. Oromo peasants, academics and businesspeople who are suspected of supporting the nationalist movement have been killed, disappeared, tortured and detained. The Oromo region is being impoverished and its environment degraded. The Oromo people have been further persecuted by famine, fire and forced conscription.

According to criteria included in the 1951 UN Convention on the Prevention and Punishment of Genocide, the Ethiopian government is committing genocide against the Oromo and other oppressed southern peoples in Ethiopia. International financial institutions and foreign aid, on which Ethiopia depends, are complicit in this genocide.

Notes

1. The orthodox Christian people of Abyssinia, the Amhara, Tigre and Tigrinya speakers, are based in the Amhara and Tigray Regional States of Ethiopia and in Eritrea.

2. Eye witness report by Oromo Relief Association health-worker trainer, midwife Sue Pollock, interviewed by author, July 1992.

3. Clandestine group of Oromo ex-prisoners, Addis Ababa, 1995.

4. Hizbaawi Adera, Volume 4, No 7, December 1996 -February 1997.

5. Oromia Support Group, *Press Release*, No. 34. August, 2001.

6. Interview with Horn of Africa desk officer, International Committee of the Red Cross, Geneva, 8 March 2001.

7. Fiseha Hailemariam Tedla, *Indian Ocean Newsletter*, 25 November 2000. Paris.

8. Personal communication, Dima Nogo, former Minister of Information in transitional government of Ethiopia, 1991-1992, who interviewed Yonatan Dhibisa in Asmara. Frankfurt, 15 July 2001.

9. Asylum statement by Hassan Ali. 7 December 1998.

10. Amnesty International Report 2000 (Index POL 10/001/00). London.

11. Human Rights Watch. Press Release, "Ethiopia, the targeting of human rights defenders," 16 May 2001. New York. Press Release 32, November 2000, p. 5.

12. Committee to Protect Journalists, *Clampdown in Addis: Ethiopia's journalists at risk*. October 1996.

13. *Attacks on the press. Yearly reports from 1993-2000*. Committee to Protect Journalists. New York.

14. Oromia Support Group, *Press Release 33*, May 2001, p. 30.

15. International Federation of Journalists. 27 January 2001.Brussels.

16. Interview with former Minister of Education, Ibsa Gutama, Germany, August 1994.

17. For example, see *Press Releases* 26, p. 26, and 27, p. 7.

18. S. Pollock, *Ethiopia - Human tragedy in the making*. March 1996.

19. Press Releases 15, October-November 1996, p.1, and 18, May-June 1997, p. 1-4.

20. For example, Urgent Action (Index AFR/25/07/98). Amnesty International. London.

21. Oromia Support Group, Press Release 31, July 2000, p. 11,

22. Interview with Elfnesh Qanno, July 2000. Munich.

23. Interview with Dhaba Wayessa, July 1995, reported in Oromia Support Group, Press Release 7, August 1995, p. 3.

24. Oromia Support Group, Press Release 29, August-October 1999, p. 3.

25 Sagalee Haaraa 31, July 2000, p. 15, newsletter of Oromia Support Group, Malvern, UK.

26. Investment in Ethiopia and the Oromo question. Oromo Liberation Front, North America Office, Washington. June 1997.

27. Oromia Support Group. *Sagalee Haaraa* 28, May-July 1999, p. 15.

28. Oromia Support Group. *Sagalee Haaraa* 29, August-October 1999, p. 7.

29. For example, see Oromia Support Group, *Press Release 30*, July 2000, p. 6, p. 7 (two cases), pp. 9, 13.

30. Oromia Support Group, *Press Release* 11, February 1996, p. 15-16.

31. A. Jalata. *The emergence of Oromo nationalism and Ethiopian reaction,* in *Oromo nationalism and the Ethiopian discourse* ... p. 5.

32. *Sagalee Haaraa* 31, July 2000, p. 8.

33. Human Rights Watch, *Evil Days. 30 years of war and famine in Ethiopia. An Africa Watch Report.* New York, September 1991.

34. Oromia Support Group, *Sagalee Haaraa* 32, November 2000, p. 3.

35. Oromia Support Group, *Press Release* 31, July 2000, p. 22-23,

36. Oromia Support Group, *Press Release* 28, May-July 1999, p. 2-3,

37. BBC Monitoring Service, 10 April 2001.

38. Oromia Support Group, *Press Release* 30, February 2000, p. 11 (AMA),

39. Oromia Support Group, *Press Release* 17, March-April 1997, and 18, May-June 1997, p. 7,

40. Oromia Support Group, *Sagalee Haaraa* 30, February 2000, p. 14.

41. Oromia Support Group, *Press Release* 31, July 2000, p. 2-11,

42. Amnesty International. Urgent Action. Fear of torture. (Index AFR/25/001/2001). 12 January 2001. London.

43. Press Release, Union of Oromo Students, Addis Ababa University, 23 December 2000.

44. Oromia Support Group, "Kenya: Ethiopian plot to kill Oromo refugees." *Sagalee Haaraa* 29 August-October 1999, p. 1-3.

45. Oromia Support Group, "Oromo refugees harassed and killed in South Africa." *Sagalee Haaraa* 30 February 2000, p. 1-3.

46. Personal communication with Lenco Lata, former Deputy Secretary General of the OLF and former member of the transitional government of Ethiopia, August, 2001.

47. Oromia Support Group, "Amhara/Oromo clash in Wallega." *Sagalee Haaraa* 33, May 2001, p. 8.

48. Oromia Support Group, *Press Release* 33, May 2001, p. 15.

49. Over 150 dead in Borana. *Sagalee Haaraa* 32, November 2000, p. 13.

50. Oromia Support Group, Oromo-Issa clashes. *Sagalee Haaraa* 32, November 2000, p. 11.

51. Oromia Support Group, "Boran under attack in Kenya." *Sagalee Haaraa* 32, November 2000, p. 5.

52. Oromia Support Group, *Press Release* 33, May 2001, p. 23,

53. United Nations, *Convention on the prevention and punishment of genocide*. Geneva, 1951.

54. E. Staub, *The roots of evil: The origins of genocide and other group violence.* 1989. Cambridge: Cambridge University Press.

55. Mekuria Bulcha. Presentation at Oromo Studies Association Conference, Toronto, 29 July 2000.

56. Mohammed Hassen, "Is genocide against the Oromo people possible in Ethiopia?" Association of Genocide Scholars Fourth International Biennial Conference. Minneapolis. 9-12 June 2001.

57. Peter Niggli. Presentation to annual congress of the Union of Oromo Students in Europe, Munich, July 2000.

58. Department for International Development, British development assistance in partnership with Ethiopia. Summary fact sheet, London, May 1997.

59. S. Rice. Presentation to African Studies Association, Cleveland, Ohio, 15 November 1997.

References

Africa Confidential, 1997. 37, 1, 5 January. London.

Amnesty International. 1995. *Ethiopia. Accountability past and present: Human rights in transition.* Index AFR/25/6/95, April. London.

Baxter, P. Introduction. In *Being and becoming Oromo,* ed. P.T.W. Baxter, J. Hultin, A. Triulzi. Lawrenceville, New Jersey and Asmara: Red Sea Press.

Human Rights Watch. 2001. "Ethiopia, the targeting of human rights defenders," Press Release, 16 May. New York.

Johnson, D. 2000. "Preliminary results of a study of Oromo refugees in Minnesota," presented at the Symposium on the international protection of human rights and the Oromo people. Minneapolis. 25 August.

Lata, Leenco. 1998. The making and unmaking of Ethiopia's transitional charter. In *Oromo nationalism and the Ethiopian discourse,* ed A. Jalata. Lawrenceville, New Jersey and Asmara: Red Sea Press.

Lata, Leenco.1999. *The Ethiopian state at the crossroads. Decolonization & democratization or disintegration.* Lawrenceville, New Jersey and Asmara: Red Sea Press.

Norwegian Institute of Human Rights. 1992. Report of Norwegian Observer Group, Human Rights Report 1. Local and regional elections in Ethiopia. 21 June 1992. Oslo: NIHR.

OSG. 1999. Oromia Support Group, *Press Releases 28*, May-July. Malvern

OSG. 1999. Oromia Support Group, *Press Release 29*. August-October. Malvern.

OSG. 2000. Oromia Support Group, *Press Release 30*, February. Malvern.

OSG. 2000. Oromia Support Group, *Press Release 31,* July. Malvern.

OSG. 2000. Oromia Support Group *Press Release 32,* November. Malvern.

OSG. 2001. Oromia Support Group, *Press Release 33*. May. Malvern.

OSG. 2001. Oromia Support Group, *Press Release 34*. August. Malvern.

US State Department. 2001. *Ethiopia: Country report on human rights practices, 2000.* February 2001. Washington.

Chapter 8

Oromo Problem
and the U.S. Foreign Policy

Hamdesa Tuso

INTRODUCTION

This essay is designed to revisit the conflict in the politically complex and culturally rich region during the post-Cold War era. We will closely examine the role of the sole super-power, the United States, in the conflict which has become even more complex than it was during the Cold War period. This examination takes place against the backdrop of the newly declared U.S. doctrine that it, as the sole superpower, will have a special obligation to support democracy and respect for human rights around the world.[1] In affirming this presumably new doctrine, the former President Bill Clinton, asserted, at his Speech to the UN General Assembly on 21 September 1999, that:

> When the Cold War ended, the United States could have chosen to run away from the opportunities and dangers of the world. Instead, we have tried to be engaged, involved, and active. We know this moment of unique prosperity and power for United States is a source of concern to many. Instead of imposing our values on others, we have sought to promote a system of government-democracy that empowers people to choose their own destinies according to their own values and aspirations.[2]

More significantly, our examination of the U.S. foreign policy toward the Horn of Africa during the post Cold War will help us to discern whether the political attitudes and behavior have changed in dealing with the social conflict in the region where traditionally major world powers have collided as the result of perceived threats by the competing parties' external "enemy."

Historically, the main interest of the major powers in the Horn of Africa has been over concerns relative to their access to the Red Sea which is adjacent to the oil fields in the Middle East deemed by the West to be vital to its economic interests and national security. Our analysis will reveal that in the final analysis, nothing has changed relative to the western approach in their quest to "ensure" the security of the Red Sea. Neither has there been a change in the strategy nor in the tactics that have been developed and employed to protect the rich oil fields and the Red Sea.

Based on the evidence available, pitting one tyrant against another at the expense of populations and as such propping tyrants to maintain control in their respective states has been a well established strategy and is still alive and well and indeed, in some cases, even more aggressive and cavalier with damaging consequences at grass root levels. What even makes the situation more extraordinary is the fact that there is not another power able to challenge the U.S. in this sphere.

The implication is that the party the U.S. anoints for its policy objectives becomes the unchallenged winner while the parties the U.S. disapproves of will have to perish in shame and despair. In our examination of the U.S. foreign policy on the Horn of Africa during the period under review, it thus seems that all the laudatory pronouncement about U.S. foreign policy commitment to advancing the cause of democracy and respect for human rights during the post Cold War era is nothing more than a side show (Dagne 1995:5).

There is another factor that should interest us: the U.S. led air strike against Slobadan Melosevic to save two million Kosovo Albainians. By its action during that conflict, the U.S. has raised the expectation that its foreign policy toward ethnic conflict caused by a dominant group should reach a new threshold with respect to the standard of acceptability to the international community. Indeed, the view of Vaclav Havel, the President of the Czeck Republic and a leading political figure in post Cold War Europe, supports such a proposition. In his speech to the Canadian Parliament on April 29, 1999, during the Kosovo crisis, President Havel declared:

> This war gives human rights precedence over the rights of the states. The Federal Republic of Yugoslavia has been attacked without a direct UN mandate for the Alliance action. But the Alliance has not acted out to license aggressiveness or disrespect for international law. On the contrary: It has acted out of respect for the law—for the law that ranks higher than the protection of the sovereignty of states. It has acted out of respect for the rights of humanity, as they are articulated by our conscience as well as by other instruments of international law. I see this as an important precedent for the future. It has been now clearly stated that it is not permissible to slaughter people, to evict them from their homes, to maltreat them and to deprive them of their property. It has been demonstrated that

human rights are indivisible and that if injustice is done to some, it
is done to all.[3]

Thus, according to Havel, the war against Melosevic set a new standard—that
ethnic mistreatment by the government of a dominant ethnic group is no
longer tolerable. Indeed, he spoke to the unresolved dysfunctional relationships
between the modern state and ethnic groups.

During the twentieth century, the U.S. has been involved four times in European wars caused by tyrants. Two of these wars took place during the 1990s. The
main goal for its involvement was to stop ethnic cleansing in the Balkans and
provide the necessary assistance for the purpose of stabilizing the social, economic,
and political system so that all groups can enjoy economic and political security
and peace.[4]

The central theme of this new doctrine was reiterated by President Clinton
in his speech to the UN General Assembly. In fact he made a linkage between
the new U.S. doctrine and the principles enshrined in the UN Charter which is
to protect the basic rights of all citizens of the world. He said:

> What is the role of the U.N. in preventing mass slaughter and dis-
> locations? Very large. Even in Kosovo, NATO's actions followed a
> clear consensus expressed in several Security Council resolutions
> that the atrocities committed by Serb forces were unacceptable, that
> the international community had a compelling interest in seeing
> them end. Had we chosen to do nothing in the face of this brutality,
> I do not believe we would have strengthened the United Nations.
> Instead, would have risked discrediting everything it stands for.... By
> acting as we did, we helped to vindicate the principles and purposes
> of the U.N. Charter the opportunity it now has to play the central
> role in shaping Kosovo's future. In the real world principles often
> collide, and tough choices must be made. The outcome in Kosovo
> is hopeful.[5]

The obvious question then is whether the U.S government is going to apply
the same standard when it comes to ethnic persecution by African tyrants. Thus
far, it seems the U.S. State Department has been sending mixed signals on this
subject. One signal came from Madeleine Albright, the Secretary of State, during
her speech at the NAACP Annual Conference in New York U.S. where she
indicated that the U.S. may do more in resolving conflicts in Africa.[6] A totally
opposite signal came from her subordinates with respect to the current crisis in
the Horn of Africa. Susan Rice, Assistant Secretary of State for African Affairs,
in her testimony before the Congressional Sub-Committee, gave a standard
Cold War style dogmatic and unreasoned, uncritical speech with a catalogue of
the "bad guys" and the "good guys." In the list of the bad guys, she once again

castigated the Eritrean government and the Oromo Liberation Front (OLF). According to her, the Eritrean government was bad because it allegedly gave weapons to the OLF. Furthermore, in her view, Isias Afeworki is going closer to Mommar Gaddaffi, the "bad guy." She also believed the OLF was bad because it was going to use those weapons for violence (Rice 1999).

About three months later Mr. Tabor Naggy, the Ambassador Designee to Ethiopia, stated in his confirmation hearings before the U.S. Senate Committee that Ethiopia is an important ally of the United States. Mr. Nagy added: "Ethiopia is one of the most important partners in Africa. Our bilateral relationship is founded on mutual strategic interests and the shared aspirations of our governments for the people of Ethiopia" (Nagy 1999). Even more startlingly, he justified the U.S. foreign policy toward the regime of Meles Zenawi by asserting that "since the fall of the repressive socialist regime of Mengistu Hailemariam in 1991, Ethiopia has made great strides toward building a democratic society"(Nagy 1999 *ibid*).

Consistent with this policy position, Mr. David Shin, the outgoing U.S. Ambassador to Ethiopia, echoed the same assertion that Ethiopia has been more democratic than in the previous periods. He even ventured to blame the victims for the conflict and devastation his government has sponsored: he specifically singled out the Oromo Liberation Front (OLF) for convenient disparagement. He accused the OLF on two main grounds; namely for failing to renounce violence, and for not accepting the Constitution of Meles Zenawi.[7] It is instructive to note that he conveniently refrained to make any references to the state sponsored violence against the other subordinate nationalities by the regime of Meles Zenawi. Neither was there any observation relative to the well-established fact that OLF was systematically prevented from full, free and fair competition during the 1992 election, and it was subsequently banned by Zenawi from legally participating in the political process. He also failed to point out that the Constitution of 1994 was drafted and ratified under political duress.

Our examination would reveal that these assertions about the democratic progress in Ethiopia could not be supported by the available evidence. This is so since the political policies of the government of Meles Zenawi in the areas of democratic processes and human rights violations against various subordinate ethnic groups should clearly demonstrate otherwise. Therefore, there are two dramatically opposing sets of views. The first set of views was expounded by the U.S. government with regard to the new doctrine of supporting democracy and human rights in the world during the post-Cold War. The second set of views was expressed about Ethiopia by the government representatives and their incongruence when compared with the evidence from the scene on the ground.

The U.S. foreign policy toward Africa's North East region can be viewed as the function of core versus periphery relations at various levels: global, regional and state.[8] The core-periphery relationship is better unravelled through a personal narrative from the periphery and the author provided this in the epilogue in this book. More specifically, since the experiences of the peoples in the periphery, particularly those in the Ethiopian empire, their grievances, hopes, and aspirations have not been exposed to the outside world sufficiently, it is hoped that such a narrative will illustrates, in some small way, the depth of the crisis by exploring the dysfunctional relationships between the core and the periphery.

The central theme of this chapter is to provide a critical review of the U.S. foreign policy toward Ethiopia. With respect to the analysis about the post-Derg Ethiopia, three entities and the treatment the U.S. government attaches to these entities will be analyzed. The three entities are: the regime of Meles Zenawi, the Oromo people, and the Oromo Liberation Front (OLF). Four areas are selected for further exploration where it is deemed that the U.S. foreign policy should be reconsidered in some fundamental ways. These are understanding the nature of the social system in Ethiopia, the possibility of democratizing an empire, the futility of suppressing national movements, and the need to consider alternative solutions including empowering the weaker parties.

THE POST-COLD WAR HORN OF AFRICA

This section will explore the nature of the post-Cold War U.S. foreign policy toward that region. In order to advance our thesis that the U.S. policies in that region are influenced by the post- Cold War, which I term as a "new Cold War," one needs to revisit the social phenomenon of the old Cold War and establish the similarities and the interconnections between them.

The Cold War was a social phenomenon which evolved during the four decades following the end of WWII. As conflict behavior, it commenced over policy disagreement between the West and the Soviet Union regarding the city of Berlin which resulted in one party unilaterally erecting the infamous Berlin Wall (Jenson 1993). It was a classic case of conflict escalation which evolves as the result of moves and counter moves by the parties in conflict. The conflict interactions between the superpowers during this period escalated and eventually encompassed the entire world community. Indeed, it was a classic case of conflict transformation. As a social behavior, conflict transformation leads to two major developments: escalation and enlargement of parties to the conflict (Rubin et al 1994:68-71). In general, in the process of conflict transformation, dramatic changes take place on three levels: cognition, attitude, and behavior of the parties both at individual and collective levels. One of the critical effects resulting from such changes in attitudes and the accompanying behavior of the parties in conflict is becoming blind to social realities—engaging in behaviors which are generated through tunnel vision—within the universes in which the social conflict takes place. During this process each party mobilizes sentiments and resources against each other (Rubin et al 1994; Kriesberg 1998:151-180).

The activities of the two superpowers during the period of the Cold War fit this frame of reference. As each superpower labored so feverishly in mobilizing sentiments and resources to undermine the other party, many societies around the world were encapsulated in a drama of social conflict which, for most part, had no connections with their direct basic interests.[9]

The Cold War had two critical dimensions. The first dimension is the one represented by the metaphor "Cold War" itself. In its conception, "Cold War" was meant to represent the non-violent aspect of the hostile activities, and those activities were limited to propaganda campaigns denigrating the ideology and political reality of the other. At the global level, the Voice of America (VOA) and Radio Moscow were among the most effective tools to achieve the goals of the two superpowers in this ideological warfare. The ideological campaigns were coupled with activities which included posturing and staging the self. This line of behavior resulted in the biggest arms race in human history which eventually bankrupted the economy of the USSR.

The second aspect of the Cold War was the violent activities sponsored by each superpower. The venues for the devastating proxy wars were the developing societies (Folz and Beinen 1985). This chapter specifically focus of how Africa was conceived as an important venue for conflict by the two superpowers during the Cold War.

Although the Cold War encompassed the entire world, there were six regions that were chosen for intense violent confrontations between the two superpowers. These were Eastern Europe, Indo-China, the Far East (the Korean Peninsula), the Middle East, Central America, and the Horn of Africa. All six regions became targets based on some material and strategic values (real or perceived) attached to each one of them.

The struggle of the Western powers over the Horn of Africa predates the Cold War, and is a continuation of the longstanding rivalry between major world powers. On the eve of the 20th Century, they fought among themselves over the Horn of Africa, resulting in their occupation by partitioning the region and the peoples therein irrespective of their ethnic, cultural, and linguistic identities. The chief participants in the colonial scramble of that era were Great Britain, France, Italy, and Czarist Russia (Melba 1988:45-61). Contrary to the craftily constructed and successfully propagated myths by Abyssinian politicians, intellectuals, and their supporters in the Western world, that Ethiopia was the bastion of anti-European colonial resistance and beacon of African independence, the Ethiopian Empire was a serious participant and beneficiary in the European colonial schemes in the partition of the continent (Melba 1988: 37).

When European global empires collapsed at the end of World War II, new leaders of independent African states retained the colonial boundaries as the legal demarcation of the decolonized states.[10] Soon the emergence of the Cold War between the West, led by the United States, and the East, led by the Soviet Union, imposed itself on the fragile material and social ecology of the Horn of Africa region. During this period each of the three major states in the region —Sudan, the Ethiopian Empire, and Somalia—were a client of one of the two superpowers, and each of these states traded, at least once, its masters with the opposing state in the process (Shraeder 1995:114-188; Chaliand 1980). For example, the Sudan was a sort of client state of the Soviet Union during the early years of Nimeiri; then after wiping out the Communist party, it began leaning toward the U.S. (Brzezinski 1983:178,179; See Habte Selassie 1980:151-165).

Ethiopia, after serving as a client state of the U.S. for some two and half decades, switched to the Soviet Union during the 1977-1978 Ethiopia-Somalia War. This period was the height of the Cold War in the region. Somalia which essentially served as the client of the Soviet Union since its inception as a new state in 1960, switched to the United States during the same war (Brezinki 1983:129-149). Indeed, it is instructive to review, though briefly, the significance the two superpowers attached to that region during this period. Zbigniew Brzezinski who served as National Security Advisor in the Carter Administration wrote the following with respect to his views valuing the U.S. attachment to the Horn of Africa in the context of the Cold War:

> However, in my view the situation between the Ethiopians and Somalis was more than a border conflict. Coupled with the expansion of the Soviet influence and military presence to South Yemen, it posed a potentially grave threat to our position in the Middle East, notably in the Arabian Peninsula. It represented a serious setback in our attempts to develop some rules of the game in dealing with turbulence in the Third World. The Soviets had earlier succeeded in sustaining, through Cuba, their preferred solution in Angola, and they now seemed embarked on a repetition in a region in close proximity to our most sensitive interest (Brzezinski 1983:178).

Chester Crocker who served as the Assistant Secretary for African Affairs in the administration of President Ronald Reagan, in his address before the Washington World Affairs Council, outlined the reasons why the U.S. was deeply involved in the conflict of the region. He stated:

> The Horn of Africa...has considerable strategic importance for the United States as it is relevant to both the security of the Middle East and to Africa. We seek access to airfields and harbors for our military forces should they, in times of crisis, be required to defend against Soviet expansionism in the Persian Gulf or the Indian Ocean.[11]

Anatoly Dobrynin, the Soviet Union Ambassador to the United States has allocated six pages in his memoirs on the subject of superpower rivalry and the ensuing conflict activities in the Horn of Africa. He vividly recorded the events which led to the dramatic escalation of the conflict both at regional and super power levels. He wrote:

> As the Soviet Union shifted its support toward Ethiopia, the United States, in its turn, accelerated the process by stopping its military assistance and accusing Mengistu's new government of human rights violations. (The real reason, of course, was the overthrow of the emperor and a clear left wing takeover.) Washington then turned its attention to Somalia, the more so because Somalia cancelled its treaty with the Soviet Union at the end of 1977 after Moscow refused to provide more arms. The Soviet Union then signed a similar treaty with Ethiopia. By the end of 1977 about two thousand Cuban troops and one thousand Soviet military advisors were sent to Addis Ababa. Somali troops were forced to retreat in Ogaden province but still held a considerable part of it.

From the long-term geopolitical point of view, the developments in that part of Africa were unmistakably of local importance, and the political leadership in Moscow regarded them as such. Nevertheless, the Soviet and Cuban interference and the deployment of Cuban task force in yet another country just two years after they had gone in Angola, plus Soviet transports and other logistic supports, caused uproar in the West, especially the United States. Suspicions were aroused that the Soviet Union had adopted a new strategy of challenging and outflanking the West in the Third World. This quickly became a priority in relations between the Carter administration and Moscow for much of the year, further complicating our relations and provoking serious discord within the administration itself (Dobrynin 1995:403).

Then, in a reflective moment reviewing the key events during the Cold War years in that region, Dobrynin wrote the following:

> In retrospect, I cannot help being surprised at the amount of energy and effort spent almost entirely in vain by Moscow and Washington on these so called African affairs. Twenty-one years later (expect historians) could as much as remember them. Even when the American marines were sent to Somalia in 1992 by George Bush to join United Nations forces to help feed the starving there, no one in the

U.S. government and a very few in the press remarked that the seeds of the anarchy then prevailing in Somalia had most probably been planted by the great power's engagement there fifteen years before. Somalia was only one of a number of countries whose local quarrels became enmeshed in the Cold War— Angola, Ethiopia, Afghanistan, among them, and all of them worse off for their involvement with two superpowers (Dobrynin 1995:407).

THE POST-COLD WAR AS A NEW COLD WAR

Ironically, as the human community was bidding farewell to the old Cold War which was fought between the East and the West, a new form of Cold War emerged; this time it took the form of religious nationalism which is to thought to pose challenge to the western sponsored state system. Religious nationalism, as a new social force, expressed itself in the form of mobilization of resources and sentiments under the broad rubric of ideology of organized religions—Sikhism, Hinduism, Islam, Judaism, Christianity, etc. While these religious based movements have different historical origin, and operate under varied social settings, they do manifest certain conflict behaviors which have common features with the old Cold War. Sociologist Juergensmeyer, in comparing the old Cold War and the new Cold War wrote:

> Like the Cold War, the confrontation between these new forms of cultural-based politics and the secular state is global in its scope, binary in its opposition, occasionally violent, and essentially a difference of ideologies; and, like the old Cold War, each side tends to stereotype the other. According to a major Islamic political strategist in the Sudan, the post Cold War West needs a new "empire of evil to mobilize against." Similarly, he and other religious politicians need a stereotype of their own, a satanic secular foe that will help them mobilize their own forces (Juergensmeyer 1993:2).

The exaggerated projection of the enemy in the new Cold War becomes clearer in his observation when he states, "Unlike the old Cold War, however, the West (now aligned with the secular leaders of the former Soviet Union) confronts an opposition that is neither politically united nor, at present time, militarily strong."[12]

Professor Noam Chomsky, a critic of U.S. foreign policy, adds another dimension to this complex social phenomenon. In comparing the world order during the Cold War and the post Cold War, he makes two interrelated conclusions: The U.S. foreign policy is the most significant factor in determining the "New World Order;" and American economic interest is paramount in shaping the "New World Order", and more specifically, the consideration of the U.S. weapons industry leads the priority in this policy enterprise (Chomsky 1994:101, 190-206).

He suggests that the current extraordinary focus on Islamic fundamentalism as the "new enemy" during the post Cold War stems from the fact that the U.S. policy makers were looking for potential "sources of threats" to the U. S. and its allies' economic interests.

The rise of Islamic fundamentalism, in the face of the failure of secular nationalism in the Middle East, made the former fit the new image of the new enemy of the West (Chomsky 1994:3,227). Dr. Trevor Trueman, a British physician and a human rights activist, using Chomsky's thesis as a frame of reference, has presented a coherent analysis relative to the rationale of the new Cold War and its intricate connection to the old Cold War. Accordingly, the West invented and overwhelmed an enemy, with dreadful consequences to the poorer sections of its societies under the onslaught of Ronald McDonald and large "investors" in the "economic miracle" of the East. After the collapse of communism the West was left without a foil to justify its support of its arms manufacturers and without a reason to endorse its profitable economic and political manipulation of world markets. Ready to fill the gap, waiting in the wings of the world stage was Islamic Fundamentalism. It was already blessed with growing unpopularity in the West, thanks in part to U.S.-sponsored Israeli interstate terrorism. Pieces in the puzzle of the "New World Order" fell into place. Islamic Fundamentalism has replaced communism as the antithesis of the western way and the excuse for the U.S.A. to subsidize its arms industry and its belligerence in its efforts to control global resources markets. Using the threat of Islamic Fundamentalism the West is able to "manufacture consent" for its foreign policy among its population (Trueman 1996:22).

There are several factors which seem to have generated the intensity of the conflict in the Horn of Africa region in the context of the new Cold War. Four are the salient ones:

a) The highly sought resources, more specifically oil and the Red Sea, are still critical factors relative to the Western security interests;

b) The emergence of Islam as one of the most articulated ideological forces under which some political individuals and groups can organize their supporters in challenging the West;

c) There are two major states in the region—Ethiopia and Sudan—whose histories have been shaped by the ideologies of Semitic religions; and

d) The existence of super ordinate and subordinate relations in the state systems—this condition of social order is present both in Ethiopia and the Sudan—which serves as the basis for the elite of the dominant groups to act as the saviors of the state (this gives them the motivation to seek outside support).

Since the selected venue for the dividing lines in the new Cold War have been the two major states, Ethiopia and Sudan, it is imperative that we review the contradictory policies of the United States government toward these two states.

THE U.S. POLICY TOWARD THE ETHIOPIAN EMPIRE

Ethiopia is the last classic empire on the African continent. The very essence of dominance which has shaped the social order in Ethiopia, is rooted in the legacy of "the chosen people" ordained by the "divine" right to conquer, subdue and rule the indigenous African peoples in their surroundings (Markakis 1974:13-26). The Orthodox Christian Church dating back to the period of the Axumite kingdom, provided the ideological doctrine of the chosen people to the Abyssinian ruling class (Markakis 1974:27-42). As a literate segment in the society, the Abyssinian rulers and clergy were able to develop a coherent ideology which they later used to instill such values in its ethnic members; in due course, this carefully fashioned ideology would successfully penetrate the consciousness of the Western world (Greenfield 1965:22-44).

By the 16th century, the crucial linkage which would last until the present period, was made between the Abyssinian rulers and the then emerging Western imperial powers. Portugal, the first European imperial power to have developed overseas colonies, intervened on the side of the Abyssinians in the raging conflict between the Abyssinian kingdom and the Muslim forces led by Gragn. That act saved the Christian Kingdom from total obliteration (Abir 1968:xx). Since then, the Abyssinian rulers have always depended on the West to find a *deus ex machina* to save them from internal as well as external adversaries. Professor John Spencer, who served as advisor to Emperor Haile Selassie for over forty years, in his lamentation of the fact that Ethiopia fell to the Soviet Union orbit during the height of the Cold War in the Horn of Africa, provides a succinct summary of the patterns of dependence on external powers for the survival of *habasha* dominance since the 16th century. To this end he wrote:

> Ethiopia's supreme crises were of external origin and were often resolved by foreign *deus ex machina*. The 16th century invasion, led by the Somali Gragn, was repelled by the Portuguese. The defeat of Italy at Adawa at the end of the 19th century was achieved in part with the French and German arms. The Emperor's rise to power in the early years of the 20th century had been achieved to a significant degree through the intervention of European states opposed to reign of Menelik's successor, Lij Iyassu. Haile Selassie fell from

power because of the European support of the Fascist invasion, went into exile in England where he was kept on hand for possible utilization against Italy. It was the British who put him back on the throne and the United States furnished the occasion for his downfall. Like Britain and Portugal before it, the Soviet Union became the third *deus ex machina*. It has spent more than two billion dollars in military aid to counter Somali and Eriterian attacks on the highlands of Ethiopia so as, in the end, to convert her to a Soviet colony (Spencer 1984:360).

There are many areas where one can observe the manifestations of the new Cold War syndrome with respect to the U. S. political behavior in dealing with Ethiopia since 1991. Due to space limitation, we will focus on three critical areas: Meles Zenawi and his TPLF, the nationality crisis with a special reference to the Oromo question; and the Oromo Liberation Front (OLF). These three entities have been selected for a closer examination because the U.S. has developed specific policies (directly or indirectly) with respect to these three entities during the period under consideration.

Is Meles Zenawi a new African democrat or a new breed of tyrant? In order to address this question appropriately, we need to examine the U.S. relations with the government of Meles Zenawi in a historical context. However, before we do that, it is imperative that we digress for a while and discuss the basic definitions of the concepts of democracy and tyranny.

We start with the concept of democracy. While the concept of democracy is too complex to be reduced to a simple definition, scholars, however, do agree on some broad conceptual outline on the notion of democracy. In a democratic system of government three key features should exist. These are competition, participation, and civil and political liberties. George Sorensen, an authority on the subject of democracy, suggests that a system of government which embodies political democracy, should posses the following conditions: Meaningful and extensive competition among individuals and organized groups (especially political parties) for all effective positions of government power, at regular intervals and excluding the use of force; a highly inclusive level of apolitical participation in the selection of leaders and policies, at least through regular and fair elections, such that no major (adult) social group is excluded; a level of civil and political liberties—freedom of expression, freedom of the press, freedom to form and join organizations—sufficient to ensure the integrity of political competition and participation (Serenson 1998).

A political figure to whom the attribute of being "a democrat" should be assigned ought to be a personality who is committed to such principles both in utterance and political behavior relative to governance.

Now we move on to the definition of the concept of tyranny which is the opposite of democracy. Daniel Chirot in his seminal work, *Modern Tyrants*, defines tyranny as such:

> Tyranny is the abuse of power. There have always been individuals who abuse their greater strength or cleverness to inflict pain and humiliation on others, and to exploit those around them for personal gain...But the scale of cruelty and the types of distress that the powerful have inflicted on others have increased as societies have become more complex. The key step toward the creation of political tyranny, the systematic abuse of power by those in position of authority, was the creation of the state. With armed soldiers at their command, and a growing body of administrators, those in charge of states could exploit their subjects much more thoroughly. They tax more, demand greater servility, and, if they so wished, were able to inflict greater cruelty (Chriot 1996:2-3).

Roger Boesche, in his work, *Theories of Tyranny from Plato to Arendt*, posed a critical question: "How do tyrannies use deception, discourse, and language?" Then he provided the answer: "One task of any tyrant is to create words of reassuring appearances." He further asked, "How do tyrants do this?" Then he assembled a list of tactics which have been used by tyrants. These include having the appearance of being religious, law abiding, merciful, and frugal without being so; having institutions of government appearing to function well while subverting the basic principles of democracy; conducting bogus elections for the purpose of deceiving the public; hiding the reality of servitude by distorting language and limiting discourse (Boesche 1996:465). Thus, a political figure (a head of state) who engages in political activities which fit such characterization can be referred to as a tyrant.

Now we will move on to our analysis of the policies of Meles Zenawi to determine whether his policies and actions fit one of these two categories. Since the U.S. and its Western allies had anointed him "as a new breed of African democrat," our examination of his policies and practices will be viewed in the context of the U.S. support of the new regime in Addis Ababa (Last 1999; Mutu 1994:31-34). The U.S. interest in the Ethiopian Empire predates the regime of Meles Zenawi. Based on John Spencer's account (as cited previously), the U.S. became the fourth *deus ex machina* in 1991 when it negotiated the peaceful departure of Mengistu Hailemariam and subsequently endorsed the takeover of government power by the TPLF. For the U.S. per se, it was the second time in about fifty years (Tuso 1997:355, 356). The first time was when it forged alliance with the regime of Emperor Haile Selassie commencing with the 1950s and lasting until the overthrow of the Emperor in 1974 (Agyeman-Duah 1994:11-157). During this period, it almost seemed that the U.S. government

161

and the Emperor were partners in running the empire. For example, it was during this period that the Emperor incorporated Eritrea under some shady political manoeuvres (Habte Selassie 1982:51-63).

The U.S. played a critical role in supporting the Emperor against oppositions that were challenging his feudal regime. For example, U.S. planes bombed the Bale armed movement in conjunction with the Israeli government.[13] Furthermore, the U.S. pressured Somalia to stop support for the movement, resulting in the surrender of the leadership, of course after some negotiation and symbolic concessions from the Emperor (Habte Selassie 1982, *ibid*). The American embassy in Addis Ababa intervened on the side of the Emperor during the 1960 attempted *coup d'etat* against the Emperor (Agyeman-Duah 1994:80-85). In return for unconditional American support for his regime, the Emperor gave the U.S. government the right to build the Kanaw air base in Asmara (Yohannes 1997:61-67). The main function of that military base was to spy on Soviet Union activities in the Mediterranean Sea, the Red Sea and the adjacent regions (Agyeman-Duah 1994:25-29). As discussed previously, during the seventeen years when the Derg ruled Ethiopia, the U.S. government sponsored various activities with the intention of snatching it, as it were, from the Soviet Union Orbit or to topple it.[14] Likewise, the Derg on its part, elevated its anti-U.S. rhetoric on its daily political menu (Korn 1986:87-116; Wolde Giorgis 19869:48-53; Spencer 1984:348-356).

The U.S., after interacting with Ethiopia for some four decades when it was under Amhara dominance, in May 1991 inherited Ethiopia which would be ruled by a Tigrayan power (Tuso 1997:355-357). Upon examining the U.S. government relations with the regime of Meles Zenawi, one finds astonishingly remarkable similarities with the policies it had with the regime of Emperor Haile Selassie. It is instructive to summarize the key policy areas the U.S. has adopted with respect to the government of Meles Zenawi.

First it endorsed the TPLF/EPRDF to enter Addis Ababa and take power in 1991, and it in effect surrendered the entire population of some 60 million in Ethiopia to the hands of a guerrilla fighter whose power base is a tiny ethnic minority; the international community knew very little about him. To be sure, at the London Peace Conference, Mr. Herman Cohen, the Assistant Secretary of State for African Affairs, and the Chairman of the Conference, announced to the international community that U.S. support for the new regime would be contingent on two conditions: support for democracy and respect for human rights.[15] However, as the records would show later with respect to the failure of the U.S. administration in dealing with human rights violations by the Meles Zenawi regime, the U.S. was not serious about the preconditions it had articulated at the London Peace Conference (Ottawa 1995:67-84; Vestal 1996:21-38).

Second, the U.S. was involved in orchestrating and managing the July 1991 Addis Ababa Conference. Third, it dispatched experts to write the New Charter. Fourth, in the diplomatic arena, it elevated the Addis Ababa post to ambassadorial level, and also allowed the Tigrayan regime to have an ambassador in Washington. Fifth, the U.S. State Department recommended to Congress the revocation of the Brooke Amendment which had prohibited foreign aid to Ethiopia during the Derg. Sixth, both the Bush and Clinton administrations supported the applications of the regime of Meles Zenawi to the international lending agencies (e.g. the World Bank, IMF). Seventh, when the Meles regime conducted fraudulent elections of June 1992, the U.S., instead of taking appropriate actions against systematic rigging and sabotaging of the internationally publicized elections, continued uncritical support for his regime.

And finally, every time the oppositions, particularly the Oromo Liberation Front, has become stronger militarily, the U.S. government conducted joint military exercises with the military of Meles Zenawi.[16] When Meles Zenawi declared war against the Oromos subsequent to those fraudulent elections, his apologists argued that he had to take such "tough measures in order to keep the unity of Ethiopia." (Bichburg 1992:A24).[17] He even reportedly claimed that he was doing what Abraham Lincoln did during the American Civil War—to save the union of the American Republic from falling apart.

In the light of such considerable investment on the part of the U.S. government and its western allies in the persona of Meles Zenawi and his government, with the specific proposition that the empowerment of him and his regime would bring about democratic traditions and more respect for human rights in Ethiopia, it is legitimate to review the performance of his regime relative to the above indicated areas.

First, all the elections conducted during the period under review have been rejected by the international community as neither free nor fair (National Democratic Institute for International Affairs 1992:6-7; Norwegian Institute of Human Rights 1992:3-4; Pausewang 1994:1-4; Tronvoll and Aadland 1995:1-3).

Second, the constitution which was drafted in 1994 and ratified in 1995 has been dismissed by external observers as a veneer for the purpose of legitimizing minority Tigrayan dominance and exclusive control over resources (Vestal 1996:21-38; Ottaway 1995:67-84).

Third, freedom of expression has been under very serious attack; according to the Committee to Protect Journalists (CPJ), Ethiopia ranks first in Africa with respect to the number of journalist in jail (CPJ 1998). The CPJ has also listed Meles Zenawi among the top ten worst enemies of the press.

Fourth, the regime's record on human rights violations is equally bleak. According to several organizations which monitor human rights conditions in post Cold War Ethiopia, the recorded violations include: imprisonment without due process, denial of rights of public demonstrations and exacting severe penalties for those who dared to assert their basic rights to undertake public demonstrations; extraordinary killings; systematic persecution of artists, intellectuals, elders, students and political leaders of the major ethnic groups—the Oromos, Amharas, Somalis, and Sidamas. [18]

Fifth, in the words of Tecola Hagos, "...the democratization process has collapsed with no prospect of revival under the present leadership of the Ethiopian government." (Hagos 1995:15). The Transitional Government commenced at the Addis Ababa Conference of July 1991 where the representatives of 29 liberation front organizations who participated and ratified the New Charter has, for all practical purposes, collapsed due to the systematic mistreatments prosecuted against members of non-Tigrean ethnic groups led by Meles Zenawi and his inner-circle (Hagos 1995:4, 5; 175-188; Lata, 1998:51-77; Mutua 1993:31).[19]

Sixth, the military is controlled by the TPLF and Meles Zenawi controls the military (Hirst, op.cit.; The Economist, 1995:46; 1992:50).

Seventh, the regime has targeted persons of certain ethnic descent for deportation (e.g. persons of Eritrean extraction) (Legesse 1998). And finally, the regime has plundered resources from the periphery and directed them to Tigray, the home base of Meles Zenawi and TPLF.[20]

In our view of the above facts, and based on his own deeds since 1991, it is legitimate to conclude that Meles Zenawi is neither a liberator nor is he a unifier. Based on his policies of gross mistreatment of various ethnic groups, Meles Zenawi is not Abraham Lincoln, neither is he Mikhal Gorbachev; he is not even W. F. de Klerk. At least all three distinguished political leaders who were confronted with inequalities in a multi-ethnic state, Lincoln, Gorbachev, and de Klerk, demonstrated having two critical qualities in common. First, all three had abiding faiths in some notion of democratic principles in the arena of governance. Even more significantly, their polices altered the balance of power in favor of the subordinate ethnic groups in their respective states. Lincoln emancipated slaves; Gorbachev, with full knowledge that the Russians would lose the historic position of dominance over the devolution of the Soviet Union in favor of democratic resolution to the historic ethnic inequities which existed between the core and the periphery of the Russian empire for centuries, allowed the process of democratization to proceed, even at great personal risk (Gorbachev 1991) and de Klerk dismantled the abhorrent Apartheid system so that the African majority could legally participate rightfully in a democratic political process in the governance of South Africa (Ottaway 1993:1-19; *The Cambridge Biographical Encyclopaedia*, 1994, 263-264; de Klerk 1999:149-341).

Meles Zenawi's policies toward various ethnic groups in the Ethiopian Empire stand in marked contrast to the demonstrated policies of Lincoln, Gorbachev, and de Klerk. To be sure, Meles neither created ethnic inequalities in Ethiopia, nor did he treat their concerns fairly and democratically. Instead, he employed the mischievous and cynical ploys from Lenin and Stalin in his creation of "ethnically-based federalism." The apt analysis by Theodore Vestal supports this observation. He wrote the following on the political reasons behind the creation of "ethnic federalism" in the post Derg Ethiopia:

> The credo of the EPRDF is rights of nations, nationalities, and peoples to self-determination, the Charter's obfuscated declaration of governance based on ethnicity. The high-sounding principle is more Machiavellian than Wilsonian however. If the outnumbered Tigreans who direct the EPRDF/TGE can keep other ethnic groups divided and roiled against each other in ethno-xenophobia or content to manage affairs only in their own limited bailiwicks, then larger matters can be subsumed by the one governing party. Thus what EPRDF views as the false ideology of nationalism for a "Greater Ethiopia" can be kept in check and its proponents divided and conquered, *ex uno plura* (Vestal 1994:21).

THE OROMO PROBLEM AND THE NEW POLITICAL ORDER

The Oromo question has come to the forefront since the fall of the Derg and the formation of the transitional government of July 1991, and the participation of the Oromo political organizations, most notably the Oromo Liberation Front (OLF) in that government. It would be recalled that the mistreatment of the Oromo people and the 1992 fraudulent elections compelled the OLF to withdraw from the government. Subsequently, all the genuine Oromo political organizations, along with other authentic ethnic organizations, were expelled from the government.[21] Before we proceed with our analysis about the Oromo question in the new political order, it is appropriate that we address one critical issue: since Ethiopia is an empire which contains about eighty (80) ethnic groups, why should this essay focus on one group? Indeed, this is a legitimate question deserving serious consideration.

We have indicated throughout this work that the imperial system oppresses all ethnic groups in the periphery in significant ways. Also we will indicate when discussing the next section on "understanding the political dynamics in Ethiopia" that there is the tradition of hierarchical legacy within the Abyssinian core that favors the winner vis-à-vis other members within the system.

In our effort to further address this issue, we need to frame it in the context of internationally accepted principles on two critical issues: the principle of democracy and majority rule, and the right for self-determination for colonized nationalities.

In our view, the most critical issue regarding U.S. policy toward the regime of Meles Zenawi vis-à-vis the Oromos lies in this: if there is any legitimacy to the two international principles listed here, then supporting an ethnic minority regime in Addis Ababa which oppresses the majority Oromo is tantamount to willingly participate in conspiratorial political schemes which systematically deprive the majority Oromo of its unalienable rights. Also, we believe this question should be considered in the context of the larger dynamics evolving in the Oromo society itself—of course, in the context of colonial experience—which have propelled the question to the forefront. There are several reasons as to why the Oromo issue has become prominent since 1991. Seven are very critical.

First, as indicated previously, the Oromos are the single majority nationality in the region, and it is estimated that they constitute more than half of the population in contemporary Ethiopia—it is estimated that they constitute around 45 per cent of the population in contemporary Ethiopia. Out of the current estimated 70 million population of Ethiopia the Oromo number more than 30 million.[22] Yet they have been the most oppressed, the most deprived, and the least exposed to modernity due to the century-old colonial subjugation and relentless exploitation (Tuso 1982:27-294).

Second, as indicated previously, the conflict in Ethiopia is essentially over power and privilege and which ethnic group and political figure is going to have exclusive control.[23] Power is based on the amount and extent of access one has to resources (Folger, Poole and Stutman 1999:70-71; 100-101). Most of the significant resources are in the periphery of the Ethiopian empire, and the Oromos are the overwhelming majority in the periphery. Thus most of the resources (e.g. coffee, gold, granary, arable land, etc.) fall within the Oromo country, Oromia (Melba 1988:25-27).

Third, the Tigrean minority regime being conscious of its own inferior numerical status has developed a scorch earth policy in dealing with the two the largest ethnic groups—the Oromos and the Amharas. In general, there has been a well-established social phenomenon that when a government inflicts increasingly harsher policies on aggrieved ethnic groups, the tendency to resist increases.[24]

Fourth, there has been a fundamental psychological transformation among the Oromos with respect to their basic demands for self-determination since 1991. In many respects, the fall of the Derg during the last week of May 1991 was the most significant event in the modern political history of the Ethiopian Empire. With the demise of the Derg, the fall of the century-old Amhara power was consummated. It seems that at a subconscious level, the Oromo populace had believed for years that the Amhara power was invincible. The earth shaking political developments of May 1991 proved otherwise. They witnessed the EPLF marching into Asmara with a triumphant victory; they watched with a great sense of envy the TPLF invading Addis Ababa like a mighty army; and of course, they observed the largest army in Sub-Saharan Africa crumbling so hopelessly like a powder house in a span of one week. Then it seems that they began to believe deep in their conscious that they too could do it. Since then, the Oromos, by and large, have shown their determination to reject the Tigrayan rule.[25] For example, the majority of the Oromos have rejected the TPLF created and managed OPDO (Oromo Peoples' Democratic Organization). The Oromo professional class, some of whose members have traditionally sided with the Abyssinian successive regimes, has for the first time rejected becoming members of OPDO.[26]

Fifth, the Oromo mistreatments in the hands of the new dominant masters, the Tigrayans, have become more transparent than any time before in their colonial experience. For example, during the June 1992 elections, it became clear that the regime of Meles Zenawi did not want the Oromos to have a chance to vote for a political party of their choice; therefore, the government, in an open manner, interfered with the process through intimidation, deprivation of the appropriate logistics to facilitate the voting process, imprisonment, and extraordinary killings. Indeed, these are infractions and gross violation of human rights known to the international community.[27]

Sixth, the Oromos are the only nationality group that has a relatively more organized armed liberation front. And finally, there exists a general view that if Oromia becomes independent there will be no Ethiopia. In our view it is partly due to this scenario that the regime develops and employs such harsh measures against the Oromo people.[28] In our view, it is these set of factors which have made the Oromo question more visible during the 1990s.

In spite of legitimate grievances the Oromos can rightfully claim concerning their subordinate status in the new political order, they still receive negative reviews from the West. It seems that such negative reviews about the Oromo people in general are based on some basic serious misconceptions about the Oromo people on the part of the Western powers. There is a common social phenomenon that occurs in all classic cases of dominant vs. subordinate interrelations by which the dominant group defines the subordinate group in the most negative light. The image of the Oromo is the one defined and perpetuated by their Ethiopian oppressors (Bosmajian 1993:356-371).

The state power holders in the modern state system usually project the subordinate groups as inferior or evil or nuisance or all of the above and that they need to be controlled by the dominant group (Adam 1978); Albert Memmi calls this social phenomenon "the mythical portrait of the colonized"(Memmi 1965:79-83). This pattern of political behavior on the part of the dominant group emanates from the fact that dominant groups need some ideologically rooted justification to continue keeping subordinate groups in perpetual subjugation (Mannoni 1964:32; Memmi 1965:xii). Throughout the known history of Abyssinian-Cushitic interrelations, the Abyssinians have always depicted the Cushitic as savages who needed to be conquered.[29] The Oromos were singled out in particular because of their superior size.

Abyssinian rulers depict the Oromo in some seriously negative light. Three are significant:

1) They were called "Gallas," a name that was imposed upon them by the Abyssinian dominant group; the term "galla" in Amharic means savage, cruel, evil, subhuman, etc;

2) They were portrayed as savages who are incapable of developing, and who deserved to be controlled by the Abyssinians. The typical metaphors which the Abyssinians used to address Oromos included "qoshasha Galla" (dirty Oromo) "tebtaba Galla" (incoherent Oromo), etc;[30]

3) To delegitimize their rightful claims to the territories they occupy, biyya Oromo (the Oromo country), intellectuals of the dominant group and a significant segment of the Ethiopianists have claimed that the Oromos are newcomers to Ethiopia. (There is a lucid discussion on this subject in Melbaa, 1988:4-8). Indeed, this has been disproved by more recent scholarship (Levine 1974:78; Lewis 1966:27-46). In this political game of negative projections, the Oromos have had a distinct disadvantage on several fronts. First they remained, for the most part, primarily an illiterate society, due in part, to the colonial legacy which deprived them of the opportunity to develop their language. Second, unlike many other societies around the world which were colonized by European powers, the Oromos were colonized by a backward feudal imperial system. Finally, Europeans in the process of colonization created a new history for the societies they subjugated; also, the very act of colonization provided legitimacy for those communities in the post WWII international order. None of these avenues were available to the Oromos.

More recently, new sets of negative ways of depicting the Oromos have emerged. Two such newly invented depictions are significant. For example, they have been described as a potential "breeding ground" for Islamic Fundamentalism.[31] This is not only a misrepresentation of a serious scope with respect to the nature of the Oromo society, in the context of the post Cold War global politics, potentially, it is a lethal designation in the light of the fact that the West has identified in some clear terms that its chief enemy during the post Cold War is Islamic Fundamentalism. There is nothing in the Oromo national character nor in the history of the Oromo national movement for self-determination which in any way suggests the presence of Islamic fundamentalism nor the ideological orientation which can be linked to such religious based political movements. Many reasons can be listed in support of this position. Four are critical. First, the Oromos, like many other African societies, have three African souls—the indigenous African belief system, Islam, and Christianity (see Mazrui 1986; Nyang 1984).

In general, an African does not become a Christian or a Muslim with the intent of renouncing his/her past (Olupona and Nayang 1993). To an African, accepting any of the Semitic religions is just another virtue which he/she hopes will fulfil his/her aspirations contained in the original indigenous paradigm. Thus an African reaches out to the indigenous doctrine as well as to the doctrine of the new religions for spiritual enrichment. Second, since 16th Century, the Oromo paradigm which is rooted in the African worldviews has mediated between the Abyssinian state and the Islamic forces from the East. Professor Donald Levine of the University of Chicago made an interesting observation relative to the role of the Oromo paradigm in mediating the devouring conflict in the Horn of Africa during the 16th Century. He wrote:

> The warfare between the Amhara kingdom and the Afar and Somali tribesmen under Gran was in some respects a clash between similar antagonists. Both were groups of Semitized Ethiopians, adherents of a Semitic religion and followers of political leaders who sought legitimacy through identification with Semitic ancestors. By contrast, the Oromo expansion represents a novel element in the politics of the empire—the assertion of a pagan, purely African force. And a remarkable force it was (Levine 1974:78).

Abbas Ganamo, a contemporary Oromo anthropologist, speaking about Oromo beliefs, writes:

> ...the Oromo society functions, in large measures, according to its customary laws, Seera, although the Shari'a is applied in some aspect of social life. The exclusive applications of Shari'a in a society where strong tradition persist cannot be materialized despite the Arabising efforts of some religious leaders. In other words, in spite of their endorsement of some Christians or Islamic ethics, after their conversion, the Oromo are still attached to their beliefs, traditional religion, culture and ancestral laws.[32]

Marina Ottaway, in her testimony before a Congressional Committee on Africa, indicated that the conflicts in Ethiopia during the post Cold War period are based on ethnicity rather than religion.[33]

Third, all three recent Oromo organizations—the Bale armed struggle (1963-1970), the Match Tuluma Association (1963-1967), and the Oromo Liberation Front (OLF) (1974-present) have constructed their political ideology in the Oromo cultural tradition not in any of the Semitic religions.[34] Fourth, during the transitional period of 1991/92 when the Oromos were given relative freedom, Oromo elders, after a century of separation from each other by government policy, instantly formed Waldaya Jarsota Biyya Oromo, the national Association of Oromo Elders.[35] The representatives to Jarsa Biyya Oromia were selected from every Oromo district from Wollo to Borana from Wollega to Harar, and from Illu Babor to the Somalia border. This act in itself was a clear demonstration of Oromo national resilience, for they rose from the ashes of the Derg and embraced each other, irrespective of diversity of region, religion, class, and the idiosyncrasies at sub-group level which had evolved as result of century long separation. One of the main objectives of this organization was to ensure that Oromo political leaders would not cause conflict among the Oromo people by using regional and religious affiliations.[36]

Is the OLF a terrorist organization or a freedom fighting force? The characterization, by the U.S. State Department, of the OLF as a terrorist organization is another area of misrepresentation about the Oromo people.[37] Indeed, this has become a source of sadness to all Oromos around the world. They are angry, and they protest when they witness representatives of the U.S. State Department regularly trashing the OLF in the U.S. Congressional corridors of power as a violent or terrorist political organization. To the Oromos, the OLF has become the embodiment of the Oromo national liberation movement.[38] Nothing in its political agenda nor its actual practice supports the allegations that the OLF is a terrorist organization. As the case has been with the other two Oromo organizations—the Bale armed struggle and Matcha Tulama—the OLF political goals have been guided by the burning desire of the peasant masses who have been yearning for freedom from the Abyssinian colonial yoke.[39]

It is instructive to examine the social context in which the Oromo Liberation Front emerged in the Oromo national history. When Emperor Menelik II conquered and incorporated the Southern peoples in the peripheries, the Oromos lost all their basic rights—political, cultural, language, land, religious liberty, etc. Haile Selassie upon his rise to power promised that he would modernize Ethiopia whereby all peoples in Ethiopia would become citizens of the Ethiopian state and enjoy all the basic rights. The Oromos waited for five decades for some meaningful reforms concerning their subordinate status in the Empire. However, there were no meaningful reforms in any areas where the Oromos were affected the most as the result of the conquest and subsequent colonization (Lefort 1983:37; Gilkes 1975:101-136). To the contrary, for every step in the modernization of Ethiopia, the Oromos were becoming increasingly marginalized on a grand scale. The escalating level of the marginalisation of the Oromo people took various decisive policy forms. They include the resettlement of *naftanyas,* systematic confiscation of land, cultural genocide, prohibition of the development and use of Oromo language for official and educational purposes, deprivation of access to modern education, discrimination relative to job opportunities in the modern economic sectors (See Melba 1988:62-124; Tuso 1982:270-293).

The contradictory Imperial policies regarding agricultural development amply illustrate this point. When the Western powers gave generous foreign aid to the regime of Emperor Haile Selassie to upgrade its agricultural productivity, the government used the assistance to dispossess the Oromo peasants from the land and gave it to the various strata of *habasha* establishment—the royal family, the church, aristocracy, the military, and the newly burgeoning educated middle class. Also, these segments received assistance in various forms from the government to introduce modern agricultural methods of farming (Stahl 1974:62-146).

For example, during this period, three distinct yet interrelated negative polices were implemented in Arsi Province. First the Province was partitioned into three parts: a new province (of Bale) was created; the Rift Valley area was transferred to Shawa Province; and some parts were transferred to Hararge province. A relatively reduced territory remained carrying the name "Arusie" (See also Tareke 1991:125-159). Second, the land was taken from the Oromos in Bale to be given to new *naftanya* settlers. Third, in the Rift Valley, Oromo peasants were evicted from their ancestral land by the absentee landlords. It was under this particular social environment that the Bale arms struggle commenced in 1963 and lasted until 1970 (Tareke, 1991, *ibid*).

When Matcha and Tulama was formed in the1963 it was essentially a civic organization. For the most part, it was organized by educated Oromos. Indeed, it was the first pan-Oromo organization in modern Oromo history. Alarmed by its successful outreach to the most oppressed rural areas such as Shawa, Arsi, and Hararge, the Haile Selassie regime banned the organization, and subsequently dismantled its leadership through intimidation, imprisonment, and physical liquidation (Human Rights/Africa Watch 1991:68, 69). When the Derg came to power in 1974, the Oromos were the first nationality group which responded positively to the changes initiated by the Derg (Rights/Africa Watch 1991:69, 70). Indeed, between 1974 and 1976 the relationship between the Oromos and the Derg were rather positive though all that changed after the 1977-1978 war with Somalia.

In due course, the Derg conceived and executed the most brutal policies toward the Oromo people. Resettlement and forced villagization represent such negative policies. (See Rights/Africa Watch 1991:211-236; U.S. Committee for Refugees 1988:14-16). It was under this milieu that the OLF emerged as a national liberation front. Its political program stipulates that its goal is to establish a non-sectarian state. Ironically, in spite of such clearly stated political objectives, some in the West, even in the intellectual circles, have unfortunately, of course, and erroneously recorded in their writings that OLF's political objective is to establish an Islamic state. For example, Halperin et al (1992:126) in their book, *Self-determination in the new political order* state that the goal of the Oromo Liberation Front is to create an Islamic state.

This, obviously, is an egregious act of misrepresentation. The OLF since its inception has been a secular and nonreligious patriotic organization. The composition of its members and leadership is highly diverse and representative by any standard. Promotion to higher positions of responsibility has been, for the most part, based on commitment to Oromo national cause and competence. To suggest that the Oromo Liberation Front is somehow linked to Islamic fundamentalism is as erroneous and as serious a misrepresentation as labeling Nelson Mandela and the African National Congress (ANC) as "Communists" and "terrorists."

Throughout human history, liberation fronts have risen to emancipate their respective peoples from national oppression. The American Revolution and many other armed liberation fronts in human history belong to that legacy. Political leaders who have earned their fame in human history such as George Washington and Nelson Mandela, in absence of any other options, have also resorted to armed struggle for the purpose of emancipating their respective peoples from the bondage of national oppression and the accompanying human misery—physical persecution, psychological injury, cultural genocide, and material deprivation. Robert Asprey, a contemporary American historian, was correct when he wrote the following regarding the role of liberation fronts—he referred to them as "guerrillas"—in human history:

> a historical sampling of guerrilla warfare should claim more than academic interest, for within the context of our day a knowledge of this history, even sharply abridged, is vital to the understanding and further study of a disturbing fact: For a number of reasons guerrilla warfare has evolved into an ideal instrument for the realization of social-political-economic aspirations of underprivileged peoples. This is so patently true as to allow one to suggest that we may be witnessing a transition to a new era in warfare, an era as radically dif-

ferent as those which followed the writings of Sun Tzu, Machiavelli, Clausewitz, and Mahan (Asprey 1994:x).

Basil Davidson, a veteran Africanist, and author of *The People's Cause: A History of Guerrillas in Africa*, writing in the same vein observed, "that such well-directed war of self-defence has been governed by an overall political and moral concept which was always paramount" (Davidson 1981:1). Thus, it can be argued that the contemporary Oromo national movement for self-determination is not a social anomaly; indeed, it is a manifestation of a social phenomenon with historically based legitimate grievances, and it deserves not a condemnation from the western powers but a better understanding and support toward the achievement of social justice for the abused and underrepresented majority in the region.

POLICY OPTIONS

In this section, we will attempt to discuss areas which need fundamental reconsideration in U.S. foreign policy toward the Horn of Africa. This effort is based on the belief that conflict is not inevitable. Conflict is a culturally constructed social phenomenon (Lederach 1995:9-10).

In this context we should challenge a view commonly held, in some quarters which suggests that in certain regions the people have been fighting each other for centuries and that the hate is so deep that it is not worth intervention for social change and peaceful co-existence. Such comments have been made about the conflicts in such places as Indo-China, the Balkans, the Middle East, and the Horn of Africa.

In our view, no individual or group is born with the love for conflict over peace or genetically programd to engage in perpetual wars. It is our belief (supported by evidence) that those regions which have been embroiled in a vicious cycle of conflict came to this state of paralysis because the peoples of such regions have been subjected to the imperial powers which have pitted peoples against peoples leading to inequalities, and exploited sentiments such as religion and ethnicity, for political reasons. In our view, the experience in the Horn of Africa fits this pattern of social conflict. Thus we believe that with appropriate policies and constructive modes of intervention, the peoples of the Horn of Africa can work out their differences based on equity and mutual respect.

The purpose of our discussion on new approaches to the conflict in the Horn is to afford external powers as well as the peoples of that region a new vision with respect to their basic values, interests, and their relationships with each other in these matters so that they will be able to control their own affairs in a more constructive and predictable manner as they confront the 21st century.

The following five issues have been selected for our consideration: (1) The need to understand the multi-dimensional internal dynamic in the empire state of Ethiopia; (2) The theoretical question: is it possible to democratise an empire; the futility of suppressing national movements; empowering the weaker parties and some alternative ideas.

UNDERSTANDING THE POLITICAL DYNAMICS IN ETHIOPIA

As has been indicated previously, since the 16th century, the West has invested considerable resources (financial, military, technical, and diplomatic) in the support of the Ethiopian Empire. While the West has procured some strategic benefits for such support for the backward and hellish empire at particular periods in history, such support did not contribute toward the internal development of a healthy and stable political system; neither did they contribute toward the development of an equitable economic system. They did not help to foster tolerant, respectful, and appreciative attitudes, the necessary qualities for a multi-ethnic state.

To the contrary, deadly social conflicts have been increasing with each decade. The exclusive support to a particular ruler has been inextricably linked with supporting one ethnic group over other ethnic groups. This, in turn, has generated resentment and rebellion against the beneficiary ruler as well as his ethnic group. The negative impact of such selective exclusive support of one ethnic group manifests at several levels. Here we will make some brief comments about three levels where conflicts have been generating. The first level is within the Abyssinian core society.

Three communities constitute the Abyssinian core society: (1) Tigray which included the Christian highland of Eritrea, (2) Northern Amhara (Gondar and Gojam), (3) and Shawa Amhara (Tarekea 1965:1).

As the result of the exclusive support given by the West to Emperor Menelik (he is a Shawa Amhara) toward the end of 19th century and beginning of the 20th century, the Shawa Amharas became dominant political actors in the most critical areas of governance and resource control during the last century (Greenfield 1965:85-95,131-146; Lefort 1983:34-37).

For example, all the heads of states during the last century originated from Shawa Amharas. The conflict within the Abyssinian core has found much more demonstrable expression in the perennial rivalry between Amharas and Tigreans. The Tigrayan resentment against the Amhara hegemony which had been manifesting itself in various forms over the century found a new and invigorated expression in the formation of the Tigray People's Liberation Front in 1975, leading to deadly violent conflict within the Abyssinian core society (Firebrace and Smith 1982:1-19; Inquay, 1983/84:5-14; Tareke 1983/84:15-29). Essentially the struggle has been over four fundamental issues, namely, control over the resources in the periphery, control of access to the Red Sea, control over access to external support, and determining which *habasha* group and which *habasha* ruler will have exclusive control over these resources.

Indeed, we can argue that the policies of Meles Zenawi and his TPLF in the post Cold War Ethiopia are more aptly designed to inflict revenge against the Amhara power for outmaneuvering the Tigreans during the last century than their claimed political objectives of introducing democracy and social justice to the peoples in Ethiopia (Hirst op. cit).

The Tigrayan grievance, perceived or real, against Amhara dominance can be categorized into six broad areas.

First, the Tigreans resent the fact that modern Ethiopia has been shaped more by the Amhara image and less by the Tigrean image. This sentiment is rooted in the Abyssinian social hierarchy. Historically, the Tigreans considered themselves more authentic *habasha*s, the pure Ethiopian (*nestuh Ethiopiawi*) than the Amharas, particularly Shawa Amharas whom they consider not to be of pure Abyssinian blood since they are supposed to have been mixed with the Oromo blood through intermarriage, a sentiment shared by the Northern Amharas, (Gondar and Gojam). (See Tibebu 1995:174-176; Bauer 1977:15-18; Markakis 1974:47-49).

Second, they feel that the successive Shawan Amhara rulers, used the resources (human and material) from the South to consolidate their position of dominance at the expense of Tigray, and deprived the Tigreans of the appropriate share of the spoils extracted from the conquest and colonization of the South (Abraham 1994:159-164).

Third, Emperor Menelik II betrayed Emperor Yohannes IV in his struggle against the Mahadist Sudanese regime in 1889 by not coming to his rescue at a critical time, and upon the death of Yohannes declaring himself the Emperor of Ethiopia (Abraham 1994, *ibid*).

Fourth, Menelik gave Eritrea to Italy and in return secured arms to conquer the South. In the process he divided the Tigrean society (the highland section of Eritrea is inhabited by Tigreans).

Fifth, they (Tigreans) feel that he made Tigray a reduced and landlocked territory (Abraham 1994; See also Firebrace and Smith 1982:18). And finally, they feel that the Shawan Amhara rulers, particularly during the reign of Emperor Haile Selassie, imposed Amhara dominance on Tigray through the Amharic language policy in schools, and when the Tigrean nationalists rebelled against unfair rule, or when they sought regional autonomy, they were treated harshly and with great cruelty, including economic deprivation through the neglect of the Tigray Province (Tareke, 1983/84:17-19). These facts are relevant to the history of the conflict within the Abyssinian core society, and it can be argued that the U.S., by supporting the regime of Meles Zenawi, is fully participating in the revengeful political activities of the new Tigrean elite against its arch-rival, the Amharas, within the Abyssinian core.

David Hirst of *The Guardian*, a British paper, captured this sense of revenge as manifested by the new Tigrean ruling group when he wrote the following astute observation:

> The collapse of the Mengistu regime was so complete that, with Eritrean help, the Tigrean could take over and dominate the Ethiopian state. They ended the "chauvinist" supremacy of ethnic Amharas through whom the Emperor Haile Selassie and then Mengistu ruled. In theory they replaced it with "unity based on equality." In practice their multi-party system, constructed on rigidly ethnic lines, was but a thin democratic façade for a Tigrean supremacy that was even more extreme than that of the Amharas. "The essence of democracy is majority rule," said a former Ambassador to Addis Ababa. "But here we have 4 million Tigreans lording it over 18 million Amharas, and 20 million Oromos—always the most oppressed." The Tigreans dominated the administration, security services, police and army. Bitter memories of Amhara chauvinism seemed to pervade and envenom their new sense of mastery. The Ethiopian state in their hands, they persisted, if surreptitiously, with a Tigrean agenda. The right of secession was enshrined in the constitution while they diverted state resources to their own people and region, and enlarged Tigray province at the expense of others (Hirst 1999).

The second level of the conflict which the outside world, including the U.S., does not understand, is that which comes from the resentment, alienation, and rebellion from the historic periphery against the colonial rule from Addis Ababa. As indicated previously, about two-thirds of the territory of contemporary Ethiopia was acquired through conquest during the late 19th century and early 20th century (Greenfield 1965:108-110; Keller 1988:36, 37).

Thus at the present time, about 70 percent of the estimated 70 million estimated population in Ethiopia reside in the periphery. By their very nature, conquest and dominance naturally generate resistance from its victims. Since the days of conquest there has been a dysfunctional relationship between the Abyssinian empire-state and the peoples of the periphery. They gallantly fought against their conquest and since then have rebelled against the Addis Ababa rule. In fact, it can be argued that the underpinning cause for all the major social conflicts since the 1960s in Ethiopia can be attributed to the unjust social system imposed on the periphery and the resistance emanating from it (Tadesse, 1993:21-27; 51-56; 1998:XXV- XL). For example, the Bale armed struggle which commenced in the mid-1960s, the Gedo rebellion of the 1960s, the Somali resistance in the Ogaden, and the Sidama resistance movement of the 1970s, are all manifestations of this social phenomenon. None of these nationalities, save the Somalis, have managed to mount major decisive wars against the government in Addis Ababa.[40] However, the disaffection and a sense of alienation is much deeper among the peoples of the periphery than the West can ever fully comprehend.[41]

The third critical element which the West has never understood about Ethiopia is the nature of the Abyssinian paradigm with respect to the creation of social order. In the Abyssinian worldview, social order is created and maintained through the application of power which is predicated on vertical relationships without compromise. Thus, for example, a ruler has to either subdue or submit. There is no concept of horizontal relationships. This practice is rooted in the Abyssinian feudal political system (see Habte Selassie 1980:11-21; Levine 1965:245-253).

A typical practice of capturing political power is by eliminating, through any means including physical, one's potential rivals at the local level, then at the regional level, and finally at the state level.[42] Once a leader reaches that level, the common practice is to seek "divine approval" through the Orthodox Church.[43] In the more recent history, the second source of approval for legitimacy has been the external world powers.[44]

Thus we can argue that it is for this basic reason that a democratic tradition which by its very nature requires the acceptance of rival parties as legitimate political entities, respect for their rights, and the necessity to make reasonable compromise with them, has failed to take root in Ethiopia.

It is in this historical context that we argue that the Western blind support of the eventual winner in the struggle to win the highest prize (i.e. the exclusive control of power) in effect has contributed toward the intensification of the vertical power relationships in the Abyssinian political systems leading to protracted social conflicts. This crisis has been aptly captured by Tekie Fessehazion, in his reflective essay.

> Who would have thought that a quarter of a century after the Emperor was deposed, the Lion of Judah's reign, in retrospect, would look the most enlightened (for Ethiopia) when compared to the last two that followed? And who would have thought that Ethiopia would suffer more bloodshed the past year and a half under TPLF than it did under the seventeen years under the Derg? These things do not add up. Only in Ethiopia does each tyrant look worse than the previous tyrant whom he deposed in the name of the people. This is Ethiopia's curse.[45]

THEORETICAL QUESTION: IS IT POSSIBLE TO DEMOCRATIZE AN EMPIRE?

An empire by definition is predicated on vertical ethnic social order: the super-ordinate nationality (the imperial core society) over sub-ordinate nationalities—the periphery (Katz 1996:25-35). Thus, social inequalities are rooted in the structural arrangement itself. It is the inherently unequal relationship between the core and periphery that generates antagonistic social conditions leading to resistance from the periphery (Memmi 1965). Throughout history, empires have collapsed, in part, as the result of rebellion from the periphery (Tilly 1997:1-16). In modern times, all empires have collapsed; the Ottoman Empire, the Austro-Hungarian Empire, European global empires, and more recently, the Soviet Union Empire, are relevant examples.[46]

Are we to assume the Ethiopian Empire possesses some unique properties and as such it is somehow immune from such ultimate fate? Then there is the corollary question: at what expense should the U.S. try to keep Ethiopia together? Or stating it differently: how long should the West continue to sponsor minority ethnic dominance in Ethiopia? If the United States government finds it fitting to orchestrate a war against Slobadan Melosevic to save two million ethnic Albanians in the Balkans which it did so magnificently, how could it justify sponsoring minority ethnic dominance and all the accompanying mistreatments against the subordinate ethnic groups in Ethiopia? If the minority rule in South Africa was unacceptable to the U.S., which it was, then why should it be acceptable in the case of the Tigreans in Ethiopia? Other related questions should include: what can be done so that the Western world can understand the perspectives from the periphery relative to the protracted saga of the devouring social conflict in the Ethiopian Empire?

THE FUTILITY OF SUPPRESSING NATIONAL MOVEMENTS

Nationality movements have shaped the history of the 20th century, in large measure. Indeed, the century commenced with a war in the Balkans which eventually led to the collapse of two empires—the Ottoman Empire and Austro-Hungarian Empire—giving rise to a new political doctrine, self-determination, in the international legal system (Halperin, et al. 1992:20-25). Ironically, the last century is ended with violent conflicts in the Balkans, all emanating from the dysfunctional relationships between ethnic groups and the modern state, leading to the collapse of Yugoslavia. Much more significantly, a great deal more has taken place around the world in terms of ethnic related conflicts since the end of WWI. The global European empires collapsed, in large measures as the result of rebellion from the non-European colonized nationalities (Laue 1987:239-271). However, while decolonisation ended direct rule from European metropolis, ironically, in a rather remarkable way, it further legitimized the modern state—a uniquely European institution—globally (Mazuri 1990:54-58).

Nevertheless, contrary to the predictions by Western scholars—both liberal scholars as well as Marxist scholars—ethnicity did not wither away with increased modernity and the proximity of peoples of different ethnic backgrounds as the result of modern communication (Connor 1972:319-355; McGarry 1995:121-142). Instead, ethnic conflicts have increased greatly since the era of independence. As an American sociologist, Donald L. Horowitz observed:

> Ethnicity is at the center of politics in country after country, a potent source of challenge to the cohesion of states and of international tension. Connections among Biafra, Bangladesh, and Burundi, Beirut, Brussels, and Belfast were at first hesitantly made—isn't one "tribal," one "linguistic," another "religious"—but that is true no longer. Ethnicity has fought and bled into public and scholarly consciousness (Horowitz 1985:xi).

A more cogent explanation has been suggested for such widespread dysfunctional relationships between the modern state and ethnic groups by another scholar, McIver J. Weatherford, who wrote:

> The nation-state absorbed the remaining "tribal" people but has proven incapable of incorporating them fully into the national society as equal members. The state swallowed them but could not digest them. The state could destroy the old languages and cultures, and it easily divided and even relocated whole nations. But the state proved less effective at incorporating the "detribalised" into the national culture. Even though the state expanded across the frontier, it could not make the frontier disappear. The frontier moved into the urban areas with the "detribalised" masses of defeated nations, emancipated slaves, and exploited laborers (Weatherford 1994:289).

The newly emerging field of conflict resolution has developed even a much stronger theoretical concept—the human needs theory—which attempts to explain the reasons why ethnic-based deeply rooted conflicts have persisted around the world. Simply stated, the human needs theory posits that there are certain basic needs universal to every individual and group which are non-negotiable (Burton 1988:187-204). There are several elements constituting basic human needs.

Azar has identified five such elements. They are: identity; recognition; security; participation; and control of environment (Azar and Burton 1986). Paul Sites has made a successful linkage between these basic needs and individual allegiance to identity groups (Sites 1973). Proponents of the human needs theory indicate that the social phenomena associated with ethnic groups can be identified with the above listed basic elements. John Burton, one of the most influential intellectuals in pioneering the field of conflict resolution (in the western historical context), has forcefully argued that no amount of force exerted by the state can succeed in suppressing these basic human needs. Expounding his views on this subject he wrote:

> The implication of this observation is that there are needs of individual development and control that will be pursued, regardless of consequences. State manipulation, socialization, coercion and repression merely postpone the inevitable. The inevitable is foreseeable, given the universal availability of the means of violence. There is a historical continuity in protest against authoritative controls. The state has the means of repression and can survive for a long period of time at great cost; but finally suitably led peoples' power, reflecting human needs that will be pursued, prevails (Burton 1988:193).

Burton further articulated on the futility of the power holders in the state and international systems in controlling the ethnic identity-based conflicts. He wrote:

> In the international and inter communal fields we are dealing with issues for which men and women are prepared and give their lives. We are dealing with conflicts that are protracted and even institutionalized, with no end in sight. Our task is not to find means of containment and suppression, as done by traditional efforts of conflict settlement, but to determine the hidden data of motivation and intentions, and thus seek to resolve conflicts (Burton 1988, *ibid*).

It has only been about half a century since the U. S. became a global power. However, during this short history, in the name of national security interest, it has participated in the suppressions of nationality movements in various regions in the world; invariably, the failures in these endeavors have been demonstrated, resulting in serious implications. It suffices to cite the following few examples in support of this observation: Indochina, Southern Africa, the Middle East, and Horn of Africa (Burton 1988 *ibid*).[47]

EMPOWERING THE WEAKER PARTIES

Power is the most significant factor in dominant-subordinate interrelations. The dominant ethnic group, with its ability to control the state resources, controls the events on their own terms. In addition, the ruling class of dominant groups controls communication with the international system (Yetman 1975:1-

8). The subordinate nationalities engage in various forms of resistance to balance those power relationships (Himes 1966:1-10).

The U.S. government and Western allies have established the tradition of empowering the weaker parties in situations where the conflicts are between the state power holders and the less powerful entities—such as human rights activists, members of persecuted religious groups, members of subordinate ethnic groups, etc., when the conflicts involve the violation of the basic rights of the disadvantaged parties.

The forms of empowerment have included symbolic gestures as well as substantive steps. Symbolic gestures include having audience with prominent members of the aggrieved parties, issuing statements of support for their cause and demanding the respect of their basic rights. Substantive actions have included cutting foreign aid, initiating economic boycott, putting diplomatic pressures including the severing of relations, maximally providing resources for the aggrieved parties to empower themselves in the manner which will enable them to defend their basic interests, and intervening militarily to create a balance of power in the conflict. For example, the U.S. and its Western allies have participated in one form or another in both the symbolic and substantive actions in supporting the disadvantaged parties in Eastern Europe and the former Soviet Union.[48]

More recently, the U.S. and it allies have formulated much more open and discernable policies in the empowerment of the weaker parties in Balkan conflicts.[49] In our view, the U.S. and its Western allies should do the same in the Horn of Africa with all the manifestations (symbolic gestures and substantive steps) to empower the weaker parties (i.e. the peoples in the peripheries) who have been paying a heavy price in these protracted conflicts. As our review in this essay has shown, the Western powers bear more responsibility in the creation of the conflicts in the Horn of Africa than in the Balkans.

SUMMARY AND CONCLUSION

The central theme of this essay is to critique the U.S. foreign policy toward the Horn of Africa during the post-Cold War years. The discussion, in main, focused on the U.S. relations towards the Tigrean dominated regime in Addis Ababa and the implications for the basic rights of the Oromo people. We selected to use the concept of the new Cold War as a frame of reference for our analysis. Three other interrelated concepts—state structural system as source of social conflict, nationalism, and human needs theory- were employed for the purpose of explaining the dysfunctional relationships between the modern state and various ethnic groups leading to protracted and deep-rooted social conflicts.

181

More significantly, viewing U.S. foreign policy toward the Horn of Africa during the post Cold War era on its own merits (i.e. considering the U.S. national interest), we are compelled to conclude that, by and large, it has been a dismal failure. For example, democratic tradition has not taken root in Ethiopia during the last fifteen years. Instead, there have been established substantive reports of gross human rights violations perpetrated against members of different ethnic groups by the government of Meles Zenawi.

Ethnic conflict has proliferated by government policy design. Ironically, the strategy of using Meles Zenawi and Isaias Afeworki against the current regime in Khartoum has not worked. In fact, the conflict between TPLF and Eritrea has strengthened the regime in Khartoum.

Two other ironies with respect to the U.S. foreign policy toward the Tigrean dominated government were noted. First, the unconditional support for Meles Zenawi has not made him a loyal ally of the U.S. for he has been touring the capitals of the states such as Libya and Iran whom the U.S. considers "rogue" states. Second, lately, Mr. Mesfin Seyoum, the Foreign Minister of the Addis Ababa government has been bashing the United States for not taking a more aggressive stance against Eritrea.[50]

And finally, recently it has been revealed that there is a distinct fear on the part of the U.S. government that Meles Zenawi, having occupied a half of Somalia, may launch another attack on Eritrea which will create a military monopoly in the region.[51] It is based on this line of concern that Mr. Benjamin A. Gilman, a Republican from the State of New York, the Chairman of the International Relations Committee of the U.S. Congress (House) has called on the U.S. government to condemn the regime of Meles Zenawi for refusing to sign a peace treaty which has been supported by the U.S. and OAU. In his article which appeared in the Washington Post, he stated:

> By rejecting this plan, however, Meles has dashed hopes to a peaceful resolution to the war. The time has come for the United States and the international community to condemn the Ethiopian's intransigence and urge them not to launch an attack (Gilman 2000:A19).

In light of these stark contradictory policies with serious consequences for the peoples in the periphery, the following five areas which the U.S. government should reconsider relative to its foreign policy toward the region were explored: the understanding of social dynamics in the Ethiopian empire; the perils of reforming empires; the futility of suppressing national movements; empowerment of the weaker parties; and alternative approaches to dealing with Sudan.

The author preceded this critical essay with a personal narrative (in the epilogue). This technique was employed in the hope that it may advance our effort to demythologize the Ethiopian Empire State and, in some small ways,

assist the reader to comprehend the stark social contradictions in the relationships between the core and the periphery in the states in the Horn of Africa in
general, and the Ethiopian empire in particular. We deem appropriate that we
conclude this essay with voices of oppressed human communities which have
elevated their grievances against systems of repression and control by placing
their legitimacy in terms of human needs, before scholars ever recognized the
validity of the human needs theory in matters relating to social conflict. Since
we wish to place this crisis—the dysfunctional relationships between the core
and the periphery in the modern states system—in historical and global contexts, we will present selected voices from the past and present. One such voice
from comes European history—it was a Jewish voice through the brilliant pen
of William Shakespeare. In *Merchant of Venice*, he captured with his magnifi-
cent imagination the plight of the Jewish community in Continental Europe
during his era. He wrote:

> I am a Jew. Hath not a Jew eyes? Has not a Jew hands, organs, dimen-
> sions, senses, affections, passions? Fed with the same food, hurt with
> the same weapons, subject to the same diseases, healed by the same
> means, warmed and cooled by the same winter and summer, as a
> Christian is? If you prick us, do we not bleed? If you tickle us, do
> we not laugh? If you poison us, do we not die? And if you wrong
> us, shall we not revenge? If we are like you the rest, we will resemble
> you in that.[52]

The European political, religious, and community leaders did not heed the
central message in that voice; mistreatments of the Jews continued in one
form or another, and eventually culminated in the Holocaust of the 1930s and
1940s.

Another significant voice comes from North America, the voice from a
freed slave. It was the eloquent voice of Frederick Douglas. He roared in indignation in his speech of 1862 entitled, *No Man is by Nature a Slave*:

> We ask nothing at the hands of the American people but simple
> justice and an equal chance to live, and if we cannot live and flour-
> ish on such terms, our case should be referred to the Author of our
> existence. Injustice and oppression has been tried with us during a
> period of more than two hundred years. Under the whole heavens
> you will find no parallel to the wrongs we have endured. We have
> worked without wages, lived without hope, wept without sympathy,
> and bled without mercy. Now, in the name of common humanity,
> we simply ask the right to bear the responsibility of our existence.[53]

America did not heed the plea of Frederick Douglass, and African Americans
had to endure another century of racism and the resultant brutalization and

human misery before they were accorded equal status in American society. Even after emancipation which was a significant achievement from the status of slavery, they were allowed to live in subjugation which manifested its negative effects in various forms-deprivation of basic needs as the result of legal segregation, physical violence in the form of lynching, and psychological violence as the result of the cruel nature of the prejudice they experienced on daily basis.

Turning to the voices of the contemporary scene, we will conclude this section with three representative voices from peoples in distress. The first one comes from the Americas, the voice of the indigenous people. It was contained in the Manifesto of the Zapatista of the National Army, issued on January 8, 1994, at the occasion of the implementation of the NAFTA (North American Free Trade Agreement). The Manifesto declared:

> We are the product of 500 years: first against slavery; then during the war of Independence against Spain led by insurgents, then to avoid being absorbed by North American imperialism, to promulgate our constitution and expel the French empire from our soil, later the dictatorship of Porfirio Diaz denied us the just application of the Reform laws and the people rebelled and leaders like Vila and Zapata emerged, poor men like us. We have been denied the most elementary preparation so they can use us as a cannon fodder and pillage the wealth of our country. They do not care that we have nothing, not even a roof over our heads, no lands, no work, no health care, no food, and no education. Nor are we able to freely and democratically elect our political representatives, nor is there independence from foreigners, nor is there peace nor justice for ourselves and our children.[54]

Equally as eloquent and as relevant is the voice form the Kurdistan country which came from Leya Zana, a Kurdish woman, a member of the Parliament in Turkey, who chose imprisonment over renunciation of her Kurdish identity and forsaking her friends and her Kurdish people who had been under attack by the Turkish dominant ethnic group. Zana wrote the following exactly three days before the above cited Zapatista Communiqué was issued:

> I am 33. For 14 years I have lived with persecution and watched many friends tortured or killed for wanting to live in peace and democracy with Turks on the sole condition they respect Kurds' identity and culture. I have two children, a husband and many dear friends. I love life. But my passion for justice for my people, who are suffering for dignity and freedom is greater. What value is a life of slavery, humiliation and contempt for what you hold dearest—your identity? I will not knuckle under Turkey's inquisition (Zana, 1994:A23).

Now we conclude this line of observation with a representative voice from the periphery in the Horn of Africa. This particular narrative is from Oromia, the Oromo country. It stated:

> The Abyssinian government is always advocating Ethiopian superiority over other nations and nationalities, whereas Ethiopia means actually the Abyssinia culture and tradition, while a liability to all conquered nations, is masked. In Africa Watch report, it was clearly stated that, to be a "genuine" Ethiopian you have to follow Orthodox Christianity and have Amahra or Tigre names. In short to be an Ethiopian you will have to wear Amhara and Tigre masks. Oromos were and are subjected to such empty superior mentality and destruction of cultural heritage and traditional invasion of the *habasha*s. This may not be a big deal when compared to the regular harassment, torture, imprisonment and rape. Oromia is a common place for such activities by the *habasha* and their henchmen. Being an Oromo in itself is crime enough to be put in jail or be killed under *habasha* repressive rule. It is not today that we became the target of cultural destruction and replacement; the tragedy started when the Oromo lost their independence to Menilik and Haile Selassie who unsuccessfully tried to Amharanize and Orthodoxize the Oromos. The repression in all aspect has continued from the early Amhara colonizers to the present Tigre colonizers. The systematic identity destruction of both colonizers of is the same; their interest is to destroy you beyond recognition of yourself, through abolishment of cultural heritage, traditions and ritual Oromo ceremonies.[55]

Of course, the subordinate status of the Oromos in the new political order of post-Cold War Ethiopia has been confirmed by independent sources, *The Economist* being one of them. In its reflective analysis with respect to the results of the internationally publicized June 1992 fraudulent elections, and the negative consequences for the Oromo people, *The Economist* wrote:

> The well being of the passion lies in a tangled and unhappy history. The people who now feel themselves most aggrieved speak for the Oromos, some 40% of the Ethiopia's population, inhabiting the centre of the country. For more than a century they were ruled and despised by autocrats from farther north: first by feudal emperors, then for 17 years by military Stalinists. Both autocracies ruled through, if not openly in the name of, the Amharas, highlanders with ancient Christian tradition. Last year guerrilla soldiers from another northern group, the Tigreans, seized Addis Ababa and ousted the dictator Mengistu Haile Mariam in the name of Ethiopian People's Revolutionary Democratic Front. History weighs heavily. For now, Ethiopia is run by an army of Tigrean farm boys, while the Oromo dwell on humiliations, past and present (*The Economist* 1992:47).

185

The relevance of presenting these five representative voices from the peoples in distress from the past and present lies in this: each of these cases has had some connections with the policies of the American government. The U.S. helped the Jews to rise from the ashes of the Holocaust and build a powerful state in the Middle East. Today the U.S. pays to the tune of 5 billion dollars for the security of Israel a year (Israel receives 3 billion and Egypt, the chief partner in the U.S. sponsored peace initiatives receives about 2 billion/year) (Ball and Ball 1992:255-282).

Representatives of American Jews play significant roles in running the federal agencies including the State Department. The African Americans in whose behalf Frederick Douglass pleaded some 144 years ago have been sufficiently empowered through a series of civil rights legislation and many other enabling provisions made in the American systems (governments and business) to participate productively in the American dream. Today they play a critical role in the formulation of the U.S. foreign policy including matters relating to the continent of Africa. However, the contrast is disturbing when one compares these remarkably successful achievements by the two oppressed nationalities (the Jews and African Americans) as the results of U.S. government positive policies with the negative records the U.S. has accumulated with respect to the oppressed nationalities in developing societies; in most cases, the U.S. government has sided with regimes headed by dictators and tyrants belonging to the dominant ethnic groups ostensibly in the presumed pursuit of "national interests." Interestingly, the situation in Kurdstan has changed since the recent American war in Iraq. Today Kurdstan is an autonomous region and it is a Kurd, who is the current president of Iraq. Only a few years ago no one thought of such a possibility. What brought about such dramatic change is the fact that Kurdstan has been seen as furthering American national interest in Iraq. Thus, it is not surprising that the other two voices—Chiapas, Oromia—share one thing in common: these nationalities in these territories have been further marginalized in all significant aspects of their lives as the result of U.S. support for the oppressors in the name of "national security interests." Currently, about two-thirds of the conflicts around the world are connected in one form or another to group identity-based conflicts (Rasmussen 1997:23-50).

These human communal groups do not have effective constituencies within the power centers in the modern global system. Thus, they are the faceless and voiceless masses around the world condemned for neglect, abuse, and exploitations by the tyrants who occupy the seat of power in the modern state system. Neither the promise of democratization (Zakaria 1997:22-43) nor globalization (Black 1999; Holm and Sorensen 1995), nor the civil society paradigm,[56] nor the free market economy (Ibister 1998; McMurtry 1998). is succeeding in mitigating the compounding effects of marginalization on such groups.

The fundamental problem centers around the issue of power— that the marginalized groups lack sufficient power to protect their basic interests. The U.S. and its allies, deeply fearful that the potential of ethnic based social movements around the globe may lead to the break-up of the states system resulting in many more states, thus undermining their basic "national interests", have engaged in supporting twin policies—pseudo conflict resolutions activities and military solution. These proposed solutions are usually made for the purpose of maintaining the sovereignty of the states rather than genuine empowerment for the aggrieved ethnic groups.[57] Undoubtedly, the ruling class of the dominant groups find solace in this pattern of policy propositions. This may be the gravest crisis facing the human community during the 21st century. The peoples of the periphery of the Horn of Africa share the burden of this crisis.

Notes

1. The Congressional Record, Foreign Operations, Export Financing and Related Programs Appropriations Act, 1997, House of Representatives, Washington, D. C. June 5, 12, Jun 12, 1996; See also, Madeleine Albright, "Sustaining Democracy in the Twenty-First Century" *The Rostov lecture series,* School of International Studies, Johns Hopkins University, Washington, D.C., 18 January 2000; "Statement on U.S. Commemoration of Human Rights Day" December 10, 1999, Washington, D. C.

2. Presidential Document, Administration of William J. Clinton, Vol. 35, No. 38 (27 September 1999), pp. 1783, 1984.

3. Vaclav Havel, Speech before the Canadian Parliament on the subject of human rights over the state rights, 29 April 1999, Ottawa, Canada.

4. For a detailed philosophical position of the U.S. foreign policy toward the conflict in the Balkans, see *Time Magazine,* 17 May 1999, pp. 27-35.

5. Presidential Document, op. cit., p. 1782.

6. A speech by Madeleine Albright at the NAACP Annual Conference, New York. See *Agence France Presse,* 13 July 1999.

7. The views of Ambassador David Shin on this subject were summarized in *Ethiopian Register,* September 1999, pp. 8-10.

8. The concept of core-periphery is also used interchangeably with "center-periphery." This has evolved to constitute a model of analysis relative to the structural relationship between the advanced or metropolitan "center" and a less developed "periphery" within a state. It is also applied to describe the relationship between the industrialized capitalist states and the developing societies. The concept is used to describe the structural relationship between the imperial core society and the subordinate societies in classic imperial systems. This model assumes that power is the most critical factor-the core has the military, economic, political, trade power to impose its will on the periphery (see Marshall 1994:47-48).

9. The literature on the subject of the Cold War is voluminous. Since we are not interested in the discussion of multi-dimensions of the Cold War, we only cite sources which support the major points in this article. The seminal work of H. Von Laue presents a coherent historical evolution of the Cold War with its significance to the entire global community. See his work, The world revolution of Westernization: The twentieth century (New York: Oxford University Press, 1987).

10. The OAU Charter Article II, No. 1, c; III, No.1, 2, 3.

11. Chester Crocker, "U.S. interests in regional conflicts in the Horn of Africa," address before the Washington World Affairs Council, Washington, D.C. November 13, 1985, p. 3.

12. Ibid. Juergensmeyer does strongly argue that these religious nationalist movements should be taken more seriously not for the purpose of military confrontation but for the purpose of recognizing the values attached to these ideological paradigms. See pp. 26-41; 193-202.

13. Interview with Adam Jillo, 23-24 July 1999, Mineapolis, Minnesota.

14. For example, Ethiopian Democratic Union (EDU), a political organization which had ties with the royal family and the nobility was funded by CIA.

15. Herman Cohen, Press Statement, May 28, London, UK.

16. Confidential Sources.

17. See also, Lucy Hanson, "Ethiopia: Democracy or Deception," Focus on Africa (nd).

18. Many reports about the human rights violations under the current regime have been issued by various organizations. The following reports are representative of such records. Amnesty International. Ethiopia: Accountability, past and present-Human rights in transition, April, 1995; Amnesty International, Report on Ethiopia for 1995, London, July 1996; Abdullahi An-Na'im, Human Rights in Ethiopia, Testimony Before U.S. Congress (House) Sub-committee on Africa, July 27, 1994 (He gave the testimony on behalf of Human Rights/Africa Watch); Sue Pollock, Ethiopia: Human Tragedy In the Making [A Report], Glasgow, Scotland, March 1995. Also, Oromo Support Group (OSG), UK, has produced press releases which contained credible information on human rights violations in Ethiopia.

19. See also Africa Confidential, Vol. No. 19 (Sept. 22, 1995), p. 5

20. See Sagalee Haaraa, OSG Newsletter No. 29, (August-October, 1999), p. 7; Sue Pollock, Ethiopia: Tragedy in the Making, op. cit. pp. 10-12.

21. See the Central Committee of the OLF, Memorandum, On "Why the OLF was forced to withdraw from elections," 17 June 1992, pp. 2, 3; Interview with Beyene Petros, published in Ethiopian Review, November, 1993, pp. 14-18; SEPDC, [North American Office] A Statement by the Southern Ethiopian People's Democratic Coalition on its "Expulsion From the Transitional Council," 16 April 1993.

22. It is predictable that in a political system where a minority ethnic group is dominant, the population number of the subordinate majority becomes in question. Thus, this has been the case with respect to the Oromo population in the Ethiopian empire. With respect to the Oromo population in Ethiopia, it has been consistently estimated to be about 50-60 percent. For example see Grey 1927:35-45.

23. See Hamdesa Tuso, "Ethiopia: Conflict within the Abyssinian core and the fall of Amhara power" (part I, and II) Unpublished paper, 1997.

24. Oromo Support Group (OSG) has documented serious human rights violations against the Oromos. Some of the reports on this subject have appeared in its newsletter, Sagale Haaraa.

25. This became more distinctively clear to this author during the last week of May 1991. The Oromos were calling each other around the world. For example, I was in London to attend as an advisor to one of the parties at the London Peace Conference; the OLF leaders informed us that they were receiving calls from Oromos around the world. This was a great surprise to the OLF leadership for they had never received so much attention from the Oromo people. In Oromia itself, we also learned from the grass roots level that expectation was for the OLF to march to Addis Ababa and declare independence for Oromia. Indeed, during the subsequent months, the Oromo elders confirmed this sentiment when they recommended to the OLF essentially to reject the Charter—this was the legal document ratified during the July 1991 Addis Ababa Conference upon which the transitional government was supposed to govern Ethiopia and pursue activities which would ensure self-determination for the Oromo people.

26. Hassen Ali, whom the TPLF used as the President of Oromia and then demoted to the Vice Presidency later, had a unique experience with Oromos in the Diaspora. When he came to Minneapolis to recruit members for OPDO in 1997, the OLF supporters overtook the meeting and dressed him up with the OLF flag. About two years later, he defected to the U.S. and applied for political asylum.

27. For example, Sue Pollack, a human rights activist from Scotland (UK) produced a detailed account of human rights violations against the Oromos (cited previously). In addition, her interviews and articles have appeared in several papers and magazines. Other reports include: Guddaa 1997:23; Packer 1996:117-127).

28. The OLF, since the reorganization that followed its Extra Ordinary Congress of May 1998, has repositioned itself to wage armed struggle against the Ethiopian Empire; indeed, it has reformed its organizational structure and began working with the Oromos in the Diaspora and at home more effectively. The Sidama Liberation Front and the Ogaden National Liberation Front are the other two fronts currently waging armed struggle against the Addis Ababa regime. Both of these have collaborative working relations with the OLF.

29. It was British Historian, Margery Perham, who captured the essence of the Abyssinian attitude toward the Oromos. Of Emperor Tewodros, she wrote, "He showed a fierce hostility toward the Galla people, and a large number mutilated and thrown over the towering natural fortress of Maqdalla, which he made his headquarters" (Quoted in Melbaa, 1988:46).

30. See Hamdesa Tuso, "The colonizer and the colonized: An exploration on the psychology of oppression and psychology of liberation-Abyssinians vs. the Oromos," unpublished paper, 1997.

31. This designation emerged during the post Cold War. It became popularized by the members of the naftnanya (colonial settlers) during the aftermath of the demise

of the Derg which was accompanied by the fall of Amhara power and the ensuing uprising for self-determination by the Oromo masses. For example, Tamene Amare, the editor of the Ethiopian, [An Independent Newsletter] promoted this propaganda in his editorial page. See the February 15, 1992 issue. Also, some western reporters became hooked to this line of projection. See the articles by the reporter for the New York Times, Jane Perlez, "Ethiopia, Islam's tide laps at the rock of ages" New York Times, January 13, 1992, p. A2; "New glance for a fractured land" New York Times Magazine, September 22, 1991, pp. 49-85.

32. Abbas H. Ganamo, "Islam, the Orthodox Church, and Oromo Nationalism" (unpublished paper) 1998, p. 15.

33. Marina Ottway, Testimony before U.S. Congress Committee on Sub-Sahara Africa, May 5, 1993. To be sure, both Abbas Genamo and Marina Ottaway do state the possibility that the Moslem population may use Islam as an ideology for political goals should not be ruled out. Both make a reference to the Islamic Front for the Liberation of Oromia (IFLO). However Abbas goes further and explains that even the leader of this political organization has adopted an Oromo name, Jara Abba Gadaa. Three more points should be added: First, the conflict between Jara the OLF was a political one, not a religious one; indeed, he is one of the founders of the OLF. Second, Jara never received large support from the Oromo masses for his organization. And finally, several small organizations in the region have a history of taking names which has connection with Islam for the purpose of obtaining resources from some quarters in the Middle East.

34. Adam Jillo, who participated in the formation of all of these organizations informed me that in all three cases, the leaders made Oromo national cultural values to be the corner stone of these organizations.

35. Interviews with B. Badasso (Summer 1994, Portland, Oregon); Leencho Laata, (Toronto, Canada, May, 1999); and Adam Jillo (Minneapolis, Minnesota, July 22-24) on the peace activities of the Jarssa Biya Oromo (the Oromo Elders) during the transitional period (1991-1992).

36. Leenco Lata generously shared with me rather extensive written official documents by the Jarssa Biya Oromo during the 1991-92 period.

37. On 29 July 1998, Susan Rice, Assistant Secretary for African Affairs, in her testimony before the House of Representative Committees on International Relations—Africa Sub-committee, listed the OLF as one of the "terrorist" organizations sponsored by the NIF regime in Khartoum. The protest was universal and immediate from the Oromos around the world. Then on May 25, 1999, in her testimony before the same body, she repeated a similar accusation against the OLF. Susan Rice, Assistant Secretary for African Affairs, in her testimony before the House of Representative Committees on International Relations—Africa Sub-committee, listed the OLF as one of the "terrorist" organizations sponsored by the NIF regime in Khartoum. The protest was universal and immediate from the Oromos around the world. Then on 25 May 1999, in her testimony before the same body, she repeated a similar accusation against the OLF.

38. The unconditional support the Oromo people gave to the OLF was rather a surprise to many parties including the OLF itself. For example, the U.S. government has been putting pressures on Oromos to join the sham elections which Meles Zenawi has been conducting. The Matcha and Tulama Association refused to participate in it. The others such as the OPDO and Oromo National Congress have not won the confidence and support from the Oromo populace.

39. This urgent need to organize for armed struggle was well captured in the historic document, "The Oromos: Voice Against Tyranny" in 1971. The document served as the blue print for the OLF. It was reprinted in the Horn of Africa, Vol. 3, No. 3 (1980), pp. 15-23.

40. The struggle of the Somali people in the Ogaden predates the creation of newly independent state of Somalia. However, with the independence of Somalia, the liberation activities took on state to state conflict between Somalia and Ethiopia. Thus, commencing with the early 1960s, there were a series of wars between Ethiopia and Somalia over the Ogaden which culminated in the 1977/78 war. However, since the demise of the Somali state, the struggle has been directed by the Ogaden Somalis themselves.

41. For example, when the Derg deposed the ailing Emperor in 1974, it declared self-determination "within Ethiopian unity." It was very clear that it did not anticipate the real challenge which would emerge from the periphery. It was thought that because the Derg had abolished the feudal system which included the ending of the absentee landlords would solidify the support of the populace from the periphery for the Derg. However, the events during the subsequent months and years proved the contrary. For more detailed discussion relative to the responses of the periphery to the Derg policies (see Ottaway and Ottaway, 1978: 82-98).

42. All modern emperors of Ethiopia-Tewodros, Yohannes IV, Menelik II, and Haile Selassie I came to power through this process.

43. Berry B. LaVerle's study of the Solomonic Monarchy at Gondar during the 17th and 18th centuries suggests this pattern of seeking legitimacy by the eventual winners of the power struggle by the emperors. See his work, "The Solomonic Monarchy at Gonder, 1630-1755: An Institutional, Analysis of Kingship in the Christian Kingdom of Ethiopia," Ph.D. Dissertation, Boston University, 1976.

44. Commencing with Emperor Menelik II, all the heads of states in Ethiopia had to depend on external powers for resources and legitimacy. After the fall of Emperor Haile Selassie the Orthodox Church ceased to serve as a source of legitimacy for the heads of states in Ethiopia. The Derg depended on the Soviet Union, and the TPLF currently depends on the U.S.

45. Tekie Fessehazion, "Pity the accursed land", Dehai-The Electronic Network of the Eritrean Community, October 6, 1999.

46. The authors of the above referenced book focus on comparative analysis relative to the collapse of the four contiguous classic empires listed here.

47. In Indochina, the nationalists fought against Japanese imperialism, French imperialism, and then the two decades of American war during the Cold War. They eventually won their independence. In southern Africa, the U.S. sided with the

minority white regimes in Rhodesia and South Africa vis-à-vis the black majority. It sided with the Portuguese in Angola, Mozambique. Eventually, it was the nationalists who won the struggle of self-determination. In the Middle East, the Israeli government with the support of the United States laboured to stem out Palestinian national movement; in particular, every effort was made to destroy the PLO. Yet, in a dramatic reversal of policy, the government of Itzhak Rabin signed the Oslo Accord with the PLO. In the Horn of Africa, a similar case can be cited with respect to the Eriterean struggle. Both the U.S. and the Soviet Union sided with the Ethiopian empire. However, after three decades, in May 1991, the EPLF marched to Asmara with a military victory; the Eritrean struggle for self-determination culminated in their attaining formal independence in 1993.

48. The remarkable collaboration between Pope John Paul II and President Ronald Reagan in undermining the Communist party in Poland eventually leading to the fall of the Communist Party in the Soviet Union has been well documented by Carl Bernstein and Marco Politi, in their book His Holiness: John Paul and the Hidden History of Our Time (New York: Dobleday, 1996).

49. The NATO policies to empower the parties to the conflict in the Balkans were articulated by Dr. Javier Solona, the NATO General Secretary. See his remarks made at his news conference on April 12, 1999 as in http://www.nato.int.doc/speech/1999/s990412a.htm.

50. Session (Washington, D.C.: U.S. Government Printing Office, 1993), pp. 51-64. His remarks on this subject originally appeared in Tigrigna quarterly magazine "Azer" and was translated by Walta Information Centre.

51. See "Somali wars: US. fears Ethiopian aggression confirmed." Sagalee Haaraa, OSG Newsletter, No. 28, (May-July, 1999), pp. 7, 8. Trevor Trueman, "Time to reflect: OLF at threshold," Sagalee Haaraa, OSG Newsletter, No. 28 (May-July, 1999), pp. 9, 10; Kevin Kelly, "U.S. criticizes Ethiopia over Eritrea conflict," The East African [Distributed via Africa News Online (www.africanews.org)].

52. The Merchant of Venice. Act iii, sc. I, 1. 61. [Shylock]

53. Rictchie 1968:90.

54. The Zapatista Army of National Liberation Declaration, "Today we say enough is enough", January 8, 1994. (Unpublished policy statement).

55. A statement of appeal by the Oromo people (elders, professionals, women, etc.) posted on O-Net (Oromo internet community).

56. The concept of civil society is a relatively a new theoretical construct to be applied to practical social policy. In particular, it has become more popular during the post Cold War era. The central thesis of this concept is that in order for the citizens to maximize their potential there should be a space between the state and the individual. Then the individuals can come together and create and control productive activities without the interference of the state. However, recent experience in a variety of settings is showing that there is more complexity to the basic proposition. For example, the issue of a differential power base in a given social order has not been addressed. In the burgeoning corruption in the post Soviet Union Russia where the former elite in the Communist system took advantage of the new liberty

and developed a scheme of kickbacks and money laundering the funds which were generated internally as well those which came from outside as foreign aid. Neera Chandhoke, in his book State and Civil Society (London Sage, 1995) argues that the existence of civil society does not ensure the evolution of a functioning of democracy.

57. See David Callahan, Unwinnable Wars: American Power and Ethnic Conflict (New York: The 20th Century Fund Book, 1997), pp. 3-43; David Bainder with Barbara Crosette, "As Ethnic Wars Multiply, U.S. Strives for Policy," New York Times, February 7, 1993, p. A1.

References

Abir, Mordechai. 1968. *Ethiopia: The era of the princes.* New York: Praeger.

Abraham, Kinfe. 1994. *Ethiopia: From bullets to ballot box.* Lawrenceville, NJ: Red Sea Press

Adam, Barry D. 1978. *The survival of domination: Inferiorizations and everyday life.* Elseview.

Agyeman-Duah, Baffour. 1994. *The United States and Ethiopia: Military assistance and the quest for security, 1953-1993.* Lanham: University Press of America.

Amnesty International. 1995. *Ethiopia: Accountability, past and present— Human rights in transition* April, 1995.

Amnesty International. 1996. *Report on Ethiopia for 1995.* London, July.

Asprey, Robert B. 1994. *War in the Shadows: The guerrilla in history.* New York: Marrow.

Azar, Edward E. and John W. Burton, eds. 1986. *International conflict resolution: Theory and practice.* Wheatsheaf and Lynne Rienner.

Ball, George W. and Douglas B. Ball. 1992. *The passionate attachment: America's involvement with Israel, 1947 to present.* New York: W. W. Norton Co.

Bainder, David and Barbara Crosette. 1993. "As ethnic wars multiply, U.S. strives for policy," *New York Times,* 7 February.

Bauer, Dan F. 1977. *Household and society in Ethiopia.* East Lansing: African Studies Center, Michigan State University.

Bernstein, Carl, and Marco Politi. 1996. *His Holiness: John Paul and the hidden history of our time.* New York: Dobleday.

Bichburg, Kieth. 1992. "International observer team criticizes Ethiopian elections," *The Washington Post.* 24 June.

Black, Jan K. 1999. *Inequality in the global village: Recycled rhetoric and disposable people.* West Hartford, CT: Kumarian Press.

Boesche, Roger. 1996. *Theories of tyranny: From Plato to Arendt.* Pennsylvania: University of Pennsylvania.

Bosmajian, Haig. 1993. From the language of oppression. In *On prejudice: A global perspective,* ed. Daniela Gioseffi, 56-371. New York: Doubleday.

Brzezinski, Zbigniew. 1983. *Power and principle: Memoirs of the National Security Adviser, 1977-1981*. New York: Farrar, Straus, Giroux.

Burton, John W. 1988. Conflict resolution as a function of human needs. In *The power of human needs in world society*, ed. Roger A. Coate and Jerel A. Rosati. Boulder: Lynne Rienner Publishers.

Callahan, David. 1997. *Unwinnable Wars: American power and ethnic conflict*. New York: The 20th Century Fund Book.

Chaliand, G. 1980. *The struggle for Africa: Conflict of the great powers*. New York, St. Martin's Press.

Chandhoke, Neera. 1995. *State and civil society*. London: Sage.

Chomsky, Noam. 1994. *World orders: Old and new*. New York: Columbia University Press.

Chriot, Daniel. 1996. *Modern tyrants: The power and prevalence of evil in our Age*. Princeton: Princeton University Press.

The Committee to Protect Journalists. 1998. *Country report: Ethiopia*. 31 December.

Connor, Walker. Nation-building or nation destroying. 1972. *World Politics* vol. XI, No. 3:19-355.

Dagne, Ted. 1995. "Ethiopia: An overview of the Transitional period," Congressional Research Service Report For Congress Washington, D. C.

Davidson, Basil. 1981. *The people's cause: A history of guerrillas in Africa*. Essex: Longman.

De Klerk, W. F. 1999. *The last trek: A new beginning—An autobiography*. New York: St. Martin's Press.

Dobrynin, Anatoly. 1995. *In Confidence, Moscow's ambassador to American's six cold War Presidents*. New York: Time Books.

The Economist. 1992, June 27, p.7.

The Economist. 1995, May 6.

Fessehazion, Tekie. 1999. "Pity the Accursed Land", Dehai–The Electronic Network of the Eritean Community, 6 October.

Firebrace, James and Gayle Smith. 1982. *The hidden revolution*. London: War On Want.

Folger, Joseph P., Marshal S. Poole and Randall K. Stutman, 1999. *Working through conflict*. 3rd edition. New York: Longman.

Folz, W. J. and H. S. Bienen, ed. 1985. *Arms and the African military influences on Africa's international relations*. New Haven: Yale University Press.

Ganamo, Abbas. 1998. "Islam, the Orthodox Church, and Oromo Nationalism" unpublished paper.

Gilkes, Patrick. 1975. *The dying lion: Feudalism and modernization in Ethiopia*. London: Julian Friedmann.

Gilman, Benjamin A. 2000. "Ethiopia needs a push toward peace." *The Washington Post*, 3 January.

Greenfield, Richard. 1965. *Ethiopia: The new political history*. London: Pall Mall Press.

Grey, C. F. 1927. *In the country of the Blue Nile*. London: Duckworth.

Guddaa, Lammi. 1997. "Victimization of the Oromos," *New African*. February.

Habte Selassie, Bereket. 1980. *Conflict and intervention in the Horn of Africa*. New York: Monthly Review Press.

Hagos, Tacola W. 1995. *Democratization? Ethiopia 1991-1994: A personal view*. Cambridge, MA: Khedera Publishers.

Halperin, Morton and David J. Scheffer with Patricia Small. 1992. *Self-Determination in the New World Order*. Washington, D. C.: Carnegie Endowment for International Peace.

Himes, Joseph. 1966. The functions of racial conflict. *Social Forces*. Vol. 45 September.

Hirst, David. 1999. "In Tsorona, On the Eritrea-Ethiopia border," *The Guardian*, 18 May.

Holm, Hans-Henrik, and George Sorensen, ed. 1995. *Whose global order: Uneven globalization and the end of the Cold War*. Boulder: Westview Press.

Horowitz, Donald. 1985. *Ethnic groups in conflict*. Berkley: University of California Press.

Human Rights/Afrcia Watch. *Evil Days:30 years of war and famine in Ethiopia*. New York.

Ibister, John. 1998. *Promises not kept: The betrayal of social change in the Third World*, 4th Edition. West Hartford, CT: Kumarian Press.

Inquay, Solomon. 1983/84. *Revolution in Tigray: A historical background Horn of Africa*. VI,4.

Jensen. J. ed. 1993. *Origins of Cold War: The Novijov, Kennan, Roberts long telegram of 1946*, Revised Edition, Washington, D.C.: U.S. Institute of Peace Press.

Juergensmeyer, Mark. 1993. *The new Cold War? Religious nationalism confronts the secular state*. Berkeley: University of California Press.

Katz, Mark. 1996. Collapse of empires. In *Managing global chaos: Sources of and responses to international conflict*, ed. Chester Crocker, Fen O. Hampson, 5-35. Washington, D. C.: U.S. Peace Institute Press.

Keller, Edmond. 1988. *Revolutionary Ethiopia: From empire to people's republic*. Bloomington: Indiana University Press.

Kelly, Kevin. "U.S. criticizes Ethiopia over Eritrea conflict" *The East African* [Distributed via Africa News Online www.africanews.org].

Korn, David, A. 1986. *Ethiopia, the United States and the Soviet Union*. Carbondale ands Edawrdsville, Ill.: Southern Illinois University Press.

Kriesberg, L. 1998. *Constructive conflicts: From escalation to resolution*. New York: Rowman & Littlefield.

Lata, Leenco. 1998. The making and unmaking of the Ethiopia's Transitional Charter. In *Oromo nationalism and the Ethiopian discourse: The search for freedom & democracy*, ed. Asafa Jalata. Lawrenceville, NJ: Red Sea Press.

Last, Alexander. 1999. "Eritrea says shot down two Ethiopian MIGS", *Reuters*. 17 June.

Laue, H. Von. 1987. *The world revolution of Westernisation: The twentieth century.* New York: Oxford University Press.

LaVerle's, Berry. 1976. "The Solomonic monarchy at Gonder, 1630-1755: An institutional, analysis of kingship. In the Christian kingdom of Ethiopia," Ph.D. Dissertation, Boston University, 1976.

Lefort, Rene. 1983. *Ethiopia: An heretical revolution.* London: Zed Press.

Legesse, Asmarom. 1998. "The Uprooted: Case material on ethnic Eritreans deportees from Ethiopia concerning human rights violations," A report by Eritrean Human Rights Task Force, USA.

Levine, Donald N. 1965. Ethiopia: Identity, authority, and realism. In *Political culture and political development.* Lucian W. Pye and Sidney Verba, 45-253. Princeton: Princeton University Press.

Levine, Donald. 1965. *Wax and gold.* Chicago: University of Chicago.

Levine, Donald. 1974. *Greater Ethiopia: The evolution of a multiethnic society.* Chicago: University of Chicago Press.

Lewis, Herbert. 1996. The Origins of the Galla and Somali. *The Journal of African History.* 7, 1:7-46.

McMurtry, John. 1998. *Unequal freedoms: The global market as an ethical system.* West Hartford, CT: Kumarian Press.

Mannoni, Dominique. 1964. *The psychology of colonization.* New York: Praeger.

Markakis, John. 1974. *Ethiopia: Anatomy of A traditional polity.* Oxford: Oxford University Press.

Marshall, Gordon. 1994. *The concise Oxford dictionary of sociology.* Oxford: Oxford University Press.

McGarry, John. 1995. Explaining ethnonationalism: Flaws in Western thinking. *Nationalism & ethnic Politics.* 1, 4 :21-142.

Mazrui, Ali. 1986. *The Africans: A triple heritage.* Boston: Little, Brown & Company.

Mazrui, Ali. 1990. Cultural Forces. In *World Politics.* London: Heinemann Educational Books.

Melba, Gadaa. 1998. *Oromia: An introduction.* Khartoum.

Memmi, Albert. 1965. *The colonizer and the colonized.* Boston: Beacon Press.

Mutu, Makau wa. 1994. "Ethiopia: The anointed leadership." *Africa Report.* 39, 6:1-34.

Nagy, Tibor. 1999. A statement before the U.S. Senate Committee on Foreign Relations-African Affairs Sub-committee, on the occasion of his confirmation hearing, 5 August.

National Democratic Institute for International Affairs. 1992. *An evaluation of the June 21, 1992 elections in Ethiopia.* Washington, D.C.

Norwegian Institute of Human Rights. 1992. *Local and regional elections in Ethiopia.* 21 June: Report of the Norwegian Observer Group, Oslo.

Nyang, Sulayman. 1984. *Islam, Christianity, and African identity.* Brattleboro, Vermont: Amana.

The OAU Charter Article II, No. 1, c. III, No.1, 2, 3.

Olupona, Jacob K. and Nayang. 1993. *Religious plurality in Africa: Essays in honor of John S. Mbit*. New York: Mouton de Gruyter.

Oromia Support Group. 1998. "Atrocities and abuses against Oromo in Kenya." *Press Release*, August—October, No. 29.

Oromia Support Group. 1999. "Fighting talk: Students and captured soldiers of forced conscription and horrors of battle", *Sagalee Haara*. May-July.

Oromia Support Group. 1999. *Sagalee Haaraa*. August–October.

Ottaway, Marina and David Ottoway. 1978. *Ethiopia: Empire in revolution*. New York: Africana.

Ottaway, Marina. 1993. *South Africa: The struggle for a New Order*. Washington, D.C.: Brookings Institution.

Ottaway, Marina. 1995. The Ethiopian transition: Democratization or new authoritarianism. *Northeast African Studies*. 2, 3:7-84.

Packer, George. 1996. Ethiopia's prisoners of blood. *Dissent*. 17-127.

Pausewang, Siegfried. 1994. *The 1994 election and democracy in Ethiopia*. Oslo: Norwegian Institute of Human Rights.

Perlez, Jane. 1992. Ethiopia, Islam's tide laps at the rock of Ages," New York Times, 13 January, "New glance for a fractured land," *New York Times Magazine*. 22 September.

Pollock, Sue. 1995. Ethiopia: Human tragedy in the making [A Report], Glasgow, March 1995.

Rasmussen, J. Lewis. 1997. Peacemaking in the 21st century: New rules, new roles, new actors. In *Peacemaking in the international conflict: Methods & techniques*, ed. I. William Zartman and J. Lewis Rasmussen, 3-50. Washington, D. C.: U.S. Institute of Peace Press.

Rice, Susan. 1999. Testimony before the U.S. Congressional Committee on International Relations-Africa Subcommittee, 25 May.

Rictchie, Barbara. 1968. *The mind and heart of Frederick Douglass: Excerpts from speeches of the great negro orator*. New York: Crowell.

Rubin, J. Z., D. G. Pruitt and S. H. Kim. 1994. *Social conflict: Escalation, stalemate, and settlement*. New York: McGraw-Hill.

Shraeder, Peter J. 1995. *United States foreign policy toward Africa: Incrementalism, crisis, and change*. Cambridge: Cambridge University Press.

Sites, Paul. 1973. *Control: The basis of social order*. Dunellen.

Sorensoen, George. 1998. *Democracy and democratization: Processes and prospects in a changing world*. Boulder: Westview, 1998.

Spencer, John H. *Ethiopia at bay: A personal account of the Haile Selassie years*. Algonac, MI: Reference Publications.

Spencer, John. 1984. *Ethiopia at bay*. Algonac, Michigan: Reference Publications.

Stahl, Michael. 1974. *Ethiopia: Political contradictions in agricultural development*. Stockholm: Raben and Sjogren.

Tareke, Gebru. 1983/84. Resistance in Tigray: From Weyane to TPLF. *Horn of Africa*. IV, 4:15-29.

Tareke, Gebru. 1991. *Ethiopia: Power and protest: peasant revolts in the 20th century*. Cambridge: Cambridge University Press.

Tadesse, Kiflu. 1993. *The generation—Part I*. Trenton, NJ: Red Sea Press, Part II Lanham:

Tadesse, Kiflu. 1998. *The generation Part II*. Lanham: University Press of America. XXV- XL.

Tibebu, Teshale. 1995. *The making of modern Ethiopia, 1896-1974*. Lawrenciville, NJ: Red Sea Press.

Tilly, Charles. 1997. How empires end. In *After empire: Multiethnic societies and nation-building, The Soviet Union and the Russian, Ottoman, and Habsburg Empires*, ed. Karen Barkey and Mark Von Hagen. Boulder: Westview Press.

Time Magazine, 1999. 7-35.

Tola, Babile. 1998. *To kill a generation: The Red Terror in Ethiopia*. Washington, D. C.: Free Ethiopia Press.

Trueman, Trevor. 1996. *Ethiopia: Democracy or dictatorship? New World order*. August.

Trueman, Trevor. 1999. "Time to reflect: OLF at threshold." *Sagalee Haaraa*, No. 28 May-July.

Tronvoll, Kjetil and Oyvind Aadland. 1995. *The process of democratization in Ethiopia: An expression of popular participation or political resistance*. Oslo: Norwegian Institute of Human Rights.

Tuso, Hamdesa. 1982. "Minority" education in Ethiopia. *Africa*. 37,3:7-293.

Tuso, Hamdesa. 1997. Ethiopia: New political order, Ethnic conflict in the post Cold War Era. *Africa* (Roma) 52, 3.

Tuso, Hamdesa. 1999. "The demise of the mythical Ethiopia: Multi-dimensional conflict in a collapsing empire," A paper presented at the African Studies Association Annual Conference, 11-14 November, Philadelphia, Pennsylvania.

Urjii. 1995. II, 24, 29 August.

U.S. Committee for Refugees. 1988. *Beyond the headlines: Refugees in the Horn of Africa, Issue Paper*. Washington, D.C.:4-16.

Vestal, Theodore. 1994. Democratic deficits in the Transitional Government of Ethiopia. *Ethiopian Review*. July.

Vestal, Theodore. 1996. Analysis of the new Constitution of Ethiopia and the process of its adoption. *Northeast African Studies* 3, 2:1-38.

Weatherford, Mclver. 1994. *Savages and civilizations: Who will survive?* New York: Crown Publishers.

Wolde Giorgis, Dawit. 1989. *Red tears: War, famine, and revolution in Ethiopia*. Trenton, NJ: Red Sea Press.

Yetman, Norman and C. Hoy Steele. 1975. *Majority and minority*, 2nd. edition. Boston: Allyn & Bacon.

Yohannes, Okbazghi. 1997. *The United States and the Horn of Africa: An analytical study of pattern ad process.* Boulder: Westview Press.

Zakaria, Fared. 1997. The rise of illiberal democracy. *Foreign Affairs.* 76, 6. November-December.

Zana, Leya. 1994. "On trial for being a Kurd." *The Washington Post*, 5 December.

Part III

Nationalism, Democracy and Self-Determination

Chapter 9

Languages, Nations, and National Self-determination in Ethiopia

Seyoum Hameso

On the one hand, conflicts over such matters as language policy, representation, education curriculum, land claims are by definition among collectives rather than individual persons. For instance, an individual right to freedom of expression does nothing to resolve the question of language of instruction in schools, the individual right to vote does not resolve the issue of how electoral boundaries are to be drawn. If such matters are to be mediated through an individual rights paradigm, one would need to assume that the State is a 'neutral' guarantor of non-discrimination among the holders of competing claims about the issue. Since no State can possibly be neutral regarding these matters, its policies and practice will in reality be a system of group rights' that support the majority language, history, culture, and calendar....The need for the collective rights model is clear in view of the fact that most of the recent and current conflicts and civil wars around the world are about rejection of assimilation or pursuit of multiple national cultures (An-Na'im 1998:150).

THE POLITICS OF LANGUAGE

This chapter begins with the exploration of the historical background to the elements of collective rights, languages, cultures, nations and nationalisms of oppressed peoples. The present day Ethiopia comprises of several ethno-national groups. Over 70 languages are spoken in a country with a population of 70 million people. The major ethno-linguistic groups are Cushitic, Semitic, Nilotic and Omotic. The Cushitic group constitutes the majority, but for over a century, they remained a "political minority." They include Oromo, Sidama, Afar, Somali, and Hadiya. These people of Cushitic descent are believed to constitute about 60-70% of the empire's population and they live in the southern, western, eastern and central areas of Ethiopia. Semitic groups, who form the other major group, include Amhara, Tigre, Gurage and Adere. With the exception of the last two, most Semetic groups live in the northern and north-central parts of Ethiopia. The Nilotic and Omotic groups live in the western and south-western regions. Like elsewhere in the world, all or most of these groups have their own distinct cultures, languages and socio-political structures. Due to the process of conquest and concomitant settlement of the Northern people in the South, there are sizeable minorities who speak northern languages.

Languages are the markers of national identity. For obvious reasons, systematic study into the languages and linguistic groups in Ethiopia is lacking as it has been discouraged by the state system. Both the cultural and the political landscape has been dominated by northern languages and *ethnie*. One of these languages is Amharic that assumed special status accompanying Amhara dominance momentarily interrupted by Italian occupation (1935-1941). When Italian army was defeated by the Allied armies, the Emperor received external support and attempted to upgrade absolutist feudal autocracy by introducing some measures such as promulgating the constitution, the formation of professional military service, and the establishment of schools.

The first state school was opened in 1908 to promote French language. After 1917 until the late 1940s, Amharic and Geez (the languages associated with the Coptic Orthodox Church) were promoted. Between 1947 and 1958, English was made the medium of instruction in all schools and Amharic being given as a subject. This was changed in 1958 when the medium switched to Amharic in primary schools while English retained its place in secondary schools. The move toward Amharization of curriculum was all too apparent with the associated measures of power centralization which precipitated, in the early 1960s, in armed conflict in Eritrea and a failed coup attempt against the Emperor. The move by the imperial regime was a clear indication yet of the policy of assimilation into Amhara culture. The imposition of language of a single ethnic group as the medium of instruction in primary schools and as official language helped secure the dominant position of Amhara elite in other spheres of life for a considerably long time. On the other hand, it caused enormous socio-political imbalance crowding out other indigenous languages, and by implication peoples.

Through time, the very existence of modern education posed informed challenge to the autocratic feudal system and the whole system crumbled in the face of devastating famine and oil price hike. What followed the 1974 event sounded like a revolution but there was hardly a fundamental change in the nature of Ethiopian state. In the name of socialism, the military regime pursued centrist and assimilationist policies. In the sphere of education, it introduced mass literacy program with the prime aim of mass mobilization for its political goals. A limited literacy program in indigenous languages was introduced, but in Geez or Ethiopic script and all formal education continued to be delivered in Amharic.

In a country where the majority of the people—over 80 per cent—live in the rural areas without speaking nor writing Amharic, maintaining the status of Amharic had perverse role in higher education. In primary schools, the use of Amharic language as a medium of education in the majority non-Amharic speaking areas was fiercely resisted as unfair and unjust as it favors Abyssinian settlers at the expense of indigenous speakers at the state level. According to Edmond Keller, the Oromos, Eritreans, and Somalis, among others, resented the use and imposition of Amharic language "not only because it disadvantaged them in the competition for university places, but also for the implication it had for the destruction of their own languages and cultures" (Keller 1991:140). It goes without saying that the imposition had serious implications on jobs and other social and political activities.

Like any other foreign language, the imposed medium served as a constricting and restricting factor for non-native Amharic speakers who score poorly on Amharic language (see Hameso 1997a). At one time, passing Amharic at a secondary school leaving examination was a requirement to join the only university that existed in the country. The development of indigenous languages and education through mother tongue were denied the opportunity to thrive. Many people were compelled to change their names or attempt to hide their cultural identities. Daily life in a prison house of nations is a constant misery.

The issues of socio-political domination coupled with resentment over linguistic, cultural and political symbolism led to protracted struggle often involving intense conflict and warfare. In the early 1990s, the armed conflict was concluded in favor of yet another northern-based rebellious group, namely the Tigray People's Liberation Front (TPLF). The Front, after assuming control over political power in 1991 with professed commitment to socio-political justice, promised guarantees for languages and cultures, as well as administrative structures based on federal arrangement. At the level of theory, these promises were unprecedented in the history of Ethiopian empire. Within a year, the regime which included the leaders of southern national liberation movements, drafted an interim education and language policy. The elite from oppressed national groups supported the project, in manners not dissimilar to what Dmitry Gorenburg observed elsewhere:

> Although native-language education is particularly important in promoting nationalism, the level of education in general is likely to be positively correlated with support for minority nationalism

because individuals with higher levels of education are more likely to retain a strong sense of common ethnic identity. Highly educated people, regardless of the language in which they received this education, are more likely to be interested in history and culture generally, leading to greater exposure to information about the ethnic group and its history. In many cases this exposure can lead to a sense of community with other members of the ethnic group that is similar to that imparted by being educated in the native language. Individuals with a more extensive education are also more likely to follow current political events closely, leading to more knowledge of the local nationalist movement's activities (Gorenburg 2000:123).

The support for new direction was not limited to nationalists from oppressed nations who joined the Transitional Government whose role, without exaggeration, was important. The commencement of primary school education in indigenous languages was received with greater enthusiasm among non-Amharic speaking peoples. Most languages became official languages of respective "administrative zones" temporarily protected by constitutional guarantees. For example, Articles 2 and 3 of the Constitution stated that "all Ethiopian languages shall enjoy equal state recognition" and "the member states of the Federation shall determine their respective official languages" (Ethiopian Constitution 1994).

The implementation of such broad constitutional provisions is doubtful. A decade after the pronouncements, there is no clear direction of language of education policy and it is not clear how indigenous languages are to be treated in the future. Except the brief interlude of the transitional arrangement in the early 1990s, there has been no open discussion into language policy in Ethiopia. Secrecy still underpins language policy.

Initially, it seemed that there was a semblance of policy shift which had important implications for indigenous languages. The idea of conducting primary education through the medium of a child's mother tongue augurs well with the United Nations Scientific and Cultural Organization's (UNESCO) recommendations. In areas where the new policy was implemented, education in mother tongue was embraced with great enthusiasm. In one such area, in Sidama for example, a development worker wrote:

> I visited about 25 elementary schools mainly those built by our development program. I see that the children are very much interested and motivated to learn in their mother tongue. One child said: 'We now know what we are learning because it is our own language' (personal correspondence).

The issue here is not only of indigenous languages but also of developing the scripts for these languages that have so far been denied the opportunity to develop their own language. In adopting a new script, most Cushitic languages are compatible with the Latin script which is phonetically more suitable than the Geez script. (Note that Cushitic languages have sounds that cannot be fully spelt and pronounced in Semitic languages and Geez or Ethiopic script). The use of indigenous languages was politically emancipating from the bond of cultural domination.

The reasons for the objection to language imposition and the search for alternatives are political, social and pedagogical. Politically and socially, Amharic, as the language of the ruling elite, was an instrument of domination and a device to screen out disfavored *ethnies* away from public office. Initially, children from non-Amharic speaking areas find themselves in tremendous disadvantage in translating, and attempting to understand and reflect new concepts which is not the case for native Amharic speakers. To non-native Amharic speakers, the language imposition restricts access to education and knowledge. Moreover, the early childhood disadvantages transcend directly to later life in which the same mechanism is used as a means of discrimination.

Pedagogically, as far as non-Abyssinian nations are concerned, Amharic language is difficult to learn with Geez or Ethiopic script which has 275 character symbols as opposed to 26 in Latin alphabet. The adoption of the latter scripts is found to be more suitable compared to the Ethiopic script with restrictive impact on children from non-Amharic speaking origin. It means that pupils starting at elementary schools were diverted from studying their immediate environment, language, culture and history and they were forced to learn about issues, languages, cultures and histories that are remote to them, their life and their environment.

There is also the issue of access to existing computerized ASCII formats in Latin script without the need to incur additional costs to develop new language software for non-familiar and difficult scripts. This presents a vast potential opportunity to translate written materials in English and other languages from around Africa and from the world without the constraints of Ethiopic script. Finally, as far as the majority of people are concerned, such a policy is perceived to pave the way for linguistic and national independence from alien, repressive and abusive central authority. Yet the new initiative and policy are not without problems.

The fact that Amharic is still the official language of the government carries all the weight that it acts as a medium of instruction in schools. In the so-called southern region, more than ten language groups were merged to form one region for the sake of administrative expediency. This regional grouping uses Amharic language as official language because it found it impractical to use all the constituent peoples' languages. Besides, as the northern settlers in the South do not speak the local language, they prefer Amharic as official language and the medium of education in Ethiopia. This makes it difficult for the region to continue using any of the constituent languages other than Amharic. In effect, this makes it likely that the old policy will revive, forcing a switch to Amharic at secondary schools. This causes what the conflict between Kiswahili and English did in Tanzania. There, the language of education, instead of "becoming a liberating, door-opening agent, it becomes constricting and restricting factor where basic concepts which should grow with a child, and be added constantly as the child learns more, are shaken midway by an ineffective change of medium" (Yahya-Othman 1990: 51).

Today, as before, various problems confront access to knowledge. Like other poor countries, the perennial problems of illiteracy and low levels of income limit access to educational materials. In the context of Ethiopia, the lopsided "development" based on few urban centers resulted in phenomenal neglect of peripheral areas which also happened to be homes of the majority of people.

One consequence of uneven distribution has been that libraries are limited to the few urban centers. The most affected are the marginalized groups, women and people in the rural areas. In one instance, in the South, there were only a couple of public libraries for a population of over three million people and there are only three libraries in three high schools for that population group. The problem of insufficiency of libraries was compounded by the shortage of books. The lack of reference and supplementary books meant that students could hardly develop their analytical understanding of textbooks. The knowledge industry is controlled by the political centre which applies discriminatory principles in the sphere of education as in anything else.

The real problem remains political. The oppressive and authoritarian nature of the polity causes the suppression of ethno-national diversity and dissent. Though the TPLF regime promised reforms on state monopoly and censorship of published information, the rhetoric falls far behind the deeds as changes were half-hearted, minuscule, and extremely slow in pace. In 2003, even the slightest gains by the oppressed people from the arrangement of the early 1990s were reversed worsening the social, political and economic imbalance. In the field of literacy, most schools and higher education establishments are still concentrated in and around the capital. The major publishers and small to medium-sized private printing presses are located in Addis Ababa. The biggest printing houses are owned and controlled by the government. School textbook publishing is monopolized by the government's Educational Materials Production and Distribution Agency (EMPDA). The same agency publishes children's books and controls the suitability of content and availability of materials for schools.

In another context, there is an obstinate political resistance to the new initiatives particularly from the benefactors of the old regime. The adoption of

Latin script and the new initiatives in primary schools seemed to reduce the role of Amharic. Adherents of Coptic Church around Addis Ababa tried to excommunicate the use of indigenous languages in non-Amharic or Ethiopic script as the work of the devil. Similar loathing exists among institutions predominantly peopled and created by Amharic or Amharanized technocracy.

The leaders of the ruling party, who paid attention to language issues in their own nations, lacked the political will to pursue and encourage the same policy throughout the country. This reluctance caused intense uncertainty as to how far the policy of education in indigenous languages will continue. There are also serous concerns over human rights situation of independent writers, editors, publishers, and educationists many of whom were jailed or exiled.

As the result of political problems regarding the future of the teachers trained in indigenous languages, the students who started their schooling in their mother tongue, and indeed the future of education policy are in a limbo. To compound the problems, the pupils rarely have access to supplementary materials. When translated from Amharic and other foreign languages, the books are inaccessible because they are direct translations and not developed in accordance with the local reality. Therefore, children who started their primary schools in their mother tongue are trapped in the process of language instruction where there is scarcity in written materials. In sum, the key areas of national development (namely language, culture and education) are overly controlled and undeveloped.

NATIONS, NATIONALISM AND SELF-DETERMINATION

The concept of nation derives from the word *nasci* (to be born). A nation consists of a group of people who belong together by birth and/or through familially inherited language and culture (see Kellas 1991:2). These characteristics could be objective or subjective. Objective characteristics include common language, territory, common descent and religion as well as shared historical experience. Subjective characteristics refer to people's awareness of their nationality and affection for the nation. Emotional feelings and elements of patriotism play important part in the latter.

The above characteristics of commonalty are widely recognized but perceptions slightly vary in defining and tracing the origins of nations. For Ernest Renen a nation is a form of morality; for Max Weber it is a form of cultural/ethnic "prestige community" (Renen 1882; Hobsbawm 1990: 5). Joseph Stalin (1912: 8) defined a nation as "a historically constituted, stable community of people formed on the basis of common language, territory, economic life and psychological make-up manifested in a community of culture." Those who draw from the latter tradition seem to prefer the term "nationality" to "nation" linking the latter with demands for national liberation while the former is restricted to cultural aspirations (Kellas 1991: 3).

Social constructionists hold the view that nationalism invents nations (Hobsbawm 1990). In other words, no matter what the past is, nationalists can construct new nations out of completely diverse materials. This could be true to a certain extent; but it is more accurate to concur with Anthony Smith (1986) who noted that nations, like their constituent people, have their social and natural roots. Mazrui and Tidy (1984: xii) assert that nations have strong biologically-derived origins. According to Smith, most nations in the modern world are products of previously existing historic ethnonational or ethnoreligious communities and the history of nations is such that they have ethnic origins (Smith 1986: 11). The same author laments:

> It is fashionable for Western observers, securely ensconced in their own national identities forged in toil and blood several centuries ago, to pour scorn on the... nationalist intellectuals in nineteenth-century Europe or twentieth-century Africa and Asia. Those whose identities are rarely questioned and who have never known exile or subjugation of land and culture, have little need to trace their 'roots' in order to establish a unique and recognizable identity. Yet theirs is only an implicit and unarticulated form of what elsewhere must be shouted from the roof-tops: 'We belong, we have a unique identity, we know it by our ancestry and history' (Smith 1986: 2).

Nations have become one of the most preferred model and means of large-scale communal identification. They are indispensable institutions to the organization of the contemporary world to the extent that "to be truly modern, we are told, one must belong to a nation, better still to a nation-state. In the secular age a man without a soul may be forgiven, but a man without a nation is truly lost and to be pitied!" (Williams 1994:1). Quite understandably, such a perspective of nation-state does not fit with situations where people are forced to live in nations without states which in itself is incomplete, if not tragic. " It is noted that a group of people forming a nation could prefer to have their own state due to their commonalties and due to their distinctive characteristics that separate them from other human groups (Szirmai 1997: 304).

WHAT IS NATIONALISM?

Nationalism is an ideology which helps organize and mobilize people for the cause of their nations. According to Ernest Gellner, it "is about entry to, participation in, identification with, a literate high culture which is co-extensive with an entire political unit and its total populations (Gellner 1983:95). As an ideology, nationalism has often been a powerful force in politics. The mobilizing capacity of patriotism, the emotional attachment to ancestral lands (fatherland or motherland), the love for and solidarity with the fellow beings, the desire and passionate commitment to protect and preserve collective heritage, etc.. are all the works of nationalism which make up a huge store of armory for ready application of nationalist goals. No "ism" has been as powerful as the one linked to the nation. Nationalism is a powerful element of modern society which inspires people in their attachment to their nation, love for the land and the people, thus lending legitimacy to state. The reading of contemporary history of nations affirms that no economic development or even progress is possible without the backing of nationalism. Behind every national development endeavor (small or big) stands collective commitment to the nation (and even to an empire to the extent that the latter stands to the critical elements of a particular nationhood). By appealing to nation-building, national consciousness, and patriotism, nationalism unleashes powerful social forces for change and continuity. The authenticity and the justness of a national cause solicit swift action. No sacrifice is too great to pay for a cause as sigificant as one's nation. Indeed, nationalism accounted for various kinds of social changes including the building and later the break-up of empires. The major role of nationalism, in African context, was in the process of decolonization. In the case of Mau Mau movement, for example, nationalism helped to rally support and mobilize people against oppressive rule. It took the form of anti-colonial nationalism, which is relevant to our inquiry.

The principles of nationalism initially grew in protest against and in conflict with the existing state patterns—not primarily to transform the state into people's state, but to redraw the political boundaries in conformity with ethnographic demands (Sugar and Lederer 1969: 10; Kedourie 1993: 1). Thus, nationalism primarily involves political processes. It requires that a national group needs to have an independent state that can maintain its distinction and reproduce its unique cultural and linguistic heritage.

In his philosophical articulation of this principle, John Mill (1910: 364-66) observed that:

> Where the sentiment of a nationality exists in any force, there is a *prima facie* case for uniting all the members of the nationality under the same government, and a government to themselves apart. This is merely saying that the question of government ought to be decided by the governed. Free institutions are next to impossible in a country made up of different nationalities. Among a people without fellow feeling, especially if they read and speak different languages, the united public opinion, necessary to the workings of the representative government, cannot exist. [Therefore], it is in general necessary

of free institutions that the boundaries of governments should coincide in the main with those of nationalities...

Where state and nation are coterminous (i.e. when the boundaries of state
and nation are the same), then there exists an ideal nation state. The term nation
state refers to the community of people with shared descent, language and
cultural values who reside within the jurisdiction of territorially defined state.
Examples of nation states include the Somali, Japanese and German states. It
does not follow, however, that many a state in contemporary world are nation
states in the strictest sense of the word. Though the international state system is
increasing in number, the large majority are multi-ethnic or even multi-national
states. The viability of these entities always depends on their formation and
their operation in conserving and promoting the critical elements of respective
national cultures. For example, the British Empire once extended to vast territories across the world lending credence to the adage that the sun never sets in
the British Empire. Today that is history and the British state exercises devolved
authority over England, Scotland, Wales and Northern Ireland with the English
language, shared history and enlightenment values as critical elements of British
nationhood. The fashionable term today is multi-culturalism which attempts to
capture diversity within existing statehood.

Where statehood diverges significantly from nationhood, nationalists
demand that the boundaries of the political unit to be congruent to the national
unit. That is, if the rulers of a political unit belong to a nation other than that
of the majority of the ruled, it constitutes an outstandingly intolerable breach
of political propriety. This situation develops through either the incorporation
of national territory in larger empires (colonialism) or the local domination by
minority group, as the case of settler colonialism (Gellner 1994: 1). Nationalists
often seek to reverse such a situation with the motto "Let all nations have their
own political roof."

NATIONAL SELF-DETERMINATION

National self-determination as a principle that a "people should have the
right and opportunity to determine their own government" (Heather 1994: 3).
The "self" of determination relates to the group who seek a common goal of
greater political, social and economic freedoms based on their common language, culture, religion, ethnicity and history.

According to Rupert Emerson, the principle of self-determination

> derives from a familiar set of doctrines, whose apparent simplicity
> conceals a multitude of complications. The prime starting point is
> presumably the eighteenth-century proposition that governments
> must rest upon the consent of the governed, to which the nineteenth

and twentieth centuries added the assumption that, since man is a national animal, the government to which he will give his consent is one representing his own nation. For full-blown self-determination to emerge it was only necessary to secure recognition of a new principle of natural law which entitles nations to possess their own states and, as the other side of the coin, renders illegitimate states with a non-national base. As Woodrow Wilson put it, the Central Empires had been forced into political bankruptcy because they dominated "alien peoples over whom they had no natural right to rule." With the aid of a little sleight of hand the original claim that individuals must consent to or contractually establish the governments ruling them is thus transmuted into the natural right of nations to determine their own statehood (Emerson 1960:296).

Given an opportunity, all people are potentially capable of self-government. An explicit articulation of the policy of national self-determination was made in 1917 when Woodrow Wilson, the U.S. President during the First World War, promoted it as a national and international policy (Heather 1994: 3). At almost the same time, V. I. Lenin also advocated the same idea by defining self-determination as the right of oppressed nations for referendum including complete political secession from oppressor nation or empire: "the self-determination of nations means the political separation of these nations from alien national bodies, and the formation of an independent national state" (Lenin 1964:397).

As a form of international justice, the principle is enshrined in the first article (Section 2) of the United Nations Charter rendering legitimacy to anti-colonial movements. The International Covenant on Economic, Social and Cultural Rights, states in Article 1(1) that "All peoples have the right of self-determination [by virtue of which] they freely determine their political status and freely pursue their economic, social and cultural development." The African Charter on Human and People's Rights of 1981 affirmed, in Article 20.1, that the right of all peoples to the unquestionable and inalienable right to self-determination."

The need for one's own government is necessitated as a result of people being continuously humiliated, undervalued and exposed to harsh treatment. The burning cause for the quest for self-determination is the subjugation, oppression and exploitation by alien rulers and it is born out of the aspiration for ethnic groups to rule themselves and not by others. Aligned to this aspiration is the desire to be primarily associated with one's own group in terms of family, clan, language, traditions, culture, religion, etc...(Neuberger 1986). A feature of self-determination is the building of common hopes, interests and aspirations of people thus bringing them together and helping them by developing their individual and collective potentials. According to McGarry and O'Leary (1993:14), the demand for self-determination is initiated as a

> reaction against ethnic discrimination and humiliation, by the pragmatic expectation that the new nation-state will have greater economic and political freedom, by the wish to have state in which different public policies will be pursued ... or to protect a given ethnic culture from extinction.

These motives are morally sound and justifiable under circumstances but the wind of change caused by nationalism and the concomitant growth of national consciousness may not blow simultaneously across all corners of the earth. The strength of national consciousness varies from place to place. That is one of the reasons why the quest for national self-determination and national liberation do not necessarily emerge everywhere at one and the same time. Where the needs are felt and when the call for national liberation falls on receptive ears, as Williams (1994: 1) argues "a new system of nation-states" is established sometimes by inventing or re-discovering them from the ashes of antiquity. But "where either nature or the political carelessness of past generations had failed to establish such a nation, then serious consequences for state legitimacy and popular involvement would be sure to follow." In the case of Ethiopia, serous consequences have already followed. In his exploration of the post-colonial African states, An-Na'im concluded that:

> [The] state, once perceived as the essential prerequisite for the achievement of the peoples' right to self-determination, is now seen by many people(s) as a major obstacle to the realization of that right. Unless the present nation states of Africa redress this situation by responding to legitimate demands for self-determination, they should expect to be treated by their peoples as colonial states to be combated in struggles and wars of liberation (An-Na'im, 1993:106).

The same author added that "an oppressed or disadvantaged minority or group will revolt, and will always find the means and resources to make its revolt effective." When there is no adequate political redress, the revolts "cannot be suppressed through policies of shifting domestic and regional alliances and maneuvers..." (An-Na'im, 1994:134).

While the motives and the principle of self-determination are, more or less understandable, their practical implementation is fraught with difficulties. First of all, the process involves systems of authority that are foreign and often hostile. This happens, as Pierre Manent (1997) maintains, when a "vote for self-determination, a democratic act par excellence, takes place within a framework previously established by undemocratic means and principles, generally by tradition, corrected or confirmed by force" posing a problem for democracy. It is particularly so, if those who have been ruling over a given people are hostile to the idea of self-determination as they may not willingly give up the favors arising from control and domination. Under such circumstances, the process leading up to self-determination might not be sweetly smooth. Just as it is unrealistic to expect a free government to arrive in divine fiat, a rough ride is expected since self-determination entails a number of changes including those on people's attitude, structures of authority and boundaries of power. As in all social changes, fear is involved which can be allayed by the promotion of understanding.

In resolving a colonial problem through national self-determination, two issues need attention. The first is the issue of linguistic or cultural minorities living within a nation. That it should be possible for the latter to maintain their rights while abiding by broader rules of the nation state to be established. Yet the very existence of such minorities cannot be used by forces of empire or its advocates to block the majority to exercise their rights, to use their language, to promote their culture and, more importantly, to be governed by their own rules and their own governments. Secondly, there is concern over the "domino effect" of self-determination in which a successful conclusion of one case may lead to endless demands within a given territory. Unless common boundaries of a nation are delimited by broader reference to language, culture and other characteristics, various clans and sub-clans within liberating territories might lodge similar claims with destabilizing effect. Indeed, the ground for self-determination need to be laid carefully, for it is of little value to have anachronistic personal rulers replace departing imperial autocrats. A nation to be curved out of old empire ought to command moral and material superiority to its predecessor for it to survive and thrive. Yet irrespective of the extent of these, there is an overriding rationale for authentic nations, uncoerced nationalism and self-determination in a democratic system.

NATIONS AND NATIONALISM IN ETHIOPIAN CONTEXT

On the basis of the above conceptions of nationhood, the present day Ethiopia is far removed from being a nation. The contemporary Ethiopian state is founded on conquest which resulted in a multi-ethnic empire.

Whether it is called the "museum of cultures" by Ethiopian palace historians or "a prison-house of nations" by critical observers, for the peoples who failed under domination, the Abyssinian state was nothing but an empire state whose origin lies in colonial past. In fact, much of the twentieth century was consumed by wars waged to deal with the problems engendered by the colonial conquest whether they were dubbed as "the problem of nationalities" or the "nationality question", colonial conquest or forced unity.

The colonial nature of Ethiopian state produced political movements whose motive is change. The discourse on nationalism and self-determination in the 1970s was dominated by the communist movements that sought direction and aspiration from the then Soviet Union and China both of which stood, at least in rhetoric, against colonialism. A number of movements including the military Derg, radical students and other progressive forces of the time bantered about the "problem of nationalities" without coming any closer to solve it. The simmering problems also gave rise to organic intellectuals and authentic nationalist liberation voices of the 1970s and 1980s. In the 1990s, the political manifestation of these voices succeeded in partially altering the political map of Ethiopia.

These movements, be it in Eritrea,[1] Oromia, Tigray, Sidama, Afar, Ogaden or anywhere in Ethiopian empire, had struggled for national liberation. The extent of the problems of conquest was such that, at one time or another, almost all of the above-mentioned nations produced politicians and political movements whose declared goal was "liberation." Examples include the Oromo Liberation Front, the Tigray People Liberation Front, the Eritreans People Liberation Front, the Sidama, Ogaden and Afar liberation fronts. In more than one instance, the people who were forcibly brought under unyielding arrangement have refused to be sacrificial lambs on the altars of pernicious forced union.

To the Abyssinian rulers who invented the myth of timeless independence in Hobsbawian sense (Hobsbawm and Ranger 1983), the words "liberation" and "self-determination" present anathema. They espoused "Ethiopian nationalism" for the purpose of self-promotion but it has "failed to embrace most of the peoples of the Southern Ethiopia as well as those whose religion was not Coptic" (Lata 1999:165). For Menelik, Ethiopian nationalism was the symbol of Shawan Amhara hegemony. With Haile Selassie, the same hegemony continued, for the most part with the image of a modernizing monarch. With the demise of the feudal autocracy, Mengistu Hailemariam's Derg attempted to reconstitute the empire along communist mould still maintaining Amhara hegemonic core. It resorted to fervent nationalism couched in terms of "Ethiopia First" and "Ethiopia or Death" both based on aggressive, militarist patriotism. It also used force ruthlessly with the support of the then Soviet military and economic aid. Mengistu was later overthrown by a different variety of nationalists.

In 1991, the military regime was replaced by the TPLF. As soon as they seized power, the TPLF leaders embraced two competing nationalisms. First, they were upright in being known as Tigrayan nationalists whose symbolism emanates from Woyane resistance of the 1940s and the political direction of later day student radicals. Secondly, they ambivalently upheld "Ethiopian" state nationalism which they claimed to be represented by their own invention, the Ethiopian People's Revolutionary Democratic Front (EPRDF). The latter is only symbolic as both the TPLF and the EPRDF were dominated by the Tigrean core. For the first time in the empire's history, the prevalence of Tigrean ethno-nationalism whose origins and popular support lie in Tigray led to the politicization of ethnicity and nationalism.

The usefulness of "Ethiopian" nationalism to oppressed nations was put to the final test in the early 1990s when it failed once again with the TPLF/EPRDF choosing to keep the legacies of the past. The superficial construct of Ethiopian nationalism is embraced by Abyssinian ruling elite. It is devoid of true sense of nationhood other than being the projection of Amhara nationalism. Its symbols and idols have little to say about Oromo, Sidama, Ogaden or other nations and their cultural identities. Its rhetoric is full of adjectives to belittle the nationalism of others as "narrow nationalism" or "ethnic politics."

The scene in contemporary Ethiopia involves the forces of the past, namely, the forces that dominated and owned the empire state for almost a century, and the forces of authentic nationalism of aggrieved majority who vie to re-establish their nations in the world community of nations. There is a serious confrontation between these forces and we see, in some detail, the central themes of these forces.

COLONIAL STATISM

Colonial statism is a form of ethno-racial hegemony of Abyssinian elite imposed through the control of state. By imposing such hegemony upon disparate nations, it aims to keep the colonial status quo. It perceives history through its own perspective and traces its foundation to antiquity. Its longing for endurance underlies a set of values and myths that symbolize a historic civilization in the continent. It is this same memory lane, which worships the polity of brutality, power centralism and unitary institutions that stood against deep social diversity. Through these institutions, the ruling ethnic group had literally owned the state to its own advantage. It used single party centralism, as Donald Horowitz (1985) rightly observed, as a mask for ethnic domination.

Those who shared similar myths, though they differ in their action, are divided into two. One variety looks backward to eventual return to recent past including a forced reunion with Eritrea, whose referendum it considers as illegal. This variant is referred here as outdated colonial statism. The second variant is "transitional statism" which presents a deceptively simple "reformed" face of the empire. It speaks for "Ethiopia" whose history starts and ends in Axum, Tigray. For the purpose of building Tigrean nation and nationalism, it does not object to use Amharic-based structures and language. This is termed as incomplete colonial statism. The question now is what do these two variants represent in detail?

The outdated colonial statism is a polity of necessarily authoritarian centralization, which breeds superficial nationalism. For it is non-organic, it suffers discomforts in identifying with Amhara nationalism, disguising itself as "Ethiopian nationalism." Its basics will break asunder if one separates Amharic nationalism, culture and language from its perception of Ethiopia and see to it that whether the same zeal exists for "Ethiopian" nationalism which is merely the form of Amhara elitism.

Here the question of language is important since it becomes the most potent tool of domination and material advantage. While all this discourse of nation and language makes little sense to the majority of the Amhara poor living in the rural areas (save psychic riches) it makes every sense to Amhara ruling elite whose dependent and predatory relationship is maintained by a state that hardly understands the language of change and development.

Those who belong to this current react convulsively to the demand for the right of self-determination equating it with opening a Pandora's Box. Unable to comprehend the currency of the demand by disparate people within the empire, they search for justification to destroy the social and cultural fabric of the oppressed peoples. In the quest for national self-determination, they perceive an ill intent of dismemberment. They fail to tolerate the rights of people to decide their destiny, to govern themselves, to use their own language, to express dissent and opposition against injustice. Given this inherent tendency, they find it extremely difficult to function with anything resembling democratic tenets of contemporary world.

No one other than Mengistu Hailemariam said this more vocally: "unity or death." That is precisely how death, the inevitable, is offered as a choice. This is also inculcated in the traditional Abyssinian psyche, which is preoccupied by and reveres death more than life. Such invitation to the unity of death repels most nationalists from non-Abyssinian backgrounds. At the moment, not even the Abyssinian elite are ready to die for it. The Tigrayans died to free Tigray, Eritreans for Eritrea and others for their nations. To nations other than the oppressor, the products of fundamentalist unity are war and devastation, poverty and famine, and permanent dependency on alms. One should not be in any delusion to expect growth, progress and prosperity while having a predatory group for whom imperial power is everything and socio-economic growth is peripheral. The Abyssinian fundamentalism of this sort is practically disastrous and morally bankrupt because it was proven in the last hundred years to lead to where things are now in Ethiopia: the last and the poorest empire in the world. Having conquered resourceful people and nations, those to whom "unity or death" was a national motto, unabashedly exploited the resources of nations, repressed other cultures, and attempted to destroy the idea of autonomy, freedom and democracy.

The fundamentalist unity seeks to continue the known patterns of domination. The return to the past is visible by looking into the symbols of this type of unity which include a) an uninterrupted history that predates history itself, b) the personality cult of tyrant feudal autocrats, and, c) an Amharic language and values. Anything outside these are viewed with contempt. The products of empire who learnt to speak and think in terms of Amharic through centrist education system, uphold Amhara values and culture as superior, they disregard other values as inferior. They loathe the ideals of self-determination and they are puzzled by its practice elsewhere in the world. They often cite "narrow nationalism" and "ethnic politics" as foes without questioning what they themselves have been promoting since the invention of the empire are precisely "narrow nationalism" and "ethnic politics." Less surprisingly, they continue to pursue failed policies without questioning their outcome.

Colonial statism leads to the perpetuation of an already unequal and unjust pattern. What, if anything new, happens with this is the repetition of the past with greater cruelty and ferocity, and possibly genocide. For it creates hardly anything new, it attempts to destroy everything on its way. For this task, it is guided by aggressive, expansionist militarism and scorch earth policies which disregard the aspirations of different people to national self-determination. For the protagonists of this view, what happened by colonial conquests to population numbers in Wolayta, Oromia and other nations does not matter. Even of recent, the disastrous and bloody thirty years of violence, the "red" and "white" terror, and the instability and poverty that ensued does not matter. What it looks forward is the glory of violence and destruction near and far. If we have anything nearer to perfect failure, it is but Abyssinian colonial "statism."

The second variety of colonial statism, on the other hand, presides in the midst of undemocratic past and uncertain future. Centering on Tigrean nationalism, it tries to take hold where Amhara nationalism failed. Even if the Tigrean TPLF was briefly refurbished as an Ethiopian EPRDF, the social base of this nationalism does hardly cross the boundaries of Tigray. Far removed form its ethnic homelands, it floats over a remote city contested by almost any group. By happily conceding to Eritrean independence, it failed to live up to its promises in relation to other nations for whom it grants the minuscule social and cultural rights. This incomplete colonial statism revolves around establishing Tigrayan ethnic hegemony by holding fragile unity at the center and repressing other nationalisms. Finally, it makes use of diplomacy and deceit as a tactic in its relations with the main protagonists in international fora.

Uncomfortably perched on one side of a precarious balance, it compares itself favorably with the vices of the past. It seeks to gain legitimacy from its struggle to topple the Derg tyranny. By introducing, or at least appearing to introduce cosmetic changes, it appeals to external support some of which it receives in terms of humanitarian aid and institutional support (including police training and equipment to keep the oppressed masses at bay). The changes it banters about include a "broad based" constitution, multi-party, regional and national elections, formation of federal, democratic government for the "first time in Ethiopian history" and power decentralization, the revival of the culture and languages, the rule of law, freedom of expression and association none of which stand to the test of the times. Since practice falls considerably short of words, the verdict on this regime is that it is the last vestige of empire statehood which is fading but uncertain of a graceful departure.

ANTI-COLONIAL NATIONALISM

In contrast to colonial statism, anti-colonial nationalism is embraced by people who consider themselves as being forced to live under oppressive colonial arrangement which they find it necessary to change. The reference and the guide for anti-colonial nationalists are their people, their languages, their cultural and political structures that had been egalitarian and to a certain extent democratic, but which had become subservient to despotic Abyssinian structures.

The nationalism of colonized nations in the empire grew significantly since the cumulative effects of the past misdeeds went beyond tolerable limits. There is broader realization that no government formed on the basis of the principles of conquest can help bring about development and prosperity to the wretched of the earth. On the contrary, the very concept of nationhood of the oppressed people is antithetical to the tenets of centralism, predation and exclusion unique to the empire state system.

National liberation movements that understood the urgency for self-determination have formed a collective block to develop a system of ideas that serve the aspirations of the colonized nations. They know that the implementation of these ideas does not take place within the existing apparatus of domination and colonial rule.

The social movements for change have several justifications to invoke the right to national self-determination. First, the colonized people in Ethiopia have suffered systematic discrimination and abuse, not to mention systematic genocide, perpetuated by colonial rule. They were denied opportunities to improve their lot. It is now evident that the people of the oppressed nations cannot expect to be served fairly and reasonably by colonial elite. No hope, progress, or freedom is forthcoming from predatory class that preaches ignorance, imposes dark rule of the jungle and ignites violence. Neither decent living standards nor modest growth is possible in the colonized nations with a dependent and poverty-perpetuating colonial rule. The people of the colonized nations can only be served better if they govern themselves and if they are ruled by their own laws and by their own people.

Second, the gap between the worldviews of the colonized nations and that of the predatory ones is ever widening. As historical symbols are increasingly contested, differences in aspirations are deepening. For example, the heroes and the symbols of oppressors from the northern core are the symbols of subordination of the colonized nations. In other words, the symbols of pride of the oppressor are the very symbols of suffering for the colonized people. Some of these include Menelik's conquest, imposition of a belief system based on Coptic Orthodox Church, and the socio-linguistic dominance of northern highland language(s). Since the perceptions of the past are different, the diagnosis of the current problems and the prescribed solutions of the future too are divergent if not diametrically opposed. The scenario of centralized empire state is unacceptable to the oppressed, but that is what the oppressors want to impose.

Third, there is a degree of evolving consensus in the demand for national self-determination among the oppressed nations. It has become ever increasingly visible that the Ethiopian empire's national composition and internal constitution remains unstable, unbalanced, abnormal and backward. The quest for liberation is strongly felt by nations that developed the political culture of resistance against growing repression by violent state. As An-Na'im maintains

> The higher the degree of the internal cohesion and self-identification of the people, the greater their historical claim to separate identity; the more they are deprived of their basic human rights under their present "nation" state, the stronger would be their case for secession. (An-Na'im 1993:114)

Indeed, the case of the oppressed nations fulfils most of the criteria enumerated for the validity of claims for self-determination such as: (i) the degree of internal cohesion and self-identification of the group claiming self-determination, (ii) the nature and scope of their claim, (iii) the underlying reasons for the claim, and (iv) the degree of deprivation of basic human rights for the people in question (Nanda 1981:275-78).

Fourth, the principle of self-determination is based on the notion of democracy that a government should be based on the consent of the governed and its free association and entry into the political bond. The very basis of the conquest state and the culture that was built around it preclude both possibilities requiring the fulfillment of the principle by forms other than the existing constitutional arrangement. In the Ethiopia context, there is no consent of the governed; neither there is agreement on the rules of the game. Dissent is meted out with flagrant violation of human rights and acts of genocide.

The execution of the goal of liberation depends on conscious and farsighted leadership. In every African country since independence, political leadership has proved so decisive. The leaders, intellectuals, and opinion makers need to be acutely well informed and responsible in accomplishing their duties. The need to promote scholarship and research on the problems and prospects of the nations is significant. Indeed,

> Africans must develop and learn to operate their own nation-states in order to exercise their right to self-determination in the modern world. In my view, the necessary resources for this already exist in African cultural traditions, albeit in somewhat rudimentary form. To the extent that one can speak of African culture in general, there are certainly rich traditions of political consultation or government by consensus and communitarian welfare which can now be utilized to promote African constitutional models (An-Na'im, 1994:121).

In the absence of success in realizing the demand for self-determination including the formation of a separate political roof, there is a grave danger for any other method to protect and promote the collective rights of a social group, and the individual rights of its members. In the case of Ethiopia, the failure of constitutional forum to resolve the outstanding claim by national liberation movements, has forced the default option of resort to violence.

Cognizant of the fact that there is no going back, nationalists bear the burden to retrieve their past, to re-invent and relive their collective memories and to master the ways of how contemporary world operates. In Gramscian sense of organic intellectuals, they are self consciously aware of their vanguard position. In all that they do, they require a vision, clear-minded, determined and dynamic leadership and workable organizations peopled by skillful characters adept at strategic thinking. The challenge of nationalists is to reconcile their past socio-political systems including the *Gada*, the *Luwa* and other forms with the contemporary world setting of political and social democracy.

In their quests for freedom, they evoke democratic rights enshrined in the UN Charter—the right of peoples to national self-determination. They also indicate an alternative future with organic nation building on the ashes of unyielding and imposed empire. The implications are many, both local and global. The tasks are huge but they are never insurmountable for one simple reason that, at one time or another, all great nations and nationalists have done it and are doing it.

In this task, nationalist intellectuals have a historic, moral and social responsibility in codifying the national language of their people, generating a national literature, creating political vision, establishing and promoting diverse civic associations. The basis for their vision and societal model should never be the dying "lions" but living people with humane aspirations.

Their aim towards achieving national self-determination requires the promotion of nationalism, national consensus and the sense of belongingness. They need to develop hitherto neglected cultures, languages and histories with the aim of re-creating solid national identity (via symbolism, events, personalities, places and historical experience). They also aim at developing national symbols including promoting music, recording folklore, legend and history—the elements of national "iconography."

What is important for those who want to get rid of the burden of colonial domination is far removed from fanaticism and fatalism (be it religious or ideological). Precisely, they ought to avoid articulating regional, class and religious divides and they must keep on protecting and achieving, be it the revival of language and culture, development of education and people's political awareness.

Finally, as far as the future of nations and nationalism in Ethiopian empire is concerned, what matters most are the forces of the future, of justice, and of democracy. By either making mistakes or working towards the creation of their nations, their action would carry the heaviest of weight in determining any future arrangement. The success to bring lasting and speedy end to Abyssinian tragedy depends on their determination. To wait for the current power holder to give away its position and take on board the unity based on equality and respect is merely wishful thinking.

Note

1. Eritrea was an Italian colony from 1890 until 1941 by which time the UN/British protectorate was set up. The trusteeship ended in 1952 when Eritrea was federated with Ethiopia. In 1962, Haile Selassie dissolved the federation and with that action, the longest war for independence in Africa had begun culminating in a de facto freedom in 1991 and formal independence in 1993.

References

An-Na'im, Abdullahi. 1993. The national question, secession and constitutionalism: the mediation of competing claims to self-determination. In *Constitutionalism and democracy: Transitions in the contemporary world* ed. Stanley N. Katz, Doug Greenberg and Steve Wheatley. New York: Oxford University Press.

An-Na'im, Abdullahi. 1994. Eritrean independence and African constitutionalism: A Sudanese perspective. In *Eritrea and Ethiopia: From conflict to cooperation,* ed. Amare Tekle. Lawrenceville: The Red Sea Press.

An-Na'im, Abdullahi. 1998. Human rights and the challenge of relevance: The case of collective rights." In *The role of the nation-state in the 21st century: Human rights, international organizations and foreign policy, Essays in Honour of Peter Baehr,* Monique Castermans-Holleman, Fried van Hoof & Jacqueline Smith, eds. The Hague: Kluwer Law International.

Emerson, Rupert. 1960. *From empire to nation: The rise to self-assertion of Asian and African peoples.* Boston: Beacon Press.

Gellner, E. 1983. *Nations and nationalism.* Oxford; Blackwell.

Gellner, E. 1994. *Encounters with nationalism.* Oxford: Blackwell.

Gorenburg, Dmitry. 2000. Not with one voice: An explanation of intra-group variation in nationalist sentiment. *World Politics.* 53, 115-142.

Hameso, Seyoum. 1997a. The language of education in Africa: The key issues, in *Language, Culture, and Curriculum.* 10, 1, 1-13.

_____ 1997b. *Ethnicity and nationalism in Africa.* New York: Nova Science Publishers.

Heather, D. 1994. *National self-determination: Woodrow Wilson and his legacy.* Houndmills, Basingstoke: Macmillan.

Hobsbawm, E. J. and T. Ranger., eds. 1983. *The invention of tradition.* Cambridge: Cambridge University Press.

Hobsbawm, E. J. 1990. *Nations and nationalism since 1870: Program, myth, reality.* Cambridge: Cambridge University Press.

Horowitz, D. 1985. *Ethnic groups in conflict.* Berkeley: University of California Press.

Kedourie, E. 1993. *Nationalism,* 4th edn. Oxford, Blackwel.

Kellas, J. 1991. Politics of nationalism and ethnicity. London: Macmillan Press.

Keller, E. 1991. *Revolutionary Ethiopia: From empire to people's republic.* Bloomington and Indianapolis: Indiana University Press.

Lenin, V.I. 1964. *Collected works,* 4th English edn. Progress Publishers: Moscow.

Lata, Leenco. 1999. *The Ethiopian state at crossroads:Decolonization & democratization or disintegration.* Lawrencevill, NJ and Asmara: The Red Sea Press.

McGarry, J. and B. O'Leary, eds. 1993. *The politics of ethnic conflict regulation: Case studies of protracted ethnic conflicts.* London and New York: Routledge.

Manent, P. 1997. Democracy without nations? *Journal of Democracy.* 8,2, 92-102.

Mazrui, A. and M. Tidy 1984. *Nationalism and new states in Africa.* London: Heinemann.

Mill, John. 1910. *Utilitarianism, liberty and representative government.* London: Dent.

Nanda, Ved. 1981. Self-determination under international Law: Validity of claims to secede. *Case Western Reserve Journal of International Law.* 13:257-280.

Renen, E. 1882. *Qu'est-cequ'une nation.* Paris: Calmann-Levy.

Smith, A. 1986. *The ethnic origin of nations.* Oxford: Balckwell.

Sorenson, J. 1993. *Imagining Ethiopia: Struggles for history and identity in the Horn of Africa.* New Burnswick: Rutgers University Press.

Stalin, J. 1912. *Marxism and the national and colonial question*, np.

Sugar, P. and I. Lederer. 1969. *Nationalism in Eastern Europe.* Seattle: University of Washington Press.

Szirmai, A. 1997. *Economic and social development.* Hempstead: Prentice Hall.

Williams, Colin. 1994. *Called unto liberty! On language and nationalism*: Multilingual Matters.

Yahya-Othman, S. 1990 When international languages clash: The possible detrimental effects on development of the conflict between English and Kiswahili in Tanzania. In *Languages in Education in Africa,* ed. C. Rubagumya. Clevedon: Multilingual Matters

Chapter 10

Sidama Nationalism and National Identity Problems in Ethiopia

Mulugeta Daye

THE RISE OF SIDAMA NATIONALSIM

The onset of Sidama nationalism can be traced back to the decades of conquest and colonialism. Spontaneous and less articulated anti-colonization movements in Sidama had started in reaction to the Amharization policy of Menelik II of Ethiopia and his successors. Traditional religious movements grew stronger among the Sidama after 1931 when the Ethiopian Orthodox Church started to baptize the followers of Sidama traditional religion against their will. At that time, there was no distinction between the said church and expanding Ethiopian empire, as the clergy were facilitating the assimilation process. For the Sidama people, the period was one of severe stress. In the face of dissatisfaction with the existing world, they looked forward to the better one whose imminent arrival was articulated by local prophets.

The prophets claimed that Amhara domination would end. They announced that oppressive rulers would soon leave the Sidama, abandoning what they had collected from the people. They urged their followers to stop paying taxes to the government whose station was about to disappear. They said that the spirit of their ancestors would liberate the people from the Amhara trap, if they persisted in their loyalty to ancestors. After this prophecy, Italy occupied Ethiopia authenticating the realization of the prophecy. As far as the prophecy is concerned, Italian occupation came to represent liberation from the Amhara domination. According to the information collected by this author while conducting research on socio-political history, the Sidama nation enjoyed more freedom during the Italian occupation which was short-lived.

Prophetic movements have generally been initiated by particular individuals who predicted that if people act in a certain way, the desired state of affairs, usually involving a return to a happy and more stable existence will some how come about.

The circumstances under which anti-colonization movements had developed in Sidama were ones of acute social change, where old ways of life have been disrupted, but full assimilation into the new culture has not been achieved. Traditional culture in the Sidama placed a great deal of emphasis on exchange and reciprocity as bases for building relationships and achieving prestige. People cemented friendships, built alliances and resolved disputes by mounting large-scale exchanges with others. The Amhara settlers who arrived in Sidama did not share the same view of relationships. Taking advantage of control over extremely attractive economic goods such as gold, ivory, coffee and land, they refused to enter into proper exchange relations with the local people. Instead, they instituted oppressive administrative structures and acted as superiors. Therefore, the Sidama preoccupation with anti-colonization became a way of rebuilding a sense of independence and prestige in the face of Amhara domination.

Anti-colonial movement in Sidama had largely religious overtures offering credence to the view that religions do not always perform purely conservative functions with respect to conflictive social relationships of dominance. In other words, religions do not necessarily constitute an obstacle to the autonomy of subordinate groups or their alliance against domination. In societies like that of the Sidama, whose world outlook is predominantly religious, the Amhara influence has caused cultural disorientation and political disempowerment. When native Sidamas were in subjection to relationships of dominance, when they found themselves reduced to subordinate positions, they were directed towards developing a strategy of autonomy and striking an alliance against it.

The spirit of ancestors known as the *Akaako cults* have provided the Sidama people with the basis for reorganization, by creating conducive ground for group consciousness, organization and mobilization. Group consciousness means that the Sidamas perceived themselves as a dominated group distinct from the dominating Amhara. This perception reached not only implicit consciousness of their difference from the dominant Amhara, but also attained an explicit perception of collective opposition and rejection of domination. Akaako cults played a vital role as the active medium through which the Sidama accepted the struggle as inspired by supernatural forces, i.e. ancestors' spirit.

In terms of group organization, Akaako cults gave the Sidama the unity for continuous existence and periodically repeated collective utilization of space, time and resources to prepare themselves, to design, to plan activities and to achieve agreed upon plan. In terms of group mobilization, the Akaako served to bring together scattered resources of the Sidama not simply in spontaneous and discontinuous actions of protest expressing the demands of isolated groups, but also in the systematic and continuous actions of gradually accelerating offensive against political and economic domination.

These actions paved the way to broaden and deepen the transformative capacity of Sidama power. Through the experience of failure and success of Akaako cults, the Sidama learned and began to develop secular political organizations. Then the cults tend to loose their importance as channels of protest. This role of the cults laid the foundation for secular political organization to further the struggle. For example, the Sidama Liberation Front has been fighting against identity-based domination of Amharas, Tigreans, Gurages and others who serve as instruments to sustain colonial domination.

The survival of indigenous political institutions is due to nascent nationalism despite untold torture and sustained pressure to destroy traditional values, their religious beliefs, passing the audacious performance of the past generation by oral literature, poems and songs such as *weeddo, faaro, geeraarsha, hano,* and *haarokkise.* The latter, in turn, served as the sources of inspiration for one to be proud of being Sidama and the survival of its nationalism.

Sidama nationalism also created its heroes and villains. Great personalities like Alito Hewano fought not only black colonialism but also Italian attempt to colonize Sidama. Other personalities include Lanqamo Naare, Yetera Bolle, Taklu Yota, and Lalimo Daye. Fiisa Ficho is another great soul who laid the foundation for Sidama nationalism and organized political struggle.

Contemporary organized political struggle of the Sidama nation started in the 1970s with the Sidama Liberation Movement that later opted to be called the Sidama Liberation Front. The Front was established by few nationalist Sidamas who fought against the Derg regime for national self-determination. Those Sidamas who were willing to work with the Derg regime without loosing their national identity consciousness were killed or jailed. Matewos Korsiisa, for example, was killed by the Derg regime on false allegation instigated by Tefera Endalewu, a northern appointed administrator of the then Sidamo region.

SIDAMA NATIONALISM AND ETHIOPIAN NATIONAL IDENTITY CRISIS

The development of Sidama nationalism and the demand for national self-determination put forward by the Sidama liberation organizations contributed to the crisis of identity associated with the Ethiopian state. For the nations under domination, the demand of self-determination is the question of political identity. Political identity as a concept is associated with ethnicity, religion, class, gender, occupation or profession (Axford 1997:92). If people's political identity (for example, ethnicity or religion) conflicts with the identity associated with the

state in which they live, this might be the result of the nature of the state formation or the manner in which the ruling group exercises its power over citizens.

The current authorities in Ethiopia presume that their federal structure
effectively answered the question of various nations and nationalities. This
chapter discusses the causes and consequences of problems in political identity
conflicts in oppressed nations in general and the Sidama in particular. It also
looks into the present Ethiopian constitution in relation to the problems of
political identity conflict and the feeling it has created among those nations
that have been under the domination of a single ethnic group. Drawing on the
experience of the Southern nations, it attempts to substantiate or challenge
what Ethiopian authorities said or ignored about the issue.

One of the causes of political identity conflicts in Ethiopia is the nature of
state formation. The conquest (as defined by Rex 1995:28) and colonization
of the southern, eastern and western parts of present day Ethiopia by Menelik
of Abyssinia in the 1880s and 1890s, had laid the foundation of contemporary
Ethiopian state. Before the conquest, peoples of these nations had autonomous kingdoms and states inhabited by different nations including Oromo,
Sidama, Wolayita, Kaffa, Benishangul, Gumuz, Somali and Afar. These nations
and their respective peoples were forced to give up not only their economic
resources but also their national identity, their organic social institutions and
practices for Amharization and forced Christianization. Amharization is the
policy and process of assimilating other ethnic groups into the cultural values
of Amhara. Under this policy, the conquered nations were "forced to assimilate
into the culture of the dominant nation—mainly Amhara nation" (Mengsteab
1997:111-132).

An example is the forced Christianization as an attempt to imitate European colonizers which also served as the pretext for the conquest of independent
nations. It was also the fashion of the day to destroy indigenous political, social
and economic system and people's identity. Yet Amharization and Coptic Christianization have been far from containing the incentives for transferring loyalty
from indigenous cultural, religious and organic social structures and practices to
Abyssinian values. On the contrary, it was repressive, brutal, unjust and divergent
from indigenous values. Abyssinian colonizers found the organic social, economic
and political systems of conquered nations, such as Luwa, Akaako cult, Ayidooma
of the Sidama and the Gada and Erecha of the Oromo nations to be negative and
constrictive.

Successive Abyssinian leaders have been exerting maximum effort to dominate other ethnic groups and pretending as the master race in the region. On the
other hand, they have not been confident on the validity and rationality of their
institutions. It is observed that they have been trying to import and implement

institutions and values from the West to East without realizing the socio-economic context under which they have been operating their brutal system. This imposition of alien institutions and values has corrupted the existing values and systems including their own. Because they were not in a position to solve the contradiction that may arise between imported systems and their ambition to be master race in the region, as well as their failure to learn, understand and recognize the validity, and rationality of conquered nations' values and systems, consecutive Ethiopian governments have prevented the development of non-Amhara centered knowledge.

Non-Amharized ethnic groups were not allowed to have schools of their own, teach their culture, history and values to their children. When they speak their mother language, they were bullied and called Galla in the case of the Oromo. The few children from non-Amhara origin who went to the school in Ethiopia were forced to learn Amhara's history, culture, and language that contradicted with the values of other groups such as the Oromo, the Sidama, Wolayita, Afar, Somali, and others. The students from non-Amhara origin were forced to despise their identity. They had to change their names that reflected the meanings and values of their own identities for Amhara names.

The second cause of political identity conflict in Ethiopia is associated with the manner in which the ruling Amhara ethnic group had exercised its power over other ethnic groups and citizens in the conquered areas. The latter were dehumanized and treated as second-class subjects. The political structures were highly oppressive and highly centralized. None of these were acceptable to oppressed people who mount stiff resistance to subjugation and oppression.

The third circumstance in which political identity conflicts have arisen has been through acute political, social and economic changes, where customary ways of life have been disrupted by conquest and yet full assimilation into the new culture (of Amharization) has not been achieved. Traditional culture in the conquered areas placed a great deal of emphasis on exchange of gifts as a basis for building friendship and achieving prestige. People cemented friendships, built alliances and resolved disputes through the system of exchanges of economic materials with others (Gellner 1983: 84-87).

The people of Amhara ethnicity, who conquered and colonized the said groups, did not share the same view of how these people built relationships and alliances. They established political dominance, and control over economic resources. They refused to enter into palatable exchange relations with the local people. They instituted oppressive structures to enhance their political power and acted as superiors. Even in the parliament which was created by Emperor Haile Selassie to disguise the nature of Amhara domination, colonized people had no representatives of their own. Those hand-picked persons who assumed the role of parliamentary representatives were Amharized and served the interest of the colonial masters than the interest of their own people.

The political, economic and socio-cultural domination of one ethnic group led to a number of violent uprisings. In the center, the student movement led the opposition against the Haile Selassie rule; it conceived its struggle on class rather than national identity. In the periphery, oppressed peoples and peasants organized their struggle along nationality and ethnic identity. Eventually it was the rebellion in Eritrea, Oromia, Ogaden, Sidama, and Tigray that had shaken the foundation of Ethiopian imperial rule leading to its final downfall in 1974.

The military government that replaced the emperor emphasized unitary government. Without paying much attention to ethnicity, it stressed the enhancement of Ethiopian nationalism under the slogan "Ethiopia first" or "Ityiopya tiqdem" to mobilize, what Clapham (1989:12) calls "composite nationalism as a source of popular unity." The struggle based on national identity became gradually more popular when the student movement was crushed by the Derg. Students from different nationalities decided to further their struggle against the military regime by changing the line of struggle from class to ethnic identity. This gave birth to political struggle associated with nationality, such as Tigray People Liberation Front (TPLF), Oromo Liberation Front (OLF), Western Somali Peoples Liberation Front (WSLF), and the Sidama Liberation Front (SLF).

For these political movements in the Empire who felt oppressed, dominated and excluded from political and economic opportunities controlled by the state, national identity and group identity consciousness provided them with conducive ground of operation. Different national groups who felt oppressed by Amhara perceived themselves as a group distinct from the ruling group. This perception reached not only implicit consciousness of their difference from the ruling group, but also attained explicit potency of a collective opposition and rejection of domination. Ethnic identity played a vital role as an active medium through which oppressed people accepted the struggle as inspired by the bond of history, blood ties, common ancestry, language and culture.

National identity gave the movements more consolidated and secure organizations i.e. the unity for continuous existence and collective utilization of resources, space and time to prepare themselves, to design and plan their activities and to achieve an agreed upon plan to abolish oppressive structures. It served them as a means to group mobilization, to bring together scattered resources and people not simply in spontaneous and discontinuous actions of protest expressing the demands of isolated groups, but consisting of systematic and continuous actions of gradually accelerating offensive against the military regime.

These political struggles paved the way to broaden and deepen the transformative capacity of different national groups' power by war which inevitably resulted in the loss of human life, economic crises, destruction of infrastructure, but finally undermined the legitimacy of the Derg regime. In its struggle to remain on power the military regime diverted economic resources and precious human lives to its endless wars, and as a result the resources that could have been used for improving the horrible poverty in Ethiopia were wasted.

In May 1991, the national movements that were fighting against the Derg regime had overthrown the communist military junta. While Oromo, Sidama, Ogaden, Benishangul and other liberation organizations convened to establish a transitional government, the TPLF started to organize puppet organizations in nearly every nation in the empire to make the leaders of these TPLF-made PDOs loyal instrument of its hidden agenda. This hidden agenda was perpetuating single ethnic domination by replacing the Amhara domination by Tigrean repression.

The organizations created and controlled by the TPLF include the Oromo Peoples' Democratic Organization (OPDO) followed by mushrooming PDOs for every nation of the Empire. The strategy of the TPLF has been that the PDOs are led by corrupt individuals, who abuse and oppress their own people for position of power that rarely lasted for a year. Although all political movements based on national political identity were ready to run transitional government by setting the Transitional Charter and how it should be handled, the TPLF was not ready to allow those political organizations freedom of action fearing that they will be obstacles for its hidden agenda. Eventually, prominent political organizations that fought against single ethnic domination of successive governments left the transitional government. The TPLF also targeted to kill the leaders of political movements based on national identity. The PDOs were created by the TPLF as instruments for controlling the colonized nations and exploiting their resources. The PDOs are loyal to the TPLF. They are not loyal for the people whose interest they were supposed to serve. As instruments of oppression and subjugation the PDOs are despised by their own people whose trust and confidence they lack.

By the same token, the TPLF/EPRDF approved its constitution on 24th August 1995, officially proclaiming the establishment of the Federal Democratic Republic of Ethiopia. The implementation of the constitution may have benefited some national groups. However, in the case of the Sidama, its misapplication took away the nominal autonomy of the Sidama. To alley profound fears of domination, the constitution set out several guarantees for ethnic groups. For example, Article 39 stated that "every nation, nationality and people in Ethiopia has unconditional right to self determination including the right to secession." This article is inserted to provide psychological guarantee for ethnic groups who may feel oppressed or mistreated by their existence within Ethiopia. However, in order to control the possible separation that might result from demands for independence, the constitution specified the conditions under which this right could be exercised (see Young 1996:531).

Theoretically, the constitution allows freedom for the entire ethnic groups so that they may develop their cultures and languages. Their language becomes the media in their respective offices and schools. Their children were allowed to learn their own values and their ethnocentric knowledge. It gave minority veto power. For every 100,000 people, there is one representative in the parliament. For ethnic groups that have a population below 100,000, there are 20 identified seats. Eritrean independence was recognized as a *fait a compli*. Tigray became autonomous regional state economically most advantaged. The nationalists who fought for Tigrean autonomy settled for Ethiopian domination. Amhara, previously dispersed regions to deceive and hide their domination became the most economically, politically advantaged. Previously, the Amhara ruling class had conquered the Southern nations to escape from famine but did nothing for indigenous Amharas, living in drought and famine prone areas. Oromia got nominal regional autonomy, but it is governed by Tigrean puppets who speak Oromo language. The Sidama lost the nominal regional autonomy at least inherent in the name Sidamo since the period of the conquest. Despite its population that is estimated to be more than four million, the Sidama is denied even the status of regional statehood, despite the fact that all criteria favors the Sidama.

If the constitution and federal structures solved the nationality question the issue that was raised in the 1970s by all political movements and yet at this very moment, more than forty five nations are forced to live together against their will in a single state in the southern region. The term Southern Nations, Nationalities and People Regional State suggest that Meles Zenawi's regime is so contemptous to call these nations by their own names.

The so-called federal constitution did not lessen the burden of the Southern nations. For instance, the Sidama lost its budget allocation, possible posts and employment opportunities. The Sidamas had been made prone to famine after the establishment of this regional state. The political intrigue taking place in the TPLF-made SNNPRS machinery point to the preparation of the ground to commit mass elimination and genocide. It was the political intrigue engineered by the TPLF and its surrogate-SNNPRS that prepared the background for the mass murder of May 24, 2002. The mass murder of peaceful demonstrators was a genocide to all intent and purposes. Following the mass murder large number of innocent people were illegally detained and several individuals dismissed from their jobs.

In conclusion, the Sidama nation has fundamental democratic right to have its self-determination. Through their sacred struggle the Sidama people will achieve their self-determination.

References

Axford, Barrie et al. 1997. *Politics: An introduction.* London and New York: Routledge.

Clapham, Christoper. 1989. The state and revolution in Ethiopia. *Review of African Political Economy.* No. 44.

Gellner, Ernest. 1983. *Nations and nationalism.* Ithaca and Oxford: Cornell University Press and Blackwell.

Haralambos, M. and M. Holborn. 1991. *Sociology: Themes and perspectives.* London: Collins Educational Publishers.

Heywood, Andrew. 1997. *Politics.* London: Macmillan.

Howard, Michael. 1996. *Contemporary cultural anthropology.* New York: Harper Collins College Publisher.

Mengisteab, Kidane. 1997. New approach to state building in Africa: The case of Ethiopia's ethnic based federalism. *Africa Studies Review.* 40,3:111-132.

Rex, John 1995. Ethnic identity and the nation state: The political sociology of multicultural society. *Social Identities.* 1.

Smith, Anthony. 1995. *Nation and nationalism in a global era.* Oxford: Polity press.

Young, John. 1996. Ethnicity and power in Ethiopia. *Review of African Political Economy.* 70.

Chapter 11

The History of Oromo Nationalism: 1960s-1990s[1]

Mohammed Hassen

INTRODUCTION

Oromo nationalism is the product of the resistance movement against the Ethiopian state which was dominated by the Amhara ruling elite. The state was created by the Abyssinians and its ideological underpinning has been Abyssinian nationalism based as it was on Christianity, the Orthodox Church, the monarchy and the solidarity of the Abyssinians. The Abyssinians are the Amhara and Tigreans, who are described as "the true Ethiopians" (Levine 1974:8). These people speak closely related Semitic languages; they also share the same political, cultural and religious institutions. Of the two people, it was the Amhara of Shawa, who created the modern Ethiopian Empire during and after the 1880s. The Amhara ruling elite not only created an empire, but also transformed Abyssinian nationalism into Ethiopian nationalism which is a governmental nationalism. This means, Ethiopian nationalism is the product of Abyssinian cultural heritage and it was not based on the collective achievements and pride of all the peoples of Ethiopia. It was not based on loyalty and devotion of all people to the Ethiopian state and a feeling of solidarity with fellow citizens. There was no concept of citizenship in the Ethiopian political culture but only that of subjects. "I know of no society in Africa," Tecola Hagos observed, "where the dignity and humanity of individuals has been so thoroughly squashed or obliterated to the same extent as is the case with Ethiopian peasants and poor, uneducated men, women and children" (Hagos 19995:4).

As Ethiopian nationalism has been governmental nationalism, the Ethiopian state has been the state of the ruling elites. Up to 1991, it was the Amhara elites who dominated the political, military, economic, cultural, religious and social life of the Ethiopian state. Since 1991, the Tigray People Liberation Front

(TPLF) not only replaced the Amhara ruling elite, but has also been restructuring the Ethiopian state for the purpose of entrenching the Tigrean elites' control of the Ethiopian economy and domination of the political landscape. The Amhara ruling elites and the TPLF have managed not only to make their governmental nationalism as "Ethiopian nationalism", but also projected their own interest as national interest and their own survival as the survival of Ethiopia (Hassen 1996:72).

This chapter is divided into eight parts: Part one discusses why Oromo nationalism developed only during and after the 1960s. Part two deals with the Macha and Tulama Association (MTA) and the rise of Oromo nationalism. Part three discusses the causes and consequences of the radicalization of the MTA. Part four establishes the link between the MTA underground movement and the formation of the Oromo Liberation Front (OLF), an organizational expression of Oromo nationalism. Part five deals with the Ethiopian military government's attempt at containing Oromo nationalism. Part six deals with the transformation of Oromo nationalism from a minority movement to a mass movement. Part seven deals with the attack on Oromo nationalism. The final part suggests some solutions to the long and enduring Oromo yearning for self-determination and democratic governance.

THE DEVELOPMENT OF OROMO NATIONALISM DURING AND AFTER THE 1960S

Before embarking on the main subject, three caveats are in order. First, although Oromo nationalism developed during and after the 1960s, it is still a taboo subject among Ethiopian intellectuals and some Ethiopianist scholars, who regard the Oromo as scattered tribal groups, who lack a sense of nationhood and therefore whose nationalism is non-existent or undeveloped. I am writing this chapter not to prove the existence of Oromo nationalism; the evidence for its existence and the intellectual ferment among the Oromo both at home and in the diaspora is strong. The new Oromo nationalist spirit cuts across class, religious and regional differences and fuses the Oromo into a nation that yearns for freedom, human dignity, social justice and democratic governance (Hassen 1998:190). Second, this work heavily draws on the author's recent three book chapters (Hassen 1999a; 1998; 1996), two articles (Hassen 1996b; 2000b) and a review essay (Hassen 1997). As such it is an attempt to share some thinking about the development of Oromo nationalism from an Oromo viewpoint. It may reflect an unintended and unconscious aggrandizement of Oromo nationalism at the expense of the Ethiopian state. However, the purpose here is simply to attempt to explain why Oromo nationalism developed as it did only during and after the 1960s as a reaction to the Ethiopian state which suppressed Oromo identity. I present this chapter to serve as stimulant for substantive discussion and to encourage others to write about the Oromo, the Amhara, the Hadiya, the Sidama, the Somali, the Tigrean, the Wolayta and other nationalisms in Ethiopia. Finally, the existence of rival nationalisms in Ethiopia is usually denied and, worse still, there is a great deal of ignorance about it. Ignorance, as Ernest Gellner wrote, "has many forms, and all of them are dangerous" (Gellner 1991: vii). This writer believes that the road for a better future for all the peoples of Ethiopia lies not in denial of and ignorance about the existence of rival nationalism, but in acknowledging the reality of their existence and coming to terms with them. With knowledge and understanding, it may be possible to harness the positive aspects of rival nationalisms while institutionalizing peaceful resolution of conflicts (Hassen 1998:185-186).

Except in Egypt and South Africa, nationalism developed in colonial Africa mainly between the 1920s and 1950s. Among the Oromo in Ethiopia, nationalism developed only during and after the 1960s. Why did it take so long for Oromo nationalism to develop? There are a number of valid reasons for this. First, after their conquest during the 1880s, the Oromo were subjected to crude colonial exploitation. The conquest was characterized in some areas by indiscriminate killings, burning houses, plunder of property and selling war captives into slavery. It was Menelik, the Amhara king of Shawa (1865-1889) and later the Emperor of Ethiopia (1889-1913) who conquered all Oromo one after the other. After his conquest and occupation of Oromo territories, Menelik gave both the conquered people and their land to his armed settlers, the colonial state and the Ethiopian Orthodox church. Since the armed-settlers were neither paid salary nor engaged in productive activities, they were given Oromo gabars (serfs) in lieu of salary. Burdensome and exhausting obligations were put on the Oromo gabar.

> He had to surrender a portion of the produce of the land to the landlord as tribute. The amount varied between a quarter and a third, but it was usually more as the legal ceiling was that it should not be more than three quarters! Besides, he paid a tenth of his total produce for the tithe. He was also expected to provide his landlord with honey, meat and firewood, dried grass and sundry other items. Labor service was an added burden, he had to grind the landlord's share of the grain, transport it to his residence, build his house, maintain his fences, care for his animals, and act as a porter, an escort or a messenger. There was an obligation to present gifts on religious holidays and other social occasions. The multiple exactions imposed on the Oromo gabars meant the loss of a considerable portion of the production, onerous labor service and manifold other impositions (Hussen 1976:14).

In the sacred land of their birth, the Oromo became landless gabar (serfs) who were exploited economically, oppressed and alienated politically, dehumanized psychologically and subjugated culturally. According to Professor Teshale Tibebu, "The rise of modern Ethiopia heralded the demise of Oromo power" (Tibebu 1995:39). One would add that Menelik's colonial empire was built not only upon the demise of Oromo power, but also the destruction of Oromo lives and plunder of their property. This means, the creation of the modern Ethiopian empire was not brought about by the growth of unity of peoples but, on the contrary, through brutal conquest (Hassen 1999:128-146). The relation between the conquerors (Amhara-Tigryan) and the Oromo and other conquered peoples of southern Ethiopia has been that of the conqueror and conquered, oppressors and the oppressed, colonizers and colonized whereby the colonized peoples were "treated as second class subjects" (Baissa 1998:81). Hence, Menelik's empire was built upon twin pillars of the gabar system (serfdom) and slavery, both of which were abolished during the short-lived Italian occupation of Ethiopia (1936-1941).

In 1941, British forces together with Ethiopian resistance forces defeated Italian fascism and ejected it from Ethiopia. The British restored Emperor Haile Selassie to power. After his return to power from 1941 to 1974, the Emperor did not undertake any meaningful and substantive reform that altered feudal relationships between the landlords and peasants in conquered regions of southern Ethiopia. In short, Oromo nationalism developed in response to the continuation of the relations of oppression and colonial conquest. It took shape against several decades of economic exploitation, military subjugation "political and cultural domination" (Baxter 1994:249). It is still developing and changing.

The Oromo colonial experience makes it different from other nationalisms in Africa. It is still developing and changing. What is more, Oromo colonial experience makes it different from other nationalisms in Africa. Paul Baxter noted that the

> Oromo nationalism differs from other nationalisms insofar as the experience of Ethiopian rule differed from that of being ruled by a western colonial power. Ethiopian colonial power was centered in the country itself and not in some distant metropole. The rulers were also 'natives', and did not have immense technological superiority over the ruled nor enjoyed vastly superior standard of living (Baxter 1994, *ibid*).

The history of nationalism is such that it develops as a long, complex and slow process. It is mediated by national awakening or national consciousness which "refers to an amalgam of feelings, impressions and ways of thinking which find their expression in the psychological and physical solidarity of the

group experiencing them in common" (Dearton 1996:7). National consciousness emerges primarily as a result of several facilitator factors such as the spread
of modern education, better communication, improved transportation system,
growth of mass media and the press, higher standard of literacy and growth
of literature, and intensive interaction among people, all of which combine to
provide (Hassen 1996:69) "a crucial environment for the spread of a national
consciousness through a given population" (Alter 1987:77).

In the case of the Oromos, the overwhelming majority of the people were
peasants who lived in rural areas and therefore were not exposed to the factors
just mentioned. Even the tiny Oromo elements that lived in urban areas did not
have access to education in their mother tongue and they were legally denied to
cultivate literature in their own language. It is not surprising then for Oromo
nationalism to develop much slower than other nationalisms in colonial Africa.

Before the 1960s, the Oromo lacked an intellectual class that aspired to
create cultural and political space for itself. Professor Jordan Gebre-Medhin
is right when he writes: "We must not forget that the pathetic lack of material progress in Ethiopia circumscribed the limits of intellectual growth in the
empire" (Gebre-Medhin 1989:26). Intellectuals are "predestined to propagate
the 'national idea,'" just as those who wield power in the polity provoke the
idea of the state" (Weber 1994:25). The lack of an intellectual class not only
delayed the development of Oromo political consciousness, but it is still one of
the major weaknesses of the Oromo national movement.

The Amharization policy of consecutive Ethiopian governments delayed
the development of an Oromo intellectual class during the 1940s and 1950s.
Emperor Haile Selassie's government worked with single-minded determination to implement its policy of Amharization by imposing the Amhara language,
culture, religion and way of life on the Oromo. Its goal was to consolidate the
power of the Amhara elite "through the establishment of the hegemony of the
Amhara culture masked as 'Ethiopian' culture" (Keller 1998:121). "Amhara
culture, language and religion were imposed on the conquered peoples as well
as Eritrea after its federation with Ethiopia in 1952. The distinction between
Amhara and Ethiopian nationalism was blurred and everybody was compelled
to learn the Amhara national characteristic as if they were pan-Ethiopian traits"
(Baissa 1998:81). To hasten the pace of Amharization, Amharic was declared
as the official language of government, and it was planned to make it the lingua
franca of the empire.

From 1942 onwards Amharic was promoted as the sole national language of
the Empire and all other national languages were suppressed. The regime prohibited the use of Oromo literature for educational or religious purposes. The prohibition was further strengthened by the empowerment of an Imperial Decree No.

3 of 1944 which regulated the work of foreign missionaries and made Amharic the medium of instruction throughout the Empire (Bulcha 1993:5,11).

The Oromo were not only denied the basic right of using their language for educating their children, but also their children had very limited access to education even in Amharic. The reason for this was very obvious and the purpose very clear. It was to deny "the majority of the Oromo any educational opportunity in order to keep them illiterate and submissive so that [the colonizers] would exploit their human and economic resources" (Jalata 1998:3). In short, the ruling Amhara elites created one obstacle after another which deprived Oromo children from being taught in any language. "These obstacles had a negative impact on integrating the various ethnic groups and on the national unity of the country" (Sbacchi 1997:11).

According to Emmanuel Abraham, who served as a Director General in the Ministry of Education from 1944 to 1947, he was accused of educating "only the Gallas" [Oromo] (Abraham 1995:64). Emmanuel Abraham was one of the most Amharized Oromo, the most loyal servant of the Emperor Haile Selassie, who was committed to and tirelessly worked for the success of Amharization. He educated five times more Amhara than Oromo. Accused of teaching more Oromo than Amhara, Abraham wrote:

> The Emperor...went one day, without my knowledge, to a school which had the largest number of students and directed the head-master to make a list of the pupils in ethnic groups and present it to him. He did that and out of a total of 991 pupils, 701 said they were Amharas. The rest came from the various ethnic groups. The Emperor showed me this and, after telling me why he had asked for it, commanded me to get him in ethnic groups a list of all the pupils in the Addis Ababa schools. I presented a complete list in a few days. In April 1947, 4,795 students attended the Addis Ababa schools. Of those, 3,055 said they were Amharas and the remaining 1,740 were from the other ethnic groups. Of these, 583 said they [Oromo]. On the basis of this, it was obvious that the great majority of students of the period were not [Oromo] but Amharas (Abraham 1995:64).

From the above it is clear that the Amhara ruling elite were not interested in creating an educational system in which all children had equal access to the benefit of modern education. On the contrary, they wanted an educational system that advanced mainly the educational interests of Amhara children. Such a policy was self-defeating and it failed to produce an Ethiopian nation. Instead, it produced few Amharized non-Amhara individuals, who were despised, ridiculed and looked down upon with contempt by the members of the Amhara ruling class.

The period from 1942 to 1990 was a time when the program of Amharization and de-Oromization was intensified, through limited educational system, cultural institutions and governmental bureaucracy. In the school, nothing positive was taught about the Oromo, their history, culture, and way of life. On the contrary, Oromo children were made to feel that "their mother tongue was inferior and too 'uncultivated' to be used in a civilized environment such as the school" (Bulcha 1993:9).

> In the school, the Oromo child was not only mobbed, but was 'fed' negative biases against everything that was Oromo. Mixed in with the Amhara language and Abyssinian history, he/she was taught many of the Amhara prejudices against the Oromo. The Oromo people were depicted as subjects and dependent in relation to the Empire's rulers whereas the Amhara and Tigreans were presented as citizens. The Oromo were (are) described as a people without culture, history and heroes .... The Oromo were characterized not only as uncivilized, but as uncivilizable. The Oromo language and culture were reduced to marks of illiteracy, shame and backwardness as the school pressed Oromo children to conform to Amhara culture .... Those who were completely overwhelmed by the unmitigated assault on Oromo culture and history, dropped (or tried to drop) their Oromo identity. Among these, were some who tried to get rid of every sign of what the Oromo themselves call Oromummaa ('Oromoness'). In a desperate move to assimilate they 'forgot' the Oromo language (Bulcha 1993:9-10).

In short, the Ethiopian educational system fostered Amharization which stripped Oromo children of their language, culture and identity. This was meant to destroy Oromo youth's pride in their cultural heritage and to keep them chained with no faith in themselves, their history, and their national identity (Hassen 1990:3). It remains the belief of the Amhara ruling class and elites that to be an Ethiopian, one has to cease to be an Oromo. The two things are seen as incompatible (Bulcha 1991:101). Fourth, in the rise of nationalism in Asia, Africa and other parts of colonial territories, the educated class played a very decisive role (Lamb 1974:36). "It is hard to find a single one of the African Nationalist leaders, whether radical or conservative who was not a graduate of a western university or else had some other prolonged exposure to western life" (Clapham 1984:29). In the Oromo case, there was no western educated class that aspired to create cultural space for itself before the 1960s, much less to lead a nationalist movement.

Fifth, the Amhara ruling elite did everything possible to prevent the development of Oromo nationalism by Amharizing educated Oromo, by dividing the Oromo along religious and regional lines, and above all by undermining the development of literature in the Oromo language. Ernest Gellner, a noted scholar on nationalism, aptly described Ethiopia as "a prison-house of nations if ever there was one" (Gellner 1991:85). In that prison-house of nations, the languages of the conquered people of southern Ethiopia was not allowed to be written, much less to be used for education and local administration. From 1942 to 1974, the Oromo language was banned from being used for preaching, teaching and production of literature. As Paul Baxter, a leading authority on Oromo studies, observed in 1967 while he was conducting field research among the Oromo in the Arsi province:

> Oromo was denied any official status and it was not permissible to publish, preach, teach or broadcast in Oromo. In court or before an official an Oromo had to speak Amharic or use an interpreter. Even a case between two Oromos, before an Oromo-speaking magistrate, had to be heard in Amharic. I sat through a mission service at which the preacher and all the congregation were Oromo but at which the sermon as well as the service was given first in Amharic which few members of the congregation understood at all, and then translated into Oromo. The farce had to be played out in case a judas informed the district officer fined or imprisoned the preacher (Baxter 1978:288).

In short, the absence of modern education, the tight control of Ethiopian administration, the absence of an intellectual class, and Amharization policy of Haile Selassie's government, all delayed the development of Oromo nationalism before the 1960s.

There was also another factor which hampered the development of Oromo nationalism during and after the 1960s. From its birth in the 1960s, Oromo nationalism faced strong opposition from both the Ethiopian and Somali ruling elites. While the Amhara ruling elites feared the development of Oromo nationalism as a threat to their empire, Somali ruing elites regarded it as a dangerous movement that would abort the realization of the dream of a greater Somalia.

> Whereas the Amhara elites saw the danger to their empire in the growth of Oromo nationalism, the Somali elites perceived the frustration of their ambition in the birth of Oromo nationalism. The Amhara attitude was nourished by the specter of the disintegration of their empire for, without the resources of Oromia, Ethiopia cannot exist as a viable state. The attitude of the Somali ruling elites was nourished by the untenable ambition of building a greater Somalia (Hassen 1996:68).

Was there anything that could be described as Oromo nationalism in the 1960s? The answer is mixed. If one looks at it from the perspective of the activities of the Macha and Tulama Association (MTA) in the 1960s, there was Oromo nationalism; but if one views it from the perspectives of the Ethiopian ruling elites of the 1960s, who denied and feared its existence, it was not prevalent. I must state clearly that Oromo nationalism of the 1960s was not a mass movement. Like the early phase of nationalism in different parts of the world, Oromo nationalism of the 1960s, 1970s, and 1980s was a minority movement (Hassen 1996:69). This was because "nationalism is usually a minority movement pursued against the indifference of the members of the 'nation' in whose name the nationalist act" (Breuilly 1982:19). Nevertheless, Oromo nationalists of the 1960s knew that nationalism is "above and beyond all else, about politics, and that politics is about power. Power, in the modern world, is primarily about control of the state" (Breuilly 1982:2). The nationalist leaders of the MTA, to which we now turn, knew about this reality and attempted to capture state power in 1966.

THE MACHA AND TULAMA ASSOCIATION AND THE RISE OF OROMO NATIONALISM

The Macha and Tulama Association (hereafter the Association or MTA) was formed in Addis Ababa (Finfinne) on January 24, 1963. However, it received legal recognition from the government only in May 1964, a year and four months after it was formed. It was grudging recognition which Haile Selassie's officials later regretted (Zoga 1993:21).

Who formed the Association and why? What did it achieve? The following discussion attempts to answer these and similar questions. MTA was formed by high-ranking Oromo officers in the Ethiopian military and Oromo lawyers. Colonel Alemu Qitessa was a distinguished officer who endured pain and sorrow for the Oromo cause (Zoga 1993:387-392). Haile Mariam Gamada was a man with an encyclopedic knowledge of Oromo history, a lawyer and greatly respected leader. Colonel Alemu Qitessa was the President of the Association and the Chairman of its Board of Directors. Baqala Nadhi was Vice President, Colonel Qadida Gurmessa, the second Vice President, and Haile Mariam Gamada was the General Secretary (Hassen 2000:125). It was Haile Mariam Gamada who chaired the committee that drafted the bylaws of the Association, coined the name of the Association and produced its logo: the *Odaa* (Sycamore tree), the symbol of freedom and self-determination (Hassen 1997:207, Zoga 1993:19). The name of the association symbolized the unity of two major Oromo groups, that of Macha and Tulama, while its logo, the *Odaa* symbolized the unity of all Oromo and their return to Gada democracy. This was because the Oromo assembly (parliament) held its meeting under the life-giving shade of the *odaa* (the holy sycamore tree) which traditionally was believed to be the most respected and the most sacred of trees, the shade of which was the source of peace, the center of religion and the office of the government and the meeting place for the democratically elected Gada leaders (Hassen 1990:14).

Thus the MTA was formed by the most privileged and the best educated elements of the Oromo society, who felt a humiliating sense of exclusion from important decision-making processes within the Ethiopian political establishment. The founders wanted the Association to be the agent of social change and the Oromo voice for exercising influence within the larger arena of Ethiopian politics.

> [T]he desire to be recognized as a responsible agents whose wishes, acts, hopes, and opinions matter and the desire to build an efficient dynamic modern state. The one aim is to be noticed; it is a search for identity, and a demand that that identity be politically acknowledged as having importance, a social assertion of the self as 'being some body in the world.' The other aim is practical : it is a demand for progress for a rising standard of living, more effective political order, greater social justice, and beyond that of 'playing a part in the larger arena of world politics' of exercising influence among the nations (Geertz 1996: 30)

The founders of the Association articulated Oromo cultural nationalism rather than political nationalism and their goal was the search for and the recognition of Oromo identity within the larger Ethiopian identity. Consequently, they did not reject Ethiopian identity, the state and its institutions. But the Oromo nationalists of the 1970s and after, who articulated Oromo political nationalism rejected Ethiopian identity and its institutions (Hassen 1998:190). For those who rejected Ethiopian identity, the Ethiopian state neither embodies a consensus of beliefs, values and aspirations nor instills in them trust in its institutions, laws, leadership and administrative machinery. On the contrary, for Oromo nationalists these are the tools of oppression and subjugation that have to be removed and replaced (Hassen 1996:72).

The leaders of the MTA promoted Oromo national renaissance and cultivated an Oromo national consciousness that challenged the legitimacy of the Ethiopian political establishment claiming that it ignored or excluded Oromo national identity. The Association was formed in accordance with Article 45 of his Imperial Majesty's 1955 Revised Constitution and Article 14, Number 505 of the Civil Code of the Ethiopian Empire as a civilian self-help association. According to Article 5 of the Association's statute, its aims and objectives were, among others, to build schools, clinics, road, churches, mosques, to help the weak and disabled, to organize Ethiopian civilian and national rights, and to spread literacy and basic knowledge about health care. The framers of the statute were highly educated, well-informed, politically conscious individuals, who knew how to organize the people and mobilize their resources for solving their own problems. Article 20 of the statute provided that all Ethiopians would be accepted as members without regard to ethnic. tribal, regional, religious affiliation or sex of the applicant, in accordance with the internal regulations of the Association (Hassen 1998:195; Zoga 1993:5-36).

The leaders of the Association challenged and defied the established Ethiopian political order in two major ways. First, they created a country-wide pan-Oromo movement that launched multifaceted activities, nourishing Oromo self-respect and self-confidence, inspiring them with a renewed vigor and determination to be united and become the agents of their own freedom and equality. Before the Ethiopian government officials realized, the leaders of the Association had done something-unthinkable even in 1963. They brought the Oromo together from East and West, North and South, Muslims and Christians and believers of traditional Oromo religion and demolished the myth of Oromo disunity. The leaders of the Association exploded the myth of Oromo disunity and embarked on coordinated and united activities which alarmed the government.

This was an unheard-of-event in Ethiopia, and outraged the Amhara ruling elites. The leaders of the Association demonstrated the depth of Oromo unity. They went beyond religious taboo when Muslims ate meat slaughtered by Christians and the Christians ate meat slaughtered by Muslims. At every, mass gathering, the leaders of the Association stressed that, despite regional and religious differences, the Oromo are one people who share a common language, culture, manners, common political idioms underpinned by the *gada* system, common pride in their democratic heritage and common historical experience under an oppressive Ethiopian system which robbed them of their land, their rights, and their human dignity. The leaders of the Association made the Oromo conscious of their unity as a people and also conscious of their deprivation and their treatment as second class subjects and urged them to be agents of their own freedom and equality.

The leaders of the Association not only united the Oromo themselves but also sought to unite them with other oppressed peoples in Ethiopia. The Association:

> [p]rovided an organizational framework, not only to unite the oppressed nationalities, but also to end national oppression in Ethiopia. Consequently, membership within the Association was open to all. This was both strength and a weakness of the Association. It was strength because the Association became the first organization to unite the oppressed nationalities of Ethiopia who like the Oromo, were subjected to economic exploitation, political oppression and cultural domination. It was a weakness because open membership provided a [good opportunity] for the security agents of Haile Selassie's regime to infiltrate the Association and to expose it to destruction (Hassen 1997:217).

The Association, with its main office in Addis Ababa, had branch offices all over the Oromo region of Ethiopia. Within three short years, its membership expanded from a few thousand to probably over a million. Its members included people from all walks of life, all social and economic classes, Christians, Muslims, and believers in traditional Oromo religion, and from every corner of Oromia. They included farmers, students, teachers, men and women, civil servants, lawyers, soldiers from the rank of private to general, community and religious leaders, and top government officials (Hassen 2000b:127). An example can be cited from the Wallaga branch to show how the Association attracted the most privileged elements of the Oromo society.

Astede Habte Mariam, the only woman in the highest policymaking Board of the Association, formed the Wallaga branch office in 1966. She was a member of the Oromo royal family of Nakamtee and the sister of Oromo governor of Wallaga province. On the day when the Wallaga branch office was opened, high ranking government officials and key members of the Association were present, including Colonel Alemu Qitessa, the President of the Association, General Taddesse Birru, the most influential member of the Association, General Jagama Kello, General Dawit Abdi, Dajazmach Kebede Buzunesh, Dajazmach Fiqere Selassie Habte Mariam (the Governor of Wallaga), his sister, princess Mahestena Habte Mariam (the wife of the deceased son of Emperor Haile Selassie), Haile Mariam Gamada, and many other government officials. This means that the Wallaga branch, chaired by Mrs: Astede Habte Mariam, included even a member of Emperor Haile Selassie's royal family. There was not a single general of Oromo origin in Haile Selassie's military or police force who was not a member of the Association. There were many high-ranking civilian officials of Haile Selassie's regime who joined the Macha and Tulama Association. (Hassen 2000b:128-129).

Through these high-ranking government officials, the Association penetrated Emperor Haile Selassie's bureaucracy. After all, they were the most privileged members of the Oromo elite. Presumably, they had much more in common with the Amhara ruling class, into which they were assimilated, than with the ordinary Oromo. In fact, some of the individuals spoke only Amharic language and did not know the Oromo language. And yet they joined an Oromo organization and spoke to the Oromo audience through interpreters. By joining, however,

> they elevated the status and transformed the image of the Association. Most of all they provided the Association with their skills, knowledge, organizational capacities and leadership qualities [important connections and information] and in the process they transformed what started as self-help organization into a pan-Oromo movement with huge membership and branch offices all over Oromia (Hassen 1996:75).

It is the assessment of this writer that the Oromo elite joined the association and turned to their roots for various reasons, the main one being the result of their disillusionment with the Ethiopian political establishment. They had all the necessary criteria to be integrated into the heart and the soul of the Ethiopian system (Giorgis 1989:117). They were mainly Christians, culturally Amharized and spoke Amharic. They were ardent Ethiopian nationalists and loyal to the Emperor; and yet they were "never treated with respect or accorded equality of status" (Baissa 1998:81).

> The life of assimilated Oromos was often peripheral. In spite of their total submission to 'pressures for their cultural suicide' and to the dominance of the Amhara over non-Amhara people in all aspects of life, they were seldom treated as equals by the Amhara. The Amharization of the Oromo and other groups was attempted without integrating them as equals or allowing them to share in any meaningful way. As the 'Amhara mask' what they wore was often too transparent, assimilated Oromo rarely reached decision-making positions within the Ethiopian bureaucracy (Bulcha 1994:104).

From what has transpired thus far, it is clear that it was the conflict between the ruling Amhara elites and Amharized educated Oromo that turned the latter towards the Oromo issue. It has been said and rightly that

> when the educated professionals find themselves unable to gain admission to posts commensurate with their degree and talents; they tend to turn away also from the metropolitan culture of the dominant ethnic group and return to their own culture, the culture of the once despised subject ethnic group. Exclusion breeds failed assimilation, and reawakens an ethnic consciousness among the professional elites, at exactly the moment when the intellectuals are beginning to explore the historic roots of the community (Smith 1982:31).

THE POLITICIZATION OF THE MTA: CAUSES AND CONSEQUENCES

After the 1960-failed coup, Emperor Haile Selassie's regime followed a secret policy of limiting the number of high-ranking military officers of Oromo origin and controlling their promotion. Ironically, not a single high-ranking officer of Oromo origin supported the 1960-failed coup; on the contrary, they opposed it. Colonels (later brigadier generals) Taddesse Birru, Jagama Kello, Waqjira Serda, Dawit Abdi, and Major Qadida Gurmeysa supported the Emperor and they were instrumental in aborting the 1960 coup (Zoga 1993:349, 352). And yet, they were suspected of disloyalty and subjected to discrimination. This policy not only angered Oromo officers but also encouraged them to be involved in political activities (Zoga 1993:12). Colonel Alemu Qitessa was among the high-ranking officers who were angered by the discriminatory policy of Emperor Haile Selassie and formed the MTA to oppose that policy. Among the first of these officers that Colonel Alemu Qitessa invited to join the Association was General Taddesse Birru, the most influential officer of Oromo origin, and a rising star within the Ethiopian political establishment.

General Taddesse Birru was a deeply religious man who was Amharized, spoke Amharic and married an Amhara woman. He passed as an Amhara. It was he who established the Rapid Force, the elite riot battalion. He was famous for his mastery of military science and trained many of the best Ethiopian officers. He was loyal to the Emperor, who entrusted to him the training of a number of leaders of liberation movements in Africa, including Nelson Mandela of South Africa (Hassen 2000b:130-131). In his autobiography, *Long Walk to Freedom,* Mandela acknowledges Taddesse Birru as the man under whose guidance he received his first military training in 1962. Nelson Mandela's wrote,

> I was lectured on military science by Colonel Tadessee who was also Assistant Commissioner of Police.... In my study sessions, Colonel Tadessee discussed matters such as how to create a guerilla force, how to command an army, and how to enforce discipline (Mandela 1994:265).

It was probably in 1963 when Taddesse Birru was promoted to Brigadier General and entrusted with many responsibilities. In addition to being the Commander of the Rapid Force, he was Deputy Commissioner of the National Police Force, Commander of the Territorial Army and the Chairman of the National Literacy Campaign. In his latter capacity he enthusiastically conducted the literacy program which was conducted only in Amharic, thus facilitating the Amharization policy of the Emperor. When Colonel Alemu Qitessa invited General Taddesse Birru to join the MTA in 1963, his answer was "I cannot participate in tribal politics" (Zoga 1993:24). For him the Association was involved in tribal politics and as an ardent Ethiopian nationalist, he felt he was above tribal politics. However, the General's energetic support for the spread of literacy among the Oromo alarmed the Ethiopian Prime Minister Aklilu Habte Wold. The prime Minister assumed the General to be an Amhara and confided in him the educational policy of Haile Selassie's regime in the following words:

> Taddesse! After you have started leading the literacy campaign, you talk a lot about learning. It is good to say learn. However, you must know whom we have to teach. We are leading the country by leaving behind the Oromo at least by a century. If you think you can educate them, they are an ocean [whose wave] can engulf you (Zoga 1993:25).

General Taddesse Birru, who wanted to create an Ethiopian nation, could not believe what he heard from the mouth of the Ethiopian Prime Minister. He was shocked and awakened by the policy designed to keep the Oromo beyond the reach of modern education. It was the realization of this policy which compelled him to return to his roots. He joined the MTA on 23 June 1964. When the Ethiopian Prime Minister heard the news about Taddesse Birru joining the Association, he realized that Taddesse was not an Amhara and had mistakenly confided in him about the government's policy. To ensure damage control, the Ethiopian Prime Minister targeted General Taddesse Birru for destruction (Zoga 1993:26-27).

Ironically, the leaders of the Association wanted to use the General's fame, his charismatic personality and his loyalty for and closeness to the Emperor for the purpose of protecting and expanding the activities of the Association. The leaders of the Association did not realize that they inadvertently traded the calm activities of their organization for high stake publicity which intensified the fear of the Amhara ruling elites who were eager and ready to destroy both the Association and its leaders (Hassen 1997:211). That, for the moment, lay in the future. After General Taddesse Birru joined the Association, he became the leading personality and one of its dynamic and energetic leaders who radicalized the Association.

The radicalized Association attracted Oromo students from Addis Ababa University, including Baro Tumsa (the Chairman of Haile Selassie I University Students' Union), Lieutenant Mamo Mazamir, Ibssa Gutama, Mekonnen Gallan, Taha Ali Abdi, and many others. With the exception of Mamo Mazamir, who was martyred in 1969, the rest were founding members of the Oromo Liberation Front (OLF) in 1974. This established a direct link between the transition from the Macha and Tulama Association to the OLF (Hassen 1996:75). The university students not only energized the movement but also raised the famous slogan of "Land to the Tiller" which became the binding revolutionary slogan for the Ethiopian student movements both at home and abroad. In his recently published book, Leenco Lata, the former Deputy General Secretary of the OLF, mentions a very interesting point in connection with how the slogan of "Land to the Tiller" was first raised; that it was two Oromo personalities who first organized public demonstration at which the famous slogan was raised. These personalities were also members of the Macha and Tulama Association (Hassen 2000b:130-131).

> The first public demonstration at which the slogan 'Land to the Tiller' was hoisted took place in February 1965 mainly as a result of a secret coordination between two Oromo personalities. The Emperor's rubber stamp parliament, whose President was Tesema Negeri, was at the time debating a land reform bill that was tabled mostly under pressure from Western governments and financial institutions, like the World Bank. Effecting the kind of changes suggested by these pressure groups and desired by the tenant farmers was opposed by most of the deputies who were mostly absentee

landlords themselves. It was to circumvent this opposition that the President of the Parliament and his fellow Oromo Chairman of the University Students' Union, Baro Tumsa, secretly arranged for the staging of the first ever "Land to the Tiller" demonstration. From that day until the unseating of the imperial government, this slogan was never missing from the almost annual event of student anti-government demonstrations (Lata 1999:191-192).

Besides Baro Tumsa, Lieutenant Mamo Mazamir was among the university students who contributed to the radicalization of the Association. A graduate of, and instructor, at the prestigious Harar Military Academy, he later joined Addis Ababa University Law School, where he completed his legal education.

Mamo Mazamir was a very intelligent, hardworking and highly motivated and immensely dedicated to the cause of the Oromo. He widely read socialist literature and knew a great deal about the Third World revolutions. He was angered with the grotesque distortion of Oromo history in the Ethiopian historiography and outraged with the Ethiopian government's policy of banning the writing of the Oromo language. He made writing Oromo history and production of literature in the Oromo language the ideological battleground for the movement (Hassen 1998:203).

It did not take long before the radicalization of the Association excited the ambition of militant Oromo nationals and aroused the anxieties of Amhara ruling elites. General Taddesse Birru and other leaders of the Association organized huge mass meetings at which through fierce oratory, dramas, poems and prayers in the Oromo language which was proscribed in public (Markakis 1987:260), moved the Oromo into tears of anger against the Ethiopian oppressive system. Those Amharized Oromo, who did not know the Oromo language started their speech with an apology: "I was born to you; I apologize for using an interpreter to make this speech." (Taye 1993:34). This was a remarkable shift in attitude among Ahmarized Oromo, who previously prided themselves in speaking in Amharic which they regarded as a mark of civilization and a status symbol. Suddenly Amharic lost its magic for Amharized Oromo. The radical members of the association realized the importance of using Oromo language for planting the seeds of Oromo nationalism. In short, the Macha and Tulama Association developed a country-wide Oromo political awakening. For the first time, peaceful Oromo resistance was coordinated under a single leadership. This came as a severe blow to the Amhara ruling class who had never lost the feeling of sitting on top of a volcano (Hassen & Greenfield 1992:580).

The leaders of the association established links and discussed common strategic issues with the leaders of armed resistance in the province of Bale. It was land alienation, heavy taxation, maladministration and Oromo hostility to Amhara political, economic, and cultural domination that triggered armed resistance in Bale. To get support from Somalia, General Waaqo Guutuu, the leader of Bale Oromo rebellion used Islam as a resistance ideology (Tareke 1991:131). Hence, it was in the name of Islam that the leaders of Bale rebellion mobilized their people and united the Oromo with the Somalis to fight against their common oppressors. According to professor Gebru Tareke, the Bale rebellion is the longest peasant struggle in contemporary Ethiopian history, and its longevity was as much due to the resolve and competence of the insurgent and ideological matrix of organization and mobilization (Tareke 1991:149). Before 1966 the armed rebellion in Bale had already liberated more than half of the vast region of Bale and encircled Goba, the provincial capital.

The leaders of the Macha and Tulama Association not only established secret contact with the armed resistance in Bale, but also they tried to unite the Oromo and other oppressed peoples of Ethiopia. Their goal was to create a democratic country in which all the peoples of Ethiopia could live together on the basis of equality. What the leaders of the Association were opposed to was the identity of Ethiopia that excluded the Oromo. What they hated was the political and cultural hegemony of the Amhara ruling elite. What they wanted was a creation of a democratic country that would be beneficial to all the peoples constituting Ethiopia. At huge mass meetings in many places from 1964 to 1966, the leaders of the MTA, channeled Oromo anger against the oppressive regime of Emperor Haile Selassie. The Oromo became conscious of their deprivation and their treatment as second-class subjects, and expressed their determination to be free and equal with other peoples of Ethiopia. In other words, the leaders of the Association fired the imagination of the Oromo, created political consciousness, and penetrated Emperor Haile Selassie's bureaucracy. It was this success which probably raised false expectations in the minds of militant leaders that the moment was ripe for capturing state power. This was the major weakness of the leadership. A weakness because the leaders failed to realize that in Ethiopian State power is always captured through victory on the battlefield. The leaders of the Association did not make sufficient military preparation to confront the regime of Haile Selassie which was ready to destroy both the leadership and the Association. The new Oromo political consciousness and the armed struggle in Bale dominated the Amhara ruling elites' policy towards the Oromo and the thought of the two in combination became their nightmare. The destruction of the MTA was part of the strategy for dealing with that nightmare (Hassen 2000b).

THE DESTRUCTION OF MACHA AND TULAMA ASSOCIATION 1967

It was Prime Minister Aklilu Habte Wold who spearheaded and coordinated the destruction of General Taddesse Birru and the Macha and Tulama Association. Up until 1966, the leaders of the Association, including General Taddesse Birru, remained loyal to Emperor Haile Selassie. For them, the Emperor was not part of the conspiracy to destroy the Association and its leaders. However, when the Emperor refused to heed their plea for justice, the leaders of the Association, under the influence and guidance of General Taddesse Birru, decided to assassinate the Emperor and capture state power. For that purpose, a hastily called meeting was held at General Taddesse's residence on the evening of 2 November, 1966. The objective of the meeting was to plan the physical elimination of the Emperor on 3 November, 1966. Never was a plot to assassinate the Emperor so poorly and hastily planned as this one.

This, more than anything else, demonstrates the pressure under which Taddesse Birru was operating. He was a brave general, who was outraged by the Ethiopian leaders plot to destroy the association. He was angered and provoked into rush action without any preparation. He was a very trusting leader who was victimized by the Abyssinian intrigue and double dealings. To complete the tragedy, General Taddesse wanted to assassinate the Emperor, who knew all about it through his planted agents within the movement itself. Worse still, the general had no contingency plan, if the planned assassination failed to materialize as it did (Hassen 2000b:132-33). Those who planned the destruction of General Taddesse Birru and the Association were delighted with the speed with which he fell into their trap (Hassen 1998:210).

While Haile Selassie knew all about the plot, the General did not know what the Emperor had in store for him. Those who participated in the hastily-called meeting to assassinate the Emperor included Ketema Yifru, the Ethiopian Foreign Minister, who was not even a member of the Macha and Tulama Association. It is impossible to understand why General Taddesse Birru included Ketema Yifru, the godson of the Emperor, in that plot. Either the general was too trusting, or naive, or both. Ketema Yifru, a leading member of the Amhara elites was probably a planted agent at the highest level of the Association. Ketema Yifru, had nothing to gain by participating in the plot to assassinate the Emperor. He had everything to gain by betraying the trust which Taddesse Birru placed in him (Hassen 1997:220).

That fateful meeting at the house of General Taddesse Birru lasted only for a few hours. Weapons were distributed and the meeting ended. The government security men who knew about the episode detained those who were returning home with weapons in their hands. According to Olana Zoga, the author of the *History of Macha and Tulama Association*, it was the key planted agent within the top leadership of the Association that enabled the government to foil the plot (Zoga 1993:122-123). Who was this high level planted agent within the movement? Olana Zoga does not directly mention that agent by name but he drops many hints, all of which point to Ketema Yifru. Of more than ten individuals who participated in the plot to assassinate the Emperor, only Ketema Yifru escaped any punishment and remained the most popular Ethiopian Foreign Minister until 1974!

For the purpose of imprisoning all the key leaders and dissolving the Association, the government used an explosion at the Cinema Hall in Addis Ababa. The government security men planted the explosive devices, one of whom lost a hand while planting the device. Mamo Mazamir, the most radical member of the Association was blamed for causing the explosion (Zoga 1993:138-148). The government imprisoned the prominent members of the Association, all of whom were severely tortured, brutalized, and dehumanized. For instance, Haile Mariam Gamada, the Secretary of the Association was brought to court on a stretcher because of the brutal beating from which he died shortly afterward (Hassen 1998:211). Before his death, Haile Mariam Gamada spoke these words:

> Neither the imprisonment and killing of the leaders nor banning of the Association will deter the[Oromo] nation's struggle. What we did is like a snake that entered a stomach. Whether it is pulled out or left there, the result is one and the same. It has spread its poison (quoted in Zoga, 297).

Haile Mariam Gamada stated that through the activities of the Association, the leaders of the Association have spread poison in the body politic of the Ethiopian State. The said poison was a metaphor for Oromo nationalism which was challenging Ethiopian political establishment. He went on to say that "whether we die or not, our ideas [about the freedom of the Oromo] will be realized by our children or grandchildren"(Zoga 1993:402). In his defense, General Taddesse Birru argued that:

> What makes the freedom of a people complete are many, the most fundamental of which is their equality before the law. I am denied equality before the law because of my nationality. Officers, who were imprisoned before me were paid their salary until their case was decided in court. Because of my nationality, I am treated differently. What is more, other officers were neither disgraced, nor tortured, while in police custody. Why am I disgraced and severely tortured? Spreading literacy among the Oromo, who are left behind in terms of education became my crime. I have been the victim of national oppression. I have been wrongly accused of things I did not do (quoted in Zoga 1993:257-258).

The court which demonstrated the Ethiopian justice system as a mockery, never considered General Taddesse Birru's argument in its deliberation. The court sentenced General Taddesse and Lieutenant Mamo Mazamir to death (Zoga 1993:261). Although Emperor Haile Selassie changed General Taddesse's death sentence into life imprisonment, Mamo Mazamir was hung in Addis Ababa prison in 1969, thus becoming a great martyr for the Oromo cause. His final words still resonate with the new generation of nationalist Oromo:

> I do not die in vain. My blood will water the freedom struggle of the Oromo people. I am certain that those who sentenced me to death for things I did not do, including the Emperor and his officials, will receive their due punishment from the Ethiopian people. It may be delayed, but the inalienable rights of the Oromo people will be restored by the blood of their children (quoted in Zoaa I 993:278).

THE MTA UNDERGROUND MOVEMENT AND THE FORMATION OF THE OLF IN 1974

In 1967, by imprisoning its leaders and dissolving the Association, the government of Emperor Haile Selassie won a pyrrhic, short-term victory. However, within seven short years, by 1974, its policy unwittingly transformed Oromo politics beyond recognition. The Association's demand for equality within Ethiopia was transformed into the Oromo Liberation Front (OLF)'s commitment to self-determination of Oromia. The Association's efforts to spread literacy in the Amharic language and Ethiopic script were transformed into literacy in *Afaan* Oromoo (the Oromo language) using the Latin alphabet. What was unthinkable in 1967 became feasible by 1974. In short, the Ethiopian government's unwarranted cruelty and brutality-produced the Oromo elite's rejection of Ethiopian identity itself. As a consequence, after 1974 Oromo politics was never the same again. What the Ethiopian government wanted in 1967 by destroying the Association was the destruction of Oromo political consciousness. What it got in 1974 was a mature form of Oromo nationalism which challenged Ethiopian nationalism itself (Hassen 1998:212).

After the Association was banned in 1967, the movement was forced to go underground. Some members of the Association went to Bale and joined the armed struggle there. Other members went to Somalia from where they went to the Middle East and formed two separate organizations; one based in Beruit and the other in Aden. Others went to the Sudan, where they formed a branch of the Macha and Tulama Association (Zoga 1993:298-99). Those who remained behind in Addis Ababa transformed the banned Association into an underground movement that organized members into study groups and cultural committees. For political agitation, the leaders of the underground movement produced literature in the Oromo language, Amharic and English.

Among the Addis Ababa based underground movement, the brothers Rev. Gudina Tumsa and Baro Tumsa played a very crucial role in keeping alive the spirit of resistance (Zoga 1993:300-301). They both gave their lives for the Oromo cause. In fact, Baro Tumsa was instrumental in the formation of the Oromo Liberation Front. It was he who organized a secret conference in Addis Ababa in December 1973. Among the participants, Hussein Sura (Sheik Hussen), the leader of Beruit based organization, Ellemo Qilixxu, the leader of Aden based Oromo National Liberation, and Baker Yusuf, came from the Middle East. Several individuals from different regions of Oromia also participated in that conference, out of which the OLF was formed in early 1974. According to Olana Zoga, under the leadership of Baro Tumsa, underground members of the Association which gave rise to the OLF took advantage of the February 1974 Revolution and contributed to the overthrow of Haile Selassie's regime in four ways.

First, its members effectively used the limited freedom of the press which flourished in Ethiopia from March to June 1974 for the purpose of exposing Oromo colonial experience. Second, its parliamentary members regularly challenged many of the regime's policies. Third, its members conducted agitation among the university and high school students. Fourth and most important, the underground members of the military and police forces were instrumental in organizing the committee of the men in uniform *(Derg* in Amharic) that overthrew the Emperor in September 1974 (Zoga 1993:301-302). From this aspect it is very clear that the OLF grew out of the underground MTA, and it is firmly rooted in Oromo national consciousness and it bases its ideological fire on Oromo nationalism.

> Consequently, it can be said that the emergence of a national movement indicates that a population or social group has reached a new stage on the road to nationhood: the transition to political action. The nation, or the sections of a population that consider themselves to be a nation, attempt to create their own state (Alter 1989:22-23).

The 1974 OLF political program which was amended in 1976, traces the historical background of the Oromo national liberation struggle. It briefly mentions the supporters and opponents of that struggle and states the ultimate goal of that struggle in the following words: "The fundamental objective of the struggle is the realization of national self-determination for the Oromo people and their liberation from oppression and exploitation in all their forms. This can only be realized through the successful consummation of the new democratic revolution ... and by the establishment of the people's democratic republic of

Oromia" (OLF Program 1976:15-16). The OLF Political Program stresses not only the establishment of a democratic republic of Oromia but also the importance of voluntary unity of the peoples of Ethiopia. This reflects the political maturity of the Oromo national movement (Hassen 1996:77).

In Ethiopia, 1974 saw not only the formation of the OLF but also the end of Haile Selassie's regime. In February 1974 Ethiopia heard the death-knell of Emperor Haile Selassie's regime. The Emperor, who dominated the Ethiopian political landscape since 1916, was too old to grasp the magnitude of the 1973 catastrophic famine which resulted in the death of over two hundred thousand people-the majority of whom were either Oromos from Wallo or Afars and Tigreans. Strikes and demonstrations in Addis Ababa reverberated throughout the country and the military which has always been the pillar of tyranny, turned against Haile Selassie's regime (Hassen 2000b:137).

THE MILITARY REGIME'S ATTEMPT TO CONTAIN OROMO NATIONALISM, 1974-1991

The 1974 revolution offered Ethiopia an opportunity not only to democratize itself, to heal the old wounds, to redress old injustice, to right the old wrongs, but also to decentralize power in the county. "Most Oromos had assumed that the revolution of 1974 would lead to decolonization and equality of all peoples in Ethiopia" (Jalata 1998:10-11; Lefort 1981:110). The formation of the OLF and the 1974 Ethiopian revolution stirred Oromo aspirations to regain their political rights, human dignity and equality. The revolution not only aroused Oromo pride in their national identity, language and culture, but also raised their expectation to regain their land. After the 1974 revolution, land reform of some kind was a foregone conclusion, without it, it would have been impossible to take impetus out of the flood of spontaneous Oromo peasant uprisings, especially in Hararghe (Hassen and Greenfield 1992:590, Lata 1999:192-193). According to Rene Lefort, it was the fear of Oromo uprising and the desire to prevent it from happening that forced the military regime to take radical measures including land reform (Lefort 1981:110). Asafa Jalata convincingly argues that the military regime took some radical measures not only to address Oromo grievances, but also to get their support and consolidate itself (Jalata 1998:10-11). Thus, the *Derg*'s nationalization of all rural lands in March 1975 was a legal recognition of *a fait accompli*, especially in Oromia, designed to arrest the tempo of peasant uprisings. Instead of devolving power to the peasantry, the land reform of 1975 centralized the power of the state in Ethiopia (Clapham 1988:6).

> What was achieved in effect was not ending landlordism but transferring the right previously enjoyed by individual landlords to the state. The state became a vehicle that centrally appropriated the labor

and produce of peasants to the descendants of the original landlords, as primarily people of such a background manned the new regime's state structures. The poverty of peasant farmers in the process rose to new heights while that of the descendants of the conquerors did not suffer a similar fate (Lata 1999:195-196).

In April 1976, the *Derg* declared the National Democratic Revolution Program (NDRP). This program which became the blueprint for the transformation "Ethiopian socialism" into "scientific socialism" was "the first official policy that recognized Ethiopia's national diversity" (Lata 1999:200). The NDRP stated:

> The right to self-determination of all nationalities will be recognized and fully respected. No nationality will dominate another one since the history, culture, language and religion of each nationality will have equal recognition in accordance with the spirit of socialism (Clapham 1988:199).

However, the NDRP was never implemented and it remained on paper, an empty gesture. In fact, the *Derg* used the NDRP not only as a showpiece of its radicalism to impress the Soviet Union, but also for waging war against "narrow nationalism" a new euphemism for Oromo nationalism. The *Derg* used the NDRP as an ideological cover for destroying Oromo nationalism. Narrow nationalism was proclaimed as the main enemy of the unity of the country and the *Derg* began a policy of physically destroying the best elements of the Oromo society, especially the intelligentsia. As a result, under the pretext of liquidating "narrow nationalists" or "anti-unity elements," "anyone concerned with the self-determination of the Oromo and the development of their language, culture and history and anyone who showed pride in the Oromo democratic heritage or possessed a strong sense of Oromo national identity and dignity became subject to "revolutionary measures," a euphemism for instant extrajudicial executions.[2] The Amhara military officers, who dominated the *Derg*, abandoned their pretensions about self-determination, having reached the peaks of hypocrisy and cynicism with their declaration of the National Democratic Revolution Program in April 1976, embarked on the massacre of peasants and the killings and detentions of educated Oromos. The purpose was to deprive the Oromo of educated leadership.

For years the military regime was engaged in the systematic destruction of the Oromo. Here it should suffice to say that the destruction of the Oromo and their resources was carried out on three levels. First and most obvious was the destruction and displacement of the Oromo. Through the regime's warfare, especially through the campaign of "search and destroy," thousands of Oromo people were killed and several hundred thousand driven into refugee camps in the neighboring countries of Somalia, Djoubti, the Sudan and Kenya. Internally, the *Derg* regime massively displaced the Oromo. Following the Ethio-Somali War of 1977-78, the regime claimed that there were six million internally displaced people in the southern and eastern parts of Ethiopia, of which over half were Oromo. To control their movements and prevent them from supporting the OLF, the Oromo in the regions of Bale, Arsi and Sidamo were herded like cattle into 506 "protected hamlets."

Second, while herding the Oromo into these hamlets, the regime started a program of resettling three million northerners in the South, mainly in Oromia. This was done behind the facade of rehabilitating drought and famine victims from northern Ethiopia. The political motive behind such massive transfer of population was to alter the demography of Oromia.

Third, the regime embarked on massive villagization and collectivization programs that were different from the resettlement program mentioned above. The goal of the resettlement program was to deprive support for guerrilla movements in northern Ethiopia by moving the people to the south, thus altering the demography of Oromia, while the goal of villagization and collectivization was to control the labor, produce, and resources of Oromo peasants (See Hassen & Greenfield 1992:584). The massive villagization and collectivization programs impoverished millions of Oromo peasants adding to their misery and suffering (Clay and Holcomb 1985:70-189; Clay & et al., 1988:103-228, 247-295; Kaplan 1988:1-8). Within a few years, the *Derg* "uprooted and regrouped over 8 million Oromo peasants into the so-called "new villages" a euphemism for [*Derg*'s] version of concentration camps where Oromo labor and resources [were] totally controlled and dominated by the military regime" (Hassen 1990:98, Clay et al., 1988:115-224).

For seventeen years, the peoples suffered under brutal military dictatorship, whose historic mission was nothing but destruction. It is believed that no less than two million peasants lost their lives between 1974 and 1991, not to mention millions of Oromo who were internally displaced and thousands who were scattered as refugees to many parts of the world. When the authors of sorrow and destruction were overthrown in May 1991, it was a sigh of relief, a time of joy and a moment of hope for the peoples of Ethiopia in general and the Oromo in particular .

THE TRANSFORMATION OF OROMO NATIONALISM FROM A MINORITY MOVEMENT TO A MASS MOVEMENT

The OLF which was formed in early 1974, articulated Oromo nationalism and also became its primary organizational expression (Jalata 1998:11). For seventeen years, the OLF struggled against the Ethiopian military regime and made a significant contribution to the combined effort which defeated the regime in May 1991. It was in recognition of this fact that the OLF was invited to participate in the London Conference of May 1991 and Addis Ababa Conference of July 1991. Thirty-one parties, including five Oromo organizations, also participated in the Addis Ababa Conference, where the parties met to discuss the future of Ethiopia and agreed upon a Transitional Charter that laid down the principles as well as the program of transition towards a new democratic order. The OLF co-authored, with the Tigray People Liberation Front (TPLF) and the Ethiopian People's Revolutionary Democratic Forces (EPRDF), the Transitional Charter and then joined the Transitional Government of Ethiopia, TGE (1991-1992).

During the short period when the OLF was part of the Transitional Government of Ethiopia, OLF cadres and soldiers were operating, openly and clandestinely, in every corner of Oromia. This provided opportunity for the transformation of Oromo nationalism from a minority movement to a mass movement. The rapid development of Oromo nationalism since 1991 is partly a response to the TPLF's occupation of Oromia, partly to the weakness of the Ethiopian state but, above all, to the activities of five Oromo organizations. Since 1991 the Oromo have experienced a vigorous rebirth of their distinctive national self-assertion and a remarkable flowering of literacy in *Afaan Oromo,* the Oromo language.

> Today Oromo children learn in their mother tongue and the Oromo society is engaged in intellectual reconstruction, using its own resources to create its own knowledge system. The speed with which the Oromo challenged the ... monopolization of knowledge in Amharic is remarkable (Hassen 1996:78).

With the collapse of the military regime in May 1991, the Ethiopian state was "deprived of its most potent weapons, the ability to inspire fear." With the transformation of Oromo nationalism into a mass movement the Oromo challenged Ethiopian state terrorism. The Transitional Government was "billed as a coalition government representing three main interests : the Oromo interest, the Amhara interest and the Tigrean interest, with others ... being considered important but secondary" (Hagos 1995:97). According to Leenco Lata:

> The Charter envisaged four elements that fundamentally departed from the autocratic and imperial tradition of Ethiopia to transform the relationships between the colonizers and the colonized nations. These four components were, the supremacy of the law, power sharing, the construction of a multinational democratic state and the establishment of a just peace (Lata 1998:56).

Secondly, while all independent Oromo organizations, especially the OLF, placed the hope of their people in the promise of democratic election, the TPLF leaders systematically sabotaged the democratization process in Ethiopia. In any free and fair election, the TPLF leaders knew and still know that they would lose. They would lose because, the TPLF which established Tigrean hegemony in Ethiopia, represents less than ten percent of the population of Ethiopia, while the Oromo represent around half the population of Ethiopia (Keller 1998:110, 114). In 1992, while all independent Oromo organizations and the Oromo people were prepared to play by the democratic rules of politics in any free and fair elections, the TPLF-dominated government closed more than 200 OLF campaign offices, imprisoned hundreds and killed several OLF cadres and supporters, in an effort to politically weaken or destroy all independent Oromo organizations and frighten the Oromo people before any elections were held (OLF Bulletin 1992:1-10).

For its grand design of imposing and perpetuating one-party domination of the Ethiopian political landscape, the TPLF-dominated regime made free and fair election impossible in 1992. In fact, the TPLF-dominated regime was interested in election for one and only purpose. That is: "through election of its card-carrying members and supporters to positions of leadership, it hoped to legitimize its illegitimate, vicious, undemocratic and brutal misrule" (OLF Bulletin 1992:3-4). Consequently, through the TPLF-controlled National Election Commission, the regime hijacked the democratic process and embarked on massive electoral fraud and deception for the sole purpose of putting "all legislative, executive and judicial powers under its total control" (OLF Bulletin 1992:4-10). It was the well-documented widespread irregularities in the electoral processes, the harassment, imprisonment, and even killings of supporters of independent organizations which forced the OLF and several other independent organizations to pull out of the June 21, 1992 election. The election according to many independent international observers was neither free nor fair (McDonald 1992:2-9). On 24 June 1992, the OLF was forced to withdraw from the transitional government of Ethiopia. Kulick Gilbert observed that

> Ethiopia's leaders blow a golden opportunity to set their country on a new course... The promise of a chance to choose their leaders and manage their own affairs had aroused great popular excitement for this thing called democracy. Millions of Ethiopians registered to vote often despite huge obstacles because they believed that this time it was going to be different. What they got was more of the same, broken promises, betrayed hopes and yet another permutation of age-old imperial intrigue (Kulick 1992:41-45).

No words can aptly describe the bitterness of the Oromo whose hope for peaceful devolution of power was shattered by the TPLF which wanted and still wants total elimination of all independent Oromo organizations and to control the resources of Oromia. Thus, what was promised to be the dawn of a democratic beginning turned out to be a new chapter for the rise of Tigrean hegemony in Ethiopia. In short, what was billed to be the first multi-party elections in June 1992 "were turned into a single party exercise" (Ottaway 1995:238-239). The TPLF leaders learned an important lesson from the election that they openly and deliberately rigged. That lesson is that they can manipulate any election as they did in 1994, 1995 (Hassen 1999:252) and May 2000 without provoking an outrage and condemnation from the Western powers that support them politically, financially and morally. The TPLF leaders also learned another lesson from the unfolding drama of 1992 which is that they can use their formidable military muscle for abusing power, dominating the Oromo, destroying all independent Oromo organizations and waging war in Oromia, all in the name of democracy (Hassen 2000b:2000b:147-148).

The TPLF quickly assimilated itself into the embodiment of the Ethiopian state, transformed its army into the national army, created its police force and huge security apparatus. "Worst of all, it has rehired the assassin squad used by the dictator Mengistu Hailemariam for the purpose of eliminating those suspected of opposing the regime" (Hassen 1999:245). According to Tecola Hagos, a former supporter of the TPLF leadership and now its bitter critic,

> the Ethiopian government is being transformed into a fascist type administration picking up the pieces where the government of Mengistu left...From his actions it is clear that Meles is not a democrat, he is a despot and the ultimate nightmare of all democratic minded Ethiopians everywhere. He has decimated opposition political organizations, and non-political as well as non-profit organizations that are not affiliated with EPRDF. The capital outlay and expenditure for the security of the current Ethiopian government and the leadership is almost double that of the previous government. He had created a security force, even larger and pervasive than the one that was protecting Mengistu (Hagos 1999:50).

From what has transpired thus far, it is clear that the Oromo and other peoples of Ethiopia have never been given an opportunity to enjoy a truly democratic government in more than a century. The TPLF leaders are not interested in democracy as a form of government or as a political system (Sorenson 1993:3, 12). They are interested in democracy only as an instrument for perpetuating their monopoly of state power in Ethiopia.

> What is very important to consider is the significance of the fact that the people who control TPLF and the Government are very parochial minded and appallingly arrogant charlatans. They are extremely violent, insanely suspicious ...with twin character flaws of excessive love of consumer goods and obsession with status and hier-

> archy . .. Fear, blackmail, intrigue, deception, suspicion, and brutal-
> ity are its defining characteristics. It is absolutely insane for anyone
> to expect democracy from a secretive and tyrannical organization
> such as the TPLF and its spawn (Hagos 1999:56).

"What remained in power since 1991," Tecola Hagos wrote, "is an illegitimate power structure, a reestablishment of feudalism and autocracy dressed in
new symbols with the descendants of yesterday's feudal warlords as the main
actors in this sickening Ethiopian political tragedy" (Hagos 1995:5).

Members of the TPLF army were transformed from being "fighters for
freedom" to an instrument of state terrorism. It was through the weapon of
state terrorism that the TPLF leaders aborted the democratization process in
Ethiopia. Tecola Hagos further notes that "Ethiopia's feudal structure represents one of the worst structures of oppression in the world, and it was/is a
system that gave birth to some of the most degenerate leaders who obstructed
very much needed social, economic and political changes" (Hagos 1995, ibid).
The TPLF leaders are the products of feudal culture, and it is these leaders, who
in the name of "democracy" have been systematically destroying all independent
Oromo organizations. "What is tragic in all of this", Hagos concludes,

> is the fact that Ethiopians have lost some of their greatest heroes
> to the gargantuan appetite of Leviathan-the monster of power. It
> is particularly painful for me to witness people like Meles Zenawi,
> who I once admired and wished a great future and creative leader-
> ship, someone who could have been a great statesman, becoming a
> despot and sellout, leader of degenerate liberation movement and
> collaborating with some of the worst opportunists and turncoats
> from the brutal government of Mengistu (Hagos 1995:234).

THE ATTACK ON OROMO NATIONALISM

Since 1992 the TPLF/EPRDF forces have been busy destroying the military, organizational and political capacity of the OLF and other independent
Oromo organizations. Though defeated militarily, dismantled organizationally
and disabled politically, the OLF will not be destroyed. This is for an obvious
reason. For the majority of the Oromo, the OLF is much more than an organization. It is an idea and an organization that stands for the freedom, and human
dignity of the Oromo nation. Even if the TPLF leaders manage to destroy the
OLF as an organization, they will not be able to destroy the OLF as an idea that
is deeply rooted in Oromo nationalism. It is precisely for this reason that the
Ethiopian government has intensified the attack on Oromo nationalism.

Starting in 1997 the ruling TPLF has declared war on Oromo nationalism.
This was clearly expressed in *Hizbaawi Adera* (Vol. 4, No 7, December 1996 - Feb-

ruary 1997). This publication, is the official quarterly of the ruling party. It is used to disseminate its policies to its party members for implementation at the local levels of government. In this publication, the TPLF dominated regime has articulated its fear of "narrow nationalism." which it says is stronger in Oromia than anywhere else in Ethiopia. The publication is written in rather dated Marxist-Leninist terms which closely match the style of the internal dialogue between the TPLF and the organizations it created and still controls. References to intellectuals and businessmen in Oromia as part of the problem permeate the document.

> Higher echelon intellectuals and big business people (narrow nationalists) have endangered the process of peace, democracy, development, and the interests of the masses in Oromia. Unfortunately, these individuals have not been isolated and exposed as much as required .... So it is necessary to crush narrow nationalism before it has a chance to gather momentum at a country level (emphasis added, Hizbaawi Adera. 9).

Narrow nationalism is a code name for Oromo nationalism. In order to destroy Oromo nationalism, TPLF's position is that it is necessary to isolate, expose and crush Oromo intellectuals and wealthy merchants, who are accused of nurturing it (Hassen 2000b). In short, *Hizbaawi Adera* argues that:

> only by eliminating the Oromo educated elite and capitalist class will the Oromo people be freed from narrow nationalism. Recent murders and disappearances of Oromo and the detention of members of the Matcha/Tulama Association and the Human Rights League are part of the implementation of policies put forward in this document" (Trueman 1998:6).

It should be noted however that despite the designation of "narrow nationalism," Oromo nationalism grew out of shared common heritage and it is also a response to a century long colonial experience. As a collective sentiment of a nation that has been wronged for too long, Oromo nationalism is a progressive, revolutionary and democratic force for change. It is this nationalism that has sustained the Oromo struggle for a quarter of a century against all odds. It is this nationalism which motivates the Oromo to endure incredible sacrifices. Their sacrifices are the measure of their worth as a people (Hassen 1998:215).

> From this perspective, the attack on an independent Oromo organization that does not receive its marching orders from the TPLF/ EPRDF is not only an attack on Oromo nationalism but also a clear assault on the right of the Oromo people to have their own independent organizations. The attempt to destroy the OLF is a cruel revenge of history. The TPLF which attempted and failed to bring the OLF under its wing from 1984 to 1990, is now using the cover

of the EPRDF and the governmental resources at its disposal to militarily, destroy the organization that has the support of the overwhelming majority of the Oromo. The attempt to destroy the OLF angers not only the Oromo but all who have concern for the future of democracy in that country. The attack on an independent organization is the greatest setback to the hopes and ideals of peaceful democratic change in Ethiopia since the overthrow of the military dictatorship in May 1991. Democracy cannot be built by militarily destroying an organization that expresses the profound aspirations of a given national group. Trust cannot be built between the rulers and the people, whose leadership is destroyed, whose property is confiscated, and who are treated as if they were under foreign military occupation (Hassen 1999a:251).

As the examples of the Macha and Tulama Association, the OLF and other independent Oromo organizations indicate that too often the Oromo develop their own independent leadership not to harm and dominate others but to run their own affairs and administer themselves, only to see their aspirations shattered and their independent leadership destroyed by those who have unquenchable thirst to dominate the Oromo and control their resources (Hassen 1994:105). The Oromo want, and it is their right, to be their own masters and assume for themselves as they have the right to do, the responsibility of their own existence and the exercise of their power, without harming the rights and interests of others.

The TPLF assault on all independent organizations and its tight control of Oromia brought to the Oromo the painful realization that the archaic Ethiopian political culture has not changed at all. It is an oppressive political culture in which the minority dictates the fate of the majority. It is sad to conclude that since the 1960s, Ethiopia has not produced a single government that did not destroy Oromo organizations, a single government that respected Oromo national dignity, a single government that did not kill Oromo leaders, a single government that treated the Oromo as full citizens of that country, a single government that did not practice arbitrary arrest, years of detention without trials, extra judicial executions, disappearances (euphemism for secret killings) denial of equal protection under the law, a single government that did not restrict freedom of expression, freedom of association, and political participation, and above all, a single government that did not attempt to destroy Oromo nationalism. However, one thing is for certain, Oromo nationalism has recalled to life the crushed Oromo self-respect and their self-confidence and it inspires them with renewed determination to achieve their self-determination. The Oromo now realize that people without self-respect and self-confidence are without the essential dignity of humanity. Nationalism has already given the

Oromo freedom of mind and spirit and a new sense of unity and nationhood. Nothing will divide them again. And no force will kill the spirit of freedom, self-respect and human dignity that now resides in the Oromo nation (Hassen 1990:99). Since their colonization during and after the 1880s, the Oromo have always struggled for their freedom and human dignity. But never more than since the 1960s. The blood of the fallen heroes such as Haile Mariam Gaamada, Lieutenant Mamo Mazamir, Ellemo Qilxxuu, General Taddesse Birru, Barro Tumsa, Rev. Gudina Tumsa, Magarsaa Barii, Jahatani Ali, Mulis Abba Gada, and thousands of others nurture the unquenchable Oromo desire for freedom and human dignity. In short, Oromo nationalism has captured the heart, mind and soul of the Oromo who will find inner fountains of fire to continue with the struggle for self-determination. The sooner the TPLF leaders realize this reality and change course, the better it will be for the future of all the peoples of Ethiopia and for consolidation of democratic order in Ethiopia.

A PROPOSED SOLUTION TO THE OROMO YEARNING FOR SELF-DETERMINATION

For more than a century, the Oromo have been and still are subjected to powerlessness, oppression and denial of all forms of political expression. To end their oppression, the Oromo have several options, two of which are crucial. The first is the establishment of an independent Republic of Oromia, separate from Ethiopia, while the second is self-determination for Oromia within a democratic federal republic of Ethiopia.

I have been away from Ethiopia for over two decades and do not know which option the majority of the Oromo favor in Ethiopia. However, from readings of current Oromo literature, participation in numerous Oromo conferences held in Africa, Australia, Europe, and North America and extensive discussion with the Oromo diaspora, there appears that the option of independent Oromia, separate from Ethiopia, resonates more with the new generation of Oromo youth than the option of self-determination for Oromia within Ethiopia. What is more, there are a number of scholars who argue convincingly that the declolonization of Oromia and the self-determination of the Oromo are incompatible within the framework of United Ethiopia (see for instance Asafa Jalata, 1993, 1998 and 2001, Bonnie Holcomb and Sisai Ibssa, 1990, and Mekuria Bulcha, 1992, and 2002. See also the contributions of Hamdesa Tuso, Mekuria Bulcha, and Temesgen Erna in this book).

> Basing their reasoning on their analysis of the Ethiopian colonization of Oromia, they argue that the Oromo self-determination requires the construction of a self-organized Oromia, independent from Ethiopia, as a necessary part of decolonization. This is one pos-

sible scenario for finding a lasting solution to the Oromo colonial experience (Hassen, 1999: 110).

I believe the decolonization of Oromia and the self-determination of the Oromo are compatible within a democratic Federal republic of Ethiopia. I maintain this position for the following broad reasons. First, to me the Oromo colonial experience is that of settler colonialism. As settler colonialism in South Africa was dismantled through democratic election, I believe that if a genuine democratic election is held in Oromia, settler colonialism will be dismantled and Oromia will be decolonized. Dismantling settler colonialism will enable the Oromo to form, without any interference and control from the outside, their own autonomous government, autonomous parliament, independent judiciary, and a national guard that protects the autonomy of Oromia. Secondly, I am an idealist who believes in the unity of free people in a free country. Today the Oromo are not free people and Oromia is still a colony. That is why I argue for the decolonization of Oromia is absolutely necessary for peace, economic development and democratization in Ethiopia. To me, there is no better prospect for the future of the peoples of Ethiopia than the establishment of a working federal system based on freedom with justice and equality in that country. I believe that only a federal system unites separate nations, nationalities, peoples and groups without sacrificing the rights and vital interests of its members (Hassen, 1999: 110).

It is only a genuine federal arrangement that will save the peoples of Ethiopia including the Oromo from vicious cycle of misery and destruction. A genuine federal arrangement will enable the Oromo, the Amhara, the Sidama, the Somali, the Tigreans and other peoples of Ethiopia to live in peace with each other instead of destroying their future.

The nations and nationalities that constitute the peoples of Ethiopia are all conscious of their identities and they are struggling to preserve their identities and cultures (Hassen 2000b:151). Of all the political systems that have been invented by human ingenuity only "federalism has proved useful in accommodating diversity" (Elazar 1987:248).

> Federalism is politically sound because of its compound features, that is, because it establishes polities that are compounded from entities which maintain their respective integrities and thus work to preserve the liberties of their citizens. Moreover, by providing for a constitutional diffusion of power, federalism enables 'ambition to counteract ambition.' It is a system designed to prevent tyranny without preventing governance; and it seeks to provide a political remedy for political diseases (Elazar 1987:29).

In the multi-ethnic, multi-cultural and multi-religious country, the ideology of Ethiopian ruling elites which opposes diversity and embraces a single nation state has proved failure. The notion of the Ethiopian state which holds "sovereignty to be indivisible" and the state power to be monopolized either by the Amhara or Tigrean elites has failed. In other situations such as the United States, Canada, Germany, India and Nigeria (Everett 1997:28-148) federalism has proved useful not only in accommodating diversity, but also in providing for power-sharing, creating joint or cutting around the issue of sovereignty and strengthening "prior organic ties where they exist" (Elazar 1987:12).

> Federalism in its most limited form is usually defined as having to do with the distribution and sharing of power, but even in that limited form there is an implicit commitment to a conception of justice that holds, among other things, that a distribution of power is necessary and desirable. On the other hand, federalism in its broadest sense is presented as a form of justice—emphasizing liberty and citizen participation in governance, but one which is inevitably linked to political reality because it must be concerned with the distribution of powers. One of the primary attributes of federalism is that it cannot, by its very nature, abandon the concern for either power or justice but must consider both in relationship to each other, thus forcing people to consider the hard realities of political life while at the same time maintaining their aspirations for the best policy (Elazar 1987:84).

How could this ideal be implemented in the TPLF-dominated Ethiopia? One cannot give an adequate answer to this important question. Three unsatisfactory points can, however, be suggested. First, if such a system is to be established in Ethiopia, the TPLF leaders must change their attitude towards federalism. The TPLF has to institute important changes in order to pave the way for peaceful political work. Moreover "the period when the EPRDF was looked at, by some people, as a genuine coalition of quasi-autonomous groups is over. Its bogus nature is now almost unanimously and openly acknowledged, even by TPLF supporters" (Lata 1999:230). In other words, the TPLF leaders must practice democracy within the organizations that they created and still control. Second, Western powers, especially the government of the United States, that has supported the TPLF regime financially and politically, must realize that the power structure in Ethiopia is unstable.

> At present, this unstable power edifice is being propped up by TPLF security and military machinery as well as by the support and endorsement of foreign powers. These factors are clearly inadequate to sustain the stability of the present power structure. Thus, its sudden collapse appears very likely. This should worry all those who

are interested in averting another round of tumultuous change in Ethiopia (Lata 1999:227).

Finally, if the peoples of Ethiopia, including the Oromo, are to avoid the tragedies of Somalia, Rwanda, the Democratic Republic of Congo, Liberia, Sierra Leone, and several African states that are collapsing, they have to establish a federal system grounded in maximum human liberty. Such a system facilitates citizens' participation in governance and above all enables them "(1) to institute workable political arrangements, (2) to create a workable polity, (3) to establish a just polity, and (4) to achieve a just moral order" (Elazar 1987:104). Only a workable federal arrangement allows people to achieve all these and much more (Everett 1997:4-9).

The strength of federal arrangement is that it combines self-rule which satisfies the aspiration of the Oromo and other oppressed peoples of Ethiopia, and shared rule which takes into consideration the geography, demography, culture, history, and above all, economic interdependence of the peoples of Ethiopia. As the experience of the last eleven years demonstrates, the TPLF federal arrangement does not work, simply because it was designed by the leadership of a single party and its partners, and above all, the TPLF lacks legitimacy and support of the overwhelming majority of the peoples of Ethiopia. The failure of the TPLF imposed federal arrangement in Ethiopia does not reflect on federalism itself. It reflects only on the TPLF leadership that aborted the democratization process in Ethiopia and abused federal principles. What is needed is to eliminate TPLF abuses and create necessary conditions for implementation of federal principles. This could be done in two ways. First, the realization that a federal arrangement works when it is designed by all the peoples of Ethiopia and their representatives and implemented with their freely and democratically expressed consent for its purpose and framework (Hassen 2000b:165-166). The new federal arrangement will, in effect, be a universally designed agreement for power sharing and to maintain a just order "in such a way that all reaffirm their fundamental equality and retain their basic rights" (Elazar 1987:4).

> Federalism involves a commitment to partnership and to active cooperation on the part of individuals and institutions that also take pride in preserving their own respective integrities. Successful federal systems are characterized not only by their constitutional arrangements in the narrow sense of the word but by their permeation with the spirit of federalism as manifested in sharing through negotiation, mutual forbearance and self-restraint in the pursuit of goals, and a consideration of the system as well as the substantive consequences of one's acts (Elazar 1987:154).

When and where will these conditions emerge? It is only after decolonization of Oromia and democratization of Ethiopia that these conditions will emerge. The spirit of federalism is absent from the Ethiopian political culture; genuine power-sharing through negotiation is unknown and; above all, forbearance and self-restraint on the part of the leadership in the pursuit of goals is utterly lacking. It is only a decolonized Oromia, with its democratically elected government and its own national guard and police force that can enter into federal partnership with other states in Ethiopia The second is the realization that federal relationships are established only through a written constitution endowed with legitimacy and based on consent of the people. So far, Ethiopia has not produced a constitution endowed with legitimacy based on the consent of the people. Like "every political and economic idea that was tried by the Ethiopian governments over the last fifty years, did not solve Ethiopia's political and economic problems" (Hagos 1995:4), the four Ethiopian constitutions that were produced since 1931 have failed to solve the question of power-sharing in Ethiopia simply because none of the constitution was a genuine federal constitution.

> First, the federal relationship must be established or confirmed through a perpetual compact of union, ... embodied in a written constitution that outlines, among other things, the terms by which power is divided or shared in the political system which can be altered only by extraordinary procedures .... Juridically, federal constitutions are distinctive in that they are not simply compacts between the rulers and the ruled but involve the people, the general government, and the polities constituting the federal union. Moreover, the constituent polities often retain constitution-making rights of their own (Elazar 1987:157).

In 1994 the TPLF drafted and ratified its constitution at the cost of more than 50 million Ethiopian birr. That constitution failed to bring about a democratic form of government and social change in Ethiopia because of the absence of popular support for its drafting (Hassen 1999:153) and because the TPLF itself disregards its own constitution with reckless abandon.

> The Constitution crafted for and by the TPLF has many shortcomings, but one can live with many of these if one condition is made possible: that the authorities which granted this constitution to the Ethiopian peoples be the first ones to start treating it with respect. Freedom of assembly and of expression are guaranteed on paper. International humanitarian and human right conventions are declared as part of the law of the land on paper. Hence, torture, extra judicial killing, disappearance, and unlawful detention are proscribed on paper. But the regime, according to local and foreign

observers, has routinely violated these same principles that it has written into its constitution. It is extremely hypocritical for the regime to insist that others accept its constitution as a precondition for dialogue when it is the first to treat its own constitution with total contempt (Lata 1999:232).

Like Emperor Haile Selassie's constitutions of 1931 and 1955 and the military regime's constitution of 1987, the TPLF constitution of 1994 will remain on paper. To have their own constitution is good politics and useful propaganda for the TPLF leaders, but their failure to abide by it, is the worst form of deception and hypocrisy. The TPLF leaders artfully drafted their constitution. However, they conveniently forgot to realize the basic principle of federal constitutions (Hassen 1998:185-186).

> It is an even greater art to bring the constituency to endow the constitution with legitimacy. Constitutional legitimacy involves consent. It is certainly not a commitment that can be coerced-however much people can be coerced into obedience to a particular regime. Consensual legitimacy is utterly necessary for a constitution to have real meaning and to last. The very fact that, although rule can be imposed by force, constitutions can exist as meaningful instruments only by consent, means that constitutional documents cannot be treated in the abstract, divorced from the power systems of which they are a part and the political cultures from which they grow and to which they must respond (Elazar 1987:164).

The TPLF leadership must be forced to change direction from dependence on bullets for governance to the use of the ballot box for self-government in Oromia. Non-interference in the internal affairs of Oromia, respect for the capacity of the Oromo to run their administration, respect for the rule of law will be necessary steps for the decolonization of the Oromo. Righting the wrongs inflicted on the Oromo by the TPLF-dominated regime will be the first challenge facing the government of autonomous Oromia. For the Oromo to be their own masters in their own state, Oromia must have its own freely elected assembly, autonomous government, independent judiciary, police force, and national guard. In short, Oromia must be as autonomous as Tigray itself. That is the prerequisite for decolonization of Oromia, the self-determination of the Oromo and the realization of the ideal of equality among the states that constitute the democratic federal republic of Ethiopia. If the TPLF leaders create the condition for establishing an autonomous government in Oromia, they need our support and deserve it. Above all, they will create trust and confidence—the precondition for building a democratic system. Trust and confidence will begin loosening the grip of hatred, mistrust, and suspicion among people and prepare the necessary climate for building a democratic system the only way it can be built -by the people from the bottom up. By cooperating with other organizations (on the basis of equality, the TPLF leaders can give new hope for a democratic future for all the peoples of Ethiopia (Hassen 1999a:256).

The prospect for a democratic Ethiopia will be greatly enhanced if the Oromo and other oppressed peoples of Ethiopia are united in their opposition to the TPLF dominated regime. At the same time if the Western powers, especially the Government of the United States, want to give a chance for a new democratization process in Ethiopia, they must stop financing tyranny in Ethiopia. Instead, they must support those who are struggling to end that tyranny. Such support will enhance the process of democratization in Ethiopia and create an environment of free expression, tolerance of a diversity of cultures and opinions, respect for the dignity of the human person, and, above all, the supremacy of the rule of law (Hassen 1999a:234).

CONCLUSIONS

For more than a century, the Oromo have been and still are subjected to powerlessness, oppression and denial of all forms of political expression. It was for ending their political oppression, economic exploitation and cultural dehumanization that the Oromo developed their nationalism.

Oromo nationalism first emerged in the 1960s when Oromo nationalist leaders developed a peaceful resistance movement against the Ethiopian state. One of the goals of these leaders was the transformation of the Ethiopian state from being dominated by the elite of one ethnic group into the state of all its citizens. That goal was never realized. It is the belief of this writer that it is only such a profound transformation will make the Ethiopian state, the state of all its citizens, "the accepted source of identity and the arena of politics . . the decision-making center of government" (Zartman 1995:5) and the institution that maintains law and order, enhances societal cohesion, respects the human and democratic rights of its citizens and allocates fair and equitable distribution of resources for all the peoples of Ethiopia.

I believe that without unity, the future of the peoples of Ethiopia, including the Oromo, appears to be bleak. Besides governmental tyranny, there are competing nationalisms in Ethiopia. The nations and nationalities that constitute the peoples of Ethiopia are all conscious of their distinct identities and they are struggling to preserve their identities and cultures (Hassen 2000b: 151). The days when Ethiopia was projected as the land of a single nation, with a single language, single culture and a single religion are over. Today there are rival nationalisms in Ethiopia. To avoid the vicious cycle of misery and destruction, the nations and nationalities who constitute the Ethiopian peoples must develop a working federal system that will enable them for handling conflict generated by rival nationalisms. At the bottom of the conflict between rival nationalisms in Ethiopia is the issue of national identity. In one way or the other, the peoples of Ethiopia have to figure out how competing nationalisms can live together without destroying the material basis and moral foundations of their future. It is precisely for this reason that the federal structure that exists on paper in Ethiopia must be implemented, broadened and strengthened. Only a federal system which is "a preferred scheme for human organization in heterogeneous societies" (Tekle 1991:48) can guarantee the survival of national identities in Ethiopia nurturing the flowering of tolerant political culture and renaissance of various cultures, and above all which allows the diverse peoples of Ethiopia to exercise their human and democratic rights without infringing upon the rights of others (Hassen 1990:100).

> In a truly democratic federated Ethiopia, the Oromo will lose nothing but they will have a great deal to gain. What is needed is to decolonize Oromia and democratize Ethiopia. The decolonization of Oromia is fundamental to the self-determination of the Oromo and one cannot be achieved without the other. The decolonization of Oromia will ensure self-determination for the Oromo, while democratization will create a necessary political climate in the country in which conflict will be resolved through dialogue, genuine search for mutual benefit characterized by the spirit of tolerance, consensus and compromise. The creation of a self-governing Oromo state is a necessary condition for the establishment of a federated democratic Ethiopia. Because of their numbers, geographical position, and rich natural resources in Oromia, the Oromo are destined to play an important role in the future of Ethiopia and the Horn of Africa. Consequently, Ethiopians should make an earnest effort to understand the reasons for, and come to terms with, the Oromo quest for self-determination (Hassen 1996:80).

I must state clearly that the Ethiopian state must accommodate Oromo nationalism through actualization of the decolonization of Oromia and the self-determination of the Oromo. The failure to decolonize Oromia in the long run will result in total alienation of the Oromo from the Ethiopian political process. Such a prospect will mark the end of Ethiopia as a viable country. This is for obvious reason. The Oromo constitute more than forty percent of the population of Ethiopia. Oromia, the Oromo regional state within Ethiopia, is the richest, the biggest and the most densely populated region of that country. Oromia forms the economic backbone of Ethiopia. Hence, it is in the best interest of the Ethiopian state and the future well being of all the peoples of Ethiopia to accommodate Oromo nationalism and harness its positive aspects for strengthening the unity, peace, stability and economic development of that country.

Finally, if this work makes the discussion of Oromo nationalism more informed and kindles enthusiasm to produce an objective and dispassionate scholarship on the subject, its purpose will have been fulfilled adding to our understanding of the Oromo yearning for self-determination.

Notes

1. The early draft of this paper was presented at the Conference on the Horn of Africa, held at Columbia University, New York, April 6, 2001. I am indebted to the Copen Foundation for its grant which enabled me to conduct research at the National Archives in July 2005 for the purpose of revising this chapter.

2. I have drawn on my "Review Essay: Gezetena Gezot," *The Journal of Oromo Studies,* Vol. 4, Numbers 1&2 (July 1997), p.220.

References

Abrah, Emmanuel. 1995. *Reminiscences of my life.* Oslo, Norway: Lunde Forlag.

Alter, Peter. 1989. *Nationalism.* Stuart Mckinnon-Evans (tr.), London: Edward Arnold.

Baissa, Lemmu. 1998. Contending nationalisms in the Ethiopian Empire State and the Oromo struggle for self-determination. In *Oromo nationalism and the Ethiopian discourse: The search for freedom & democracy.* ed. Asafa Jalata. Lawrenceville, NJ: The Red Sea Press.

Baxter, Paul. 1978. Ethiopia's unacknowledged problem. The Oromo. *African Affairs.* 77, 283-296.

Baxter, Paul. 1998. Towards identifying some of the moral components of on Oromo national identity. In *Ethnicity and the State in Eastern Africa,* ed. Mohamed Saleh and John Markakis, 50-61. Upsala: Nordiska Afrikanistitate.

Breuilly, John. 1982. *Nationalism and the state.* New York: St Martin's Press.

Bulcha, Mekuria. 1993a. Language, ethnic identity and nationalism in Ethiopia. *The Oromo Commentary.* III, 1:8-16.

Bulcha, Mekuria. 1993b. Language, ethnic Identity, and nationalism in Ethiopia, Part Two. *The Oromo Commentary.* III, 2:5-18.

Bulcha, Mekuria. 1994a. The state of human right in Ethiopia. *The Oromo Commentary.* IV,1; 21-24.

Bulcha, Mekuria. 1994b. Priests, religion and language in Ethiopia: A Commentary. *The Oromo Commentary.* IV,1, 8-11.

Bulcha, Mekuria. 1994c. The language policies of Ethiopian regimes and the history of written Afaan Oromo: 1844-1994. *The Journal of Oromo Studies.* 2,1 & 2:91-115.

Clapham, Christopher. 1988. *Transformation and continuity in revolutionary Ethiopia.* Cambridge: Cambridge University Press.

Clay, Jason and Bonnie Holcomb. 1986. *Politics and the Ethiopian famine of 1984-1985.* Cambridge, MA: Cultural Survival, Inc.

Clay, Jason, et al. 1988. *The spoils of famine: Ethiopian famine policy and peasant agriculture.* Cambridge, MA: Cultural Survival, Inc.

Elazar, Daniel. 1987. *Exploring federalism.* Tuscaloosa: University of Alabama Press.

Everett, William Johnson. *Religion, federalism and the struggle for public life: Cases from Germany, India and America* Oxford: Oxford University Press. 1997.

Gebre-Medhin, Jordan. 1989. *Peasant and nationalism in Eritrea: A critique of Ethiopian studies.* Trenton, NJ: The Red Sea Press.

Gellner, Ernest. 1983. *Nations and nationalism.* Ithaca and Oxford: Cornell University Press and Blackwell.

Hagos, Tecola. 1995. *Democratization? Ethiopia 1991-1994: A personal view.* Cambridge, MA: Khepera..

Hagos, Tecola. 1999. *Demystifying political thought, power, and economic development.* Washington, D.C. Khepera Publishers.

Hassen, Mohammed. 1990a. *The Oromo of Ethiopia: A history 1560s-1860.* Cambridge; Cambridge University Press.

Hassen, Mohammed. 1990b. "The militarization of the Ethiopian state and the Oromo." Proceedings of the Fifth International Conference on the Horn of Africa, 91-102. New York: Marsden Reproductions.

Hassen, Mohammed. 1992. "A new battle in and over Oromia." Proceedings of the International Conference on the Prospects for the Liberation of Oromia and its Impact on the Politics of the Horn of Africa, ed. Mohammed Hassen, 81-93. The University of Minnesota. August 1-2.

Hassen, Mohammed. 1994. Eritrean independence and democracy in the Horn of Africa. In *Eritrea and Ethiopia from Conflict to Cooperation*, ed. Amare Tekle, 85-113. Lawrenceville, NJ: The Red Sea Press.

Hassen, Mohammed. 1996. The development of Oromo nationalism. In *Being and becoming Oromo historical and anthropological enquires*, ed. P.T. W. Baxter et al, 67-80. Upsala: Nordska Africa Institute.

Hassen, Mohammed. 1997. Review essay on Gezatena Gezot Macha and Tulama Association. *The Journal of Oromo Studies* 4, nos. 1 & 2:203-238.

Hassen, Mohammed. 1998. The Macha-Tulama Association and the development of Oromo nationalism. In *Oromo nationalism and the Ethiopian discourse: The search for freedom and democracy,* ed. Asafa Jalata, 183-221. Lawrenceville, NJ: The Red Sea Press.

Hassen, Mohammed. 1999a. Ethiopia: Missed opportunities for peaceful democratic process. State building and democratization. In *Africa: Faith, hope, and realities*, ed. Kidane Mengisteab and Cyrie Daddieh, 233-260. Connecticut and London: West Port.

Hassen, Mohammed. 1999b. A short History of Oromo Colonial Experience: Part One 1870-1935. *The Journal of Oromo Studie.* 6, nos 1 & 2:109-158.

Hassen, Mohammed. 2000a. A critical account of the history of the Oromo national liberation movement: setbacks and prospects. Sagalee Oromoo. *Journal of Oromo Students in Europe.* 25,1:48-94.

Hassen, Mohammed. 2000b. A short history of Oromo colonial experience; Part two, Colonial consolidation and resistance 1935-2000. *The Journal of Oromo Studies* vol.7, nos 17 2 July.

Hassen, Mohammed and Greenfield, Richard. 1992. "The Oromo nation and its resistance to Amhara colonial administration." Proceedings of the First International Congress of Somali Studies, ed. Hussien M. Adam & Charles I. Geshekter, 546-599. Atlanta: Scholars Press.

Hussen, Abdul Mejid. 1976. The political economy of the Ethiopian famine. In *Rehab: Drought and famine in Ethiopia,* ed. Abdul Mejid Hussen. London: International African Institute.

Hizbaawi Adera. 1997. Vol. 4, No. 7, December 1996-February.

Jalata, Asafa. 1993. *Oromia and Ethiopia: State formation and Ethnonational conflict.* 1868-1992, Boulder & London: Lynne Rienner.

Jalata, Asafa. 1998. The emergence of Oromo nationalism and Ethiopian reaction. *Oromo Nationalism and the Ethiopian discourse: The search for freedom & democracy,* ed Asafa Jalata, 1-26. Lawrenceville, NJ: The Red Sea Press.

Karaa Walabummaa. *Information Bulletin of the Union of Oromo Students in Europe,* 6, nos.3:2-7.

Kaplan, Robert D. 1988. *Surrender or starve: The wars behind the famine.* Boulder, Co: Westview Press.

Keller, Edmond. 1995. Remaking the Ethiopian state. In *Collapsed states: The disintegration and restoration of legitimate authority* ed. I. William Zartman, Boulder, CO: Lynne Rienner Publishers:

Keller, Edmond. 1996. Africa in the new international order. In *Rethinking state sovereignty and regional security,* ed. Edmond J. Keller and Donald Rothchild, Boulder, CO: Lynne Rienner Publishers.

Keller, Edmond. 1998. Regime change and Ehno-regionalism in Ethiopia: The case of the Oromo. In *Oromo nationalism and the Ethiopian discourse: The search for freedom & democracy,* ed. Asafa Jalata, 109-124. Lawrenceville, NJ: The Red Sea Press.

Kulick, Gilbert D. 1992. Ethiopia's hollow election observing the forms, *Foreign Service Journa.l* September, 42-45.

Lamb, Margaret. 1974. *Nationalism.* London: Heinemann Education Books.

Lata, Leenco. 1999. *The Ethiopian state at the crossroads: Decolonization & democratization or disintegration.* Lawrenceville, NJ: The Red Sea Press.

Lata, Leenco. 1998. The making and unmaking of Ethiopia's transitional charter. In *Oromo Nationalism and the Ethiopian discourse: The search for freedom & democracy,* ed. Asafa Jalata, 51-77. Lawrenceville, NJ: The Red Sea Press.

Lefort, Rene. 1981. *Ethiopia: An heritical revolution?* London: Zed Press.

Levine, D. N. 1974. *Greater Ethiopia: The evolution of a multiethnic society.* Chicago: The University Press of Chicago.

Mandela, Nelson. 1994. *Long walk to freedom.* Boston: Little Brown Company.

Mcdonald, P. 1992. Testimony prepared for presentation to the House of Foreign Relations Subcommittee on African Affairs Hearing.

Markakis, John. 1987. *National and class conflict in the Horn of Africa.* Cambridge: Cambridge University Press.

Memorandum. 1992. Why the OLF is forced to withdraw from the election. *Oromo Bulletin.* I, 2:1-10.

Monshipuri, Mahmood. 1995. *Democratization, liberalization and human rights in the Third World.* Boulder, CO. LynneRienner

The Oromo Liberation Front Political Program. Finfinne: 1976.

Ottaway, Marina. 1993. Testimony Prepared for presentation to the House of Foreign Relations Subcommittee on African Affairs hearing, March.

Ottaway, Marina. 1995. Democratization in Collapsed States. In *Collapsed States,* ed. I. William Zartman, Boulder, CO: Lynne Rienner.

Smith, Anthony D. 1982. Nationalism, ethnic separatism and the intelligentsia. *National separatism,* ed. Colin H. Williams. Vancouver: University of British Columbia.

Sorenson, George. 1993. *Democracy and democratization: Dilemmas in world politics.* Boulder, CO: Westview, Press.

Sbacchi, Alberto. 1985. *Ethiopia under Mussolini: Fascism and colonial experience.* London: Zed Books.

Sbacchi, Alberto. 1997. *Legacy of bitterness: Ethiopia and Fascist Italy. 1935-1941.* Lawrenceville, NJ: The Red Sea Press.

Tareke, Gebru. 1991. *Ethiopia: Power and Protest Peasant Revolts in the Twentieth Century.* Cambridge: Cambridge University Press.

Taye, Gemechu, 1993. The history of Macha-Tulama Association. Addis Ababa University, Essay.

Truman, Trevor. 1998. *Sagalee Haaraa* no. 21 January-February:

Truman, Trevor, 2000. *Sagalee Haara,* no. 30:1-3.

Wolde Giorgis, Dawit. 1989. *Red tears: War, famine and revolution in Ethiopia.* Trenton, NJ: The Red Sea Press.

Zoga, Olana. 1993. *Gezatena Gezot and Macha and Tulama Association,* Addis Ababa.

Chapter 12

The Oromo Movement and the Crisis of the Ethiopian State

Asafa Jalata

The Oromo[1] movement which seeks self-determination for the nation known as Oromia[2] is a central factor for the current crisis of the Ethiopian state. This movement, as an anti-colonial national struggle, aims at dismantling Ethiopian settler colonialism and its institutions that have been legitimated by the ideology of racism.[3] It specifically fights against economic exploitation, cultural destruction and repression, and the denial of individual and national rights.

In the Ethiopian Empire where the colonized nations, oppressed groups and classes have been forced to live under rigid racial/class hierarchy, the state itself has become an instrument of oppression, exploitation, and cultural destruction used by one group against the others. Hence, the central contradiction that is built into Ethiopian politics is the racialization and ethnicization of state power leading to further rigid ethno-class stratification and dependence on big powers without accountability to the ruled (Jalata 1993; 1996). The acute political and economic crises in Oromia and Ethiopia, and the policy response to them, have contributed to social unrest and social movements. These crises stem from the political behavior of the Ethiopian state and structural factors, such as internal social forces, and global forces that have become involved on the side of this state without requiring accountability, the rule of law, or the implementation of at least 'limited democracy.'

Two assumptions emerge from this statement. The first assumption is that racialization of Ethiopian state power, the lack of accountability and democracy have prevented the construction of a legitimate state that reflects multinational interests. The second assumption is that since cultural systems of the peoples that traditionally provided the material and social needs have been broken by the alliance of the Ethiopian state and the capitalist world system, peoples are exposed to cultural, economic and political crises. The Ethiopian state and its external counterparts could not promote meaningful social changes and they have contributed to recurrent crises in the form of political crisis, famine, poverty, conflict, and war.

Currently, the emergence of the Eritrean state, the intensification of nationalist struggles, and the conflict between Eritrea and Ethiopia have increased the severity of the crises. The national struggles of Oromos, Sidamas, Afars and Ogadenis demonstrate the intensity of these problems (see Katsuyoshi and Markakis 1994; Jalata 1998). These crises and conflicts are grounded in specific historical and structural features built into the Ethiopian ethnocratic colonial state. A critical understanding of these problems requires to identify and examine the conditions that facilitate hostilities and mutual cultural destruction among various national groups.

As these recurrent conflicts and crises show, the Ethiopian government has failed to play its state roles and unable to provide basic social services to the majority of the population. The failure to fulfill its obligations raises serious theoretical and practical problems for academics, progressive political actors and policy analysts. Therefore, a deep understanding of structural forces (e.g., social and national inequality, global and regional structures) and conjunctures (e.g., state behavior, conflict) are necessary to enrich our social scientific knowledge that informs pragmatic policy approaches to these problems.

The interplay of multiple social structural and historical factors and conjunctures in the global capitalist world system facilitated the development of Oromo nationalism. The inability of the colonizers to totally control or crush human spirit, individual and collective resistance to colonial domination, the immortality of certain cultural memory, changes in social structures because of economic and political changes, urbanization and community formation, the development of institutions, the emergence of an educated class, politicized collective grievances, and the dissemination of knowledge through global and local networks interacted and facilitated the development of this nationalism. A better understanding of the Oromo national struggle requires to critically explore the social structural factors, historical and sociological processes, and conjunctures that interplayed to develop human agencies in Oromo society necessary to challenge the Ethiopian colonizing and racist structures. The development of these human agencies cannot be understood without linking it to the processes of ideological formation and cultural revitalization, institutional and organizational manifestations, and alternative knowledge production and dissemination. Gurutz Bereciartu (1994) calls these processes "national revindication" in which the colonized people reclaim and attempt to recover their lost

cultural, political, and economic rights by developing their collective consciousness of nationalism.

This chapter situates the emergence and development of Oromo nationalism in history and explains how resistance to slavery, racial hierarchy and
colonial domination was gradually transformed into the Oromo movement,
the phases and objectives and the problems of this movement, the successes and
failures of the movement, and its role in the crisis of the Ethiopian state. By
drawing on historical and ethnographic analyses, the chapter combines a social
constructionist model of social and national movements with a social structural
approach to explain the development of Oromo nationalism and the crisis of
the Ethiopian state.

HISTORICAL BACKGROUND

The development of Oromo nationalism was slower than that of other
Africans who were colonized directly by the European powers during the
scramble for Africa, the same period Oromos and others were colonized by the
alliance of Ethiopian warlords and European powers (see Holcomb and Ibssa
1990; Jalata 1993). Oromos were colonized directly by the Ethiopian (Amhara-
Tigray) minority colonial settlers that attempted to destroy Oromo peoplehood through genocide or ethnocide and selective assimilation. The Ethiopian
colonial government with the help of the weapons, mercenaries, and advisors
from Great Britain, France, and Italy liquidated half of the Oromo population
(five million out of ten million) and their leadership during the last decades
of the nineteenth century (see de Salviac 1901; Hassen 1998). The Ethiopian
colonial settlers established their main geopolitical centers in Oromia through
which racist and colonial policies have been formulated and implemented to
keep the remaining Oromos as second class citizens and to exploit their economic and labor resources by denying them access to state power. These geopolitical centers are garrison cities surrounded by the Oromo rural masses who are
denied meaningful health, education and other social services, despite the fact
that these colonial settlers and their collaborators depend on resources of the
Oromo majority.

These "garrison cities were geopolitical headquarters from which Ethiopian soldiers were dispatched to impose colonial rule through enslavement
and expropriation of the basic means of subsistence such as cattle, land, and
other valuables. Through these centers expropriated goods flowed for local
consumption and an international market" (Jalata 1993:62). The settlers also
created semi-slavery (*nafxanya-gabbar*) system to divide the Oromo farmers
between colonial officials and soldiers and their collaborators to force them to
produce agricultural commodities for local consumption and an international

market; the farmers were also coerced to work without payment for the settlers, intermediaries, and the colonial state for certain number of days every week. The Ethiopian state introduced the process of forced labor via slavery and the *nafxanya-gabbar* system. Bonnie Holcomb and Sisai Ibssa (1990:135) noted that "the gun (from Europe) and the gun carrier (from Abyssinia) arrived in the colonies as one unit and this unit basically expresses political alliance that created the *neftenga-gabbar* [sic] relationship, the relation that lay at the heart of the emerging Ethiopian colonialism." Whenever the Oromo farmers and other colonized peoples failed to provide services or pay taxes or tributes, the settlers enslaved their children or wives; during the colonial wars, millions of Oromos and other colonized peoples were sold (Jalata 1993:67-68; Schmitt 1994:32-34; Bulcha 1997:19-33). The Ethiopian colonialists continued to depopulate Oromia through slave trade until the 1930s when the Italians abolished slavery to recruit adequate labor for their agricultural plantations in the Horn of Africa. Emperor Menelik, the founder of the Ethiopian Empire, and his wife at one time owned 70,000 slaves, and he was considered "Ethiopia's greatest slave entrepreneur" (Pankhurst 1968:75; Marcus 1975:73).

It is known that colonialism does not exist for a long time without collaborators from the colonized population. The Ethiopian state destroyed the Oromo leadership that resisted Ethiopian colonialism, and co-opted those submissive Oromo leaders who accepted the role of intermediary (*balabbat*) in the colonial system. After expropriating the three-fourth of Oromo lands, the settlers gave the remaining one-fourth to these Oromo intermediaries who were integrated into the colonial system and acted against the interest of the Oromo majority. As a result, the majority of Oromos became landless serfs and share croppers. The major objectives of the local *balabbat* system were to ensure the maintenance and reproduction of the Ethiopian colonial system in order to facilitate the continuous supply of grain, labor, and other necessary materials for the settlers. A few Oromos, who became collaborators and served the interests of their classes and that of the settlers, were Ethiopianized while the Oromo majority were kept under darkness by denial of education and information.

Paradoxically, Italian fascist colonialists created new conditions for the emergence of Oromo resistance and nationalism by removing all these archaic Ethiopian institutions between 1935-1941. By abolishing the *nafxanya-gabbar* and *balabbat* systems, slavery, the Ethiopian landholding system, and by introducing wage-labor and colonial capitalism, Italian colonialism created social structural and conjunctural factors that would allow Oromos to express their grievances and Oromoness (Jalata 1993:83-85). The Italians attempted to win Oromos and to mobilize them against the Ethiopians by broadcasting in the Oromo language and employing it in the court and schools (Hassen 1993:77), and by giving "many of them full rights to the land they had cultivated under

Amhara landlords" (Sbacchi 1985:160). Although the Ethiopian state was restored with the help of the British government, Italian colonialism laid down an economic infrastructure that facilitated the development of colonial capitalism in Oromia. The development of colonial capitalism between the mid-1930s and the 1960s produced structural and conjunctural factors for the emergence of Oromo consciousness and nationalism.

The new social forces that emerged with the development of capitalism began to challenge the Ethiopian state and its archaic ideology. One of the political forces that started to challenge the Ethiopian state was the Oromo movement. Despite the barbaric nature of Ethiopian colonial rule that restricted leadership development in the 1960s, Oromia began to produce a centralized leadership somewhat linked to a farmer rebellion. Lack of educational opportunity delayed the development of an Oromo leadership for a long time. Even in the early 1990s, one source estimated that less than 0.01% Oromos received modern education out of the total population of about thirty million (see Baasaa 1994:30).

THE RISE OF OROMO NATIONALISM

Oromo nationalism only developed into a mass movement in the early 1990s (see Jalata 1997). This development occurred after a long period of resistance. Initially, Oromos resisted slavery and colonization without systematically organizing themselves; their cultural and political resistance continued after their enslavement and colonization because they were assigned to the status of slaves and colonial subjects and second class citizens by the Ethiopian state. Because of the seriousness of Oromo resistance to slavery and colonialism, it took more than thirty years to establish Ethiopian settler colonialism and its institutions in various Oromo regions. Various Oromo groups continued to challenge Ethiopian settler colonialism to regain their freedom and independence. There were numerous local uprisings in different parts of Oromia; sometimes these local groups expelled the Ethiopian colonial settlers from their country. Although unsuccessful, some Oromo groups tried to use European powers, such as Italy and Great Britain, to regain their independence by ejecting the Ethiopian colonial settlers from some part of Oromia. The Oromo's search for freedom and

> decolonization was clearly manifested when thirty-three Oromo chiefs held meetings in 1936 and decided to establish a Western Oromo Confederacy. The document they signed to establish this confederacy expressed the desire of the people of Western Oromia to become a League of Nations protectorate with the help of the British government until the Oromo could achieve a self-government (Jalata 1993:153).

Despite all these resistance struggles, it took a long time to develop Oromo nationalism when nationalism in different parts of colonial Africa developed between the 1920s and the 1950s. The denial of education, the nature of Ethiopian colonialism and its structures that have kept almost all Oromos in rural areas by limiting their division of labor to agriculture, and tight political repression delayed the development of Oromo nationalism.

Furthermore, Ethiopian colonial state and its institutions have prevented the emergence of Oromo leadership by co-opting submissive elements and liquidating the nationalist ones, and by suppressing Oromo autonomous institutions, and erasing Oromo history, culture, and language. Mohammed Hassen (1998:194) noted that "from the 1880s to the early 1960s, the Oromo suffered a great deal from the lack of central leadership. It should be remembered that in the 1880s during the conquest and colonization of Oromo territory, a large number of the Oromo people, together with their leaders, were decimated ... Other Oromo leaders were co-opted into the Ethiopian political process. The basis for independent Oromo leadership was destroyed." Despite the fact that Oromo individuals and various Oromo groups resisted and fought against the combined forces of Ethiopian settler colonialism and global imperialism, a few Oromo elites and urbanites started to develop and manifest Oromo collective consciousness and nationalism only in the early 1960s.

The destruction "of Oromo national leadership, the tight control of the government, the meagerness of a modern educational establishment, lack of transport and communication systems and mass media, the absence of written literature in the Oromo language and the limited nature of interaction among the Oromo in different regions ... may have contributed to retarding the growth of an Oromo national consciousness before the beginning of the 1960s" (Hassen 1998:193). For a long time, Oromos lacked formally trained and culturally-minded intellectuals. The christianized Oromo ex-slave scholar, Onesimos Nasib who was trained in Europe, and his team Aster Ganno, Lidya Dimbo, and Feben (Hirphee) Abba Magaal, and another religious scholar, Sheik Bakri Sapalo, pioneered the production of written literature in *Afaan* Oromo and tried to introduce literacy to educate Oromo society in the first half the twentieth century (Bulcha 1993; Hassen 1993). To deny Oromos education, the Ethiopian colonial government and the Orthodox Church suppressed the efforts of these scholars.

It was not only the Ethiopian government and its international supporters that hindered the progress of Oromo society. The opposition of Somalia to the Oromo interest also contributed to the slow development of Oromo consciousness and nationalism. The Somali state that emerged with the liberation of Somalia in 1960 tried its best to Somalize some Oromos and to incorporate a part of Oromia to Somalia. While the Ethiopian elites "feared Oromo nationalism as a major threat to the disintegration of the Ethiopian Empire, Somali ruling elites regarded it as a dangerous movement that would abort the realization of the dream of greater Somalia" (Hassen 1998; 189). All these obstacles hampered the development of Oromo nationalism. Although the national struggle of the Oromo people had been the continuation and culmination of previous resistance, it emerged from certain social structural, historical and sociological factors.

The development of colonial capitalism in Oromia, the emergence of a few conscious Oromo intellectual and bureaucrats, the cumulative experiences of struggle, and politicized collective and individual grievances had facilitated the development of Oromo nationalism (Jalata 1993; 1998). Since the 1960s, some Oromos started to move to cities where colonial settlers have been concentrated. As some Oromos flowed from rural areas into cities, the condition of urban areas began to change. While a few were successful and became petty traders, most became laborers, semi-laborers, or unemployed. These groups and students brought the Oromo language and culture to urban areas where the colonialists were concentrated. An example of this was the formation of musical groups, such as the Arffan Qallo and Biftu Ganamo musical groups in Dirre Dhawa (Jalata 1993:161). It was not only the Oromo masses who were mistreated by the Ethiopian colonizers. Those Oromo elites who joined the Ethiopian colonial institutions were not treated as equal citizens. Since the colonial government ignored them, those few Oromo individuals who joined colonial institutions (such as schools, parliament, the army, and the administration) and Oromo merchants began to think about ways to improve the Oromo living standard. Despite their relative achievements, these individuals had inferior status to Ethiopians due to their Oromo national identity.

Paradoxically, the idea of developing the collective consciousness of Oromos was mainly initiated by a few Oromos who were educated to be members of an Ethiopianized Oromo collaborative class. "Exclusion breeds failed assimilation," Anthony Smith (1982:31) writes, "and reawakens an ethnic consciousness among the professional elites, at exactly the moment when the intellectuals are beginning to explore the historic roots of the community." Since there has been a fundamental contradiction between the Ethiopian colonizing structures and the colonized Oromos, Ethiopian society could not culturally and structurally assimilate the Oromo elites. The formation of the Macha-Tulama Self-Help Association in the year 1963-1964 marked the popularity of Oromo nationalism. Since the Ethiopian Constitution did not allow to establish a political organization, emerging Oromo leaders formed this association in accordance with Article 45 of his Imperial Majesty's 1955 revised Constitution and Article 14, Number 505 of the Civil Code as a civilian self-help association.

These Oromo elites through forming this association in Finfinnee (Addis Ababa) started to politicize the collective grievances of the Oromo people, and formulated programs to solve some economic, social and educational problems of Oromo society. Since the association was open to all interested national groups in Ethiopia, it embraced the principle of multicultural diversity. Members of the colonized national groups, such as the Sidama, Wolayita, Kulo Konta, Issa, Gimira, Gamo, Benishangul and Adare joined the association; non-Oromos held twenty-six positions in different committees of this association (Zoga 1993:75-77). Within short time, the association "transformed itself from a self-help development association in Shawan administrative region, into a pan-Oromo movement that coordinated peaceful resistance, and in turn gave birth to Oromo political awareness. This means that since their conquest in the 1880s, the Oromo developed a single leadership ... for two interrelated purposes: economic, educational and cultural development and to establish the political equality of the Oromo with other peoples of Ethiopia" (Hassen 1998; 183).

While Oromos provided the resources to build Ethiopian infrastructures and institutions, they were denied access to social amenities. Reflecting on this reality, this association, at its Itaya meeting in May 1966, expressed that: "(1) less than one percent of Oromo school age children ever get the opportunity to go to school; (2) ... less than one percent of the Oromo population get adequate medical services; (3) ... less than fifty percent of the Oromo population own land; (4) ... a very small percentage of the Oromo population have access to [modern] communication services. [And yet] the Oromo paid more than eighty percent of the taxes for education, health, and communication" (quoted in Hassen 1998:205-206). When the Ethiopian government and Ethiopian elites intensified to mistreat these Oromo elites and conspired to deny Oromos opportunities, and even attempted to destroy the leadership of the association, the association under its charismatic leader, Taddasa Biru, unsuccessfully attempted in 1966 to take over the control of the Ethiopian state by assassinating Emperor Haile Selassie (Zoga 1993:118-133). The Oromo nationalist elements of the 1960s recognized what Clifford Geertz (1994:30) describes:

> The one aim is to be noticed; it is a search for identity, and a demand that identity be publicly acknowledged. The other aim is practical: it is a demand for progress for a rising standard of living, more effective political order, great social justice, and beyond that of 'playing a part in the larger arena of world politics', of exercising influence among the nations.

The Ethiopian colonial state and the Ethiopian settlers in Oromia did not tolerate any manifestation of Oromo consciousness. The Haile Selassie government banned the association in 1967, and its leaders were imprisoned or killed. Since the association started "to articulate the dissatisfaction of the Oromo with the government and particularly with their position in society," it was not tolerated (Wood 1983:516). The Ethiopian government did not even tolerate the existence of Afran Qallo and the Biftu Ganama muscial groups because they manifested themselves in the Oromo language and culture. They were banned like the association. Similarly, the Bale Oromo armed struggle that started in the early 1960s was suppressed with the assistance of Great Britain, the United States, and Israel between 1968 and 1970 (Gilkes 1975:217-218). The banning of the Macha-Tulama Self-Help Association, the destruction of the Afran Qallo and Biftu Ganama musical groups, and the suppression of the Bale Oromo armed struggle forced Oromo nationalism to go underground. The Macha-Tulama "movement marked the beginning of a new political experience that was crucial to the growth of Oromo nationalism in the 1970s, an experience that taught the Oromo elites that they needed a liberation movement that would marshal the resources of their people, harmonize their actions and channel their creative activities and innovation against the oppressive Ethiopian system" (Hassen 1998:196).

The suppression of Oromo reform nationalism forced some Oromo nationalists to go underground in Oromia, and others went to Somalia, the Middle East, and other countries to continue the Oromo national movement. When Oromos were denied the right to express themselves in the late 1960s and the early 1970s, a few Oromo militant elements produced political pamphlets, such as *Kana Bekta* (Do you know this?), and historical documents such as *The Oromos: Voice Against Tyranny*. For the first time the original name of this people, Oromo, was used in publication by rejecting the derogatory name, Galla. *The Oromos: Voice Against Tyranny* (1980:23) pinpointed the Oromo question as a colonial and defined the future direction of the Oromo national struggle:

> [F]or an Oromo worthy of the name ... there is one and only one way to dignity, security, liberty and freedom. That single and sure way is to hold a common front against his oppressors and their instruments of subjugation. In this, he [or she] is ready and willing to join hands in the spirit of brotherhood, equality and mutual respect, with oppressed nationalities and all persons and institutions of goodwill, he is equally ready and prepared to pay any sacrifice and oppose any person or groups that in any way hinder his mission for liberation from all forms of oppression and subjugation. An Oromo has no empire to build but a mission to break an imperial yoke, that makes this mission sacred and his sacrifices never too dear.

The denial of individual, civil, and collective rights, and the suppression of all forms of Oromo organizations and movements forced Oromo nationalists to engage in clandestine forms of struggle. Explaining how the Ethiopian National

Liberation Front (ENLF) was formed in 1971 and the Oromo Liberation Front (OLF) in 1974, Holcomb and Ibssa (1990:299) note that "intellectuals who had survived the banning of Macha-Tulama had gone underground to find a new approach. Those who had been able to leave the country were also searching together for alternative tactics and strategies to achieve the objective they had espoused and to find a new model for effective organization."

The main objectives of ENLF were to reform Ethiopia, introduce democracy, and bring civil equality for all peoples by removing the imperial and racist nature of Ethiopia (Jalata 1994:5-7). However, most Oromo nationalists did not endorse these objectives recognizing the nature of Ethiopian elites, but rather determined to develop revolutionary nationalism that attempts to dismantle Ethiopian settler colonialism and to establish a people's democratic republic of Oromia as an independent or autonomous state within a federated multinational democratic society (OLF Program 1976). Oromo revolutionary nationalism emerged with the birth of the OLF in the early 1970s. The OLF states that the main "objective of the struggle is the realization of national self-determination for the Oromo people and their liberation from oppression and exploitation in all their forms. This can only be realized through the successful consummation of the new democratic revolution ... and the establishment of the people's democratic republic of Oromia." This organization also recognizes the significance of creating a multinational democratic state through voluntary association by dismantling the Ethiopian colonial, dictatorial, and racist structures. As Oromos intensified their national struggle, the crisis of the Ethiopian state and its terrorism increased.

OROMO REVOLUTIONARY NATIONALISM AND STATE TERRORISM

A few Oromo revolutionary elements established an underground political movement and transformed reform nationalism into revolutionary one because the Ethiopian colonial government totally denied Oromos any channel through which to express their individual and collective interests. These revolutionary elements understood from the beginning the significance of the reconstruction of Oromo culture and history for the survival of the Oromo national identity and the development of Oromo nationalism. The Oromo leaders produced political pamphlets and expanded their sphere of influence by organizing different political circles in different sectors of Oromo society, such as students, professionals, workers, farmers, soldiers, students, and the army. Those Oromos who fled to foreign countries and received military training returned to Oromia to initiate armed struggle. The group that initiated the Oromo armed struggle in 1973 and the revolutionary elements together created the OLF in 1974. As soon as the OLF began to challenge Ethiopian colonial domination ideologically, intellectually, politically, and militarily, the Ethiopian state initiated terrorism against Oromo nationalists and the Oromo people.

Due to lack of international support and suitable sanctuary coupled with Ethiopian state terrorism and internal disagreement within Oromo elites, the growth of Oromo nationalism was slow in the 1970s and the 1980s. Because of all these factors, the Oromo movement played a secondary role in overthrowing the military regime of Mengistu Hailemariam in May 1991. With the demise of this regime, the Ethiopian Peoples Revolutionary Democratic front (EPRDF) dominated by the Tigray People Liberation Front (TPLF) came to power with the support of the Eritrean Peoples Liberation Front (EPLF) and the endorsement of the U.S. government. It established a minority Tigrean-based authoritarian-terrorist government. To obtain political legitimacy, in the beginning, the new regime invited different liberation fronts and established a transitional government. It persuaded these organizations that it would prepare a ground for the formation of a multicultural federal democratic government of Ethiopia. However, in less than a year, this regime expelled major coalition partners by using intimidation, terrorism, and war, and established an ethnic-based party dictatorship without any opposition from the U.S. and other Western countries (Trueman 1997; Pollock 1996 1997). The US, other Western countries, and the Organization of African Unity called the sham elections the regime used to legitimize its power satisfactory, fair, and free (see *Reuters Business Briefing* July 5, 1994; Reuters May 15 1995). However, the feat was accomplished through systematic intimidation and outright terrorism.

During the transitional period, Oromo nationalism was transformed from an elite initiative to a mass movement. The development of the Oromo movement representing the largest national group in Ethiopia prevented the Tigrean-led regime from establishing its hegemony. Therefore, Oromos are the main target of Ethiopian state terrorism. Since the discourse on terrorism is dominated by those groups who control the political, intellectual and economic resources of the world, it is not adequately articulated. That is why Annamarie Oliverio (1997:48) notes that "relatively little scholarly attention has been devoted to the relationship between the politics of the state, the politics of terrorism, and the production of injustice in the world."

State terrorism is a systematic policy of a government through which massive violence is practiced to impose terror on a given population group to change their behavior of political struggle or resistance. The essence of Ethiopian state terrorism can be clearly understood within this context. The state that engages in terrorism is not a protector of citizens; it rather violates civil and human rights through assassinations, mass killings and imprisonments, and display of corpses on streets so that people accept the violent state due to fear of terror. The main assumptions of such a state are that it can control the population by destroying their culture of resistance and leaders. States, such as the Ethiopian state, that fail to establish ideological hegemony and political order are unstable and insecure; hence they engage in terrorism (Oliverio 1997; Gibbs 1989).

The Tigrean-led government has accepted state violence against Oromos and others as a legitimate means of establishing political stability and order. Explaining how state terrorism is associated with the control of territory and resources and the construction of political and ideological domination, Oliverio (1997:52) says: "First, the state reinforces the use of violence as a viable, effective, mitigating factor for managing conflict; second, such a view is reinforced by culturally constructed and socially organized processes, expressed through symbolic forms, and related in complex ways to present social interests. Within increasing economic and environmental globalization, gender politics, and the resurgence of nationalities within territorial boundaries, the discourse of terrorism, as a practice of statecraft, is crucial to the construction of political boundaries."

The regime practices state terrorism with the support of global capitalist elites against Oromos who have challenged Ethiopian cultural and ideological domination. The massive human rights violations of Oromos had first taken place in rural areas and then expanded to cities. Since this regime mainly survives on Oromo economic resources, it uses terrorist actions mainly against the Oromo People. According to the Oromia Support Group,

> Because the Oromo occupy Ethiopia's richest areas and comprise half of the population of Ethiopia, they are seen as the greatest threat to the present Tigrean-led government. Subsequently, any indigenous Oromo organization, including the Oromo Relief Association, has been closed and suppressed by the government. The standard reason given for detaining Oromo people is that they are suspected of supporting the OLF (OSG Nov. 1997:1).

The terrorist activities of this regime include systematic assassinations of prominent Oromos, open and hidden murders of thousands of Oromos, re-initiation of villagization and eviction of Oromo farmers and herders, expansion of prisons in Oromia, forcing more than forty-five thousand Oromos into hidden and underground detention camps, and looting economic resources of Oromia to develop Tigray, enrich Tigrean elites and their collaborators (see Seifa Nabalbal, No. 94, 8 November 1996; Urjii 1994, 1995, 1996 and 1997 series; Amnesty International, 1995 and 1996; Oromia Support Group, 1996 and 1997). Comparing the state terrorism of the military regime with that of the Tigrean, the OLF (1996:6) asserts that "the *Derg*'s terror was conducted officially, and the regime actually tried to justify its actions and took responsibility for it. Executions and extra judicial killings were announced officially. But the current regime carries out its crimes mostly in secret and unlike the *Derg's* period, there is no official records ... The present regime's policies ... actually amounts to a policy of genocide ..." Umar Fatanssa (Fossati et al 1996:43), an elderly Oromo, also says the following: "We had never experienced anything like that, not under Haile Selassie, nor under the Mengistu regime: these people just come and shoot your son or your daughter dead in front of your eyes."

The video smuggled out of Ethiopia in 1997 shows horrifying mass graves in Eastern Oromia (Hararghe) and proves the correctness of what the OLF and Fatanssa assert (Oromia Support Group 1997). Without any doubt Oromos are exposed to systematic state terrorism so that their lands and other economic resources are looted by Tigrean elites, their collaborators, and transnational corporations (Jalata 1997). History repeats itself in different forms and contexts. The Amhara elites systematically destroyed an independent Oromo leadership through extermination with the help of European colonial powers. Later they used the so-called socialism and the Soviet bloc to suppress the Oromo national movement. Currently, state terrorism manifests itself in this empire in different forms: Its obvious manifestation is violence in the form of war, assassination, murder, castration, burying alive, throwing off cliffs, hanging, torture, rape, confiscation of properties by the police and the army, forcing people to submission by intimidation, beating, and disarming citizens (Pollock 1996; 1997; Trueman 1997; Amnesty International, Human Rights Watch/Africa, 1997; Survival International 1995; Oromia Support Group 1997 series).

Several interviews made by Bruna Fossati, Lydia Namarra, and Peter Niggli (1996) reveal the means used in Ethiopian state terrorism. Since 1992 several thousands of Oromos have been killed or arrested for suspicion of being OLF supporters or sympathizers or for refusing proposed membership of the EPRDF. Based on their field research, these three scholars report that former prisoners testified that their arms and legs were tied tightly together on their backs and their naked bodies were whipped; large containers or bottles filled with water were fixed to their testicles, or if they were women, bottles or poles were pushed into their vaginas; there were prisoners who were locked up in empty steel barrels and tormented with heat in the tropical sun during the day and with cold at night; there were also prisoners who were forced into pits so that fire could be made on top of them. Based on the testimonies of former victims of torture, the Oromia Support Group (May/June 1997:18) also notes the following:

> The physical torture of rural prisoners was systematic and prolonged and seemed a form of punishment as well as a means of pressing prisoners to provide information or to confess to collaboration with

armed groups. Testimonies also revealed the wide use of threats against and the actual detention of family members, particularly mothers, wives, and daughters, to force fugitive suspects to turn themselves in for interrogation.

The government soldiers have openly shot thousands of people in rural Oromia and left their bodies for hyenas, or buried them in mass graves, or threw their corpse off cliffs. As the Oromia Support Group documents in its series, there have been other methods of killings, including burning, bombing, cutting throats or arteries in the neck, asphyxiation by tightly binding the chest or by strangulation, and burying people to their necks in the ground. Prompted by hate for Oromos, TPLF soldiers never spared even pregnant women or youth; they killed several pregnant women and hundreds of Oromo children between the ages of 12 and 16 (the Oromia Support Group, August/September 1996). According to the Oromia Support Group (1997:8), "A 7-month pregnant woman in Robe, Bale, was arrested and beaten ... She miscarried and later died in custody. When relatives went to claim her body, they were told to replace the remains with a living relative. When asked to explain, the TPLF soldiers said 'She died with OLF objectives still stuck in her brain and we could not get what we wanted from her.'" The way these soldiers have treated women and girls demonstrates widespread inhumane behavior. Fossati at al (1996:10) report that "in prison women are often humiliated and mistreated in the most brutal fashion. Torturers ram poles or bottles into their vaginas, connect electrodes to the lips of their vulva, or the victims are dragged into the forest and gang-raped by interrogation officers."

Despite all these inhumane and criminal activities, U.S. officials deny the existence of torture in Ethiopian prisons or camps (see U.S. Department of State, 1993). Explaining how systematic terrorism takes place through a tightly organized party that functions from the central government to the grass-root committee, the Oromia Support Group (May/June 1997:18) notes the following: "Testimonies of victims of abuse by rural security personnel persistently pointed to the role of security committees, consisting of local officials, political cadres of the EPRDF and its affiliates and army officers, in control of the 'peasant militias.' The committee system made the militia an integral part of the national political structure and placed them under the control of the central government through the ruling party apparatus. They provided the interface between local authorities, the militia, the army and the ruling party, in practice subordinating local security structures to the federal authorities." Being misled or intentionally accepting the Ethiopian Constitution at its face value, U.S. officials praise the Ethiopian government for its goal of a "decentralized system that brings justice closer to the people" (U. S. Department of State, 1997:4) and reject the idea that "real power is retained at the center and used repressively" (the Economist, August 16,

1997:36). It is paradoxical that when Oromos and others assert that the Tigrean-dominated regime has brought terrorism to their neighbors and families, U.S. officials argue that it has brought justice closer to the people.

Another form of state terrorism is economic violence. The government confiscated the properties of some Oromos and others who have been imprisoned; those who were released from prisons paid a huge amount of 'ransom money' collected by relatives for TPLF/EPRDF soldiers and agents (see Fossati et al, 1996). "The persecution of suspected and real political opponents and the widespread campaigns of intimidation against the Oromo population produce a considerable booty which is pocketed by the government's representatives on the ground" (Fossati, et al 1996:23). It seems that the TPLF/EPRDF leaders have implicitly decided that they and their close associates use state resources and international connection to enrich themselves, and regional and local officials and soldiers use violence and repression to loot and accumulate wealth (see Negash 1996). Fossati et al (1996:35) concur: "Some privileged members of the TPLF have managed in dubious circumstances to privatize and run former state enterprises and are now successful in business. They are considerably better off than their former little 'comrades in arms' who do the dirty work of repression." The military and political leaders of TPLF have emerged as a new capitalist class through illegal means and dominate the Ethiopian political economy.

Using state power this new class has expropriated state corporations in the name of privatization and established joint businesses with either local investors or foreign corporations (see the Indian Ocean Newsletter 1996). Assefa Negash (1996:73) writes that "practically every important business sector of Ethiopia is now controlled by Tigreans [sic]." The plan of developing Tigray at the cost of Oromia and other regions is becoming clear: "... nearly 45% of Ethiopia's total private investment funds went to the Tigray region between 1992 and 1997... Tigray, with a population of 3.5 million, receives the lion's share of 2.1 billion birr investment, while [the] Amhara and Oromo regions, with five and seven times as many people, get 146 million and 613 million respectively. Tigray now has 250 projects in transport, construction, manufacturing, agriculture and mining, while the Amhara and Oromo regions have just over 200, much smaller projects between them" (Oromia Support Group, November/October 1997:5).

The Ethiopian government has decided to destroy Oromo merchants and intellectuals by labeling them "narrow nationalists" and "the enemy of the Ethiopian Revolution" (Hizbawi Adera, Tahisas to Yekatit 1989 E.C.). One prominent Oromo businessman, who was forced to run away from his family, property and country and now lives an impoverished life in Djibouti, describes his predicament: "They stole 162,000 Birr in cash, took my cattle, slaughtered my herd of goats, 150 animals. Both my vehicles, a land cruiser and a small lorry, were confiscated. Soldiers moved into my home, and my warehouse became the new prison in Kobbo" (quoted in Fossati et al 1996:34). Hundreds of Oromo business people have been harassed, killed or imprisoned and robbed of their properties. Currently it has openly begun its plan of destroying prominent Oromo intellectuals, community leaders and businessmen in Finfinnee (Addis Ababa) and its surrounding; extrajudicial killings on the streets of Finfinnee, massive imprisonment, torture and disappearance have become common practice of this regime. "The current wave of arrests appears to be concentrating on all prominent Oromo, whether or not they are associated with the OLF. More than twenty officials of the Matcha-Tulama self-help organization including Gabissa Lameessa, Beyene Abdi, Beyene Ballissa, Hussein Abdi and Haji Sahlu Kabte, were detained on November 5th [1997]" (Oromia Support Group, November 1997:1-2). Several prominent Oromo journalists such as Solomon Namarra, Tesfaye Dheressa and Garoma Bekele were arrested illegally.

The regime never trusts non-Tigrean intellectuals who refuse to be recruited to EPRDF. Several scientists and professors were arbitrarily fired from Addis Ababa University by this regime and others were imprisoned. When this regime implemented the programs of structural adjustment, it fired non-Tigrean employees and replaced them with that of Tigrean and their collaborators (see Negash 1996). Denying jobs to these scientists, professors and other employees by firing them and canceling their contracts and denying their retirement and other benefits are also another form of economic terrorism. Trueman (1997:145) expounds that "Ethiopian academicians who opposed the government have been sacked. Deans and administrators of Addis Ababa University are now appointed by the government. Educational institutions in Tigray are burgeoning while the renowned Agricultural College at Alemaya [Haromaya] on Oromo territory has been dismantled. Teachers, other numbers of the civil service and employees in state industries have lost their jobs unless [they were] willing to become members of the EPRDF." The American Association for the Advancement of Science expressed that these scientists and professors were "arbitrarily deprived of their human rights and academic freedom" and requested that "the Ethiopian government release the imprisoned scientists from detention and allow them to leave the country if they so desire, [and] reinstate those professors who were dismissed from Addis Ababa University." (quoted in Oromia Support Group, March/April 1997:8-9). But the regime rejected this request, and the positions of these scholars were filled by Tigrean intellectuals and their surrogates (Negash 1996).

Oromos are not even allowed to have a meaningful relief association in Ethiopia and neighboring countries. Realizing that the Ethiopian government and international organizations care very little about the welfare of Oromo society, a few Oromo leaders created the Oromo Relief Association, ORA, in exile as an independent humanitarian Oromo association in the late 1970s to assist Oromo refugees in the Horn of Africa (Dibaba 1997:7). Terfa Dibaba (1997:9) estimated that in 1984/85 there were more than a half million Oromo refugees in Sudan, Somalia and Djibouti. Assuming that the political change of 1991 would allow a peaceful and democratic political resolution for the Oromo problem, ORA moved its head office to Finfinnee and shifted its program from relief work to rehabilitation and settlement activities, and developed projects that included health, education, agricultural and forestation activities (see Dibaba 1997). According to the Oromia Support Group (August/September 1996), one thousand three-hundred fifty-two ORA orphans moved to Oromia from Sudan, when ORA decided to locate its headquarters in Oromia in 1991; some of these children were killed by TPLF soldiers or drowned by big rivers while being chased by these soldiers, and others were captured and taken to the Dhidheessa concentration camp where they were beaten, tortured, raped, and some died of hunger and infection. The regime closed ORA regional offices in August 1995, and its headquarters in February 1996 and confiscated all its properties. ORA activities were banned not only in Ethiopia, but also in Djibouti, Somalia and Kenya. Explaining the banning of ORA in Djibouti, Fossati et al (1996:3) comment that "the only organization that for some years looked after the Oromo refugees, the Oromo Relief Association (ORA), was banned ... in June 1995 by the Djibouti government at the request of the Ethiopian government." Most international humanitarian organizations did not object (Dibaba 1997).

Impoverishing people by transferring their wealth and capital from non-Tigreans to Tigrean elites and Tigrean society and their local and international collaborators via the state machinery are a form of hidden economic violence. Thousands of Oromos have lost their lands through eviction and their cattle through looting; Oromo forests have been set on fire in an attempt to destroy the Oromo Liberation Army; Oromo forests have been cut for use by Tigreans and their collaborators. This regime uses economic violence to impoverish Oromo society and destroy it. According to Trueman (1997:147-8), "natural resources in Oromo and other areas in the South, agricultural products, natural forests and minerals, are being plundered and the environment destroyed. Villages close to areas of conflict with OLF have been subject to waves of arrests, beatings and disappearances. There are reports of families being burned alive in their houses and many reports of looting of property..."

Using the leverage of Western countries, the regime pressures neighboring governments to return or expel Oromo refugees from their countries. The alliance of the West with this regime has frightened neighboring countries, such as Djibouti, Kenya and Sudan and turned them against the Oromo struggle and Oromo refugees. The United Nations High Commission for Refugees

(UNHCR) has even failed to provide reasonable protection for thousands of Oromo refugees in Djibouti: "The Oromo refugees are generally regarded by the Djibouti authorities as unwelcome aliens or illegal immigrants, despite the fact that Djibouti is a signatory to the Geneva Convention on Refugees. Every day the refugees fear being caught in one of the frequent police raids and forced back across the border. Only a small minority has legal refugee status" (Fossati et al 1996:3). The burdens of Oromo women refugees are heavy; many of them would be raped while crossing the border on the way to Djibouti or they would be forced to work as slaves by Djibouti households or the Djibouti police. Sebida Musa says that "[t]hey take the women home and treat them as their personal property. If one of the women gets pregnant, she is mercilessly thrown out into the street, where she and her unwanted child have to try and survive by begging" (Quoted in Fossati et al 1996:10).

Oromo refugees have been abused by the Djibouti authorities and the Ethiopian government, and ignored by international organizations, such as UNHCR. In addition to lack of food, Oromo children are denied education in Djibouti. "Our difficulty is that as Oromo we are threatened and endangered both at home in Ethiopia," Zeinaba Ibrahim says, "and as refugees in Djibouti..." (quoted in Fossati et al 1996:28). Probably following the instructions of the Ethiopian and Djibouti governments or due to the fear of these governments, the UNHCR provides no material help to Oromo refugees in Djibouti. Fossati et al (1996:44) recount that: "The Oromo council of elders told us they believed they were entitled to a small portion of the international aid available to refugees, but did not even get a glass of water from the UNHCR and had been completely forgotten..."

Some refugees also faced terrorism and forced repatriation. Hussein Sora, a young Kenyan Oromo lawyer, accused the Ethiopian regime of international terrorism and compiled a report on the criminal activities of the Ethiopian security forces in Kenya since 1992. According to this report, the TPLF forces assassinated prominent Oromo refugees, bombed the houses of some Kenyan Oromos and abducted civil servants, and shot some citizens in Kenya (cited in Oromia Support Group 1997). This lawyer died the same year he compiled and distributed the report to the Kenyan authorities and international organizations; the agents of the Ethiopian government were suspected of killing him by poisoning. The TPLF forces have continued to enter into Kenya murdering and looting the economic resources of some Kenyan Oromos by accusing them of harboring the Oromo Liberation Army. "The Tigrean incursions are ostensibly to punish Boran Oromo suspected of supporting the OLF. The soldiers bear characteristic facial markings of Tigrean culture: they wear Ethiopian army uniforms ... The raids are of two kinds. The bombing, murder, rape and plunder of Boran Oromo and assassination of prominent elders suspected of supporting the OLF is one kind. Simple banditry or robbery with violence and murder is the other" (Oromia Support Group, March/April 1997:10).

When it comes to Oromos, international organizations care less even if international laws are broken. Oromos are even denied a sanctuary from neighboring countries and are denied the right to be refugees. Oromos have been assassinated or murdered by the regime, denied burial rights, and eaten by hyenas and other wild animals. Since Oromo refugees are not welcomed by neighboring countries and international organizations, there are thousands of 'internal' Oromo refugees in Oromia and Ethiopia. Fleeing from Ethiopian state terrorism, these internal refugees hide in the bush and remote villages. Fossati, et al (1996:36) assert that "there are not only Oromo refugees abroad, but probably just as many refugees in their homeland -displaced, in hiding, hunted, who still see a slim chance of staying in the country." Suspecting that these internal refugees support the Oromo national struggle, the regime attempts to control their movements and the movement of other Oromos. Trevor Trueman (1997:146) notes that "[t]he movement of rural people is closely watched. Peasants are repeatedly searched on the way to market and goods are likely to be confiscated. Those traveling by bus are subjected to body searches, beatings, robbery and imprisonment. Peasants avoid being seen talking to foreigners." Democratic discourses have been used by the government and its international supporters to hide state terrorism and massive human rights violations. Why do Oromos still face state terrorism? Why did not they yet achieve national self-determination?

THE PROBLEM OF OROMO NATIONALISM

Ethiopian settler colonialism, state terrorism, cultural destruction or repression, political slavery, and denial of education have stagnated the development of Oromo indigenous institutions. Indigenous institutions and organizations provide "a favorable structure of political opportunities" for the oppressed group (McAdam, et al 1988:697). Hence, the destruction or suppression of Oromo institutions denied Oromos "organizational infrastructure" that could evolve from Oromo indigenous and institutions. McAdam (1997:178) asserts that "the ability of insurgents to generate a social movement is ultimately dependent on the presence of an indigenous 'infrastructure' that can be used to link members of the aggrieved population into an organized campaign of mass political action."

Explaining the significance of informal groups, friendship networks, churches, mosques, and other forms of institutions for collective movement and action, D. McCAdam et al (1988:709) also note that:

> The key concept linking macro-and micro-processes in movement
> emergence is that of the micro-mobilization context. A micro-

> mobilization context can be defined as any small group setting in
> which processes of collective attribution are combined with rudi-
> mentary forms of organization to produce mobilization for collec-
> tive action.

Oromos have never been allowed to develop autonomous institutions under
Ethiopian colonial rule. The government has been imposing absolute control
both on Oromo nationalists and the Oromo masses. It allowed Oromo elites
to establish a self-help association in 1966 only to ban it in 1967 when this
association tried to provide educational and health services to Oromo society,
and when it also openly expressed the collective grievances of the Oromo.

The indigenous Oromo institutions and organizations have been suppressed
and denied freedom of development. As a result, Oromo society still lacks
organizational infrastructures. Movement scholars consider "the strength and
breadth of indigenous organizations as the crucial factor in the rapid spread of
the movement" (McAdam et al 1988:703). The lack of development, state violence, and tight control have handicapped Oromo society by maintaining what
McCarthy (1987:49-66) calls "infrastructure deficits." Oromo nationalists and
activists have been prevented from educating and helping the Oromo masses.
Since Oromo society has been penetrated by Ethiopian agents and spies, their
informal groups or associational networks that "serve as the basic building blocks
of social movements" have been tightly controlled (McCarthy 1987:711). The
Oromo national movement, particularly the Oromo Liberation Front, has been
struggling under this dangerous condition. Almost all Ethiopians are against
the Oromo national movement. The ethnocratic-authoritarian terrorist Ethiopian state has only a limited space for an Ethiopianized Oromo intermediaries.
This state is above the rule of law and it has liquidated some Oromo activists
without any hesitation. That is why the Oromo national movement has been
an underground movement in Oromia. The nature of the Oromo struggle has
been difficult and dangerous. As a result, several thousands of leaders, activists,
and sympathizers have been killed or imprisoned. The statement that Mamo
Mazamir, one of the leaders of the Oromo movement, expressed in 1963, when
he was to be hanged captures this reality: "I do not die in vain. I am certain that
those who sentenced me to death ... will receive their due punishment ... It may
be delayed, but the inalienable rights of the Oromo people will be restored by
the blood of their children" (quoted in Hassen 1998:211-212).

Movement scholars further explain that the level of infrastructure in a
given population is itself "shaped by the type of macro factors ... Broad macro-
processes such as industrialization, urbanization, mass migration, and the like,
largely determine the degree to which groups in society are organized and
the structure of that organization. The extent and structure of that organiza-

tion in turn imply very different potentials of collective action" (McAdam et al 1988:711). Oromos still lack such macro-structural political opportunities since they are geographically dispersed and impoverished rural people. More than ninety percent of Oromos are still poor farmers and herders. In garrison cities in Oromia, Oromos have become a minority. Since Ethiopian settlers dominate these cities, this condition created serious obstacles for the development of Oromo nationalism and collective action. Because of the lack of modern communication and transportation networks, and domination of the media (television, radio, newspaper) by the colonial government, Oromos have limited communication among themselves. Oromos are denied to have their own independent media in Oromia.

The Ethiopian colonial system did not leave any cultural space for Oromos to develop their institutions and educate their children. Most of those few Oromos who had an opportunity of education were forced to be Amharized or Ethiopianized and reject their Oromo identity. Those educated elements that tried to maintain their Oromo identity and promote the interest of their people were systematically suppressed. Explaining how writing about Oromo by Oromos can lead to death, Hassen (1998:203-204) says: "Mamo wrote History of the Oromo which was confiscated by the government when his house was searched in 1966. In addition to writing history, Mamo prepared a plan for a new government, a new constitution and distribution of land among the landless tenants. This was too much for the ruling Amhara elites, and Mamo Mazamir was martyred for producing that document." The denial of intellectual freedom still prevents Oromo scholars and Oromo society from developing freely an alternative knowledge.

The Oromo literature that started to mushroom when the OLF joined the Transitional Government of Ethiopia between 1991-1992, was suppressed. Oromo scholars and journalists who tried to express themselves today perish in Ethiopian prisons. Today Oromo scholars in the diaspora produce and disseminate an alternative knowledge that is considered illegal in Ethiopia and Oromia. Challenging how the Ethiopian knowledge elites and Ethiopinists treated Oromos, the diaspora "publications on Oromo cultural and social history challenge a top-down paradigm to historiography and make the Oromo subjects rather than objects of history. Studying people as subjects or agents helps scholars avoid producing false knowledge" (Jalata 1998:253-254). The Ethiopian elites and the Euro-American scholars who supported them attempted to erase Oromo history and culture from the world map. Therefore, until Oromos have intensified their struggle in the 1990s, the world did not even recognize the existence of 30 million Oromos. Oromos were seen as a people without history who were to disappear through assimilation or through other means. William Shack (1994:642-643) pointed out that "the lack of critical scholarship has inadvertently distorted the human achievements of conquered peoples like the Oromo including transformations of their social, cultural, and political institutions." Oromo nationalism influenced several Oromo scholars and friends of Oromos to produce and disseminate an alternative knowledge in Oromo studies. The emergent Oromo studies in North America and Europe, and the formation of the Oromo Studies Association in the diaspora attest to this reality (Jalata 1998:253-292; Lata 1998:125-152). Some Oromos do not have intellectual freedom in Oromia and Ethiopia, the Ethiopian elites are keeping Oromos in the darkness of ignorance to maintain the colonial system.

Since Oromo organizations are clandestine organizations in Oromia they cannot practice democracy within themselves and among themselves. The idea of tolerating diverse ideologies and diverse approaches and forming the unity of purpose is just started in the Oromo movement. Despite all these problems, the Oromo movement has gained some cultural, intellectual and ideological success in Oromo society. Today the Oromo nation has emerged out of century-old historical obscurity, and the Oromo people have achieved some level of cognitive liberation. Because of the development of Oromo nationalism, Oromo organizations have begun to embrace Oromo democratic tradition known as *gada*, and recognized the importance of the unity of purpose and started to work toward building a united front. By challenging the Ethiopian ideological and cultural hegemony, the Oromo movement has introduced political instability to the empire which survives by sheer military force. McAdam (1997:177) states that "generalized political instability destroys any semblance of a political status quo, thus encouraging collective action by all groups sufficiently organized to contest the structure of a new political order."

The Oromo organizations need to improve the degree of their organizational readiness by creating a united front and by combining research, politics, policy formulation and implementation to mobilize the whole population for collective action. One of the central problematic of insurgency "is whether favorable shifts in political opportunities will be defined as such a by large enough groups of people to facilitate collective protest" (McAdam 1997:182). Since the Ethiopian government does not allow a peaceful struggle, the only avenue that Oromos have is armed struggle. The suppression of emerging indigenous Oromo associations and organizations such as the Oromo Relief Associations, the Oromo Human Rights League and various professional, political, and economic organizations negatively affected the expanding political opportunities for the Oromo national movement.

The Oromo movement is recognizing the diversity and unity of the Oromo people because "people who participate in collective action do so only when such action resonates with both an individual and a collective identity that makes such action meaningful" (Buechler 1993:228). Moreover, collective identities are not automatically given, but "essential outcomes of the mobilization process and crucial prerequisites to movement success.... One critical intervening process which must occur to get from oppression to resistance is the social construction of a collective identity which unites a significant segment of the movement's potential constituency" (Buechler 1993, *ibid*). The Oromo collective identity has been constructed from past cultural memory, political grievances, popular historical consciousness, and the hope for freedom and democracy. Oromos have also different religions, various cultural and economic experiences, class divisions, and different ideologies.

Therefore, Oromo nationalists and activists are recognizing the Oromo unity and diversity that are central to the further development of Oromo nationalism and its transformation into collective political and military action. "If the social construction of a collective identity is an on going, never-completed task in social movements," Buechler (1993:229) writes, "this is because movements are often composed of diverse and heterogeneous individuals and sub-groups." However, the Oromo movement has only focused on collective identity and paid less attention to movement diversity. As a result, some Oromo organizations fought against one another ideologically, militarily and politically. This factor has also contributed to the weakness of the Oromo movement. Buechler is of the opinion that "intra-movement diversity can be a potential asset or a liability although it is perhaps most often viewed as a liability which will lead to factionalism and thereby reduce a movement's chances for success. However, diversity can also be beneficial by expanding a movement's potential constituency and resource base as well as by broadening the arguments which can be made for movement objective" (Buechler 1993:229). Oromo leaders and organizations have not yet utilized their diversity to effectively mobilize most of the Oromo people for collective political action. Since Oromos are the largest national group, the crisis of Ethiopia continues until their political problems are solved by mobilizing almost all of them to take a unified political action. While Oromo political actors and organizations prepare the Oromo nation to liberate itself from Ethiopian settler colonialism, they also need to consolidate their political coalition with other colonized nations.

CONCLUSION

Oromos have been suffering under Ethiopian settler colonialism that practiced slavery, the *naftanya-gabbar* system, forced villagization and collectivization, and total subjugation without freedom for more than a century. Ethiopian settler colonialism cannot be explained without locating it in the global capitalist world system since it has been an integral part of this system. Global capitalism and the imperial interstate system facilitated the enslavement and the subjugation of Oromos. In the capitalist world-economy, those peoples who have state power or access to state power enjoy relatively various political, economic, and cultural advantages. They are recognized internationally and regionally by the imperial interstate system and by multinational organizations and corporations. Business and state elites who get resources from these linkages and who control domestic resources suppress the colonized peoples and deny them meaningful access to state power (Enloe 1986:39). One among such peoples, the Oromos, have been dominated by Ethiopian colonial settlers and their government. The incorporation of Oromia into Ethiopia made Oromos invisible in the world. Since Oromos were identified with Ethiopians, the existence of Oromos and their national liberation struggle were hidden until the early 1990s (see Lata 1998:125-152). Even today Oromos in the diaspora are having difficulty in introducing themselves and their struggle to the world.

The Tigrean-dominated regime has significantly racialized the Ethiopian state by making the Tigrean ethnonational minority the core of repressive government, and by hindering the construction of a legitimate state that can be accountable, democratic and reflect a multicultural society. All these are done in the name of "self-determination" and "democracy." The U. S.-sponsored Ethiopian "democracy" utterly failed to resolve the main contradiction of racialization/ethnicization of state power that has been built into Ethiopian politics since the creation of this empire. The replacement of the Amhara-based regime with that of Tigray under the guise of "democracy" and "self-determination" could not change the nature of the Ethiopian state. This state has remained an instrument of oppression, exploitation, terrorism, genocide and cultural repression by one group against the other.

Without an accountable, democratic and legitimate state, the colonized nations, and particularly Oromos, face disastrous conditions similar to Bosnia, Rwanda, and Kosovo. If the current Ethiopian state terrorism and massive human rights violations are tolerated by the world community to continue, these conditions may soon lead to full genocidal war. The intensification of the Oromo, Ogaden-Somali, and Sidama armed struggles, the brutal response of the regime in the form of terrorism and repression, the emergence of war between Ethiopia and Eritrea, and recurrent famine show the deepening crisis of the Ethiopian state. The world conflicts that are racial or ethnic-related cannot be easily contained or stopped once they erupt into violent conflict and confrontation. Therefore, the world community needs to become capable of mediating these processes in Ethiopia and to develop procedures and criteria by which to resolve these dangerous conflicts before it is too late. On their parts, Oromos and other colonized nations must make their problems known to the world and be prepared to resolve these contradictions through creating a genuine multicultural democratic state.

Notes

1. Oromos are the largest nation in Northeast Africa; during the 1990s, they are estimated to be about 30 million in the Ethiopian Empire alone. See Feyisa Demie, "Population Growth and Sustainable Development: The Case of Oromia in the Horn of Africa," *The Journal of Oromo Studies*, vol. 4, nos. 1 & 2, July 1997, pp. 83-114.

2. The Oromo used to call their country "Biya Oromoo." This name was changed to Oromia by Oromo nationalists in the early 1970s. Presently the name Oromia is used interchangeably with the Oromo nation indicating "the geographical location of the nation in the Horn of Africa. Oromia comprises almost three-fourths of the Ethiopian Empire ..." A. Jalata, Oromia & Ethiopia: *State formation and Ethnonational conflict 1868-1992*, Boulder: Lynne Rienner Publishers 1993, p. 3.

3. For further discussion on Ethiopian racism, see Asafa Jalata, "The impact of a racist U.S. foreign policy on the Oromo national struggle," *The Journal of Oromo Studies*, vol. 6, nos. 1 & 2, 1999, pp. 49-89.

References

Amnesty International. 1995. *Ethiopia: Accountability past and present -Human rights in transition,* see also reports of 1996 and 1997.

Baasa, D. 1994. "Oromo Students in the higher education system: An outline," *Oromo of Finfinnee University 1993-1994 Graduates.* Finfinne Addis Ababa, no name of publisher.

Bereciartu, G. J. 1994. *Decline of the nation-state,* trans. W.A. Douglas. Reno, Las Vegas: University of Nevada Press.

Bulcha, M. 1997. Religion, the slave trade and the creation of the Ethiopian Empire. *The Oromo Commentary.* VII,2:19-33.

Buechler, S. M. 1993. Beyond resource mobilization? Emerging trends in social movement theory? *The Sociological Quarterly.* 34, 2:217-235.

de Salviac, M. 1901. *Un peuple antique au pays de Menelik: les Galla, grande nation africaine.* Paris: Oudin.

Dibaba, Terfa. 1997. "Humanity forsaken: The case of the Oromo Relief Association (ORA) in the Horn of Africa," Paper presented to the Oromo Studies Association annual meeting at the University of Minnesota.

The Economist. 1997. "Ethiopia: Federal sham." *The Economist.* 16 August .

Enloe, C. H. 1986. Ethnicity, the state, and the international order. In *The primordial challenge: Ethnicity in the contemporary world,* ed. J. F. Stack, Jr. New York: Greenwood Press.

Fossati, Bruna, L. Namarra, and Peter Niggli. 1996. *The new rulers of Ethiopia and the persecution of the Oromo: Reports from the Oromo refugees in Djibouti,* Dokumentation, Evangelischer Pressedienst Frankfurt am Main.

Fatanssa, Umar. 1996. Quoted in *The new rulers of Ethiopia and the persecution of the Oromo*. Bruna Fossati, Lydia Namarra, and Peter Niggli. Frankfurt.

Geertz, C. 1994. Primordial and civic ties. In *Nationalism*, ed. J. Hutchinson and A. D. Smith. Oxford: Oxford University Press.

Gilkes, Patrick. 1975. *The dying lion: Feudalism and modernization in Ethiopia*. New York: St. Martin's Press.

Gibbs, Jack. 1989. Conceptualization of terrorism. *The American Sociological Review* 54:329-340

Hameso, Seyoum, Trever Truman and Temesgen Erena, eds. 1997. *Ethiopia: Conquest and the quest for freedom and democracy*. London: TSC.

Hassen, Mohammed. 1998. The Macha-Tulama Association 1963-1967 and the development of Oromo nationalism. In *Oromo nationalism and the Ethiopian discourse*, ed. A. Jalata, 183-221. Lawrenceville, NJ: The Red Sea Press.

Hassen, Mohammed. 1993. "The growth of written Oromo literature," Proceedings of the international conference on resource mobilization for the Liberation of Oromia, University Toronto, Ontario, Canada. 31 July -1 August, pp. 65-91.

Holcomb, B. and S. Ibssa. 1990. *The invention of Ethiopia: The making of dependent colonial state in Northeast Africa*. Trenton, NJ: The Red Sea Press.

Hizbawi Adera, an EPRDF political pamphlet, Tahisas-Yekatit, 1989 E.C. [1997].

The Indian Ocean Newsletter. 19 October 1996.

Jalata, Asafa. 1993. *Oromia & Ethiopia: State formation and ethnonational conflict, 1868-1992*. Boulder: Lynne Rienner Publishers.

Jalata, Asafa. 1994. Sheik Hussein Suura and the Oromo national struggle. *The Oromo Commentary*.IV,1: 5-7.

Jalata, Asafa. 1996. The struggle for knowledge: The case of emergent Oromo studies. *The African Studies Review* 39:95-123.

Jalata, Asafa. 1997. Oromo nationalism in the new global context. *The Journal of Oromo Studies*. 4:1 & 2:83-114.

Jalata, Asafa. ed. 1998. *Oromo nationalism and the Ethiopian discourse: The search for freedom and democracy*. Lawrenceville, NJ: The Red Sea Press, Inc.

Katsuyoshi, Fukui, and John Markakis, eds. 1994. *Ethnicity & conflict in the Horn of Africa*. London: James Currey.

Lata, L. 1998. Peculiar challenges to Oromo nationalism. In *Oromo nationalism and the Ethiopian discourse*, ed. A. Jalata, 125-152. Lawrenceville, NJ: The Red Sea Press.

Marcus, H. 1975. *The life and times of Menelik II, Ethiopia, 1844-1913*. Oxford: Clarendon.

McAdam, D., J. D. McCarthy and M. N. Zald. 1998. Social Movements. In *Handbook of sociology*, ed. Neil J. Smelser. Newbury Park, CA: Sage.

McAdam, D. 1997. The political process model. In *Social movements: Perspectives and issues*. ed., Steven M. Buechler and F. Kurt Clykes, Jr. Mountain View, CA: Mayfield Publishing Company.

McCarthy J. D. 1987. Pro-life and pro-choice mobilization: Infrastructure deficits and new technologies. In *Social movements in an organizational society*, ed. Mayer N. Zald and John D. McCarthy. New Brunswick, NJ: Transaction Books.

Negash, Assefa. 1996. *The pillage of Ethiopia by Eritreans and their Tigrean surrogates*. Los Angeles: Adey Publishing Company.

The Ogaden Relief Association. November 1996.

OLF. *The political program of the Oromo Liberation Front*. Finfinne, 1976.

Oliverio, Annamarie. 1997. The state of injustice: The politics of terrorism and the production of order. *International Journal of Comparative Sociology*. 38, 1-2:48-63.

Oromia Support Group. Press Release, October/November 1996; August/September 1996; May/June 1997; March/April 1997; January/February 1997; Urgent Action -November 1997; Summary Press Release -September/October 1997; Human rights abuses in Ethiopia-Press Release -September/October 1997; Scale of EPRDF nepotism revealed, September/October 1997.

The Oromo Liberation Front. 1996. "Statement on the current state of the Oromo people's struggle and the situation in the Horn of Africa." The Oromo Liberation Front. June.

The Oromos: Voice Against Tyranny, originally produced in 1971 and reprinted in 1980. *Horn of Africa*. 3, 3.

Pankhurst, R. 1968. *Economic history of Ethiopia 1800-1935*. Addis Ababa.

Pollock, Sue. 1996. Ethiopia-human tragedy in the making: Democracy or dictatorship? In *Oromia Support Group*. Press Release.

Pollock, Sue. 1997. Politics and conflict: Participation and self-determination. In *Ethiopia: Conquest and the quest for freedom and democracy*, 81-110. ed. Seyoum Hameso, et al. 81-110. London: TSC.

Reuters Business Briefing, July 5, 1994.

Reuters, May 15, 1995.

Seifa Nabalbal, no. 94, 8 November, 1996.

Shack, W. A. 1994. Book review, The Oromo of Ethiopia: A history 1570-1860. *American Ethnologist*, 21/3:642-643.

Survival International. 1995. Ethiopia: Human rights hypocrisy must end now. *Press Release*, July 14.

Sbacchi, A. 1985. *Ethiopia under Mussolini: Fascism and the colonial experience*. London: Zed Books.

Schmitt, K. 1994. Machbuba – An Oromo slave-girl who won the heart of a German Prince. *The Oromo Commentary.* IV, 2:32-34.

Smith, Anthony. 1982. Nationalism, ethnic separatism and intelligentsia. In *National separatism,* ed. C. H. Williams. Vancouver: University of British Columbia Press.

Trueman, Trevor. 1997. Democracy or dictatorship? In *Ethiopia: Conquest and quest for freedom and democracy,* ed. Seyoum Hameso et al. 141-150. London: TSC.

Urjii, August 26, 1997. See also the 1994, 1995, 1996, 1997 series.

U. S. Department of State. 1993, 1997. US Department of State on Human Rights.

Wood, A. P. 1983. Rural development and national integration in Ethiopia. *Review of African Political Economy.* 26.

Zoga, O. 1993. *Gezatena Gezot and Macha-Tulama Association,* Addis Ababa: np.

Conclusions

Asfaw Beyene

From the arguments well narrated in this book, and from several other publications authored by Abyssinian and non-Abyssinian scholars as well as statistical data compiled by international and regional institutions, even wishful Ethiopians who only see their country's greatness should come to a consensus that Ethiopia is indeed one of the poorest countries in the world. This disappointing news has been sustained for decades by images of a ghostly skeleton of children headed for death, an insignia that symbolized Ethiopia of the last three decades. Revamping this gruesome image has been a dear interest of all human beings, not just the peoples in Ethiopia who, of course are most concerned as subjects of this anguish. The international community has mobilized, sympathized, and agonized with this unsettling level of poverty.

Oblivious to this situation for about a century, Ethiopian leaders dedicated their concerted efforts to building and cultivating Abyssinian political and cultural Puritanism, a transgression blamed for keeping the country and the population in dearth. Sufficient call has been made by non-Abyssinian scholars to mainstream Abyssinian historians, politicians, and activists to refocus their collective thinking and political yielding towards a progressive and positive resolve.

In this sense, this book comes as a good news for all peoples of Ethiopia, the oppressor and the oppressed, because at an intellectual level the authors point at the core reasons of the Ethiopian poverty, amassing the grand political issues of the empire and implying a desired road to a solution. The stubborn defense of a cultural supremacy and brassy exploitation of the land and the people have left an empire so intensely distressed that one should see no survival at the cost of collective death. Seyoum Hameso eloquently surmises, "this state of being cannot be considered as normal state of national being." And yet one wonders

how Ethiopian politicians could be so condemned to repeat the past and duplicate the same *faux pas* over and over again.

Reasons that led to the abject Ethiopian poverty have been narrated time
and again by various authors. But, this work is unique because it is an in-depth
treatment of the subject covering socio-political history, contemporary political
economy, and politics of nationalist struggle. Furthermore, the diverse cultural
predisposition, academic training, and scholarly caliber of the contributors
make their messages a timely work of immense role and great importance.

The power of this book also comes from the accord of the authors. As a
unity of purpose among scholarly voices of the non-Abyssinian population and
as an assembly of reasoned views, this book marks one of the beginnings of what
must be understood as an emissary of a broader intellectual leadership networking to lay the knowledge base for a protracted effort towards a better future of
the South. Hence, the very gathering of studious ideas is no mean achievement;
the outstanding messages of refuting myths of the empire and exposing aggressive occupation are far reaching historical missives.

Hamdesa Tuso brings the sadness of colonial tyranny close to the readers'
imagination by sharing his personal experience. Himself an Oromo, he admits
he received the history lesson in the old Oromo tradition, by way of oral recitation from his parents. The killings of his grandfather with five family members,
the loss of his uncle, the confiscation of the entire cattle and property of the
family leaving nothing for the widows, are atrocities Oromo families from north
to south, west to east can recount to this day with deep and profound sadness.
The 30,000 Oromo political prisoners now herded in TPLF's secret prisons will
one day tell similar stories to their kin and to their people. As a witness to Abyssinian rulers' historical aversion to Oromo freedom, Hamdesa Tuso also refers
to a British historian, Margery Perham, who wrote about Emperor Tewodros
fierce hostility toward the Oromo people.

As Mekuria Bulcha notes the brutal Abyssinian conquest threatened extermination of the entire nation and caused forced displacement of the Oromo
people. Records of European travelers, historians, and missionaries spanning
over several decades back his claims. Graphic recitation of cruelties of the conquering Abyssinian army discussed here and elsewhere, sends a chilling imagination of pain the Oromo and other peoples of the South continue to conjure
to this day. Unsatisfied by the quantity of looted properties, the conquering
army from the North turned the entire conquered population into a pool of
financial commodity, capturing and selling all war captives. This short-sidedness
deprived the land of its young and strong, farming diminished, and famine and
devastation followed.

Whenever the Oromo farmers and other colonized peoples failed to provide services or pay taxes or tributes, Asafa Jalata writes, the "settlers enslaved their children or wives; during the colonial wars, millions of Oromos and other colonized peoples were sold. This use of slavery to depopulate the nation continued until the 1930s. In fact, Menelik, "Ethiopia's greatest slave entrepreneur" and the founder of the Ethiopian Empire at one time owned 70,000 slaves. Grand children of that enslaved generation still suffer under brutal repressions by the grand children of the slave owners of yester-decades, changing only the format of the market silhouette.

Slavery was common throughout the post-invasion South. Achame Shana writes that from 1912 to 1924, as the northern Ethiopian grip on Shekacho society tightened, more than 160,000 people were sold into slavery from Shekacho region alone. He states that based on a 1993 census, 75% of the Shekacho people are female. This tragic demographic imbalance is due to political and military ventures of successive Ethiopian regimes.

After decades of hopeless struggle to unchain themselves from such hostility and brutal bondage, Southern people resorted to whatever they thought could bring them some ease against such tyranny. For example the Sidama people, Mulugeta Daye writes, "looked forward to the better [future] whose imminent arrival was articulated by local prophets. The prophets claimed that Amhara domination would end." This also became a form of resistance as the prophets promised that "the spirit of their ancestors would liberate the people from the Amhara trap, if they persisted in their loyalty to ancestors." But prophecy helped little to stop the colonial might, and Abyssinian rulers continued demanding what would have been considered inhumane by any leap of imagination. Achame Shana's recount of a well-known episode from 1968 puts this helplessness in fresh perspective. It is about Inqu Selassie, one of the emperor's governors for whom the native population was press-ganged to build an 18 km of road for his convenience while driving over a muddy road. When a mud caught the car, the people were forced to carry the car out on their shoulders using two heavy logs, while the governor sat inside the car. Such was the quintessence of Ethiopian colony.

For about a century, the Ethiopian rulers have "abused the concept of sovereignty and statehood to deprive the rights of other peoples living under the oppressive rule," writes Abdurahman Mahdi. To maintain the colonial state, he continues, "the rulers had to build massive military machine and embark on forcefully maintaining one of the most vicious authoritarian rules in the Third World."

Over the years, the Naftanya system, an old tradition whereby the settler army was fed and sheltered by the colonized farmer population, was tailored into a centralized semi-modern army of the same purpose and ferocity breeding, what de Waal describes as, "pathological violence". The military has consequently become a tool of repression, a symbol of brutality whose interest conflicts the very existence of a united and democratic state. "By imposing itself on diverse modes of existence," Seyoum Hameso writes, "the Abyssinian colonial rule corrupted the *gada* system of the Oromo, the *luwa* of the Sidama and similar cultures of other nations forcing them into what Pausewang calls 'anarchic accommodation of individual self-interest.'"

Few today believe in TPLF's version of the Ethiopian unity, even if the government advocates token regional autonomy, which "assures themselves (the rulers) of continued oppression and conflict". So, the abuse continues under the "Federal" government as it did under the imperial rule, and human rights organizations continue to register thousands of human tragedy. Most dreadfully, the Derg continued to undermine farming by recruiting Oromo farmers for its war against the OLF, EPLF, etc. The TPLF repeated the same during its war against Eritrea. Not surprisingly, the recent famine in Oromia and the South followed the Ethio-Eritrean war.

In the backdrop of all these abuses and their expose, and naturally, there is a sense of *aluta contiua*, the victim population persistently fighting against subjugation of a human being by another human being. For many reasons, the continued harassment of the southern people demonstrates careless political ferocity in bogus defense of, or under the pretext of, unity. In fact, the only discernible and well-dressed Abyssinian politics that was built in favor of peace over the last several decades is a political scarecrow baring the image of an untouchable unity. Designers of this scarecrow attempt to fake the existence of true unity within the forcefully assembled "empire-states", simulating unity as an upshot of such a primitive political ferocity. A sentiment of regret acknowledging the violent past of Abyssinian leadership is not in sight, and there is still a stern and fierce will of dominance. Chances and hopes for fraternity to conjure up a peaceful common future can come far behind expression of such regret. To the contrary, Prime Minister Meles Zenawi and his TPLF cadre simply added pain to the historical injury, leaving little or no room for trust and meaningful talks for peaceful coexistence, as neighbors or as partners, whatever the people may choose. Hamdesa Tuso excellently portrays the essence of TPLF's occupation through the words of David Hirst of *The Guardian*, "The Ethiopian state in their hands, they (Tigreans) persisted, if surreptitiously, with a Tigrean agenda. The right of secession was enshrined in the constitution while they diverted state resources to their own people and region, and enlarged Tigray province at the expense of others." So, what does the future hold for this continued mauling of peoples in this gloomy country?

In this era of media, emails, faxes, videos, telephones, cellular, and digital pictures, it is easy to register atrocities, chronicle all criminal activities, and keep them for history, or for a record to one day bring perpetrators to justice. Oromo, Sidama, Somali, Shekacho, etc. observers are busy taking photographs, interviewing victims, and registering disappeared activists of their population. When overlooked records of the 1880s are revealed from rare history books a century later by nifty scholars whose numbers are sure to grow, it is hard to imagine any brutal human abuse of the 2000s will pass unnoticed by the eyes and ears of the thousands of upcoming guardians of a new born hope for freedom. Even non-Oromo organizations and foreign governments cannot keep up with ever-growing list of human rights abuses in Ethiopia. Trevor Truman's extensive data on extra-judicial killings, disappearances, arbitrary detention, torture, and rape paint the true color of today's Ethiopia as a prelude to the possibly more violent future. Truman cites "credible reports of 2,754 extra-judicial killings and 842 reports of disappearance since 1994". Thus, the real agenda of TPLF for Ethiopia is conquest. This is clearly stated in the TPLF's journal, *Hizbaawi Adera*, which targets "the higher intellectual and bourgeoisie classes (of Oromo) in a very extensive and resolute manner". Today, several government reports including that of the U.S. State Department assert that suspicion of belonging to the OLF is the most common cause for detention in Ethiopia.

So, one continues to ask, what drives Ethiopian leaders for such all out and persistent attack on the Southern peoples, ignoring the lessons learnt from Eritrea that achieved its indpendence from the empire, exhausting all its options to assert its national and human rights peacefully? Where does the political vision for such a forbidding and destructive future come from? Is it conceivable that Abyssinian scholars, who continue to so stylishly articulate all the political intrigues that the empire thrives on, fail to see the pending dangers of so excessively stored anger and anguish? The answer that percolates from the painstaking details of essays presented in this book is that this known danger is simply overruled by obnoxious ambition. The Ethiopian experience clearly shows that this obnoxious ambition is primarily revered by emotions, the non-emotional part of the politics being the deliberate concealment of this emotion. The lack of political vision in the courts of Abyssinian leaders, their derision of a growing Southern frustration towards an ever declining rights of these peoples, and the potential retort that would undermine even their own peaceful existence within the empire, in short, their obnoxious ambition, which often comes across as chauvinistic arrogance, is astounding.

Distressfully, this ambitious ignorance has become, perhaps deliberately so, a trait of too many Abyssinian scholars. This has created a steep political fault within the empire demarcating two highly antagonistic schools of thoughts. On one side, those who promote Abyssinian interests to dominate the socio-political panorama of the empire continue to demoralize rising sentiments for equality. On the other side those who foster the rights of the Southern peoples for equality, self-determination and indpendence, continue to press these agendas with a greater determination than ever before. During the last decade and particularly after the fall of the brutal Derg regime, Abyssinian scholars failed to sieze the moment once again, and continue to give at least a subtle support for Northern hegemony. So, the paradox continues, as the resistance literature increased exposing historical injustices and ongoing moral corruptions of domination bare-naked, the occupation propaganda also continued to rise with more and more deceit, at times resorting to criminal conduct in defense of the status quo. Clearly, the peace mentors of the empire preach two antagonistic views, offering their own collective versions and revelations of the same occupier-occupied relationship. Before this contradiction is resolved, there cannot be any chance for peace, and this is another major reading of essays presented in this book.

Some authors in here, including Jalata, Hameso, and Hassen explain the revolutionary and evolutionary changes that the Southern movements underwent since the 1960s. But, Abyssinian reactions to the continued resistance of the Southern peoples' struggle also showed some degree of adoptive transformation. These changes in Abyssinian schools of thought have not been given sufficient attention especially from a Southern point of view. So, what is the reaction of Abyssinian mainstream thinkers to this growing Southern revolutionary mood and resistance?

Since the creation of the empire, no Ethiopian regime, except perhaps the short-lived rule of Lij Eyasu, ever showed genuine interest in ethno-political diversity and attenuation of Amhara or Tigrean political dominance. So, Abyssinian scholars have observed little changes towards accommodating the demands of southern peoples. Most noticeable of all advances in the Abyssinian political maturity over the last 20 or 30 years is the transformation of the Abyssinian Marxist intelligentsia of the 1970s and 1980s into anti-South political cartel of the 2000s. The transformation bore no substantial change in its political outlook and ideological content, but mastered the form of repackaging and recycling the same potent ideology of supremacy. This ideology of supremacy ranges from simple reformist solutions to outright return to Abyssinian monarchy. The latter is an extreme form of unapprised political ambition, and the reformist mood, often adopting a form of sham ethnic federalism, is a savvy manifestation of the same ambition.

Most political writings of the monthly, weekly, and daily Abyssinian publications show great engagement to suppress nationalistic resistance, resuscitate positive sentiments of the feudal monarchy, and maintain Abyssinian state dominance. Almost exclusively, these papers reject nationality struggles as anti-unity while promoting ethnic domination of the North as non-ethnic politics. No realistic alternative ideology is offered to this one-dimensional ideology of dominance, leaving a vacuum in Abyssinian political vision of the empire. This is the type of a vacuum that, in the case of Rwanda led to ethnic genocide and, in the case of Somalia, led to chaos and state-less anarchy. But why are these fairly smart Abyssinian elites so bent on destructive ideology of supremacy, and why do they demonstrate sympathy for a stubborn and abhorrent ethnic dictatorship?

The primary reason, as stated earlier, is obnoxious ambition, oblivious to Ethiopia's place on the world's map of development. Too many Abyssinian elites view themselves and their nation as a power capable of colonizing, and this has been a crucial vigor to keep a moral high when every measure of growth and development indicates an otherwise miserable portrait of the empire. The elites of course have their own disagreements and petite quarrels among themselves, particularly burdened by the superimposition of two beings: one group of intelligentsia advocating modernity at least for posterity, and another intelligentsia they guard the interests of their former feudal class. At the heart of this duplicate disposition lies the Abyssinian ideological vacuum and lack of political vision.

The disputing monarchic and modernist groups of Abyssinian elites have aspects of genealogy and intelligentsia, respectively. The intelligentsia aspect of Abyssinian elitism has misgivings towards genealogy politics within the Abyssinian domination. For a system that predetermined who-is-who of the individual by blood and genealogy, modernity means fairer diffusion of opportunity for Abyssinians than the pre-appropriated aristocratic authority. At times, a feudo-elitist group dominates all Abyssinian political events, suggesting the emergence of Abyssinian political cartel promoting a return to monarchy, with whatever changes that can be afforded by the suggested reform. At other times, a federal ethnic empire is advocated, but without shaking the Abyssinian socio-political supremacy. For a country and a feudo-elitist system that favored its political supremacy defined by ethnicity and more firmly by birth, modernity is most appealing even to those Naftanyas who benefited from the system, but thought and dreamt to do better ruling than audaciously monarchic governance that could be viewed as archaic by others.

The inter-Abyssinian contradiction was born when the ambitious children of the aristocrats and non-aristocrats discovered considerably less room than that available at the top of the power pyramid. Hence, the mushrooming of Abyssinian political groups differing on the role of monarchy and on what really constitutes modernity in domination. However, both modernists and monarchists defended Abyssinian domination with identical doctrines of unity. Thus, Mengistu Hailemariam's and Meles Zenawi's regimes defended their modernist and feudal pedigree, provided they did not threaten their political statute. Thus, the

313

dominant contradictions and conflicts in the late 1970s and 1980s of Ethiopia either reflected national struggle, or were inherently inter-feudal by nature. The crash of contending feudal elites by the Derg seems to have seriously weakened the inter-feudal conflict, ordaining an entrenched ethno-militant group that continued nurturing and protecting Abyssinian supremacy. And as a matter of historical reality, the nationalist movement continues with no end in sight.

Another important question remains: what is the primary reason for such continued success of repressive Abyssinian regimes and weaknesses of generations of victimized peoples? Historians and political analysts suggest that the oppression continues because of lack of significant political consciousness. Mohammed Hassen blames the "lack of an intellectual class" among Oromos for delayed development of Oromo political consciousness, which he also thinks is "still one of the major weaknesses of the Oromo national movement". He gives a case references to support how and why "the Amhara ruling elites were not interested in creating an educational system in which all children had equal access to the benefit of modern education," a case also reitrtated by Hameso. In addition to lack of access to modern education and development, lack of optimistic politics and unrelenting extreme violence by Abyssinians rulers continue to frustrate the Southern peoples. Often times, the domination is wrapped with political mischief to justify human rights abuses and ruthless aggression. Kulick Gilbert puts Oromo frustration eloquently, rephrased by Mohammed Hassen who adds candid flavor to this truth. Writing about this relentless political stratagem, Gilbert is quoted as saying "what the [people] got was more of the same, broken promises, betrayed hopes and yet another permutation of age-old imperial intrigue". This age-old imperial intrigue gave rise to widespread mood of mistrust vis-à-vis a state of siege. So, Temesgen Erena correctly asks, "can the people of Oromia try to function and develop their economy in this state of siege?"

Most of the challenges that the Southern peoples face as oppressed nations are symptoms of a general problem with a particular pattern, persistency, and consistency. These challenges cannot be ignored as arbitrary or universal human ethos. The symptoms bespeak a collective weakness embedded in the attitude of the middle class organizations, in their confidence or lack of confidence, in their nationalist manifestations or lack of nationalism thereof. What is the root cause of these clues, which we see as endemic problems of our society?

Nationalists and organizers of the oppressed peoples are often frustrated by the poor determination, hesitant devotion, and confined persistency of the individual toward national aspirations. A question is often paused: what should we do to awaken this sleeping South? Or, why does such and so happen that way, contradicting a perceived common sense? It seems too much of commotions are out of the "ordinary," that the issue must be discussed in an organized manner. Why do the oppressed individuals demonstrate meager commitment, and why so skimpy on resource contribution to liberation? Why are they less participants and more of observers to their peoples' struggle? To even partly answer these questions, we need to understand the colonial synthesis of Ethiopia and how the Southern individual perceives it. This means, accepting Mohammed Hassen's thesis, that shortage of an intellectual class contributed to delayed consciousness, which in turn contributed to weaknesses of national movements, we need to examine factors that limited the growth of an intellectual class among the oppressed people. The answer probably lies in the colonial synthesis of the empire.

The Southern people suffered greatly under Abyssinian colonization. But the colonizers mingled with the colonized population both in class and in geography. Such mingling of class structure while aggressively aiming to preserve the dominating ethnic culture or national edifice is unique to Ethiopia. In fact, Ethiopian politicians used the mingling to cover-up ethnic and cultural supremacy of the North over the South. The geographic proximity and poverty of Amharas have been repeatedly suggested as the equalizing factor of Ethiopia, concealing their cultural hegemony. The political implications of this "economically almost peer" colonizer is a distorted political order, tainting the true meaning of colonial intensity in favor of faking national equality/unity. It is true that the excessive taxation of the South by the Northern settlers in the South barely reached the pockets of Northern farmers. It however created a wealthy supra-class of settlers within the South, much unlike the European colonialism that benefited the colonial country's businessmen and population at large. This aspect can be truly confusing, say to the Gondar Amhara observer of the last few decades who neither saw the colonial bonanza, nor witnessed the cultural isolation of the South. As communications opened between various regions in Ethiopia particularly after the Second World War, considering that Italy gave more autonomy to the South than the Northern colonizers, Oromos and other Southern peoples recaptured a strong psychological ground to claim high national identity and social morale despite economic subjugation by Amhara colonizers. The defeat of Amhara leaders by Italy undermined Amhara superiority, and the fame of Oromo war heroes who fought and defeated Italy or Somalia fed the Oromo national confidence.

In the years that followed the Second World War, Oromo nationalism continued to challenge Amhara domination at all levels and corners, keeping its cultural potential intact. Gada was outlawed, but it was practiced anyway; Oromo language was forbidden as a public media, but it was spoken publicly. On the other hand, the Oromo may condemn Amhara supremacy today, but will donate to Amhara social gathering, *idir*, tomorrow; an Oromo could resent the forbidding of his/her language, but will score an "A" in Amharic language or even produce better Amharic poets and writers than Amharas themselves.

They organize semi-nationalist organizations, but the formal language of the organization would remain Amharic. So, the Amhara colonizer did not have a clear-cut economic, technical, and cultural boundary as in the case of European colonizers. The power balance was very close, the difference in moral values was not apparent, and their technical skill is no better if not for the imported armament. So, the southern confusion about this colony is real, it floats in all discussion levels and in all regions to this day. Despite the Amhara domination of the Ethiopian bureaucracy, a few Oromos see no colonial issue because the Amhara colonial capacity as they know contradicts the Euro-colony they learnt from European history. Accepting Amhara colony could also constitute accepting Amhara superiority, and this is not agreeable to the ego of some.

Due to the abstract nature of the problem, there is a vacuum of knowledge in defining the Oromo problem via its psychological underpinning as hinted here. This is as opposed to a well covered and properly addressed historical context of Amhara domination of Oromo, or the empire, by several historians. More in-depth understanding of the problem will allow designing the correct tool to tackle the problem.

The narrow economic difference between the colonized South and the colonizer North within the same empire has implied colony to be a misnomer for Ethiopia. But then due to the strong Oromo indignation towards Ethiopia, caused by the cultural imbalance, Ethiopia is viewed as a misnomer for Oromo too. Again, in the minds of many Oromos, the strong cultural domination alone, with its regional inconsistency at that, is not sufficient to compare it to old and brutal colonial rules we heard and read about. However, the cultural domination was brutal, badly damaging the identity of its victims, Oromos included. The Amharazation of the Oromo is no less, if not more, than the Anglicization of India or Francization of Algeria. Thus, animated by the poverty of his colonizer, an Oromo may on one side think he is not colonized at all, and willingly share the fable of Ethiopia's three thousand years of independence. But on the other hand, shameful of his language and Oromo name, he would attempt to deny his Oromoness, willfully abandoning his own natural bequests, thus demonstrating unequivocal symptoms of colonial subordination.

Abyssinian rulers went a great distance to Amharize the South, and this consorted effort lasted for about a century. The economic exploitation did not continue to grow in all parts as deep as cultural supremacy was perpetuated, and in fact the colonial economic tentacles died in some cases faster than the cultural domination due to structural inefficiencies to exploit the South. But it was "land to the tiller" which came in the 1970s that crippled the economy of Amhara domination. However, Amhara cultural domination survived to the 1990s, and perhaps beyond. Its effect with replaced Oromo names of cities, villages, and school children, can be witnessed everywhere even today. What is said here for Oromo is true for any other Southern nation, and Amharization is the single most dominant reason for the unsatisfactory growth of Southern intellectual class. The challenges of organizing the Oromo individual are symptoms of this identity crisis.

Thus, the identity crisis within the Ethiopian empire exists within a somewhat balanced poverty in the same empire. The crisis is at times denied to defend a Southern national ego, or to entertain the mood of Ethiopianization. In whatever fashion it manifests itself, it is this identity quandary that creates the greatest challenge to organizing an intellectual class. Amharization, at times artificially concealed and suppressed from within, is mostly responsible for the organizational failures of Southern fronts; whereas a consolidated identity and nationalism, wherever it is so consolidated, is most singularly responsible for the success of intellectual organizations. In fact, partial success of the early 1990s coincides with partial de-Amharization of the South. The hesitation in defining national goals and visions or the dilemma in accepting oneself before or after accepting Ethiopianess are reminiscent examples of this clash of cultures in transition, as a colonial legacy. Expecting the individual's full determination to support the Southern struggle in the midst of such a crisis is less than practical. It takes psycho-revolutionary transformations to calibrate the southern vision and bring a global change of attitude towards national exertions. It may indeed be a waste to spend time and energy on convincing the deeply Amharized individual, but the generation must be tolerated to the maximum as a compulsory historical transition.

Over the last decade, the changes that took place all over the South, particularly the beginning of Qube (Latin based Oromo alphabet), the surge in literature, the birth of a new group of artists, etc., have introduced what may indeed be defined as Southern cultural renaissance of the 1990s. Cultivated by this cultural rebirth and detaching itself from the century old Amhara domination, a new generation of Southern nationalism is in the making. This new generation seems to have distinctly superior confidence in its identity over its predecessors, embracing its traditional and cultural heritage. The tone in which Oromo university students in Ethiopia asserted their national feelings in the late 1990s, the courage in which Oromo, Sidama, etc. journalists continue to publish regardless of difficulties, and above all, the number of young nationalists willing to confront the abusive system gives a clear message, that the growth in nationalism has become a serious menace to the Amhara cultural domination and renewed Tigrean supremacy, and this new breed of nationalism is here to stay. In view of the slowly declining recognition of Amhara domination in the South, the evolutionary change in generational attitude in theSouth is apparent and inherent. But the change is also a tribute to the thousands if not millions who kept the torch of freedom burning, still kindling the heart of millions far into the future—until full freedom is achieved. The solution to the challenges of southern struggles may indeed rest in cultivating this culturally conscious new generation.

In the preceding arguments, I claimed that Amharization lies at the core of most ideological and organizational problems in the South. But it may also have been compounded with other unrelated or lateral circumstances to create an even greater challenge for Southern political discourse. For example, like any other third world nation, we suffer from lack of expertise. But on top of that, a good part of the few experts we have are Amharized. So, Amharization is in no way the only source of southern problems, though most political challenges can be traced to it.

As grass-root Southern movements emerged and continued to grow, the 1980s and 1990s exhibited a more balanced proportion between the two contending cultural routes: Amharization and de-Amharization of the South. The first is on the way out, the later on the way in. Due to lack of organized cultural movements in these same years, Oromization, Sidamization, Somalization, etc. in all cases have not necessarily replaced de-Amharaization. The cultural vacuum created as a result of failure in replacing Amhara culture by self-culture probably still benefited the Amhara culture, which prevailed as the underlying dominant culture. Thus, Amhara culture benefited from the no-growth of Oromo culture and language. In the wake of a declining cultural role of Amhara all over Ethiopia, Amhara settlers, who, for a century profited from the colonial structure, started panicking. They are losing the cultural front, which facilitated some economic leverage. Their outrage against Qube is typical of this panic, and the "Galla Killers" organization exhibit the extreme form of this same panic. In other words, they are all excellent proofs and as such measures of the ongoing de-Amharization process of the South.

Amharization grew nourished as dual phenomena: imposed and self-imposed. The latter emerged as a recurring phenomenon, and the first, as a psychological conditioning. There are also Southerners who subscribe to this notion and then some, volunteering for self-Amharization, an Oromo declaring his/her desire to be called by an Amhara name. The bond between the Master and the house-slave, between the true and the adopted identities is tattering, marking the beginning of effective cultural decolonization. The shame is hitting the self-Amharizing Southerner from both sides; he is rejected and despised as a Southerner among the Amharas. He is also pitied and isolated among his people as a renegade. In fact, the self-Amharizer may be more disrespected by his own people than the Amhara who claim to "own" Ethiopia. This phenomenon is on the rise even in Diaspora.

The struggle between cultural domination and cultural emancipation in the empire is also characterized by delays due to inefficiency of the emancipation process. This inefficiency is inherent to the process, because cultural domination primarily affects the social and cultural makeup of the victim society on which the ability to organize and the willingness to be organized are strongly based. Adding to the challenge, the diehard Naftanyas will trap, betray, and ambush the liberation process. Thus, like a toddler who stands and falls trying to stay in balance on a rough floor, Southern partisans have not yet developed sufficient energy and confidence in reclaiming full ownership of their culture. Exposing and eliminating these last ill-mannered parasites of the society such as "the members of Galla Killers" is one of the last phases of the de-Amharization process, but even that requires networking.

The de-Amharization process, which determines the quality of a Southern struggle, must be the primary agenda of a Southern *network* designed for this purpose. Creating a network and launching the de-Amharization process as a complex mission and as a strategic task of the Southern struggle will most likely ease the bottleneck of the struggle for equality. But this does not mean ignoring other relevant areas of the struggle.

The creation of an intellectual class favors the increase of a nationalist group with a liberated mind. It is impossible to conquer a liberated mind. So, self-awareness comes first. Liberating the land and the people come next, with significant ease. A nationalist movement of higher intricacy must be initiated to liberate the Southern mind. Only people with satiated nationalistic awareness can see the benefit of positive political collaboration among the oppressed peoples of the South and demoralize the impact of regional and religious differences that undermined unity of the oppressed. A model of struggle needs to be developed that recognizes a role for the scholars in cultivating southern nationalism as a component of social consciousness and an element of collective intellectual growth. Passion, desire, and aspiration towards freedom must link the strategy of struggle within the empire.

List of Contributors

Asfaw Beyene teaches engineering at San Diego State University, California.

Mekuria Bulcha is Associate Professor of Sociology at Uppsala University and Malardalen University, Stockholm. He is the author of *The Making of the Oromo Diaspora: A Historical Sociology of Forced Migration from North East Africa*.

Mulugeta Daye is a postgraduate research student at the University of Newcastle.

Temesgen Erena is an economist, Thames Valley University, London.

Seyoum Hameso is the author of *Development, State and Society: Theories and Practice in Africa*. He is also the editor of *The Sidama Concern*.

Mohammed Hassen is Associate Professor of African History at Georgia State University, Atlanta. He is the author of the *Oromo of Ethiopia: A History 1560s-1860*.

Asafa Jalata is Professor of Sociology and African and African American Studies at the University of Tennessee, Knoxville. He is the author of *Oromia and Ethiopia: State formation and ethnonational conflict, 1868-1992*.

Abdurahman Mahdi is a teacher and a political commentator, UK.

Achame Shana is a researcher and human rights activist, UK.

Trevor Truman is a medical practitioner and the Chair of the Oromia Support Group, UK. He trained health workers for the Oromo Relief Association from 1988 to 1991.

Hamdesa Tuso is an Associate Professor in the Department of Dispute Resolution at Nova Southeastern University, Florida.

Name Index

Subject Index